The New Muslims of Post-Conquest Iran

Tradition, Memory, and Conversion

How do converts to a religion come to feel an attachment to it? *The New Muslims of Post-Conquest Iran* answers this important question for Iran by focusing on the role of memory and its revision and erasure in the ninth to eleventh centuries CE. During this period, the descendants of the Persian imperial, religious, and historiographical traditions not only wrote themselves into starkly different early Arabic and Islamic accounts of the past but also systematically suppressed much knowledge about pre-Islamic history. The result was both a new "Persian" ethnic identity and the pairing of Islam with other loyalties and affiliations, including family, locale, and sect. This pioneering study examines revisions to memory in a wide range of cases, from Iran's imperial and administrative heritage to the Prophet Muḥammad's stalwart Persian companion, Salmān al-Fārisī, and to memory of Iranian scholars, soldiers, and rulers in the mid-seventh century. Through these renegotiations, Iranians developed a sense of Islam as an authentically Iranian religion, as they simultaneously shaped the broader historiographic tradition in Arabic and Persian.

Sarah Bowen Savant is a historian of religion and an Associate Professor at the Aga Khan University, Institute for the Study of Muslim Civilisations in London. Her publications include *Genealogy and Knowledge in Muslim Societies: Understanding the Past* (2013), co-edited with Helena de Felipe, as well as book chapters and journal articles treating early Islamic history and historiography.

Cambridge Studies in Islamic Civilization

Editorial Board

David O. Morgan, *Professor Emeritus, University of Wisconsin-Madison (general editor)*
Shahab Ahmed, *Harvard University*
Virginia Aksan, *McMaster University*
Michael Cook, *Princeton University*
Peter Jackson, *Keele University*
Chase F. Robinson, *The Graduate Center, The City University of New York*

Published titles are listed at the back of the book.

The New Muslims of Post-Conquest Iran

Tradition, Memory, and Conversion

SARAH BOWEN SAVANT
Aga Khan University
Institute for the Study of Muslim Civilisations

CAMBRIDGE
UNIVERSITY PRESS

CAMBRIDGE
UNIVERSITY PRESS

32 Avenue of the Americas, New York NY 10013-2473, USA

Cambridge University Press is part of the University of Cambridge.

It furthers the University's mission by disseminating knowledge in the pursuit of education, learning and research at the highest international levels of excellence.

www.cambridge.org
Information on this title: www.cambridge.org/9781107529854

First published 2013
First paperback edition 2015

A catalogue record for this publication is available from the British Library

Library of Congress Cataloguing in Publication data
Savant, Sarah Bowen.
The new Muslims of post-conquest Iran : tradition, memory, and conversion / Sarah Bowen Savant, Aga Khan University.
pages cm – (Cambridge studies in Islamic civilization)
Includes bibliographical references and index.
ISBN 978-1-107-01408-4 (hard covers)
1. Islam – Iran – History. 2. Conversion – Islam – History. I. Title.
BP63.I68S28 2013
297.0955–dc23 2013012348

ISBN 978-1-107-01408-4 Hardback
ISBN 978-1-107-52985-4 Paperback

Contents

Illustrations — *page* ix
Maps — xi
Preface — xiii
Acknowledgments — xv

Introduction — 1

PART I TRADITIONS FOR REMEMBERING

1. Prior Connections to Islam — 31
2. Muḥammad's Persian Companion, Salmān al-Fārisī — 61
3. Finding Meaning in the Past — 90

PART II TRADITIONS FOR FORGETTING

4. Reforming Iranians' Memories of Pre-Islamic Times — 137
5. The Unhappy Prophet — 170
6. Asserting the End of the Past — 198

Conclusion — 230

Bibliography — 237
Index — 269

Illustrations

0.1. Relief figure of an individual dressed in a kaftan *page* xxii
0.2. Throne Hall, Persepolis 8
0.3. Bowl with Arabic inscription, "He who multiplies his words, multiplies his worthlessness" 23
1.1. Ādur Gushnasp 56
2.1. The capture of Iṣfahān 74
3.1. Shahrbānū 103
4.1. *Ahriman tempts Mishyana* 142
5.1. Drachma of Queen Būrān 192
6.1. The battle of al-Qādisiyya 199
6.2. Tomb of Daniel at Susa (Sūs) 208
6.3. Vahrām (Bahrām) VI 218

Maps

0.1.	The Great Empires on the Eve of the Arab Conquests	*page* xix
0.2.	Historical Iran	xx
1.1.	Fārs	58
3.1.	Jurjān	110
3.2.	Sīstān	116
4.1.	Jibāl (Media)	152

Preface

For the period of this study, the primary language of our written sources is Arabic. I follow the *International Journal of Middle Eastern Studies*' (*IJMES*) transliteration system for Arabic; accordingly, I do not indicate final *tāʾ marbuṭa* or distinguish between *alif mamdūda* and *alif maqṣūra*. Technical terms and place names used in English appear without transliteration (e.g., vizier, Baghdad), as do Anglicized derivatives of Arabic words and dynasties (e.g., ʿAjam, ʿAbbasid). From the fourth/tenth century onward, a few, albeit culturally significant, Persian sources enter circulation, with more in the centuries that follow. My transliteration of Persian texts generally reflects that of *IJMES*, but where Persian words appear in Arabic texts, I give priority to Arabic transliteration. I hope I will be forgiven for this choice by Persianists, and by all for any inconsistencies.

For the Qurʾan, I draw primarily on the English translation by Alan Jones (Cambridge: Gibb Memorial Trust, 2007).

For dates, I generally use those in the *Encyclopaedia of Islam*, 2nd ed.; *Encyclopaedia Iranica*; and Tarif Khalidi, *Arabic Historical Thought in the Classical Period* (Cambridge: Cambridge University Press, 1994), 235–42.

Acknowledgments

Although this book is not a revision of my Ph.D. dissertation (which I now see as heavily circumscribed by time and circumstance), the seeds for it were first planted while I was a Ph.D. student, so I would like to start by acknowledging with gratitude the insights and guidance of Roy Mottahedeh at Harvard, without whom this study would never have been conceived. At Harvard, I also benefited from the advice of William Graham, Wolfhart Heinrichs, and Charles Hallisey, among other members of the faculty, and the fruitful companionship of fellow students who remain important interlocutors and among whom I would single out Kristen Stilt, Raquel Ukeles, Joseph Saleh, Greg White, Christian Lange, Kambiz GhaneaBassiri, and Bruce Fudge. At an early stage, I also profited from reading courses with Ahmad Mahdavi-Damghani. Harvard, the Fulbright-Hays Commission, and the Social Science Research Council funded work on the Arabic sources in Egypt with two extraordinarily helpful teachers from Cairo University, Rida al-ʿArabi and ʿAbd al-Hamid Madkour. The University of California, Berkeley, was a second home to me for much of the dissertation-writing process as well as afterward, when I was a Sultan post-doctoral Fellow at the Center for Middle Eastern Studies. John Hayes, Emily Gottreich, Nezar AlSayyad, Wali Ahmadi, James Monroe, and Fred Astren welcomed me and offered key expertise and friendship. It was at Berkeley that this book began to take shape.

The more recent environment in which it developed was London, and its progress was helped by the opportunities I have had since joining the faculty of the newly established Institute for the Study of Muslim Civilisations of the Aga Khan University. Abdou Filali-Ansary, the Institute's founding director, and Farouk Topan, its director since 2009, deserve special mention, as do now five cohorts of our students from across the globe who have sensitized me to the ways in which early Islamic history can today be interpreted in different Muslim-majority contexts. At an early and critical stage, I benefited from stimulating conversations with colleagues, including Stefan Weber, now of the Pergamonmuseum in Berlin. Rebecca Williamson aided me with research for an important year, which freed me to read widely and to think. Fasih Khan has throughout provided unstinting support in all matters technical, and likewise, in our library, Waseem Farooq, Jessica Lindner, Walid Ghali, and Shah Hussain. The U.K. has generally proved an exciting environment for work on historiography. I have particularly benefited from collaboration with Konrad Hirschler and James McDougall in a now annual workshop on "Arabic Pasts: Histories and Historiography." Hugh Kennedy, an early supporter of "Arabic Pasts," has been a generous friend and commentator on my work.

Several parts of this study have been presented in public talks and at conferences, and I would like to thank these audiences. *Comparative Islamic Studies* has kindly permitted me to reproduce in Chapter One material from my 2006 article, "Isaac as the Persians' Ishmael: Pride and the Pre-Islamic Past in Ninth and Tenth-Century Islam," *Comparative Islamic Studies* 2, no. 1 (2006): 5–25, © Equinox Publishing Ltd 2006. I would like to thank *Annales Islamologiques* for permission to use in the Introduction a few paragraphs from my article "'Persians' in Early Islam," *Annales Islamologiques* 42 (2008): 73–91, in which I explored ideas relating to Persians, memory, and forgetting.

Many friends read drafts at various stages of the project. Dealing with a significant variety of fields, genres, and languages was a risky endeavor requiring some familiarity with a wide range of specialist scholarship. I have often drawn on the expertise and guidance of others, who should not, however, be held responsible for the book's shortcomings. I would like to thank in particular Zayde Gordon Antrim, Fred Astren, Patricia Crone, Touraj Daryaee, Robert Gleave, Mohammadreza Hashemitaba, John Hayes, Stefan Heidemann, Karim Javan, Wadad Kadi, Aptin Khanbaghi, Majid Montazer Mahdi, Raffaele Mauriello, Christopher Melchert, John Nawas, Farid Panjwani, Richard Payne, Parvaneh Pourshariati, Kathryn Spellman Poots, Khodadad Rezakhani, Andrew Rippin, Fatemeh Shams-Esmaeli, Maria Subtelny, and Raquel Ukeles. Antoine Borrut, Peter Webb, Philip Wood, and Travis Zadeh have especially enriched this study through fruitful discussions about Arabs, Persians, memory, narrative, and historiography and through their insightful feedback on the entirety of the manuscript.

Marigold Acland of Cambridge University Press supported this project at an early stage and throughout. I also thank William Hammell, Joy Mizan, Sarika Narula; and the editorial staff at Cambridge. John Tallmadge provided critical early advice on writing, and Hanna Siurua helped me to shape the manuscript into its final form. Joe LeMonnier created the maps. Cambridge's anonymous reviewers offered encouragement and constructive criticism, which I have accepted gratefully.

Finally, I would like to thank my family: my parents, William and Susan Bowen, and sister, Julia Bowen, and numerous in-laws and "outlaws," especially John Joseph Savant and Stephanie Murphy. Above all, I thank John Paul, Johnny, Leila, and Julian, who have provided important perspective on life as on work; to them I gratefully dedicate this study.

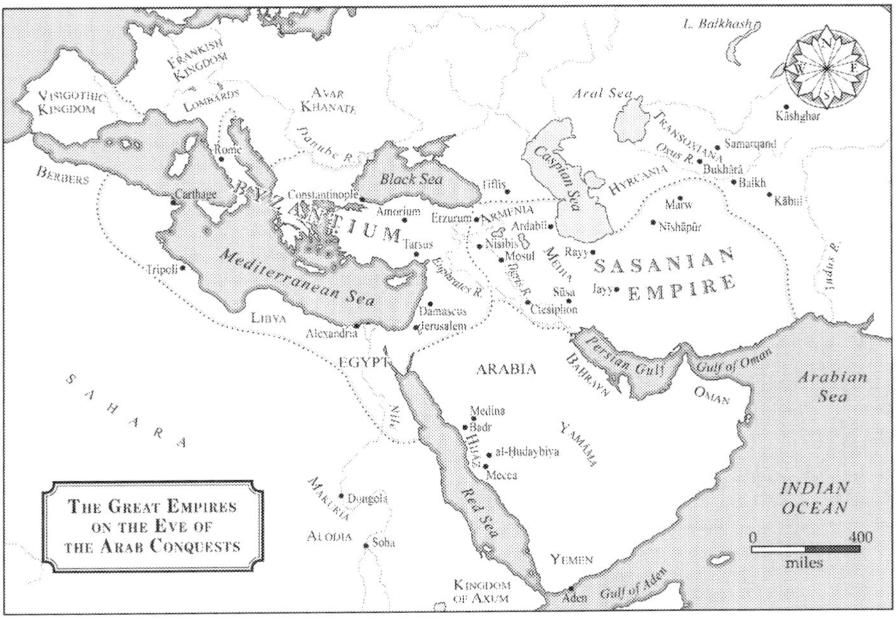

MAP 0.1. The Great Empires on the Eve of the Arab Conquests

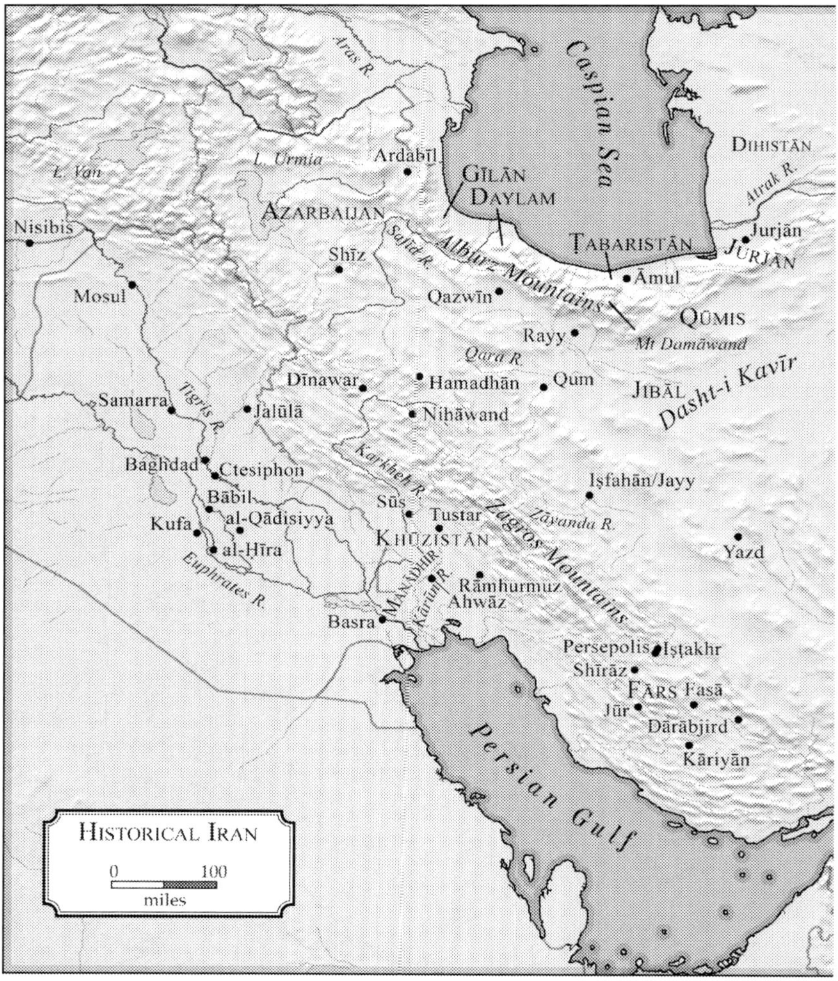

MAP 0.2. Historical Iran

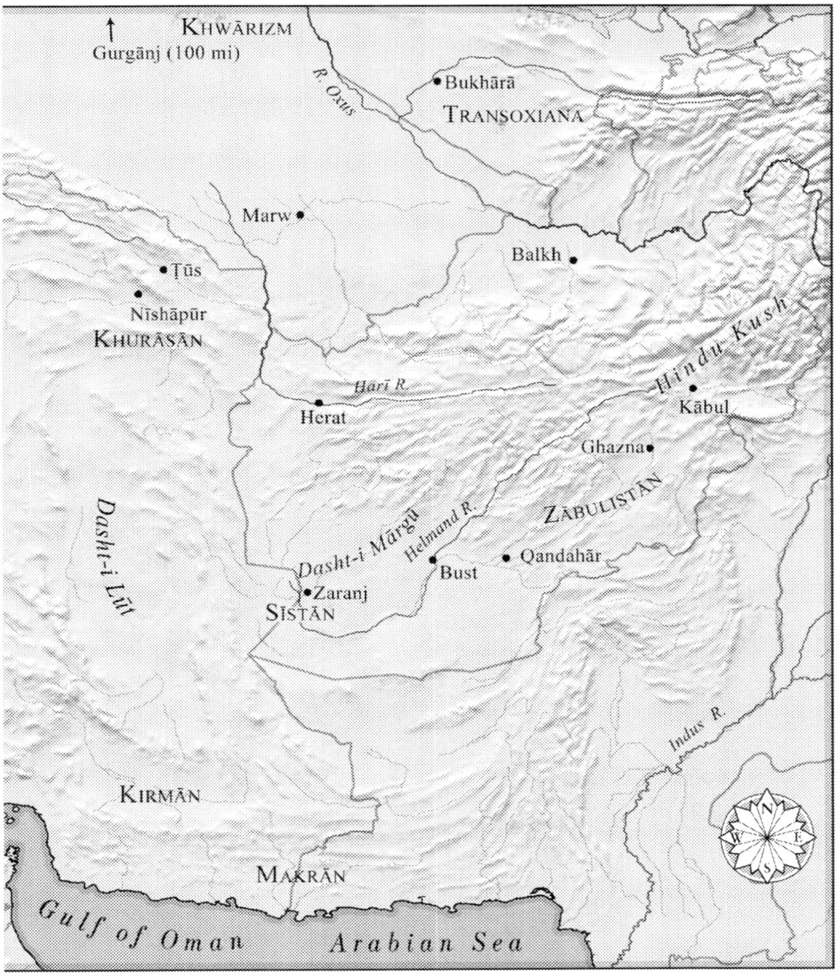
Khwārizm
Gurgānj (100 mi)
R. Oxus
Bukhārā
Transoxiana
Marw
Balkh
Ṭūs
Nīshāpūr
Khurāsān
Hindu Kush
Harī R.
Herat
Kābul
Ghazna
Zābulistān
Dasht-i Lūt
Dasht-i Mārgū
Helmand R.
Bust
Qandahār
Zaranj
Sīstān
Indus R.
Kirmān
Makrān
Gulf of Oman
Arabian Sea
N
W
E
S

FIGURE 0.1. Relief figure of an individual dressed in a kaftan. Nizamabad (south-east of Tehran), Iran, seventh–early eighth century. © Museum für Islamische Kunst, Berlin State Museums. Photo by I. Geske. (Inv. no. I.4591b.)

Introduction

Worries were at my stopping place, so I turned
my sturdy she-camel toward the White Palace of al-Madāʾin.
Consoling myself with good fortune, and sorrowing
at the traces of the camp of the clan of Sāsān.
Successive afflictions reminded me of them;
incidents make one remember, make one forget.

al-Buḥturī (d. 284/897)[1]

Amid the alluvial flatlands east of the Tigris River in Iraq stands a great hulk of a ruin known as the Arch of Khusraw, or to Iranians today as the Tāq-i Kisrā. When Robert Mignan, in the service of the East India Company, came upon the "Tauk Kesra" in 1827, he described "a magnificent monument of antiquity, surprising the spectator with the perfect state of its preservation, after having braved the warring elements for so many ages; without an emblem to throw any light upon its history; without proof, or character to be traced on any brick or wall." Mignan noted that "the natives of this country assert" that "the ruins are of the age of Nimrod," a conclusion that he seems to have found credible.[2] In the

[1] This *qaṣīda* is widely repeated in Arabic sources. The lines featured here follow the recension provided by A. J. Arberry in his *Arabic Poetry: A Primer for Students* (Cambridge: Cambridge University Press, 1965), 72–81 (no. 11); they are translated by Richard A. Serrano in "Al-Buḥturī's Poetics of Persian Abodes," *Journal of Arabic Literature* 28, no. 1 (1997): 79–80 (lines 11–13). See also al-Buḥturī's *dīwān* in the edition of Ḥasan Kāmil al-Ṣayrafī, 5 vols. (Cairo: Dār al-Maʿārif, 1963–8), 2:1152–62 (no. 470).

[2] Robert Mignan, *Travels in Chaldæa, including a Journey from Bussorah to Bagdad, Hillah, and Babylon, Performed on Foot in 1827: With Observations on the Sites and Remains of Babel, Seleucia, and Ctesiphon* (London: Henry Colburn and Richard Bentley, 1829), 71 and 73.

seventeenth and eighteenth centuries. European travelers who came upon the mysterious site assumed the majestic arch and the large columned structure flanking it to be a temple of the sun, or else the work of a Roman emperor.[3] But while the Tāq-i Kisrā was built on the remnants of past civilizations, the history of the site was much more recent, belonging to the Sasanian period and the environs of Ctesiphon, when, within the residential district of Asbānbar, it had served as the throne hall of a palace possibly built by Khusraw Anūshirvān (r. 531–79 CE).[4]

The Arab invasion of Iraq in the 630s initiated a new phase in the area's history, ultimately resulting in the fall of the Sasanian dynasty and the conquest of Iran, and so Ctesiphon and its monuments were eclipsed. The entire area straddling the Tigris became an Arab-Muslim settlement, which the Arabs called al-Madāʾin (Arabic for "the cities"). In the centuries that followed, they dismantled its buildings in order to construct new ones in Kufa and Baghdad. But even as they removed vestiges of the Sasanian architecture, they began the long process of memorializing the site. On the night of the Prophet Muḥammad's birth, according to one report, the battlements of the Tāq-i Kisrā shook so hard that fourteen of them collapsed. At the same moment, for the first time in a thousand years, the Zoroastrians' sacred fire in Fārs (Iṣṭakhr) died out. According to another account, when the Arabs' conquering hero, Saʿd b. Abī Waqqāṣ, entered the Tāq-i Kisrā he performed the special "prayer of conquest" (*ṣalāt al-fatḥ*) that Muḥammad had performed on entering Mecca.[5] Afterward, al-Madāʾin was governed by Salmān al-Fārisī (Salmān "the Persian"), a companion of Muḥammad. There were also tales of spoils so magnificent that antiquities dealers today still hunt for treasures from Ctesiphon.

The Line of Enquiry

The story of Islam's spread beyond Arabia is central to every general history of the faith and of Muslim civilizations, and to understanding the shape of the Muslim world today. Whereas the early community

[3] Oscar Reuther, "The German Excavations at Ctesiphon," *Antiquity* 3, no. 12 (1929): 440 and 447.

[4] Regarding his role, see esp. the doubts expressed by E. J. Keall, "Ayvān-e Kesrā (or Ṭāq-e Kesrā)," in *EIr*. Kisrā is the Arabized form of the Middle Persian xusrō and the new Persian Khusraw.

[5] Al-Ṭabarī, *Taʾrīkh al-rusul wa-l-mulūk*, ed. M. J. de Goeje et al., 15 vols. in 3 series (Leiden: E. J. Brill, 1879–1901), ser. I, 981 and 2443. Subsequent references to this work give the series and page number of the citation.

was based on a small, tribal, Arabian elite, Islam quickly spread beyond this narrow group and was woven into the fabric of innumerable local contexts. Today, although adherents still acknowledge the importance of the Arabian origins of their religion, Islam commands the loyalty of people of virtually every nationality and is the dominant religion in some of the world's most culturally and socially dynamic regions. About 98 percent of Iran's nearly seventy million people are Muslim; Zoroastrianism, the Sasanian state religion, claims adherents only in the tens of thousands.

One of the most important questions relating to the success of Islam worldwide is how loyalty has been fostered among the newly converted. In particular, how have they come to feel a sense of belonging to a Muslim community? This study addresses questions of loyalty and belonging in relation to Iran's Persians of the third/ninth to fifth/eleventh centuries, who represented the first large group of non-Arab converts to Islam. It does so by showing how the post-conquest descendants of the Persian imperial, religious, and historiographical traditions wrote themselves into starkly different early Arabic and Islamic accounts of the past. Although they soon developed a sense that Islam was as much an Iranian religion as it was an Arab one, nothing guaranteed that Islam would succeed among them, especially in the ways that it did.

The book addresses the issue of loyalty and belonging from the twin angles of tradition and memory. For groups, as for individuals, loyalty and a sense of belonging depend on how they make sense of the past, including their origins, their ancestry, and the achievements of previous generations. The past helps inform and stabilize group identity, particularly during times of political, cultural, or social change. Conversion to Islam led Iranians to recall their past in new ways and to accumulate new memories about their history. Despite the complexity of this process, one can trace its broad outlines by examining the deep currents of Arabic texts that circulated in the third/ninth to fifth/eleventh centuries, including not only works of local, regional, and universal history, but also biographical dictionaries, geographies, works of belles-lettres (*adab*), and "religious" texts such as Qurʾan commentaries, collections of and commentaries on Prophetic Hadith, and works of jurisprudence. These Arabic works represented only the first phase in Iran's rewriting of its past, a process that continued with the subsequent development of Persian letters from the fourth/tenth century onward.

The terms "tradition" and "memory" are central to the book and enable it to draw on a broad body of work that has developed largely outside Arabic, Islamic, and Iranian Studies and that treats memory as integral to processes of cultural and social change. By "tradition" I mean reports handed down about the past in whatever form, including but not limited to the conventional Prophetic traditions and historical reports known as Hadith and *akhbār* (sing. *khabar*). I treat transmission as evidence of the fostering of shared memories. Traditions, like objects, patterns of action, and ways of thinking, are reproduced and disseminated, and they frequently exhibit differences that suggest adaptation and therefore interpretation. I label those who transmit them "traditionists," whatever other affiliations they may have had.[6] The concept of memory, on the other hand, draws attention to the power of traditions to affect individuals and collectivities. As a tradition accumulates weight and authority, it shapes collective agreements about the past, thereby creating memories. These collective agreements are deeply held by groups and the individuals within them, but they can also be opposed, changed, and otherwise subjected to negotiation, especially by the people who consider them to represent "their" past: the descendants of the actors in the story, the residents of the country where the events took place, and the present-day believers.

The period under principal consideration here witnessed great creativity in the fashioning and circulation of traditions about the founding moments of Islam in Iran. This was when Iran's urban elite classes likely converted to Islam, as Richard Bulliet observed more than thirty years ago. Bulliet based his conclusions for Iran chiefly on biographical dictionaries composed for Iṣfahān and Nīshāpūr, thriving cities in central and northeastern Iran.[7] In adopting a quantitative methodology for the study of conversion across the Middle East (with prominent attention to Iran), he noted:

[6] This expansive notion of tradition follows especially Edward Shils, *Tradition* (Chicago: University of Chicago Press, 1981).

[7] Bulliet found that the "basic conversion process" in Iran was completed by 400 AH (1010 CE), leaving about 20 percent of the population "adamant non-Muslims, whose number was reduced only very slowly" afterward; Richard W. Bulliet, *Conversion to Islam in the Medieval Period: An Essay in Quantitative History* (Cambridge, MA: Harvard University Press, 1979), esp. 18–19 and 43. Jamsheed Choksy has hypothesized that urban Zoroastrians adopted Islam between the eighth and tenth centuries CE, whereas the countryside saw an accelerating wave of conversion from the tenth through the thirteenth centuries. See Jamsheed K. Choksy, *Conflict and Cooperation: Zoroastrian Subalterns and Muslim Elites in Medieval Iranian Society* (New York: Columbia University Press, 1997), 106–7. But see also the critique of such periodizations by Michael G. Morony, "The Age of Conversions: A Reassessment," in *Conversion and Continuity: Indigenous Christian Communities in Islamic Lands, Eighth to Eighteenth Centuries*, ed. Michael Gervers and Ramzi Jibran Bikhazi, 135–50 (Toronto: Pontifical Institute of Mediaeval Studies, 1990).

The great conversion experience that fundamentally changed world history by uniting the peoples of the Middle East in a new religion has had few modern chroniclers, the reason being that conversion plays so slight a role in the narratives of medieval chroniclers. Without data it is difficult to write history, and medieval Islam produced no missionaries, bishops, baptismal rites, or other indicators of conversion that could be conveniently recorded by the Muslim chronicler.[8]

What has not been duly appreciated, however, is that in writing about history – including their history before the conquests – Muslims were engaged in an effort to make sense of Islam in the changing and multi-religious communities in which they lived. Conversion is more than a background context for traditions; it is often a point of concern. This is the case even though, as a whole, narrators of traditions generally refer only obliquely to conversion itself and represent themselves as speaking exclusively to other committed Muslims.

Iran in the First Centuries of Islam

In terms of historical background, the following summary will be useful for readers new to Islamic or Iranian history. It represents something of a standard narrative and chronology of the first centuries of Islam, though readers should also be aware that some of its points have been subject to vigorous debates and skepticism among historians.[9] It is commonly thought that Muḥammad was born in or about 570 CE in the town of Mecca in the western Arabian region of the Ḥijāz. From around 610, Muḥammad developed a conviction that he had been specially selected by God and began to gather a small group of followers.[10] At intervals, he recited passages that, he said, were a revelation from God and formed a corpus called the Qurʾan, and which gave confidence and guidance to his followers. Facing opposition in Mecca, in 622 Muḥammad formed a new community in Medina – the moment that traditionally marks the

[8] Bulliet, *Conversion to Islam in the Medieval Period*, 4.

[9] Regarding what follows, see esp. Chase F. Robinson, "The Rise of Islam," in *The New Cambridge History of Islam*, vol. 1, *The Formation of the Islamic World, Sixth to Eleventh Centuries*, edited by Chase F. Robinson, 173–225 (Cambridge: Cambridge University Press, 2010), and Elton L. Daniel, "The Islamic East," in the same volume, 448–505 (he treats Iran's conversion on pp. 463–6).

[10] As an example of skepticism, see Lawrence I. Conrad's arguments regarding these dates; "Abraha and Muḥammad: Some Observations Apropos of Chronology and Literary *Topoi* in the Early Arabic Historical Tradition," *Bulletin of the School of Oriental and African Studies* 50, no. 2 (1987): 225–40.

beginning of the Islamic (hijri) calendar. Over the second half of the 620s, he gained the support of many Arab tribal groups as he consolidated his authority in Medina and then fixed his attention on Mecca, which he conquered about two and a half years before his death in 11 AH/632 CE. His followers were known collectively as companions (*ṣaḥāba*) and were divided into two groups: the Muhājirūn (emigrants from Mecca) and the Anṣār (helpers), those Medinans who supported him. After Muḥammad's death the Muslims engaged in military campaigns so extensive that, within twenty years, they had brought down the Sasanian Empire, which stretched from Iraq to Marw in modern Turkmenistan. Arabs settled in cities such as Hamadhān, Rayy, and Nīshāpūr, building their own quarters with palaces, mosques, and gardens. Several former villages, such as Qum, became cities as a result of such settlement, but many territories, protected by mountains and deserts, remained beyond the reach of the Arabs' armies.[11] The Byzantine Empire, meanwhile, had controlled the eastern remnants of the Roman Empire, but Syria, Palestine, Egypt, and North Africa fell quickly to the Arabs, with the net result that the Arabs acquired control over approximately half of the former territory of Byzantium.

In the emerging empire, after the first four successors to Muḥammad rule passed down along dynastic lines, first among the Umayyads in Syria (r. 41–132/661–750), and after 132/750, among the Iraq-based ʿAbbasids, who descended from the Prophet's uncle, ʿAbbās. The early ʿAbbasid period is often depicted as a golden age (as in the stories from the *Arabian Nights*), when caliphs ruled with the assistance of their able Persian viziers. Yet for all its strengths, by the second half of the third/ninth century, the ʿAbbasid state had begun to show weakness. In Baghdad, the caliphs subsequently fell under the control of Buyid (r. 334–447/945–1055) and Seljuk (447–547/1055–1152) amirs and sultans, the Buyids hailing from the Caspian region of Daylam and the Seljuks from the steppes north of the Caspian and Aral seas. While the caliphs retained nominal sovereignty, Iran and the central and eastern stretches of the empire came under the rule of these de facto rulers, as well as of other dynasties who at various times controlled portions of the ʿAbbasid realm: the Samanids (204–395/819–1005), the Saffarids (247–393/861–1003),

[11] On the persistence of belief systems in rural Iran after the conquests, see now Patricia Crone, *The Nativist Prophets of Early Islamic Iran: Rural Revolt and Local Zoroastrianism* (Cambridge: Cambridge University Press, 2012).

and the Ghaznavids (366–582/977–1186), to name but three.[12] While our earliest extant narrative sources were written in ʿAbbasid Iraq at the height of its glory through the first half of the third/ninth century, a real literary outpouring took place later, often exhibiting different perspectives, when the caliphs were weak and Iranian and Central Asian rulers patronized scholarship and learning. Throughout the period, Arabic functioned as the language of elites much as Latin did in the premodern West. Even local Iranian histories of the fourth/tenth and fifth/eleventh centuries, for example, tended to be written in Arabic (though in some cases they were later translated into Persian).

Coins give a sense of the cultural confidence and political will of Iranians from the mid-fourth/tenth century onward. The Caliph ʿAbd al-Malik (r. 65–86/685–705) and his successors had made sure that Arabic epigraphy distinguished the caliphate's gold and silver coins from those of its predecessors and current neighbors. However, semi-independent or autonomous governors, such as the Buyids, struck coins with their personal names, which were often of ancient Persian derivation.[13] When Aḥmad b. Buwayh (d. 355/967) became commander of the caliph's armies in 334/945, he quickly usurped the caliph's authority: he and his Buyid successors adopted lofty titles, including *shāhān-shāh* ("king of kings"); had their names read out in the sermon (*khuṭba*) of the weekly communal prayer, traditionally a caliphal prerogative; and inscribed their names on coins. The Buyids drew on the iconography of earlier days and reemployed the Pahlavi script in coins minted and presented to dignitaries on special occasions across their domains.[14] The ʿAbbasids could

12 There had been Iranian "statelets" throughout the early Islamic period, but these had existed on the fringes of the empire, in territories that were hard to reach and offered little material reward to the ʿAbbasid state. For a useful summary of this situation, see Hugh Kennedy, "Survival of Iranianness," in *The Idea of Iran*, vol. 4, *The Rise of Islam*, ed. Vesta Sarkhosh Curtis and Sarah Stewart, 13–29 (London: I. B. Tauris, 2009).

13 Regarding the extensive use of Persian names, see esp. Vladimir N. Nastich, "Persian Legends on Islamic Coins: From Traditional Arabic to the Challenge of Leadership," in *The 2nd Simone Assemani Symposium on Islamic Coins*, ed. Bruno Callagher and Arianna D'Ottone, 165–90 (Trieste: Edizioni Università di Trieste, 2010).

14 Regarding the Buyids, see esp. Mehdi Bahrami, "A Gold Medal in the Freer Gallery of Art," in *Archaeologica Orientalia in Memoriam Ernst Herzfeld*, ed. George C. Miles, 5–21 (Locust Valley, NY: J. J. Augustin, 1952); Wilferd Madelung, "The Assumption of the Title Shāhānshāh by the Būyids and 'the Reign of the Daylam (*Dawlat al-Daylam*),'" *Journal of Near Eastern Studies* 28, no. 2 (1969): 84–108; John J. Donohue, "Three Buwayhid Inscriptions," *Arabica* 20, no. 1 (1973): 74–80 and idem, *The Buwayhid*

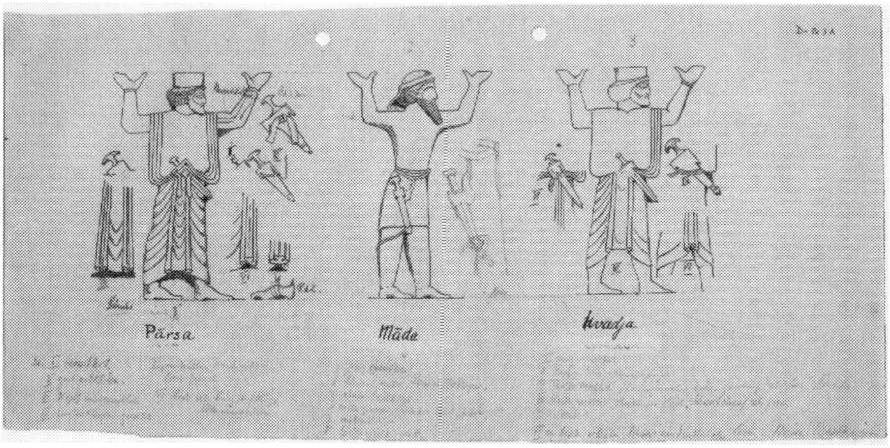

FIGURE 0.2. Persepolis (Iran), Throne Hall, standing figures drawn from rock reliefs depicting representatives of the nations of the Empire "supporting the throne," 1903–1936. Ernst Herzfeld Papers, Freer Gallery of Art and Arthur M. Sackler Gallery Archives, Smithsonian Institution, Washington, DC. Gift of Ernst Herzfeld, 1946. Drawing by Ernst Herzfeld (D-903a).

do little as pre-Islamic symbols such as Sasanian winged crowns entered the larger currency system, although there were protests. The great jurist and caliphal adviser al-Māwardī (d. 450/1058), for example, reportedly once declared a legal opinion (*fatwā*) against the Buyid ruler Jalāl al-Dawla, who in 429/1037–8 demanded from the reigning caliph, al-Qāʾim (r. 422–67/1031–75), the right to the Arabic title *malik al-mulūk* ("king of kings").[15]

The term "Persia" was used in Achaemenid (559–330 BCE) and Sasanian (224–651 CE) times to refer both to the ethnic homeland of a "Persian" ethnic group in southwestern Iran and to the vast lands under the imperial control and cultural influence of this people following its

Dynasty in Iraq, 334H./945 to 403H./1012: Shaping Institutions for the Future (Leiden: Brill, 2003); Luke Treadwell, *Buyid Coinage: A Die Corpus (322–445 A.H.)* (Oxford: Ashmolean Museum Oxford, 2001), xv–xvii; and Roy Parviz Mottahedeh, "The Idea of Iran in the Buyid Dominions," in *The Idea of Iran*, vol. 5, *Early Islamic Iran*, ed. Edmund Herzig and Sarah Stewart, 153–60 (London: I. B. Tauris, 2012).

15 Al-Māwardī declared the fatwa in 429/1037–8; see ʿIzz al-Dīn b. al-Athīr, *al-Kāmil fī al-taʾrīkh*, ed. C. J. Tornberg, 15 vols. (Leiden: E. J. Brill, 1851–76), 9:312–13; also, C. Brockelmann, "al-Māwardī," in *EI*[2] and K. V. Zetterstéen, "Djalal al-Dawla," in *EI*[2]. Ibn al-Athīr's citation of the title as *malik al-mulūk* rather than *shāhān-shāh* (as stated by Brockelmann) is noteworthy.

dispersal.[16] Scholars have traced the ambiguous usage of the geographical term "Persia" in early Islam to this prior, pre-Islamic ambiguity.[17] In early Arabic sources, one can thus find the term *Fārs/Fāris* applied both in the narrow sense to a specific province, particularly by geographers, and in wider senses to refer to a territory that includes the province but exceeds it. Likewise, the term *ahl Fārs/Fāris* (or sometimes just *Fāris*) may denote either a "Persian" people sharing a culture and a sense of historical community, in general, or the people of the province of Persia in particular, whereas the much more common term *al-Furs* most often refers to a people not limited to a province.[18] By contrast, the idea of Iran (Middle Persian, *Ērān*) has quite a different sense and history, and the term "Iran" had only limited usage in the period of this study. In the late 1980s, Gherardo Gnoli initiated reconsideration of this term and its associations with the argument that a notion of Iran reached a point of clarity only at the beginning of the Sasanian period, when it was part of a program that included among its elements an appeal to Achaemenid origins.[19] Accordingly, the Sasanians introduced the Middle Persian title of *shāhān-shāh Ērān* and invented the idea of *Ērān-shahr*, the "domain of the Iranians," to refer to their realm; the term was subsequently used as part of state propaganda.[20] Sasanian titles made extensive use of the name

16 The "Persian" rulers of both the Achaemenid and the Sasanian empires established imperial centers outside of Fārs, including Susa (Achaemenids) and Ctesiphon (Sasanians).

17 "The confusion between the two senses of the word was continuous, fueled by the Greeks who used the name Persai to designate the entire empire. It lasted through the centuries of Arab domination, as Fārs, the term used by Muslims, was merely the Arabicized version of the initial name." Xavier de Planhol, "Fārs i. Geography," in *EIr*. Cf. David Morgan, *Medieval Persia, 1040–1797* (London: Longman, 1988), 1–2, and Edward G. Browne, *A Literary History of Persia*, 4 vols. (Cambridge: Cambridge University Press, 1928), 1:4–5.

18 See, e.g., Abū al-Ḥasan al-Masʿūdī, *Kitāb al-Tanbīh wa-l-ishrāf*, ed. Michael J. de Goeje (Leiden: E. J. Brill, 1893), 77–8, where al-Masʿūdī includes in the land of the Persians Fārs as a province (quite far down his list), as well as other regions and towns, including Nīshāpūr, Herat, and Marw in Khurāsān. Al-Masʿūdī describes seven original nations (*umam*), including the Persians, *al-Furs*. The term *al-ʿAjam* is sometimes also used synonymously with "Persians"; see C. E. Bosworth, "ʿAjam," in *EIr*, and Jan Retsö, *The Arabs in Antiquity: Their History from the Assyrians to the Umayyads* (London: RoutledgeCurzon, 2005), 24–8. Writers also appear to use the term *al-ʿAjam* to avoid the ethnic sense of "Persians" (a good example being Abū Ḥanīfa al-Dīnawarī, d. ca. 281 or 282/894–5, in his *al-Akhbār al-ṭiwāl*, discussed in Chapters 3 and 4).

19 Gherardo Gnoli, *The Idea of Iran: An Essay on Its Origin* (Rome: Istituto italiano per il Medio ed Estremo Oriente, 1989), 178.

20 Gnoli argues that "This new title had a very important value insofar as, in its adoption by Ardaxšīr and his successors, we can actually detect the birth of the very idea of Iran in

Ērān, and it was also used as part of personal names.[21] Since Gnoli (and, indeed, before him as well), many scholars both inside and outside of Iran have undertaken studies that consider the meaning and significance of "Iran" as a focus of "national" loyalties from Sasanian on through to modern times. As with many studies of other, modern nationalities, opinions are deeply divided, with some scholars viewing identification with Iran as reaching back into the distant primordial Avestan, Achaemenid, or Sasanian past, while others argue for the modernity of Iranian national sentiment.[22]

In contrast to the Sasanian period, and at variance with the situation today, we find early Islam to be the era of Persia and Persians.[23] Muslims

its political, cultural and religious meaning. He who coined that title wanted to refer to the *arya* and Zoroastrian tradition so as to cement his politics and to differentiate them from those of his hated predecessors." Gnoli describes *Ērān-shahr* as "something new, though in the guise of a venerable tradition," and invokes Eric Hobsbawm and Terence Ranger's notion of the "invention" of tradition. Gnoli, *Idea of Iran*, 138, 139, and 177; Hobsbawm and Ranger, eds., *The Invention of Tradition* (Cambridge: Cambridge University Press, 1983).

21 Gnoli, *Idea of Iran*, 130. Cf. Arthur Christensen, *L'Iran sous les Sassanides* (Copenhagen: Levin & Munksgaard, 1936), esp. 108ff., 214–15, 416, and 513ff.

22 The bibliography on this subject is extensive; see especially Mostafa Vaziri, *Iran as Imagined Nation: The Construction of National Identity* (New York: Paragon House, 1993); Afshin Marashi, *Nationalizing Iran: Culture, Power, and the State, 1870–1940* (Seattle: University of Washington Press, 2008); Mohamad Tavakoli-Targhi, "Historiography and Crafting Iranian National Identity," in *Iran in the 20th Century: Historiography and Political Culture*, ed. Touraj Atabaki, 5–21 (London: I. B. Tauris, 2009), and in the same volume, Afshin Marashi, "The Nation's Poet: Ferdowsi and the Iranian National Imagination," 93–111; and Abbas Amanat and Farzin Vejdani, *Iran Facing Others: Identity Boundaries in a Historical Perspective* (New York: Palgrave Macmillan, 2012). See also the series published by I. B. Tauris in association with the London Middle East Institute at SOAS and the Faculty of Oriental Studies, University of Oxford, *The Idea of Iran*, including vol. 4, *The Rise of Islam*, ed. Curtis and Stewart (2009), and vol. 5, *Early Islamic Iran*, ed. Herzig and Stewart (2012). Regarding *Ērān* as a focus for Zoroastrian religious loyalties in the Sasanian period, see vol. 3, *The Sasanian Era*, ed. Curtis and Stewart, and especially the chapter by Shaul Shaked, "Religion in the Late Sasanian Period: Eran, Aneran, and Other Religious Designations," pp. 103–17.

23 A strain of recent scholarship relating to Iran has sought to limit strictly the size of the social group called Persians in early Islam, with the argument that early Muslim sources, when they refer to *al-Furs*, err by confusing the people of a part of Iran, that is, Fārs, for the entirety of the Iranian population. See, for example, Choksy, *Conflict and Cooperation*, 8–9. Considering that early Muslims, including Iranians, themselves used the term "Persians," such scholarship risks favoring a hypostatized notion of Iranians. One can refer to Iranians, but with the acknowledgment that this was not the primary category employed in early Muslim sources. For the term "Iran" in later centuries, however, see esp. Dorothea Krawulsky, *Īrān, das Reich der Īlḫāne: Eine topographisch-historische Studie* (Wiesbaden: Dr. Ludwig Reichert, 1978), and Krawulsky, "Zur Wiederbelebung des Begriffes 'Īrān' zur Ilkhânzeit," in *Mongolen und*

continued to use the terms *Īrān* and *Īrān-shahr* (as transliterated from Arabic and New Persian, versus Middle Persian *Ērān-shahr*), although they do not appear to have been attuned to the terms' potential. Geographers, in their entries, treat Īrān-shahr and Fārs, the province, separately. Likewise, Muslims refer to Īrān-shahr in contexts in which Iran's pre-Islamic past, especially its "national" tradition, is mentioned.[24] But otherwise the term "Persia" is generally preferred, often even in discussions of geography and of the national past.[25] Muḥammad himself is remembered to have spoken of Persia but not of Īrān-shahr. At the same time, other ethnic identities were submerged. For example, a notion of "Pahlav" as an ethnicon may have lingered, but in the early Muslim sources the term *fahlaw* has nothing of the currency of the terms *al-Furs* or *Banū Fāris*.

In what follows, I will use the term Iran to refer to a territory centered on a plateau, and in recognition of shared linguistic and cultural patterns that do have antique origins; likewise, the term "Iranians" will refer to its inhabitants and is useful for encompassing a variety of groups. But in the period under consideration, regional identities were far stronger than pan-Iranian ones. The major identity that cut across regions was a

Ilkhâne: Ideologie und Geschichte; 5 Studien, 113–30 (Beirut: Verlag für Islamische Studien, 1989).

24 Still today, historians commonly, if uncritically, apply the term "national" to Iran's epic nation, as well as to Sasanian-era historiography. For the roots of this view among modern Iranian academics, see esp. Marashi, "Nationalizing Pre-Islamic Iran," in *Nationalizing Iran*; regarding European scholarship and the lineage of the term, see esp. Theodor Nöldeke, *Das Iranische Nationalepos* (Berlin: de Gruyter, 1920); Christensen, *Les Kayanides* (Copenhagen: Andr. Fred. Høst & Søn, 1931), 35ff.; and Ehsan Yarshater, "Iranian National History," in *The Cambridge History of Iran*, vol. 3(1), *The Seleucid, Parthian and Sasanian Periods*, ed. Ehsan Yarshater, 359–477 (Cambridge: Cambridge University Press, 1983), 395ff.

25 See, for example, al-Yaʿqūbī, *Taʾrīkh*, ed. M. Th. Houtsma, 2 vols. (Leiden: E. J. Brill, 1883; repr., Beirut: Dār Ṣādir, 1960), 1:178 (where, however, Persia's kings figure as part of prophetic history, a phenomenon I treat in Chapter 1). But compare the *Shahrestānīhā-ī Ērān-shahr*, a Middle Persian text that its modern translator, Touraj Daryaee, believes reflects a sixth/early seventh-century CE imperial Sasanian vision of Ērān-shahr, although its last redactors lived under the ʿAbbasid caliphate in the eighth century CE. Touraj Daryaee, ed. and trans., *Šahrestānīhā ī Ērānšahr: A Middle Persian Text on Late Antique Geography, Epic, and History* (Costa Mesa, CA: Mazda Publishers, 2002), "Introduction." See also M. Boyce, trans., *The Letter of Tansar* (Rome: Istituto Italiano per il Medio ed Estremo Oriente, 1968), 26, n. 1, and Gnoli, *Idea of Iran*, 153–5. For another exception, see Roy P. Mottahedeh, "Finding *Iran* in the Panegyrics of the Ghaznavid Court," paper presented at the conference "Eastern Iran and Transoxiana 750–1150: Persianate Culture and Islamic Civilization," Institute of Iranian Studies, University of St. Andrews, March 9, 2013.

"Persian" one, and this imperfectly, in different ways at different times.[26] As for all times and locales, it is also important to bear in mind the extent to which identity was intersubjective and contextual. During the first century and a half of Islam, tribes from throughout the Arabian peninsula, Syria, Palestine, southern Iraq, and as far away as Khurāsān came to see themselves as sharing in a larger "Arab" identity as part of a process in which many other, non-"Arab" groups began to recognize their own distinctiveness in new ways. So a man might identify himself as a Persian relative to other ethnic groups and in recognition of shared customs, language, homeland, history, and descent, but consider himself a Kirmānī (a native of the province of Kirmān) when traveling in Khurāsān or a partisan of the Shiʿa or of the legal school of al-Shāfiʿī when sectarian or juristic affiliations mattered. Like other Muslims of their day, the inhabitants of Iran tended to affiliate themselves with many different groups based on bonds of ethnicity as well as of language, lineage, locality, and profession. Regarding sectarian loyalties, in the first centuries, the family of ʿAlī also won the affection of some Iranians, although it was centuries before Shiʿi sectarianism won the loyalty of Iranians as a whole.[27] For understanding the loyalties and affiliations of Iranians after the Muslim conquest, therefore, a number of possibilities must be considered, of which Persian ethnicity is an important but not the sole or overriding one.

Tradition

In Islamic Studies, the term "tradition" is often used in a limited sense to refer to the Hadith of the Prophet or to reports about him and the early community (*akhbār*) that circulated in "historical" texts, such as Prophetic biographies. In this book, the term is used in a more general sense to emphasize not only the common characteristics of reports about the past but also the ways in which these reports participate in larger patterns of culture. The definition itself is silent on questions of soundness, authenticity, and truth. A bowl may be faulty for a variety of reasons but still be traditional, insofar as it follows past patterns, and likewise, a

[26] For consideration of the term "Persians" in another context, that of the ʿAbbasid Revolution, with special attention to Syriac historiography, see Antoine Borrut, *Entre mémoire et pouvoir: L'espace syrien sous les derniers Omeyyades et les premiers Abbassides (v. 72–193/692–809)* (Leiden: Brill, 2011), 345ff.

[27] On this, see esp. Rula Jurdi Abisaab, *Converting Persia: Religion and Power in the Safavid Empire* (London: I. B. Tauris, 2004).

historical proposition may rise or fall depending on "rational and empirical evidence," but in either case, it can justifiably be called traditional.[28]

For a student of history, a key opportunity presents itself in the way in which our Arabic sources tend to return to a common pool of memories about locales, events, institutions, and persons, but with different methods of selecting and manipulating the record. These divergent methods can often suggest something about the hermeneutics of individual traditionists. One can compare texts so as to decipher novelties, discern goals, and understand the social and cultural stakes involved in remembering the past in one particular way as opposed to another. Ctesiphon, for example, was made into an expressive relic by reporters who made much of the spoils, including a massive carpet, the *qiṭf*, known in Persian as the *Bahār-i Khusraw* ("the king's spring"); this was divided up with a large piece given to ʿAlī, perhaps suggesting the metaphorical transfer of a portion of the kingdom of Kisrā (the Sasanian ruler) to his later partisans.[29] A different memory is encapsulated in the *qaṣīda* of al-Buḥturī, cited at the beginning of this introduction, which was composed during the reign of Caliph al-Muntaṣir (r. 247–8/861–2) and which has its own perspective on the site. The poet dwells on and even exaggerates the ruin of the monuments at al-Madāʾin as he connects the past majesty of the monuments to that of their unnamed builder. As Richard Serrano has argued, he is attentive to their present state and, most importantly, to their affective power, but for him, the ruins are positive reminders of a great though vanished empire with which he identifies as the descendant of a people that was once allied to it. Al-Buḥturī stresses the resilience of Kisrā's *īwān* (throne hall) against all attempts to plunder it and refers specifically to its carpets:

> It was not disgraced by the robbery of carpets
> Of silk brocade, or plunder of curtains of raw silk;
> Lofty, its battlements soar,
> Raised on the summits of Radwa and Quds;
> Clothed in white, so that
> You see of them but cotton robes.
> It isn't known if it's the workmanship of men for jinn
> Who inhabit it, or the work of jinn for men,
> Yet I see it gives witness that
> The builder is not the least of kings.[30]

28 For Shils's point regarding historical truth, see *Tradition*, 89–90.
29 Al-Ṭabarī, *Taʾrīkh*, I:2454.
30 Serrano, "Al-Buḥturī's Poetics of Persian Abodes," 83–4.

Al-Buḥturī profited from the patronage of several ʿAbbasid caliphs, but he appears to have composed his *qaṣīda* in a moment of upset. Through the motif of an abandoned site, he has made al-Madāʾin and its monuments, including the *īwān*, into a subject that shows the finitude of empires in general, insinuating, perhaps, the same fate for his ʿAbbasid patrons. He has also, as Serrano has proposed, imagined himself in the place of Khusraw Anūshirvān, served by the king's boon companion al-Balahbadh; his praises are for himself, not for his patrons, who we are led to believe have failed him.[31]

Wherever possible, I employ a comparative method to discern what makes a particular author's perspective distinctive. This method requires consideration for a traditionist's own particular, historical circumstances, as well as some attention to those of the genre within which he worked, since a historian of the conquests, for example, will tend to provide a perspective that differs from that of a Qurʾan commentator, though they both reflect on the same, seminal events. This method is greatly facilitated by modern technology and databases of Arabic texts, but it does have some limitations. For example, it gives little consideration to earlier, lost sources and their particular perspectives, and it leaves open the question of how much fifteenth-century Persian translations or reworkings of tenth-century Arabic texts can tell us about tenth-century views. Sometimes such views do become fossilized in later sources, with traditionists passing on reports indifferently. Historians often drew on past layers of history writing. As is frequently noted, Arabic historiography is a cumulative endeavor. Still, I believe that scholars have too often overlooked creative possibilities in their quest to uncover the origins of ideas or to establish the boundaries of genres. I prefer, then, the risk of overstating the plasticity of our sources for the benefit of querying them.

Remembering

The expansion of Islam and the birth of Islamic historiography occurred within a late antique world where techniques of memory played an important role in the transmission of knowledge. The Qurʾan was recited

[31] Serrano argues that al-Buḥturī questions the "source – and value – of imperial Arab culture" ("Al-Buḥturī's Poetics of Persian Abodes," 69). This may be so, but if anything, it won him the admiration of ʿAbbasid poets and anthologists. For example, the ʿAbbasid prince and poet Ibn al-Muʿtazz (d. 296/908) reportedly praised the *qaṣīda*, and his appreciative comments are repeated throughout Arabic literature. See, e.g., al-Khaṭīb al-Baghdādī, *Taʾrīkh Baghdād*, 14 vols. (Cairo: Maktabat al-Khānjī, 1931), 1:130.

and transmitted orally in support of ritualized prayer, but also Hadith, *akhbār*, all manner of historical lore, and poetry were passed down in oral form. Children often learned the Qur'an at a young age so as to prepare themselves for later studies (not to mention the social cachet that went with such knowledge), and they also memorized Hadith and other reports, the authenticity of which depended on continuous transmission. Those who cited the Prophet's warning against the writing down of tradition sought to combat the use of the pen and, they feared, the consequent erosion of memory.[32] As they juxtapose written and oral transmission, Muslim sources from the first centuries often depict this debate as an inquest, including questions posed and information gathered, with a high degree of anxiety about the loss of connections and information. Long after the place of written transmission was secured, the values of an oral culture, and a focus on memory, continued.[33] Throughout the first four centuries of Islamic history, the ideal of the perfectibility of memory is widely in evidence, most conspicuously in works that provide ratings on the reliability of Hadith transmitters. Such individuals are linked to each other but also backward in time, as communities in which a perfectible, if not perfect, memory inheres.[34]

Historians of Islam have long recognized the importance of memory to the work that they do, though until recently typically without considering its social or cultural dimensions. By contrast, a recent and expansive study by Antoine Borrut considered the formation of a "vulgate historiographique" at different phases, particularly in ʿAbbasid times, that filtered and reshaped memory about the Umayyad dynasty and the early ʿAbbasids, about the Syrian landscape, and about the eras' heroes and rebels, institutions, and monuments.[35] Like the Umayyad and

32 Michael Cook, "The Opponents of the Writing of Tradition in Early Islam," "Voix et Calame en Islam Médiéval," special issue, *Arabica* 44, no. 4 (1997): 437–530.

33 The relationship between oral and written transmission was complex and varied depending on the nature of the material being passed on. They also occurred simultaneously; see esp. Gregor Schoeler, *Écrire et transmettre dans les débuts de l'Islam* (Paris: Presses universitaires de France, 2002). Translated as Gregor Schoeler, *The Genesis of Literature in Islam: From the Aural to the Read*, rev. ed., trans. Shawkat M. Toorawa (Edinburgh: Edinburgh University Press, 2009). Even in later centuries, orality and memory remained integral to education; see Konrad Hirschler, *The Written Word in the Medieval Arabic Lands: A Social and Cultural History of Reading Practices* (Edinburgh: Edinburgh University Press, 2012).

34 See also Chase F. Robinson, *Islamic Historiography* (Cambridge: Cambridge University Press, 2003), 172–7.

35 See Borrut, *Entre mémoire et pouvoir*; 168–73, for a useful summary of scholarship on memory relating to Islam and early Islamic history; see also Borrut and Paul M. Cobb,

early ʿAbbasid eras, the first century of Islam also has been treated as a subject of remembrance, as have other phases in Islamic history.[36] Several studies of narrative have pursued similar goals, that is, to examine a textual tradition, its agents (or "authors"), and its plasticity and meaningfulness.[37] Consideration has also been given to memory in studies on books and book cultures.[38] As for Iran, despite work on a variety of topics, especially the transmission of pre-Islamic texts and ideas into Arabic and Persian (particularly relating to the *Shāh-nāmah* and courtly tradition),[39] and modern memories of the pre-Islamic past, so far there have been few works treating historical consciousness among Iranian Muslims in the period of conversion, and no study dedicated to the issue of their shared memories.[40]

Readers familiar with Jan Assmann's work on the representations of Moses in European history will find echoes of his methodology in my own. What Assmann calls "mnemohistory" concerns itself with the past as it is remembered: he lifts out memory from history writing, connects it to social and cultural contexts, and returns it as an object of inquiry. Memory is not opposed to history, but part of it. If scholars generally

eds., *Umayyad Legacies: Medieval Memories from Syria to Spain* (Leiden: Brill, 2010), esp. Borrut, "La *Memoria* Omeyyade: Les Omeyyades entre souvenir et oubli dans les sources narratives Islamiques" (pp. 25–61).

36 Surprisingly little work has been done on this topic; but see Asma Afsaruddin, *The First Muslims: History and Memory* (Oxford: Oneworld, 2008), to be read in the light of Robinson's review article, "The Ideological Uses of Early Islam," *Past & Present*, no. 203 (2009): 205–28. Work on prophetic biography has not typically taken up the question of collective memory, as such, though it has treated the "reception" of ideas about Muḥammad; see Uri Rubin, *The Eye of the Beholder: The Life of Muḥammad as Viewed by the Early Muslims* (Princeton, NJ: Darwin Press, 1995).

37 E.g., Fred Donner, *Narratives of Islamic Origins: The Beginnings of Islamic Historical Writing* (Princeton, NJ: Darwin Press, 1998), and Tayeb El-Hibri, *Reinterpreting Islamic Historiography: Hārūn Al-Rashīd and the Narrative of the ʿAbbāsid Caliphate* (Cambridge: Cambridge University Press, 1999). While narratives can be evidence for the shaping of memory, they should not be conflated with memory, as I argue below.

38 Such studies foreground questions about orality, with a central interest in Arabic literary history and in the ways in which knowledge was transmitted in the first centuries of Islam; see esp. Schoeler, *Genesis of Literature in Islam*, and Shawkat M. Toorawa, *Ibn Abī Ṭāhir Ṭayfūr and Arabic Writerly Culture: A Ninth-Century Bookman in Baghdad* (London: RoutledgeCurzon, 2005), esp. "From Memory to Written Record."

39 I address this body of scholarship especially in Chapters 1 and 4.

40 In Persian a few Iranian scholars have recently engaged with the question of historical consciousness after the conquests with an eye toward identifying continuities across eras in different domains, including with regard to the Persian language; see, for example, Ādhartāsh Ādharnūsh, *Chālish miyān-i Farsī va ʿArabī: Sadah-hā-yi nukhust* (Tehran: Nay, 1385 *shamsī*/[2006]).

seek to distinguish history from myth, mnemohistory seeks to identify a representation in its *Sitz im Leben*. It does not ask, "Was Moses really trained in all the wisdom of the Egyptians?" Instead, it considers "why such a statement did not appear in the book of Exodus, but only appeared in Acts (7:22), and why the Moses discourse in the seventeenth and eighteenth centuries almost exclusively based its image of Moses not on Moses' elaborate biography in the Pentateuch, but on this single verse in the New Testament."[41]

As one reviewer noted, Assmann gave a gratifyingly precise name to what many historians were already seeking to do.[42] In terms of method, Assmann's approach rests on bringing together different accounts for the purpose of noting similarities and dissimilarities, and it assigns importance to narratives as repositories of memory. Comparison of narratives can uncover the layering of memory, taking the form of stratigraphy, to borrow a term from geology, but it equally requires distinguishing a variety of perspectives: that of someone living on the frontier versus in Baghdad; that of a partisan of the Shiʿa versus that of a Sunni traditionist; that of a courtier with "skin in the game" versus that of a political outsider; that of a descendant of the conquerors versus that of the conquered.

From my perspective, the significance of mnemohistory as a method lies in its attentiveness to meaning and in the light it can shed on the renegotiation of identities and their associated loyalties. This way of reading the sources suggests something quite profound about Persians of the third/ninth to fifth/eleventh centuries that has not been noted previously, and this is the occurrence of not one but two conversions: one to Persianness, and the other to Islam. One involved a particular ethnic group, the other a religion of nonparticular, universal membership. As part of this dual process of conversion, aspects of Persian identity were contested,

41 Jan Assmann, *Moses the Egyptian: The Memory of Egypt in Western Monotheism* (Cambridge, MA: Harvard University Press, 1997), 9–10. Assmann's broader theory of "cultural memory" involves "the handing down of meaning," and within it the written, textual dimension is but one matter of concern among others (such as the institutional frameworks and technologies associated with writing). See Jan Assmann, *Cultural Memory and Early Civilization: Writing, Remembrance, and Political Imagination* (Cambridge: Cambridge University Press, 2011).

42 Daniel Boyarin, review of *Moses the Egyptian: The Memory of Egypt in Western Monotheism*, by Jan Assmann, *Church History* 67, no. 4 (1998): 842–4. Or as Assmann himself noted, "mnemohistory is nothing new.... Only the distinction between history proper and mnemohistory is new. Without an awareness of this difference, the history of memory, or mnemohistory, turns all too easily into a historical critique of memory." Assmann, *Moses the Egyptian*, 12–13.

especially the Persians' heritage of imperial rule as an elite class and their previous bonds to Zoroastrianism, the Sasanian religion. Persians became possessors of a variant Muslim culture, with common holidays, ritual practices, social conventions, and norms of behavior. This Persian Muslim culture was further characterized by bilingualism among elites, including religious specialists, but the use of dialects of Persian among ordinary members of society, and by a shared reservoir of memories, our point of investigation. A Persian collective sensibility likely varied in the extent and intensity of its hold over different populations, with possibly more consciousness among the elite and literate social strata for which we have evidence. It developed gradually, my period being only the start of the phenomenon, though events occasionally propelled it forward.[43] It was neither continuously present nor always at the forefront of groups' senses of themselves, as they could also identify along other lines, such as in terms of locale, lineage, sect, or dialect. In other words, in putting stress on Persians, I do not wish to substitute a primordial or perennial Iranian identity with a Persian one. Still, whereas other ethnic groups dissolved and fell into near or absolute oblivion, having failed to adapt effectively in the new environment, Persians were successful and indeed absorbed members of other groups. Many factors played a role, but the sense of a shared past, and therefore a future, as Persian Muslims was among the most important.[44]

The idea of collective memory itself is often traced back to Maurice Halbwachs, whose work remains remarkably prescient and insightful. His *Social Frameworks of Memory* greatly extends Durkheim's observation that knowledge is socially constructed – in other words, it cannot be discovered as a simple "given" but resides in and results from groups.[45] For

[43] Notably, the first stages of its development preceded the emergence of New Persian, on which see, for example, Ludwig Paul, "The Language of the *Šāhnāme* in Historical and Dialectical Perspective," in *Languages of Iran: Past and Present; Iranian Studies in Memoriam David Neil MacKenzie*, ed. Dieter Weber, 141–51 (Wiesbaden: Harrassowitz, 2005).

[44] In the terminology of Anthony D. Smith, Persians survived and were transformed as an *ethnie*, sharing a collective name, a mythology of common descent, a shared history, a distinctive shared culture, an association with a specific territory, and a sense of solidarity. Anthony D. Smith, *The Ethnic Origins of Nations* (Oxford: Blackwell, 1986), 21ff.

[45] Halbwachs was recognized in his lifetime for his contribution to the study of collective memory, although it was not until the 1980s that the significance of his work was extensively acknowledged. This prompted Barry Schwartz to conclude: "Halbwachs's discoveries did not cause the current wave of collective memory research; they were rather swept into it." Schwartz, "Collective Memory," in *The Blackwell Encyclopedia*

Halbwachs, memory is knowledge about the past that individuals acquire through social interaction. We remember because we are in dialogue with other members of society, and through this dialogue meaning and significance are assigned to the past and make it memorable. Groups provide "social frameworks for memory" that give an individual the means to recall the past, on the condition, Halbwachs writes, "that I turn toward them and adopt, at least for the moment, their way of thinking."[46] Individuals have their own memories, but these are in large measure part of "group memory" because an event, person, or fact leaves an impression only to the extent that "one has thought it over," that is, "to the extent that it is connected with the thoughts that come to us from the social milieu."[47] Paul Ricœur summarized Halbwachs's contribution as showing that "to remember, we need others."[48]

Halbwachs believed that the present generation becomes conscious of itself in counterposing its present situation to its own constructed past.[49] There are as many collective memories as there are groups and institutions in society. Shared memories are necessary for group solidarity, and therefore loss of memory results in loss of place in the social group, as occurs with aphasics.[50] Halbwachs illustrated how memory resides in several groups, including the family, religious groups, and social classes. In a family, the expressions and experiences of individuals in relations of kinship are given their form and "a large part of their meaning" by the domestic group, so the idea of the family as an institution is variable across societies and between families.[51] Families have their own "customs and modes of thinking" that impose their form on the opinions and feelings of their members; likewise, each family has its own mentality, "its memories

of Sociology, ed. George Ritzer, 11 vols. (New York: Blackwell-Wiley, 2007). Much of the interest in memory, and the most interesting work of a theoretical nature, has been propelled by the catastrophic events of World War II, during which Halbwachs himself died at Buchenwald.

46 Maurice Halbwachs, *On Collective Memory*, trans. Lewis A. Coser (Chicago: University of Chicago Press, 1992), 38.

47 Ibid., 53.

48 Paul Ricœur, *Memory, History, Forgetting*, trans. Kathleen Blamey and David Pellauer (Chicago: University of Chicago Press, 2004), 120. In the field of the sociology of knowledge, an analogous point is made, i.e., that knowledge cannot exist independently of social frameworks that recognize it. See Max Scheler, *Problems of a Sociology of Knowledge*, trans. Manfred S. Frings, ed. Kenneth W. Stikkers (London: Routledge & Kegan Paul, 1980), 67.

49 See Lewis A. Coser, "Introduction," in Halbwachs, *On Collective Memory*, 1–34, at 24.

50 Halbwachs, *On Collective Memory*, 43.

51 Ibid., 56.

which it alone commemorates, and its secrets which are revealed only to its members." Memories are not individual and disinterested images of the past; rather, they work on a higher plane as models, examples, and elements of teaching. These express the "general attitude of the group" and "reproduce its history," but they also, importantly, define the group's very "nature and its qualities and weaknesses."[52] Within these memories there are certain "landmarks" that stand out as points of group interest: figures that express an "entire character," or facts that recapitulate "an entire period in the life of the group."[53]

Among these landmarks would be Assmann's Moses and the Exodus, or in the case of Persian Muslim historiography, the Tāq-i Kisrā, Salmān al-Fārisī, and the Arab conquest of Iran. Such landmarks are labeled "sites of memory" (*lieux de mémoire*) by Pierre Nora, whose ideas also inform this study. Nora introduced his theory of *lieux de mémoire* both as a way of understanding what he terms the "consolidation" of a French national heritage and its most spectacular symbols and, it would seem, as a program ultimately concerned with the preservation of a catalog of a fading French national memory. Sites are presented expansively as nostalgic devotional institutions around which French society's "memory crystallizes and secretes itself," exemplified by museums, archives, cemeteries, festivals, anniversaries, treaties, depositions, monuments, sanctuaries, and fraternal orders.[54] For a study such as mine, Nora's theory offers several points of interest, first, in his explanation of how history and historical propositions themselves can become objects of collective memory, and, second, in his emphasis on the will of society and its members to remember and create *lieux de mémoire*. This means, for example, that there is a difference between the archive and the memory, between that which is recorded and preserved and that which is held and maintained by society in itself. Third, sites of memory are hot spots: they have a capacity for metamorphosis, "an endless recycling of their meaning and an unpredictable proliferation of their meaning." To take an example, a children's textbook, *Tour de la France par deux enfants*, published in 1877, portrayed a France that drew its seductive power from a past that no longer existed. The book continued to circulate, and on the eve of

[52] Ibid., 58–9.

[53] Ibid., 61.

[54] Pierre Nora, "Between Memory and History: *Les lieux de mémoire*" (trans. Marc Roudebush), "Memory and Counter-Memory," special issue, *Representations*, no. 26 (1989): 7 and 12. See also Nora, ed., *Les Lieux de mémoire*, esp. vol. 1 (Paris: Gallimard, 1997).

World War I, it was a nostalgic institution. The book eventually slipped out of the collective memory, but it returned to public consciousness when reprinted on its centennial. The same book and text now took on new meaning and significance because of the transformations undergone by French society in the interval and the effect that these had on those who now considered it memorable.[55]

Forgetting

Common ideas about forgetfulness overwhelmingly stress it as a failure of memory. The Hebrew Bible (Deuteronomy 8:11) warns against this sort of forgetfulness when it states: "Beware lest you forget the Lord your God so that you do not keep His commandments and judgments and ordinances." This forgetting, in a collective sense, occurs, as Yosef Hayim Yerushalmi has written, when "human groups fail – whether purposely or passively, out of rebellion, indifference, or indolence, or as the result of some disruptive historical catastrophe – to transmit what they know about the past to their posterity."[56] Yerushalmi points to the astounding lack of reliability of both individual and collective memory. As Ricœur has also noted, "forgetting is the challenge par excellence put to memory's aim of reliability."[57]

Arabic and Persian sources remember remarkably little about Iran's pre-Islamic and early Islamic past. Consider again the case of Ctesiphon. Despite the importance of Iraq under the Umayyad and ʿAbbasid dynasties – and even though Arabic sources often provide our most convincing literary evidence – by the late third/ninth century many of the details about Ctesiphon's origins, early history, and topography had been forgotten. Early Arabic sources refer to it in ways that suggest its displacement. It is *al-madīna al-ʿatīqa*, that is, "the ancient city." As

[55] See Jacques and Mona Ozouf, "*Le Tour de la France par deux enfants*: Le petit livre rouge de la République," in *Les Lieux de mémoire*, ed. Nora, 1:277–301, and Nora, "Between Memory and History," 19–20. Nora's ideas on memory and history can be and have been critiqued on several grounds, inter alia for creating too strong an opposition between memory and history and between premodern and twentieth-century views of the past; for seeming to possess a romantic agenda not just to describe *lieux* but to preserve and sacralize them; and for the expansiveness of the concept *lieux de mémoire* itself. For an especially lucid critique, see Hue-Tam Ho Tai, "Remembered Realms: Pierre Nora and French National Memory," *American Historical Review* 106, no. 3 (2001): 906–22.

[56] Yosef Hayim Yerushalmi, *Zakhor: Jewish History and Jewish Memory* (Seattle: University of Washington Press, 1996), 108–9.

[57] Ricœur, *Memory, History, Forgetting*, 414.

for details: when was Ctesiphon founded, and by whom? What monuments were located there, rather than in other cities? Was the White Palace joined to the Tāq-i Kisrā? Some of the answers were no longer available, whereas others were contested. That the Arabs used the name al-Madāʾin ("the cities") to refer both to the entirety of the Sasanian metropolis, of which Ctesiphon represented one piece, and to Ctesiphon itself only added to the confusion. And which cities were the *madāʾin*? Were the cities located on both sides of the Tigris, or on the eastern side only?[58]

Historians have recognized such amnesia as they have labored to construct their narratives, often performing complex recoveries of historical data, such as for the late Sasanian *Xwadāy-nāmag*, which was transmitted in some form in Arabic-language writings from the second/eighth century onward. Such gaps have generally been viewed as emerging from failures of memory that resulted from the conquests, the settlement and movement of populations, the growth of new urban centers, the emergence of new bases for elite status (even if old elites successfully negotiated their survival), and the exigencies of an empire centered, initially, outside of the former Sasanian territories. All of these factors did play a role. With time, conversion to Islam likewise undermined knowledge about past religious institutions, associations, practices, and beliefs insofar as they fell from use.

As students of memory increasingly realize, however, forgetting is an essential human practice. On a practical level, we simply cannot remember everything, nor is there a need to remember much of what we experience. Forgetting is required for new memories, since when the past is forgotten, memories can be reshaped or recreated to meet present needs. If we remembered absolutely everything, we would find ourselves in the position of Alexandr Romanovitch Luria's mnemonist, whose memory was

[58] On the confusions in the Arabic sources regarding Ctesiphon, see especially Saleh Ahmad el Ali, "al-Madāʾin fī al-maṣādir al-ʿarabiyya," *Sumer* 23 (1967): 47–65, and el Ali, "Al-Madāʾin and Its Surrounding Area in Arabic Literary Sources," *Mesopotamia* 3–4 (1968–9): 417–39. See also Guy Le Strange, *The Lands of the Eastern Caliphate: Mesopotamia, Persia, and Central Asia, from the Moslem Conquest to the Time of Timur* (Cambridge: Cambridge University Press, 1905; repr., Boston: Adamant Media, 2006), 33–5; J. M. Fiey, "Topography of Madaʾin (Seleucia-Ctesiphon area)," *Sumer* 23 (1967): 9–11; Keall, "Ayvān-e Kesrā (or Ṭāq-e Kesrā)," in *EIr*; Hugh Kennedy, "From Shahristan to Medina," *Studia Islamica*, no. 102/103 (2006): 13; and Savant, "Forgetting Ctesiphon: Iran's Pre-Islamic Past, ca. 800–1100," in *History and Identity in the Late Antique Near East*, ed. Philip Wood, 169–86 (Oxford: Oxford University Press, 2013).

FIGURE 0.3. Bowl with Arabic inscription, "He who multiplies his words, multiplies his worthlessness." Nīshāpūr, Iran, tenth century. © 2011 by The Metropolitan Museum of Art/Art Resource/SCALA Florence. © Photo SCALA, Florence.

so prodigious that he found himself incapable of functioning in society.[59] As James E. Young has explained: "Not only does every remembered past moment displace the present lived moment, substituting memory for life itself, but without forgetting there is no space left by which to navigate the meaning of what one has remembered."[60] The need to make room for new memories was well understood in antiquity. Wax tablets were used as writing instruments for everyday purposes because their surface could be smoothed out and reused. In the Platonic heritage, writers therefore referred to smoothing out the wax tablet as an archetypal image of voluntary forgetting.[61] Greek mythology knows the river Lethe as a river of forgetting: whoever drinks of its waters forgets his or her earlier

[59] Aleksandr Romanovich Luria, *The Mind of a Mnemonist: A Little Book about a Vast Memory*, trans. Lynn Solotaroff (Cambridge, MA: Harvard University Press, 1987).

[60] Young, foreword to *Oblivion*, by Marc Augé, trans. Marjolijn de Jager (Minneapolis: University of Minnesota Press, 2004), viii.

[61] Harald Weinrich, *Lethe: The Art and Critique of Forgetting*, trans. Steven Rendall (Ithaca, NY: Cornell University Press, 2004), 5.

existence and is freed for rebirth.[62] Medieval Europeans explained the process with agricultural metaphors: one cuts down groves of trees that were once sacred to the gods so that one can create arable land.[63] When the forest has been cleared, the land will appear visually quite different from its previous state, and the past of the land will seem discontinuous with its present.

But how does one clear the metaphorical forest? The answer lies only partially in omission and failure. At least as important is the new knowledge that overwrites and often confuses past memory. As Umberto Eco has observed, such "mnemonic additions" foster forgetfulness of the past "not by cancellation but by superimposition, not by producing absence but by multiplying presences."[64] Though not typically focused on memory as such, studies of "invented" traditions illustrate this well. In his iconic essay, Hugh Trevor-Roper, for example, argues that in the eighteenth and nineteenth centuries Highland Scots forgot their Irish, Celtic past in large measure through the artificial creation of new Highland practices that were presented as "ancient, original and distinctive." Through invented conventions of "traditional" dress, Highlanders came to see themselves as a distinctive people with an antique history separate from that of Ireland, which was forgotten. Highlanders themselves played a role in this, but important contributions were also made by a variety of other groups, including the British government with its formation of the Highland military regiments.[65] In times of change, such as with the advent of modernity, groups often find meaning in the image of a stable, antique past. To paraphrase Benedict Anderson, antiquity is often the consequence of novelty, as awareness of significant social, cultural, or political change generates the need for narrative explanation to erase the older historical consciousness.[66] Scholars who have studied transformations in identities have highlighted the way in which new identities and

[62] Ibid., 6–7.

[63] Patrick J. Geary, *Phantoms of Remembrance: Memory and Oblivion at the End of the First Millennium* (Princeton, NJ: Princeton University Press, 1994), 114.

[64] Umberto Eco, "An *Ars Oblivionalis*? Forget It!" (trans. Marilyn Migiel), *PMLA* 103, no. 3 (1988): 254–61.

[65] Hugh Trevor-Roper, "The Invention of Tradition: The Highland Tradition of Scotland," in *The Invention of Tradition*, ed. Eric Hobsbawm and Terence Ranger, 15–41 (Cambridge: Cambridge University Press, 1983).

[66] Anderson is concerned principally with a modern phenomenon, but I find this aspect of his theory helpful for premodern contexts. Anderson, *Imagined Communities: Reflections on the Origin and Spread of Nationalism*, rev. ed. (London: Verso, 1991), xiv.

their associated heritages have effaced past ones and the role of both a group and its neighbors in fashioning its sense of itself.[67]

The Route

The primary purpose of this study is to shed light on the shaping of memory about and among Iran's first Muslims. The book consists of two symmetrical, chronologically organized parts. In Part 1, I focus on the development of certain ideas, persons, and events as nostalgic sites of memory depicting a natural and easy transition to Islam in which Iranians themselves played a meaningful role. Chapter 1 highlights theories of ethnogenesis that placed Persians within an overarching genealogical system that included many of the world's known peoples. In this way of thinking, Persians descended from Muḥammad's spiritual ancestors, that is, the prophets who preceded him and whose progeny populated the earth. Such accounts often emphasized the Persians' deep and enduring connections to Islam and, by extension, the antiquity of Islam in their country. Iranians even came to see ancient monuments such as Persepolis as part of this history.

Chapter 2 considers the transformation of the Prophet's companion Salmān into a paragon of Persian history. In early works on Muḥammad and his followers, Salmān stands out more as a non-Arab than as a Persian; it is even stressed that with his conversion to Islam, he abandoned his Persian homeland and identity altogether. But by the fourth/tenth century, Salmān's identity as a Persian is embraced in numerous Arabic traditions that nostalgically recall his homeland as well as the Prophet's affection for it and its people. The chapter includes a discussion of the particular situation of Iṣfahān and its local histories, which feature legal texts important to Salmān's descendants.

Chapter 3 turns to memory of the Arab conquests of the first/seventh and second/eighth centuries to show how Iranians, and Persians in particular, were assigned meaningful roles in the conquests' transformative events. I argue that if one compares accounts across the third/ninth century, one can observe a transformation that parallels the transformation

[67] As but one example, Leyla Neyzi demonstrates the replacement of individual memories of a Sabbatean past with those of a Kemalist past in "Remembering to Forget: Sabbateanism, National Identity, and Subjectivity in Turkey," *Comparative Studies in Society and History* 44, no. 1 (2002): 137–58.

of Salmān discussed in Chapter 2: Iranians are increasingly given credit for their own roles, as the Iranian origins of institutions such as the military register are recognized. Local histories shared this vision to a great extent, but they also adapted it for their own audiences.

Part 1 therefore explores the role of tradition and memory in the creation of Iranian, and especially Persian, Muslim identities. In Part 2, I turn to a corresponding need to forget some elements of Iran's past. This involved the development of strategies by which traditionists undermined elements of Persian identity that were viewed in some quarters as incompatible with Islam, especially the Persians' long history of independent political rule. The pre-Islamic past has posed problems to communities ranging from medieval Egypt and Spain to modern Indonesia for chiefly two related reasons. First, the past can cast a long shadow. The ruling elites of a new and insecure society may wish to erase the traces of their predecessors. For no matter how politically quiescent the previous regime and its descendants may be, their monuments, cultural traditions, and achievements in law and economy can still provoke nostalgia. Second, the contrary values of the past can also pose a threat. Because they provide alternative frames for behavior and action, and thus alternative measures of success, they can prevent the assimilation of new cultural traits, feed the ambitions of the imperfectly assimilated, and tempt the newly converted. Such residual values remind a people of a heritage, now viewed through a different lens, which they would often prefer to forget. They challenge the antiquity and continuity of ethical standards, putting into relief and context what is otherwise presented as a given.[68] For both types of reasons, Muslim authors have frequently revised history.

In Chapter 4, I introduce three general ways in which our reporters sought to limit memory: by rewriting Persia's past within a purely local frame of reference, by replacing a Persian past with a Muslim past, and by promoting unfavorable traditions about Persia's past. Chapter 5 focuses on the last of the three methods and gives a deeper sense of how reporters filtered memory by developing labels, homologies, and icons, as well as ideas about gender. Chapter 6 explores a central impulse behind all forgetting, namely, the wish to move on, by showing how third/ninth- and fourth/tenth-century histories erased the identities of the losing side: Sasanian soldiers, religious communities, and elite families. I consider the specific problems that the past posed for authors, the agendas of elites,

[68] On such problems, see esp. David Lowenthal, *The Past Is a Foreign Country* (Cambridge: Cambridge University Press, 1985).

and the challenge of past values. The sources also permit us to recapture voices of protest against history and its outcomes.

In many ways, this book is a new attempt to consider a transformative period in knowledge regarding Iran's past. This period had a profound impact on what was subsequently available to later generations.[69] At the outset, I must make a few caveats. Memory about Iran should be considered both on its own terms and in terms of the broader historiographical tradition to which it belongs. I have tried to be cautious in my reading of the texts and to avoid asserting Iranian interests where narrators may not have intended them. Such a reading of the sources is more art than science, and it is likely some readers will interpret texts differently. Second, focusing on founding moments will bring to light particular dimensions of memory but occlude others. The themes I treat tend to mention Zoroastrians but not Christians, Jews, Manicheans, Buddhists, or Iranians of other religions, some of whom may have also considered themselves to be "Persians." While this silence may be discouraging as a view onto Iranian religions, it does reveal the way in which the constitutive myths of Persian Muslims developed with an emphasis on a Zoroastrian past and their focus on the Sasanians and their religious allegiances.

Third, when discussing Iran's new Muslims, modern interpreters since the great Hungarian Orientalist Ignaz Goldziher (1850–1921) have frequently made reference to a movement known as the Shuʿūbiyya to explain the ambitions and conflicts of Iran's early Muslims.[70] Generations of scholars afterward have adopted Shuʿūbism as an interpretive

69 Further research could probe the issue of what no longer can be imagined or thought as a result of the way history has been shaped. In the sociology of knowledge, the question of oblivion has been theorized more profoundly. See Mohammed Arkoun, *The Unthought in Contemporary Islamic Thought* (London: Saqi Books, 2002).

70 Goldziher described a "literary battle" waged by a "party" (*Partei*, *Shuʿūbijjapartei*) of Muslim Persians against Arabs. Goldziher saw an "intimate connection" between the Shuʿūbiyya and "the political and literary renaissance of the Persians" and advanced the argument that the movement arose in a "political and social atmosphere" characterized by the growth of "foreign elements in Islam," growing displacement of Arabs in places of power, and even a revival of Persian religious customs and the "defiant reaction of the ʿAjam element against Islam" itself. These foreign elements ultimately achieved foreign rule and the emergence of independent dynasties within the caliphate, breaking not only the caliphate's power but "also that of the nation from which this institution stemmed." *Muslim Studies*, ed. S. M. Stern, 2 vols. (Chicago: Aldine, 1966), 1:137, 40–4; translated by C. R. Barber and Stern from *Muhammedanische Studien*, 2 vols. (Halle: Max Niemeyer, 1889–90). The Shuʿūbīs are mentioned in three chapters: "ʿArab and ʿAjam"; "The Shuʿūbiyya"; and "The Shuʿūbiyya and Its Manifestation in Scholarship."

framework as they have sought to identify Shuʿūbī partisans, their motivations, and the movement's broader stakes, which H. A. R. Gibb wordily summed up as "the whole cultural orientation of the new Islamic society – whether it was to become a re-embodiment of the old Perso-Aramaean culture into which the Arabic and Islamic elements would be absorbed, or a culture in which the Perso-Aramaean contributions would be subordinated to the Arab tradition and the Islamic values."[71] But why – modern interpreters should ask more seriously – have historians turned up virtually no self-professed Shuʿūbīs, only their opponents? The central evidence marshaled for the existence of the movement, furthermore, pertains mainly to late second/eighth- and third/ninth-century ʿAbbasid Baghdad and to its courtly circles, and hardly ever extends beyond that first cited by Goldziher. What about the rest of the empire and centers outside of its orbit in the three centuries that followed? Accordingly, I treat the Shuʿūbiyya lightly in the first and third chapters, but otherwise not at all.

Finally, I am concerned with ways and methods of shaping memory, and I try to strike a balance between analysis of traditions as a whole and up-close readings of particular texts. But it is impossible to provide an exhaustive catalog of memory. Upon such an attempt, one would find oneself, like Luria's mnemonist, unable to take measure of meaning or significance. What one can do is focus on a set of remembered pasts and examine the strategies employed, learn something of their circumstances, and investigate how they supported or effaced memory. This might open fruitful paths of inquiry not only for historians of Iran and its conversion, but also for historians of other periods and locations interested in how memory can be retrained during times of significant social and cultural change.

[71] Gibb, "The Social Significance of the Shuubiya," in *Studies on the Civilization of Islam*, ed. Stanford J. Shaw and William R. Polk, 62–73 (Boston: Beacon Press, 1962), at 66. By way of further example, see Aḥmad Amīn, *Ḍuḥā al-Islām*, 3 vols. (Beirut: Dār al-Kitāb al-ʿArabī, [1933–6]), 1:49–78 and ʿAbd al-ʿAzīz al-Dūrī, *al-Judhūr al-taʾrīkhiyya li-l-Shuʿūbiyya* (Beirut: Dār al-Ṭalīʿa, 1962).

PART I

TRADITIONS FOR REMEMBERING

1

Prior Connections to Islam

> Every child is born in the state of *fiṭra* [with a natural disposition for Islam]. Then his parents make him a Jew, a Christian, or a Zoroastrian.
>
> Muḥammad, the Prophet

One of the central challenges the early Muslim community faced was determining the relationship between kinship-based ways of organizing Muslim society and those that claimed to transcend kinship in the name of Islam. In the end, genealogy was put to many uses and provided a common vocabulary that expressed and mobilized modes of social organization.[1] Muḥammad's family tree, enumerating his ancestors, descendants (known as *sayyid*s or *sharīf*s), and adoptive clients (*mawālī*), served as the most important paradigm. The families of *sayyid*s and *sharīf*s were, and still are, accorded enormous prestige, as their lineages underwrote dynastic arrangements, provided access to patronage, and created power brokers and mediators. Converts who adopted familial connections to other Muslims as *mawālī* gained a sense of belonging to their new faith. And other forms of kinship, such as tribal lineages or descent from Sufi saints, conferred similar forms of belonging, prestige, and benefits, including access to office and positions of leadership.

[1] Early Arab Muslims' fascination with genealogy can readily be seen in the *Jamharat al-nasab* of Hishām b. Muḥammad al-Kalbī (d. ca. 204/819 or 206/821): *Ǧamharat an-nasab: Das genealogische Werk des Hišām ibn Muḥammad al-Kalbī*, ed. Werner Caskel, 2 vols. (Leiden: E. J. Brill, 1966). See now esp. Sarah Bowen Savant and Helena de Felipe, eds., *Genealogy and Knowledge in Muslim Societies: Understanding the Past* (Edinburgh: Edinburgh University Press, 2013) and Savant, "Genealogy," in *The Princeton Encyclopedia of Islamic Political Thought*, ed. Gerhard Böwering et al., 189–90 (Princeton, NJ: Princeton University Press, 2012).

This chapter traces the importance of genealogical representation during the process of Iran's conversion to Islam, when there was a great need for a persuasive image of a Persian community with deep connections to Islam. Traditionists promoted the idea that in the distant past the Persians were descended from Muḥammad's spiritual ancestors, that is, the prophets who preceded him and populated the planet; in this way, their reports connected Persians to history before Muḥammad and God's final revelation. Islam became part of the ancient landscape and heritage of Iran, and all that followed the conquests likewise became part of a developmental progression. This primordial vision was articulated most forcefully in Iraq and western Iran, spoke for the entirety of the Persian population, and eventually was woven into the dominant narratives of the history of Islam. It ultimately even provided a creative license to claim Muslim associations for Iran's monuments of antiquity. Muḥammad b. Jarīr al-Ṭabarī (d. 310/923) – a towering figure in Muslim historiography – played a central role in promoting the idea of the Persians' primordial connections to the spiritual tradition of Islam. His work consequently receives significant attention in what follows.

The Origins of the Idea of Ethnogenesis

The Persians' prophetic genealogies were first and foremost an extension of Muḥammad's own genealogy and represented the development of ideas surrounding the history of his countrymen, the Arabs; the relationship of Muḥammad and his people to the history of monotheism; and the significance of blood ties for securing bonds within and among peoples. The parallels between biblical traditions and those of Islam have been noted, as have the ways in which Muslims developed these in their narratives about the Prophet's life and the origins of their faith. To summarize: just as the Bible traced the ancestries of patriarchs, prophets, and Jesus back to Adam, Muḥammad was shown to descend from Adam through a series of prestigious ancestors including Noah, Abraham, and Ishmael. Jesus' genealogy in the gospel of Matthew shows, in the words of one Bible scholar, that "the entire history of Israel finds its fulfillment in Jesus Christ."[2] Muḥammad's genealogy, likewise, shows that Muḥammad was the fulfillment of prior monotheisms: he completes the prophecy especially of Abraham, from whom the Arabs, as sons of Ishmael,

[2] Barclay M. Newman Jr., "Matthew 1.1–18: Some Comments and a Suggested Restructuring," *Bible Translator* 27, no. 2 (1976): 209. Jesus' genealogy is detailed in Matthew 1:1–18 and in Luke 3:23–38.

descend – in parallel to Jewish prophets, who descend from Abraham's other son, Isaac. The biography of Muḥammad by Ibn Isḥāq (d. ca. 150/767) – transmitted by Ibn Hishām (d. 213/828 or 218/833) in the edition dominant today – begins with the Prophet's genealogy and runs through key Arab eponyms and Arabized biblical figures back to Adam: "Muḥammad b. ʿAbd Allāh b. ʿAbd al-Muṭṭalib . . . b. Kaʿb . . . b. Fihr . . . b. Muḍar b. Nizār b. Maʿadd b. ʿAdnān . . . b. Nābit b. Ismāʿīl b. Ibrāhīm [Ishmael, son of Abraham] . . . b. Arfakhshadh b. Sām b. Nūḥ [Arpachshad, son of Shem, son of Noah] . . . Shīth b. Ādam [Seth, son of Adam]."[3] As Daniel Martin Varisco has written, it is in the generation after Abraham, with Ishmael, that the line is Arabized at the joining point of the biblical with the Arab genealogy that continues through Muḥammad himself.[4]

Traditionists extended these ideas by elaborating Muḥammad's ancestors. For the Arab part of his ancestry, this yielded a schematized map of Arab tribes. For the biblical part, it resulted in different peoples, all linked by blood ties to Noah or Abraham, and implicitly to Muḥammad himself. Such a genealogy was supported by a discourse according to which Muḥammad belonged to a prophetic family. He was remembered to have referred to his fellow prophets using familiar terms, suggesting a shared kinship. In one Hadith, Muḥammad is quoted as saying that the prophets are sons of one father by different mothers. In another version, he refers to them as brothers.[5] God bestowed His favor not just on previous prophets but on their progeny as well, or at least on those of their progeny who believed.[6] This family knew *islām*, or the monotheistic submission to God that He revealed throughout the ages to particular prophets and their peoples. Every time God sent a prophet, "a window onto the unseen was opened up and a glimpse of ultimate reality

[3] ʿAbd al-Malik b. Hishām, *al-Sīra al-nabawiyya*, ed. Muṣṭafā al-Saqqā, Ibrāhīm al-Abyārī, and ʿAbd al-Ḥafīẓ Shalabī, 2 vols. (Cairo: al-Bābī al-Ḥalabī, 1955), 1:1–3.

[4] Daniel Martin Varisco, "Metaphors and Sacred History: The Genealogy of Muhammad and the Arab 'Tribe,'" "Anthropological Analysis and Islamic Texts," special issue, *Anthropological Quarterly* 68, no. 3 (1995): 139–56. Cf. Franz Rosenthal, "The Influence of the Biblical Tradition on Muslim Historiography," in *Historians of the Middle East*, ed. Bernard Lewis and P. M. Holt, 35–45 (London: Oxford University Press, 1962).

[5] Al-Bukhārī, *al-Jāmiʿ al-ṣaḥīḥ*, ed. M. Ludolf Krehl, 4 vols. (vol. 4 partly ed. Th. W. Juynboll) (Leiden: E. J. Brill, 1862–1908), 2:369.

[6] Qurʾan 3:33–4: "God chose Adam and Noah and the family of Abraham and the family of ʿImrān above all created beings, the seed of one another. God is the Hearer and the Knower." Throughout this book, I rely most on the Qurʾan translation of Alan Jones (Cambridge: Gibb Memorial Trust, 2007). On these verses, see al-Bukhārī, *Ṣaḥīḥ*, 2:365. See also Qurʾan 6:83–7.

was transmitted to the earth."[7] The Qur'an therefore refers to Abraham and his sons Ishmael and Isaac as *muslims*, or "submitters" to the one God.[8]

The Persians' genealogies were, equally, an attempt to account within an "Islamic" model for Iranian ways of explaining the origins of the world and the course of human history. These ways posed a challenge to a history centered on prophets, as they proposed their own accounts of the origins of humanity, its development into distinct peoples, and the overall diversity of human relations. They were related in tales within which chronology typically moved according to a different rhythm, that of a history of kingship. Most importantly, they featured ideas of "Īrān," sovereignty, topography, and heroes and villains going back, with some interruptions, at least to Sasanian times if not further. They also featured noble Iranian families and their descendants in the present, which, insofar as prophetic history was concerned, could be reckoned, theoretically, as merely late offshoots.

Iranian accounts of the past attracted the early interest of Muslims (including Persian Muslims), who responded to them by translating them from Middle Persian into Arabic, debating their ideas, reworking them into their own narratives, and otherwise engaging with them. Such rewriting occurred within what scholars have called Iranian "national" history. Its best-known representative, the "Book of Kings," known in Middle Persian as the *Xwadāy-nāmag* (in Arabic written as *Khudāy-nāma*, *-nāmaj*, or *-nāmak*), covered Iranian history from its beginnings until the last Sasanian monarch to rule Iran, Yazdagird III (r. 631–51 CE), though a final chapter seems to have been added after that monarch's death.[9] The work seems to have been compiled at different stages, but it

7 Patricia Crone, *God's Rule: Government and Islam; Six Centuries of Medieval Islamic Political Thought* (New York: Columbia University Press, 2004), 10.

8 For the term *muslim* as applied to Abraham and his family, see Qur'an 2:127–8, 2:131–3, and 3:67–8; for Noah, see 10:72; for Joseph, 12:101; for Moses, 10:90; and for Lot, by interpretation, 51:36.

9 Much has been written about the *Xwadāy-nāmag*. See especially Nöldeke, *Das Iranische Nationalepos*, 13–15; Christensen, *L'Iran sous les Sassanides*, 53–6; Yarshater, "Iranian National History," 359–60; J. Derek Latham, "Ibn al-Muqaffaʿ and Early ʿAbbasid Prose," in *ʿAbbasid Belles-Lettres*, ed. Julia Ashtiany et al., 48–77 (Cambridge: Cambridge University Press, 1990), at 53–4; A. Shahpur Shahbazi, "On the X^{w}*adāy-nāmag*," in *Iranica Varia: Papers in Honor of Professor Ehsan Yarshater*, 208–29 (Leiden: E. J. Brill, 1990); Latham, "Ebn al-Moqaffaʿ, Abū Moḥammad ʿAbd-Allāh Rōzbeh," in *EIr*; Zeev Rubin, "Ibn al-Muqaffaʿ and the Account of Sasanian History in the Arabic Codex Sprenger 30," *Jerusalem Studies in Arabic and Islam* 30 (2005): 52–93; Rubin, "Ḥamza al-Iṣfahānī's Sources for Sasanian History," *Jerusalem Studies in Arabic and Islam* 35 (2008): 27–58; and M. Macuch, "Pahlavi Literature," in *The Literature of Pre-Islamic*

was fixed in a coherent form by the end of the reign of Khusraw Parvīz (r. 590–628 CE). It was first translated into Arabic in the ʿAbbasid period by the prolific courtier ʿAbd Allāh b. al-Muqaffaʿ (d. 139/756) and retranslated several times later. In Arabic, it served as a major source for Arabic traditionists and in some fashion as one of the likely sources for Firdawsī's Persian *Shāh-nāmah* (completed ca. 400/1010).[10] On the other hand, Muslims ignored, or were unaware of, much of Iranian historical knowledge. This was particularly true of Iranian "religious" history, namely, Zoroastrian ideas about the past; these received highly selective attention in Muslim historical works.

The greatest challenge to studying how Muslims took account of such history lies in the nature of the surviving sources, nearly all of which postdate the rise of Islam. This does not allow for a stable point of comparison, that is, a "pure" pre-Islamic national or religious historiography against which to measure interpretations by Muslims. No historical books have survived intact from Seleucid, Parthian, or Sasanian times that could chronicle Iranian national history, although there is some non-narrative evidence of it in the Avesta, Achaemenid inscriptions and tablets, Middle Iranian inscriptions, ostraca, papyri, graffiti, coins, and the Arabic and Persian Muslim sources themselves.[11] This has had the odd result that attempts to describe the *Xwadāy-nāmag* have relied on Firdawsī's epic or on al-Ṭabarī's *History of Prophets and Kings* (*Taʾrīkh al-rusul wa-l-mulūk*). Likewise, Zoroastrian Middle Persian texts, while containing much old material, came into their current forms in the eighth century CE and afterward, when Zoroastrians had been interacting with Muslims for some time.[12] A further challenge arises from the fact that while one can

Iran, companion volume 1 to *A History of Persian Literature*, ed. Ronald E. Emmerick and Maria Macuch, 116–96 (London: I. B. Tauris, 2009), at 172–81.

10 On the sources for the *Shāh-nāmah*, see also Nöldeke, *Das Iranische Nationalepos*, who holds that the *Xwadāy-nāmag* likely passed directly from Pahlavi through versions in neo-Persian to Firdawsī's epic (pp. 16–19); and esp. W. Barthold, "Zur Geschichte des persischen Epos" (trans. Hans Heinrich Schaeder), *Zeitschrift der Deutschen Morgenländischen Gesellschaft* 98 (1944): 121–57; F. Gabrieli, "Ibn al-Muḳaffaʿ," in *EI*²; Mahmoud Omidsalar, "Could al-Thaʿâlibî Have Used the *Shâhnâma* as a Source?" *Der Islam* 75, no. 2 (1998): 338–46; and Macuch, "Epic History and Geographical Works," 172–4. Cf. Dick Davis, "The Problem of Ferdowsî's Sources," *Journal of the American Oriental Society* 116, no. 1 (1996): esp. 50–1, and Kumiko Yamamoto, *The Oral Background of Persian Epics: Storytelling and Poetry* (Leiden: Brill, 2003), esp. xix–xxiv and 60ff.

11 Yarshater, "Iranian National History," 360.

12 On this problem, see esp. J. de Menasce, "Zoroastrian Pahlavī Writings," in *The Cambridge History of Iran*, 3(2):1166–95, and "Zoroastrian Literature after the Muslim

speak of Zoroastrian historiography, elements of Iranian national and religious history are often merged in the Arabic sources.[13] Other times, what once may have counted as Zoroastrian history is "nationalized," becoming part and parcel of the history of all Persians. Whatever the heuristic value of a religious/national distinction, the state of our sources should cause misgivings about any rigid categorization of contents as simply either "national" or "religious," since although it may be true that such a division held once upon a time, as the two types of history were produced and first consumed, the distinction softens in Arabic and Persian, as traditionists make use of a variety of sources.

Finally, there is every reason to believe that historical knowledge of a more local nature also served as a source for genealogies featuring the prophets and for Muslim historiography more generally, though identifying its original, pre-Islamic forms is fraught with difficulties. Some of this evidence is circumstantial: Jews and Christians, who may have served as sources of such knowledge, inhabited Iranian towns such as Hamadhān, Nihāwand, and Jayy, from which we also have testimony about prophetic genealogies. Other support is derived from pure conjecture: Iraq with its Jewish and Christian populations would have provided a fertile ground for discussions of the prophets' ancestries.[14] Local histories contain much material relating to pre-Islamic times, and they even take archaic forms, such as the Pahlavi treatise on the "Wonders and Magnificence of Sīstān."[15] Although their first audiences resided in Iranian localities, they circulated widely and transmitted their ideas about ancient history, and other matters, to wider horizons.

Conquest," in *The Cambridge History of Iran*, vol. 4, *The Period from the Arab Invasion to the Saljuqs*, ed. R. N. Frye, 543–65 (Cambridge: Cambridge University Press, 1975); Shaul Shaked, "Some Islamic Reports Concerning Zoroastrianism," *Jerusalem Studies in Arabic and Islam* 17 (1994): 43–84; M. Stausberg, "The Invention of a Canon: The Case of Zoroastrianism," in *Canonization & Decanonization: Papers Presented to the International Conference of the Leiden Institute for the Study of Religions (LISOR) Held at Leiden 9-10 January 1997*, ed. A. van der Kooij and K. van der Toorn, 257–77 (Leiden: Brill, 1998); and D. Neil MacKenzie, "Bundahišn," in *EIr*.

13 They may even have been blended in the *Xwadāy-nāmag* itself.

14 Work on the Babylonian Talmud under the late Sasanians is suggestive of the possibilities for exchange of ideas on a variety of matters, genealogy included. Also, for Mandaean appropriation of the Kayanids, see Louis H. Gray, "The Kings of Early Irān according to the Sidrā Rabbā," *Zeitschrift für Assyriologie und vorderasiatische Archäologie* 19, no. 2 (1906): 272–87.

15 For a translation, analysis, and bibliography, see Bo Utas, "The Pahlavi Treatise *Avdēh u sahīkēh ī Sakistān* or 'Wonders and Magnificence of Sistan,'" *Acta Antiqua Academiae Scientiarum Hungaricae* 28 (1980): 259–67.

When Muslims tried to account for Persians in prophetic history, they therefore had on offer a complex network of traditions from which to choose: those preoccupied with Islam's biblical heritage; those reflecting native Iranian knowledge in different forms, including that produced for particular localities and disseminated widely; and ideas originating with longstanding local Jewish and Christian populations.

The Inheritance of Noah

Let us look at the most commonly mentioned prophet-forefather for the Persians, Noah, and at the various ways in which descent from him could connect them to prophetic and Islamic history. The story of the Flood that destroyed all peoples except Noah's family has required those who subscribe to its mythology of ethnogenesis to trace their ancestries to one or another of his sons, Shem, Ham, or Japheth. This has been accomplished in a variety of ways. Although early European Christians, for example, were not mentioned in the Genesis 10 account of Noah's progeny, they traced their lines to Japheth.[16] Jewish traditions supported this ancestry, but details proved difficult to work out[17] and, in some cases, involved the recasting of a former god as a royal figure.[18] According to an unusual tradition circulating in ninth-century England, the Anglo-Saxon royal line of Wessex descended from an ark-born son of Noah named Sceaf.[19] In the complex search for roots that took place in Reformation era Germany, Christians identified Ashkenaz, a grandson of Japheth, as their forefather.[20]

[16] Genesis 10:2–5 mentions Japheth's seven sons and adds that "From these the coastland peoples spread. These are the sons of Japheth in their lands, each with his own language, by their families, in their nations." (Throughout this study, I rely on the Revised Standard Version of the Bible.) Genesis 10 mentions Japheth's grandsons through his sons Gomer and Javan, omitting mention of progeny through Japheth's other five sons.

[17] Donald Daniel Leslie, "Japhet in China," *Journal of the American Oriental Society* 104, no. 3 (1984): 404–5.

[18] Craig R. Davis has described this as a reversal of the process described by Euhemerus in the third century BCE: "The ancient gods are not glorified heroes; heroes, or at least some of them, are fallen gods." Davis, "Cultural Assimilation in the Anglo-Saxon Royal Genealogies," *Anglo-Saxon England* 21 (1992): 23–4.

[19] Daniel Anlezark, "Sceaf, Japheth and the Origins of the Anglo-Saxons," *Anglo-Saxon England* 31 (2002): 26–7.

[20] For Noah's sons in European historiography, see esp. Benjamin Braude, "The Sons of Noah and the Construction of Ethnic and Geographical Identities in the Medieval and Early Modern Periods," *William and Mary Quarterly* 54, no. 1 (1997): 103–42.

In adopting the ancient Near Eastern idea of the Flood, Muslims inherited its ethnogenic imperative as well: if all other peoples perished at that time, then Muslims and their ancestors, whatever their origins, must descend from Noah, too. There could be no autochthons. For Arabs, this was quickly addressed. The early biographers of Muḥammad, as mentioned, constructed for him a lineage that went back to Noah (and before him, to Adam). The Arabian prophets – Hūd, Ṣāliḥ, and Shuʿayb – were also given lineages. The eponyms of Arab tribes, such as Qaḥṭān, also became Noah's progeny, conferring this ancestry upon the tribes generally and upon the individuals within them.

Scholars of the genealogical sciences placed non-Arab peoples in a great number of segmented lineages that showed more than one line of descent from a given ancestor. Such lineages contain multiple branches, and are therefore well suited for different purposes. For many scholars, no matter what their own locale, a clear primary concern was the way in which kinship to Noah provided a biological explanation for the Arabs' relations with other peoples, especially the "Children of Israel" (*Banū Isrāʾīl*).[21] For others, genealogy reflected a salvific hierarchy of peoples (in which, for example, Ham's descendants tended to fare poorly), or it could root in primordial times devolution from an original Islam and therefore serve as part of a critique (as I discuss in Chapter 4).

Persians were considered in some of the earliest schemes that gave an anthropology of the world's peoples. For example, traditions attributed by al-Ṭabarī to ʿAbd Allāh b. ʿAbbās (d. 68/687 or 688) or Wahb b. Munabbih (d. 110 or 114/728 or 732) would have the Persians descend from Shem or Japheth. Ibn ʿAbbās reportedly named Shem's descendants as Moses's people (*qawm Mūsā*, i.e., the Children of Israel), the Arabs, the Persians (*al-Furs*), the Nabat (*al-Nabaṭ*, that is, the Aramaic-speaking population of Syria and Mesopotamia, not the Nabateans of Petra familiar to modern readers), and the people of India and Sind (*al-Hind wa-l-Sind*).[22] Wahb, meanwhile, specified Persians, Arabs, and the people of Byzantium as Shem's descendants, thus rendering the Arabs kin

[21] This agenda, in which Abraham also figures prominently, animates works composed across the Muslim world, including in Muslim Spain, as demonstrated by Ibn Ḥazm's (d. 456/1064) *Jamharat ansāb al-ʿArab*, ed. É. Lévi-Provençal (Cairo: Dār al-Maʿārif, 1948). For a broad study, see Zoltan Szombathy, "The *Nassâbah*: Anthropological Fieldwork in Mediaeval Islam," *Islamic Culture* 73, no. 3 (1999): 94.

[22] Al-Ṭabarī, *Taʾrīkh* I:218–19. Regarding this genealogy, see *The History of al-Ṭabarī*, vol. 2, *Prophets and Patriarchs*, trans. William M. Brinner (Albany: State University of New York Press, 1987), 17–18, n. 61.

to the two major imperial powers they conquered. For him, "the Blacks" (*al-Sūdān*) descended from Ham and the Turks (*al-Turk*) and Gog and Magog from Japheth.[23]

The Accommodation of al-Ṭabarī

The most systematic attempt to account for translocal Iranian historiography was undertaken by al-Ṭabarī in his *History of Prophets and Kings*. For al-Ṭabarī, the Persians' genealogies, including Noah as a forefather, were part of a larger project of narrating the history of Islam and the Muslim community upon the premise that knowledge of true monotheism, *islām*, came into the world with the first prophet, Adam, and was reinforced by all prophets after him. In al-Ṭabarī's work, Persians play a major role in this early history, which prepares audiences to spot them in the narratives that follow and lead to the early fourth/tenth century. By this logic, it would not be too far-fetched to view Islam as an indigenous religion, forgotten and then recovered.

Al-Ṭabarī was born in 224 or 225/839 in the city of Āmul in the Persian province of Ṭabaristān on the Caspian Sea, which developed loyalties to Islam rather late and whose control was contested at the time of al-Ṭabarī's birth.[24] His own family may well have had Arab roots, though he discouraged speculation about his ancestry.[25] He left home at the age of twelve and finally settled in Baghdad when he was about thirty, funding his studies with income from the rent of properties in his home town.[26] He was well acquainted with Iran's cultural and literary heritage but at some remove, and he was certainly no chauvinist. Rather, he likely wanted to preserve an Iranian historiographical tradition, to make other Muslims aware of it, and to give it a certain pride of place, but also to urge Iranians to see their history as part of a wider Muslim history. And so, in

23 Al-Ṭabarī, *Ta'rīkh*, I:211.

24 In 224 and 225 AH, a recent convert to Islam and member of a non-Muslim dynasty known as the Bāwandids revolted unsuccessfully against the central authorities of the caliphate; heavy taxes were imposed on the landowners of Āmul, and the city itself was laid waste. See R. N. Frye, "Bāwand," in EI^2, and Franz Rosenthal's description of al-Ṭabarī's early life in *The History of al-Ṭabarī*, vol. 1, *General Introduction and From the Creation to the Flood*, trans. Franz Rosenthal (Albany: State University of New York Press, 1989), 10–11.

25 See the comments by Rosenthal; *History of al-Ṭabarī*, 1:12.

26 Fuat Sezgin, *Geschichte des arabischen Schrifttums*, vol. 1 (Leiden: E. J. Brill, 1967), 323–8; Robinson, *Islamic Historiography*, 162; Claude Gilliot, "La formation intellectuelle de Tabari (224/5–310/839–923)," *Journal Asiatique* 276 (1988): 203–44.

his book, al-Ṭabarī presents a wealth of possible ways in which Persians might be related to prophets and other Qurʾanic figures – including Adam, Seth, Noah, Dhū al-Qarnayn, al-Khiḍr, Solomon, Abraham, and Isaac – whose lines intertwined with, and spawned, many possible Persian ones. The Persian lines include those of Gayūmart – about whom we will have much to say in this study – as the father either of the human race as a whole or of the Persians in particular; Hūshang, as the first king of the so-called Pīshdādian dynasty; Mashī and Mashyāna, figures of Zoroastrian cosmogony; Jamshīd, Farīdūn, and Manūshihr, all known from the Persian epic tradition; Kay Qubādh, who features in al-Ṭabarī's account as the first Kayanid ruler; and Yazdagird III, the last Sasanian ruler of Iran. He identifies many different advocates of varying views of Persian genealogy: Muslim *akhbārī*s, Arab and Persian genealogists, poets, and Zoroastrian priests, as well as Persians, Zoroastrians, and Jews (the Children of Israel) in general.

As a whole, al-Ṭabarī's volume presents its readers with a range of possibilities relating to the origins of humanity, its branching out, its ancient history of prophets and kings, especially in Palestine, Arabia, and Iran, and its religious and ethnic forms in his own day. The possibilities address problems in merging what al-Ṭabarī likely saw as a Qurʾanic vision of history with the Iranian views he apparently knew quite well. The thrust of his inquiry is earnest, searching, and literal, if not philosophically systematic, in its mode of thinking: With whom does the human race start? When did the major communities we know today come into existence? What role did the Flood, its devastation of humanity, and its aftermath have in shaping humanity in the present? Genealogically speaking, what are the origins of the key figures of the Persian epic tradition – especially Jamshīd, Farīdūn, and Manūshihr?

It was once held that al-Ṭabarī was unoriginal in his presentation because of his extensive citation of authorities, his reproduction of substantial portions of earlier texts, often without attribution, and the general discourse of learning in his day that was based on faithful reproduction through both memorization and scrupulous note taking. Although one still finds some adherents to such a view, the consensus of scholars now begins with the premise of al-Ṭabarī's intervention and looks for his own position in his comments on reports, his references to sources in different, distinguishing ways, and his choices regarding emplotment (how he structures his text, and with what narrative economy), weighting (by length, chiefly), and assumptions within and across portions of the text. In his general introduction to the translation of al-Ṭabarī's *History*, Franz

Rosenthal went so far as to assert that "the most remarkable aspect of Ṭabarī's approach is his constant and courageous expression of 'independent judgment (*ijtihād*).'"[27] While this is surely an overstatement, as al-Ṭabarī rarely speaks in his own "voice," it is often possible to discern his perspective.[28]

His view of the Persians' genealogy runs something like this and emerges out of the various contradictory details. The Persians' history begins with famous figures whose lineages run deep into prophetic history: they begin either at creation or, more likely, after the Flood, probably with Noah's son Shem. Afterward, pre-Islamic Persian history, particularly dynastic history, runs mostly on its own track, independent of prophetic history. It provides a useful and stable point of reference for prophetic history but is also part of prophetic history, both because it originates in the latter and because it is part of a broader narrative and telos leading to Muḥammad, the final prophet, and Islam in Iran itself.

Three aspects of al-Ṭabarī's position deserve special comment. First, he treats Zoroastrian opinions as plausible; reports them, he says, directly from Zoroastrians; and uses them to flesh out the early history of the Persians. For him, such opinions are not disqualified by the religious identity of their proponents and may even be a valid source of information, at least insofar as the Persian branch of humanity is concerned. Most interestingly, al-Ṭabarī singles them out as representing the native "Persian" view with which a history of Islam must come to terms. He does not describe them as Sasanian, nor as expressly part of the heritage of an imperial Iran.

Second, Zoroastrian ideas, though treated seriously, cannot be accepted as plausible if they contradict basic tenets of Muslim belief about the past, chiefly about human origins and the Flood. Adam, not Gayūmart, was father to the human race, whatever the relationship between the two. There was a Flood. The Zoroastrians, al-Ṭabarī notes, say there was no Flood, or they say there was, but it did not cover their lands or interrupt their genealogies, as they "assume that it took place in the clime

27 Rosenthal, *History of al-Ṭabarī*, 1:55–6. Rosenthal is speaking here of all of al-Ṭabarī's works. He cites unfavorably Carl Brockelmann, *Geschichte der arabischen Litteratur*, 2nd ed., 2 vols. (Leiden: E. J. Brill, 1943–9), 1:148, and the latter's assessment of al-Ṭabarī as "kein selbständiger Kopf," or unoriginal.

28 See "Ṭabarī's Voice and Hand," in Boaz Shoshan, *Poetics of Islamic Historiography: Deconstructing Ṭabarī's History* (Leiden: Brill, 2004), 109–54. Cf. Tayeb El-Hibri, *Reinterpreting Islamic Historiography* and "Ṭabarī's Biography of al-Muʿtaṣim: The Literary Use of a Military Career," *Der Islam* 86, no. 2 (2011): 187–236.

of Babylon and nearby regions, whereas the descendants of Gayūmart had their dwellings in the East, and the Flood did not reach them."[29] Al-Ṭabarī points to the error of this view: "The information given by God concerning the Flood contradicts their statement," he says, citing Qurʾan 37:75–7, in which the Qurʾan describes Noah and his offspring as "survivors," saved by God.[30] God therefore indicates that "Noah's offspring are the survivors, and nobody else."[31] Al-Ṭabarī repeats this assertion amid a discussion of the mythic tyrant Ḍaḥḥāk, as he notes that "some people" (*baʿḍahum*) claim that Noah lived during his reign.[32] For him, it is clear that there is in reality no uninterrupted and independent Persian line that preceded the Flood and continued after it. He goes on to discuss various theories about the Persians' genealogies that may explain the Zoroastrians' errors regarding their origins. One theory is based on a simple confusion of names: he reports that the Magians of his day believed Gayūmart to have been the same person as Adam, with 3,139 years passing between Gayūmart's lifetime and the hijra of Muḥammad.[33] He also notes that Persian scholars – whom he does not describe specifically as Zoroastrians but rather as members of a scholarly class (*ʿulamāʾ al-Furs*) – assume that Gayūmart was Adam.[34] A second explanation relies on genealogical sublimation through the depiction of Gayūmart as "the son of Adam's loins by Eve."[35] Al-Ṭabarī also reports a combination of these two methods of reconciliation with regard to Hūshang on the authority of "some Persian genealogists" (*baʿḍ nassābat al-Furs*). This theory takes the equation of Gayūmart with Adam as its starting point and further assumes that Hūshang descends from Gayūmart through Gayūmart's son Mashī, grandson Siyāmak, and great-grandson Afrawāk (Frawāk). Thus Gayūmart would be Adam, Mashī would be Seth, Siyāmak would be Enosh, Afrawāk would be Kenan, and finally Hūshang would be Mahalalel – perfectly reflecting Adam's biblical descendants.[36] Al-Ṭabarī puzzles over whether the equations would

[29] Al-Ṭabarī, *Taʾrīkh*, I:199.
[30] Qurʾan 37:75–7 says: "Noah called out to Us, and how excellent was the Answerer. We delivered him and his household from the great distress, and made his seed the survivors."
[31] Al-Ṭabarī, *Taʾrīkh*, I:199.
[32] Ibid., I:210.
[33] Ibid., I:17.
[34] Ibid., I:147.
[35] Ibid.
[36] Ibid., I:155; Genesis 5:1–12.

plausibly permit Hūshang to be a contemporary of Adam, as Mahalalel was, and concludes that it would be possible.[37]

A third important aspect of al-Ṭabarī's position is his belief that the Persians were born early in the history of humanity, whether at its inception, with Gayūmart, or more likely afterward, from Noah's sons. They are among its original stock, their history emerging before that of either Jews or Arabs. An alternative genealogy, which al-Ṭabarī also mentions, traces the lineage of the Persians to the later figure of Abraham and his son Isaac (through Manūshihr, a claim considered below), and so places them chronologically on a par with the Jews and Arabs. However, al-Ṭabarī discounts this theory; he credits it to an unnamed source or sources (*baʿḍ ahl al-akhbār*); he notes that this is a view not shared by the Persians themselves; he quotes a good Muslim source that contradicts it (Ibn al-Kalbī, d. ca. 204/819 or 206/821); and in a subsequent mention of Manūshihr, al-Ṭabarī casually refers to him as Manūshihr b. Īraj. He thus dispenses with the possibility that the Persians descend from Abraham.[38]

The cumulative result of these features of al-Ṭabarī's discussion is the placement of Persians within the story of Islam at an early stage, and in ways that respect and preserve some of their native traditions, for which Persians, and even Zoroastrians, are given significant credit. Genealogical autonomy, after a point, paves the way for autonomy in other realms. Persian history sets the pace for, and is part of, prophetic history. Toward the beginning of the *History* al-Ṭabarī remarks that pre-Islamic Persian history, beginning with Gayūmart, is the most reliable benchmark for measuring history. That is, "the history of the world's bygone years is more easily explained and more clearly seen based upon the lives of the Persian kings than upon those of the kings of any other nation (*ghayrihim min al-umam*)." Indeed, "a history based upon the lives of the Persian kings has the soundest sources and the best and clearest data."[39] This history shares much of the same Near Eastern geography as other narratives of prophetic history, overlaps in dramatic content, and runs toward the lifetime of the Prophet and the Muslim conquests, including of Iran itself.

In al-Ṭabarī's writing, one gets a sense of the challenge the author probably first encountered when, as a youth, he moved south from Āmul

37 Al-Ṭabarī, *Taʾrīkh*, I:155.

38 "As for the Persians (*al-Furs*), they disclaim this genealogy, and they know no kings ruling over them other than the sons of Farīdūn and acknowledge no kings of other peoples. They think that if an intruder of other stock (*min ghayrihim*) entered among them in ancient times, he did so wrongfully." Ibid., I:432–4.

39 Ibid., I:148; *History of al-Ṭabarī*, 1:319; see also *Taʾrīkh*, I:353.

to Rayy, located near modern Tehran and a major center of the empire in his day, to study Muslim traditions, including Ibn Isḥāq's biography of the Prophet and *Kitāb al-Mubtada'*, which treats prophetic history prior to Muḥammad's lifetime, with major figures such as Muḥammad b. Ḥumayd (d. 248/862).[40] While there and afterward in Baghdad, he certainly recognized the problem of reconciling prophetic history with knowledge otherwise available in Iran. When he sat down to write the *History*, which he finished in 302/915,[41] he ostensibly had a full range of Islamic and older Iranian materials at his disposal, and he chose to address the conflicts that they presented by assembling them in this particular way.

In contrast to his general precision in citing sources in his *History*, it is remarkable that al-Ṭabarī describes the sources of his knowledge about Gayūmart, Hūshang, Farīdūn, and Jamshīd and these very first chapters of prophetic history in such general terms, as owing to Zoroastrians or to Persians in general. He does not specify Ibn al-Muqaffaʿ, the *Xwadāy-nāmag*, or a *Siyar al-mulūk* (as Ibn al-Muqaffaʿ's translation of the latter is sometimes called), nor does he otherwise name his informants, unless they are Muslims (including Ibn al-Kalbī). Instead, he employs the passive voice (*dhukira*, "it is said that") and generally speaks ambiguously. Modern scholars have persuasively argued, however, that al-Ṭabarī's knowledge of Iran's pre-Islamic history derived in significant measure from the *Xwadāy-nāmag*, if not through a copy of Ibn al-Muqaffaʿ's translation, then through another channel.[42] His way of citing contrasts sharply with that of later traditionists writing outside of Iraq, who seem to have felt much more comfortable identifying Iranian sources by name. These other reporters include Ḥamza al-Iṣfahānī (d. after 350/961) – a particularly strong point of contrast, surely – who spent most of his life in Iṣfahān and who begins his work by listing eight sources for knowledge about Iran's pre-Islamic history, first on the list being Ibn al-Muqaffaʿ's *Kitāb Siyar mulūk al-Furs*. Ḥamza mentions a Zoroastrian priest named Bahrām who claimed to have collected more than twenty copies of the *Xwadāy-nāmag*

40 Gilliot, "La formation intellectuelle de Tabari," 205–6; Rosenthal, "The Life and Works of al-Ṭabarī," in *History of al-Ṭabarī*, 1:17–19.

41 Rosenthal, *History of al-Ṭabarī*, 1:133.

42 Theodor Nöldeke, *Geschichte der Perser und Araber zur Zeit der Sasaniden aus der arabischen Chronik des Tabari* (Leiden: E. J. Brill, 1879; repr., 1973); Arthur Christensen, *Les types du premier homme et du premier roi dans l'histoire légendaire des Iraniens*, vol. 1, *Gajōmard, Masjay et Masjānay, Hōšang et Taχmōruw* (Stockholm: P. A. Norstedt, 1917), 64–6. See also Gabrieli, "Ibn al-Muḳaffaʿ," in *EI*[2].

in order to establish the correct dates of the reigns of Persian kings.[43] The other reporters also include Balʿamī (d. ca. 363/974), who was, until the studies by Elton L. Daniel and Andrew C. S. Peacock, widely regarded as al-Ṭabarī's "translator" into Persian.[44] In his adaptation of al-Ṭabarī's work, produced under the autonomous Samanid governate of Khurāsān and Transoxiana and considered the earliest work of Persian historical writing, Balʿamī mentions a far more varied list of sources that also features Ibn al-Muqaffaʿ, a *Shāh-nāmah-yi buzurg* (attributed to the Samanid era Persian poet and writer Abū al-Muʾayyad Balkhī), and "the book of Bahrām b. Mihrān Iṣfahānī," perhaps referring to some version of what Ḥamza had on hand – among several other works.[45]

Why does al-Ṭabarī not give credit where it was likely due? It could be that such knowledge was diffusely held, with al-Ṭabarī gaining it directly from Persians, especially Zoroastrians, so it deserved the general attributions he gave to it; he also may have known it to be part of a Persian corpus already heavily filtered by the Arabic sources. But there may be more to his silence. His reluctance to name the work represents a way of dealing with two possible historical visions identified by Julie Scott Meisami in Persian-language historical texts: one is "Iranian, focusing on pre-Islamic Iranian monarchy up to the Islamic conquest," whereas the other is "Islamic," and gave rise to dynastic history. Meisami traced these visions to the emergence of Persian historical writing in the last

43 Ḥamza al-Iṣfahānī, *Kitāb Taʾrīkh sinī mulūk al-arḍ wa-l-anbiyāʾ* (Berlin: Kaviani, 1340/1921 or 1922), 9 and 19.

44 For the hugely complex history of the work's transmission, see Elton L. Daniel, "Manuscripts and Editions of Balʿamī's *Tarjamah-yi Tārīkh-i Ṭabarī*," *Journal of the Royal Asiatic Society*, n.s., 122, no. 2 (1990): 282–321. Andrew C. S. Peacock's recent study raises further, serious questions about how historians have traditionally used Balʿamī's text; see his *Mediaeval Islamic Historiography and Political Legitimacy: Balʿamī's Tārīkhnāma* (London: Routledge, 2007), esp. 73–102, "Balʿamī's Reshaping of Ṭabarī's History."

45 *Tārīkh-i Balʿamī: Takmilah va Tarjumah-yi Tārīkh-i Ṭabarī*, ed. Muḥammad Taqī Bahār and Muḥammad Parvīn Gunābādī, 2 vols. (Tehran: Zavvāl, 1974), 1:3–5 (incl. 5, n. 11); on this passage, and Balʿamī's treatment of Gayūmart generally, see esp. Maria Subtelny, "Between Persian Legend and Samanid Orthodoxy: Accounts about Gayumarth in Bal'ami's *Tarikhnama*," in *Ferdowsi, the Mongols and Iranian History: Art, Literature and Culture from Early Islam to Qajar Persia*, ed. Robert Hillenbrand, A. C. S. Peacock, and Firuza Abdullaeva (London: I. B. Tauris, 2013). Subtelny persuasively argues, however, that Balʿamī copies a passage, including a list of sources, from the so-called older prose preface to the *Shāh-nāmah* (completed in 346/957 for Abū Manṣūr b. ʿAbd al-Razzāq, the governor of Ṭūs); i.e., he would seem to overstate the variety of what he actually had at hand. For the relevant passage, see V. Minorsky, "The Older Preface to the *Shāh-nāma*," in *Studi orientalistici in onore di Giorgio Levi Della Vida*, 2 vols., 2:159–79 (Rome: Istituto per l'Oriente, 1956), 2:173.

half-century of Samanid rule (the second half of the fourth/tenth century).[46] It seems more likely, however, that these visions existed in tension much earlier and in Arabic, from the moment of Ibn al-Muqaffaʿ's translation, as can be seen in a complaint of the ʿAbbasid litterateur al-Jāḥiẓ (d. 255/868 or 869), who said that his contemporaries were overly impressed by old models.[47] In the early days extending to those of al-Ṭabarī, the conflict was often resolved with little acknowledgment of the pre-Islamic and Iranian strand. It is significant that even Ibn al-Muqaffaʿ's own Arabic translation was eventually lost – a fate that would have seemed shocking from the perspective of other fields of knowledge where the past was meticulously (if differently) recorded, such as Hadith study. The result can be seen in the fourth/tenth century, when Ḥamza cites a Mūsā b. ʿĪsā al-Kisrawī, who bemoans the instability of the *Xwadāy-nāmag*'s textual tradition. Mūsā notes that all of the copies of the Arabic text differ, and he could not find even two copies agreeing in content.[48]

Generally speaking, al-Ṭabarī's *History* played a large role in shaping the historiographical tradition that followed him, so much so that a Buyid amir was once chastened by Maḥmūd of Ghazna for having failed to read his al-Ṭabarī.[49] Besides all of the other topics al-Ṭabarī treats in his work, we have him to thank for a considerable amount of our knowledge of Iran and its pre-Islamic history. But whatever he and other giants of Arabic or

[46] J. S. Meisami, "The Past in Service of the Present: Two Views of History in Medieval Persia," "Cultural Processes in Muslim and Arab Societies: Medieval and Early Modern Periods," special issue, *Poetics Today* 14, no. 2 (1993): 249 and 257. According to Meisami, the *Shāh-nāmah* represents a pre-Islamic and Iranian narrative, whereas a variety of other texts represent an Islamic one. In speaking of Firdawsī's ambitions, however, Meisami softens the distinction. The *Shāh-nāmah* reflects a cyclical view of history and the rise and fall of states. Implicit in this structure, she argues, "is the hope for the appearance of a house which would combine both Iranian and Islamic ideals, a hope clearly expressed in the poem's panegyrics."

[47] See al-Masʿūdī, *al-Tanbīh*, 76–7 (al-Masʿūdī criticizes here a romanticization of past authorities, citing al-Jāḥiẓ). Cited by Edward G. Browne in "Some Account of the Arabic Work entitled '*Niháyatu'l-irab fí akhbári'l-Furs wa'l-'Arab*,' particularly of that part which treats of the Persian Kings," *Journal of the Royal Asiatic Society*, n.s., 32, no. 2 (1900): 200. See also al-Jāḥiẓ's skepticism regarding the authenticity of ancient Persian writings transmitted in Arabic; *al-Bayān wa-l-tabyīn*, 2nd ed., ed. ʿAbd al-Salām Muḥammad Hārūn, 4 vols. (Cairo: Maktabat al-Khānjī, 1960–1), 3:29.

[48] Ḥamza al-Iṣfahānī, *Taʾrīkh*, 15. On this passage of Ḥamza's text and its implications for historiography, see Zeev Rubin, "Ḥamza al-Iṣfahānī's Sources for Sasanian History," *Jerusalem Studies in Arabic and Islam* 35 (2008): 43–4.

[49] For this example, see Robinson, *Islamic Historiography*, 115. Robinson cites Ibn al-Athīr (d. 630/1233); see *al-Kāmil fī al-Taʾrīkh*, 9:261. Firdawsī's *Shāh-nāmah* is dedicated to Maḥmūd; the anecdote might represent a comment on the relative worth of the two texts so as to show the importance of the *History* (see also Chapter 4).

Persian letters give us, we should not underestimate the significance of the fact that first the Pahlavi and then the Arabic texts are so quietly absorbed into other texts, a process that we explore in the second half of this book. Contents cannot survive unchanged regardless of the structures in which they are encased; nor can the memories they encapsulate, especially when their origins date back to a conquered empire. And quiet absorption suggests less fidelity to an original text than diligent attribution.[50]

Abraham and a New Divine Election

A further theory regarding the Persians' genealogy enjoyed currency in the third/ninth and fourth/tenth centuries. This theory, briefly mentioned earlier, held that the Persians descended from Abraham through his son Isaac. In ancient times, Persians even made their way to Mecca for the pilgrimage that Abraham first established. In his *Murūj al-dhahab*, the historian and litterateur Abū al-Ḥasan al-Masʿūdī (d. 345/956) describes the visits: "the Persians' ancestors (*aslāf al-Furs*) would betake themselves to the Sacred House [i.e., the Kaʿba] and circumambulate it to honor their grandfather Abraham, to hold fast by his way, and to preserve their genealogies."[51] The last pre-Islamic Persian to perform the pilgrimage was Sāsān, the dynasty's eponym: "When Sāsān came to the House, he circumambulated it and mumbled prayers (*zamzama*) over the well of Ishmael. It is named 'Zamzam' only on account of his and other Persians' mumbling prayers over it. This indicates the frequency of their practice over this well."[52] Al-Masʿūdī cites two poets, whom he does not name, attesting to this "mumbling." The first states: "The Persians mumbled prayers over Zamzam (*zamzamat al-Furs ʿalā Zamzam*). That was in their most ancient past."[53] Al-Masʿūdī also cites this line in his *Tanbīh*, noting there that the Persians would bring to the Kaʿba offerings to show respect for Abraham and his son: "it is, according to them, the greatest of the seven

[50] In a related vein, see Fred Donner's caution against the "Ṭabarization" of history in his review of Hugh Kennedy's *The Prophet and the Age of the Caliphates: The Islamic Near East from the Sixth to the Eleventh Century*, *Speculum* 65, no. 1 (1990): 182–4. Also, on the same tendency in scholarship, see Antoine Borrut, *Entre mémoire et pouvoir*, 106–7.

[51] Abū al-Ḥasan al-Masʿūdī, *Murūj al-dhahab wa-maʿādin al-jawhar*, vols. 1 and 2, ed. Charles Pellat (Beirut: Manshūrāt al-Jāmiʿa al-Lubnāniyya, 1965–6), 1:283 (no. 573). Regarding al-Masʿūdī, see esp. Tarif Khalidi, *Islamic Historiography: The Histories of Masʿūdī* (Albany: State University of New York Press, 1975).

[52] Al-Masʿūdī, *Murūj*, 1:283 (no. 574).

[53] Ibid. Neither poet can be identified.

great temples (*hayākil*) and the world's noble houses of worship."[54] The second poet al-Masʿūdī cites in the *Murūj* "boasted after the appearance of Islam" because of the Persians' ancient practices, saying:

> In bygone times we kept visiting the sanctuary (*naḥajju al-bayt*),
> And setting up camp securely in its valleys.
> Sāsān b. Bābak journeyed from afar
> To support religion with a visit to the Ancient House.
> Then he circumambulated it and mumbled prayers (*zamzama*) at a well belonging
> To Ishmael that quenches the drinkers' thirst.[55]

The topos of pilgrimage to the Kaʿba before Islam is found elsewhere in Arabic historiography.[56] In genealogical terms, the significance of the idea lies in the ties it establishes with Arabs and Muḥammad, of whose genealogy the Arab portion, as noted above, begins with Abraham's son Ishmael. In this manner, Persians become Muḥammad's kin and, as is more often emphasized, kin to the Arabs; see, for example, the following poem that was recited by Jarīr b. ʿAṭiyya (d. ca. 110/728–9), an Umayyad-era Arab poet, and circulated widely:

> The sons of Isaac are lions when they put on
> Their deadly sword-belts, wearing their armor.
> When they boast, they count among themselves the Ispahbadhs,[57]
> And Kisrā and they list al-Hurmuzān and Caesar.
> They had scripture and prophethood,[58]
> And were kings of Iṣṭakhr and Tustar.

54 Here he refers to the poet as an Arab poet from pre-Islamic times (*jāhiliyya*), whom the Persians cited as proof of their ancient practice. Al-Masʿūdī, *al-Tanbīh*, 109. The "seven great temples" refers, according to Bernard Carra de Vaux, to a Sabian syncretism. The Sabians, he writes, believed these temples to have been founded by Hermès. Al-Masʿūdī, *Le livre de l'avertissement et de la revision*, trans. Bernard Carra de Vaux (Paris: Imprimerie nationale, 1896), 155, n. 2. See also Yāqūt al-Ḥamawī, *Muʿjam al-buldān*, ed. Ferdinand Wüstenfeld as *Jacut's geographisches Wörterbuch*, 6 vols. (Leipzig: F. A. Brockhaus, 1866–73), 3:166, s.v. "Zamzam." All of the preceding should, however, be read in light of Kevin van Bladel's sober *The Arabic Hermes: From Pagan Sage to Prophet of Science* (Oxford: Oxford University Press, 2009).

55 Al-Masʿūdī, *Murūj*, 1:283 (no. 574).

56 For example, in Alexander the Great's pilgrimage; see al-Dīnawarī, *al-Akhbār al-ṭiwāl*, ed. ʿIṣām Muḥammad al-Ḥājj ʿAlī (Beirut: Dār al-Kutub al-ʿIlmiyya, 2001), 75. See also G. R. Hawting, "The Disappearance and Rediscovery of Zamzam and the 'Well of the Kaʿba,'" *Bulletin of the School of Oriental and African Studies* 43, no. 1 (1980): 44–54.

57 Arabic, *al-ṣibahbadh*.

58 Regarding post-conquest characterizations of Zoroaster as a prophet bringing a book, see Stausberg, "Invention of a Canon," 268–70.

They included the prophet Solomon, who prayed
And was rewarded with distinction and a pre-determined sovereignty.
Our father is the father of Isaac;
A father guided [by God] and a purified prophet unites us.
He built God's *qibla* by which he was guided,
And so he bequeathed to us mightiness and longlasting sovereignty.
We and the noble sons of Fāris are joined by a father
Who outshines in our eyes all those who have come after him.
Our father is the Friend of God and God is our Lord.
We have been satisfied with what God has given and decreed.[59]

The "sons of Isaac" whom Jarīr so proudly claims as kin were both worldly leaders and prophets. They included "Caesar," the usual Arabic name for the Roman and Byzantine emperors, and the Children of Israel as Solomon's descendants. More unusually from a biblical perspective, they included the "Ispahbadhs," a reference to the Persian title for army chiefs of pre-Islamic Persian empires;[60] "Kisrā," referring to the Sasanian rulers collectively; and "al-Hurmuzān," referring to a famous Persian general who was defeated by Caliph ʿUmar (r. 13–23/634–44) but who later was said to have converted to Islam. Isaac's sons were kings of Iṣṭakhr in the province of Fārs, the religious center of the Sasanian kingdom and its capital. They were also kings of Tustar, a town in southwestern Persia in the province of Khūzistān, where al-Hurmuzān was captured.[61] All of Isaac's sons benefited from their ancestry with Abraham, who was a "father guided [by God]," "a purified prophet," and "the Friend of God" (*khalīl Allāh*, Abraham's common epithet).

The portrayal of Abraham as the common ancestor linking the Arabs and the Persians played a crucial role in enabling the latter to be integrated into the communal world view of Muslims. Recent work on ethnicity and nationalism has emphasized the importance of ideas of divine election for social mobilization and national coherence. The work of Anthony D. Smith, in particular, has drawn attention to the ways in which myths of divine election both promote sociocultural survival and serve as a stimulus for ethnopolitical mobilization. For Smith, divine election signifies

[59] Cited in al-Masʿūdī, *Murūj*, 1:280–1 (no. 568). Otherwise, see, e.g., Jarīr b. ʿAṭiyya, *Dīwān Jarīr bi-sharḥ Muḥammad b. Ḥabīb*, ed. Nuʿmān Muḥammad Amīn Ṭāhā, 2 vols. (Cairo: Dār al-Maʿārif, 1969–86), 1:472–4 (no. 112, lines 27–39); al-Ṭabarī, *Taʾrīkh*, I:433; and Yāqūt, *Buldān*, 2:862–3, s.v. "al-Rūm."

[60] C. E. Bosworth, "Ispahba<u>dh</u>," in EI^2.

[61] On his defeat at Tustar, see Chapter 6.

a community's shared belief in its special destiny. Ethnic election is not ethnocentrism in a simple sense, but far more demanding:

> To be chosen is to be placed under moral obligations. One is chosen on condition that one observes certain moral, ritual and legal codes, and only for as long as one continues to do so. The privilege of election is accorded only to those who are sanctified, whose life-style is an expression of sacred values. The benefits of election are reserved for those who fulfil the required observances.[62]

For Smith, there are two basic types of myths of ethnic election. "Missionary" election myths exalt their community "by assigning them god-given tasks or missions of warfare or conversion or overlordship."[63] The community believes itself to be chosen to preserve and defend the true faith. This is the most common type of ethnic election and has been invoked by, among others, Armenians, Franks, Orthodox Byzantines, Russians, Catalans, and Catholic Poles. "Covenantal" election, by comparison, is contractual and conditional upon compliance with the will of God. This type of election has been seen less often, but it has surfaced among certain Protestant communities that have seen themselves as the heirs of the ancient Israelites (including the Puritan settlers of New England, the Ulster Scots, and Afrikaners).[64]

From an early date, the Arabs often espoused a missionary sense of chosenness when they sought new converts, first among other Arabs and then among their neighbors.[65] Arabic literature is filled with claims representing them as a people of religion, set apart from others. A common identity, documented through tribal genealogies, was nurtured, and it was also their election that made Arabs out of former non-Arabs. An ideology of election was supported by the Prophet as well as by the supreme

[62] Anthony D. Smith, "Chosen Peoples: Why Ethnic Groups Survive," *Ethnic and Racial Studies* 15, no. 3 (1992): 441. See also Smith's *Chosen Peoples* (Oxford: Oxford University Press, 2003), esp. ch. 3, "Election and Covenant," 44–65, and "Ethnic Election and Cultural Identity," "Pre-Modern and Modern National Identity in Russia and Eastern Europe," special issue, *Ethnic Studies* 10, no. 1–3 (1993): 9–25, esp. 11–12. For a useful summary and analysis of much of Smith's work on myths of divine election, see Bruce Cauthen, "Covenant and Continuity: Ethno-Symbolism and the Myth of Divine Election," *Nations and Nationalism* 10, no. 1/2 (2004): 19–33.

[63] Anthony D. Smith, *Myths and Memories of the Nation* (New York: Oxford University Press, 1999), 15.

[64] Anthony D. Smith, *The Nation in History: Historiographical Debates about Ethnicity and Nationalism* (Hanover, NH: University Press of New England, 2000), 67; Anthony D. Smith, "The 'Sacred' Dimension of Nationalism," *Millennium: Journal of International Studies* 29, no. 3 (2000): 791–814, esp. 804–5. See also Cauthen, "Covenant and Continuity," 21–2.

[65] Although some members of the Umayyad elite reportedly discouraged conversion.

importance of the Arabic language in Muslim religion and ritual. It is a mature sense of Arabness that is reflected in the statement of al-Jāḥiẓ:

> Since the Arabs are all one tribe, having the same country and language and characteristics and pride and patriotism and temperament and disposition, and were cast [in] one mould and after one pattern, the sections are all alike and the elements resemble each other, so that this became a greater similarity than certain forms of blood-relationship in respect of general and particular and agreement and disagreement: so that they are judged to be essentially alike in style.[66]

As their kinsfolk, Persians were given a share in the Arabs' ethnic election through reference to the most antique source of this chosenness, Abraham. As Jarīr said: "Our father is the father of Isaac; A father guided [by God] and a purified prophet unites us." The idea may well have originated in pre-Islamic times, as extensions to Abraham's genealogy were made by eastern Jews, who were also Isaac's descendants. In any event, by ʿAbbasid times, the view was credible to Arabs because they knew it to have been voiced by earlier Arabs, who claimed kinship with Persians as a point of pride. The Arab tribal context for such claims is alluded to by al-Masʿūdī and other traditionists. Al-Masʿūdī explains to his readers that Jarīr was directing his poem against Qaḥṭān, the name given to the southern Arabian tribal alliance.[67] Jarīr, as a "northern" Arab, thus boasted of his noble kinsmen against a southerner.[68]

In ʿAbbasid times, the clearest (but by no means only) rhetorical context in which ideas about the Persians and Isaac were articulated was that of the Shuʿūbiyya movement. The name of the movement's "Shuʿūbī" proponents derived from a Qurʾanic verse they were fond of quoting, which includes the statement: "We have created you male and female and made you peoples (*shuʿūb*) and tribes so that you may know one another. The most noble among you before God is the most God-fearing" (Qurʾan 49:13).[69] The movement had its roots among the Persian court secretaries and was mainly centered in Baghdad; its members were overwhelmingly

[66] Translated by C. T. Harley Walker in "Jāḥiẓ of Baṣra to al-Fatḥ ibn Khāqān on the 'Exploits of the Turks and the Army of the Khalifate in General,'" *Journal of the Royal Asiatic Society*, n.s., 47, no. 4 (1915): 639.

[67] Al-Masʿūdī, *Murūj*, 1:280 (no. 568).

[68] Elsewhere different tribal loyalties are cited, suggesting a rivalry among "northern" Tamīmīs. See Jarīr b. ʿAṭiyya, *Naqāʾiḍ Jarīr wa-l-Farazdaq*, ed. Anthony Ashley Bevan, 3 vols. (Leiden: E. J. Brill, 1905–12), 2:991–1003 (no. 104), and Savant, "Isaac as the Persians' Ishmael: Pride and the Pre-Islamic Past in Ninth and Tenth-Century Islam," *Comparative Islamic Studies* 2, no. 1 (2006): 18–19, n. 19.

[69] Ibn Qutayba, *Faḍl al-ʿArab wa-l-tanbīh ʿalā ʿulūmihā*, ed. Walīd Maḥmūd Khāliṣ (Abu Dhabi: Cultural Foundation Productions, 1998), 109; Ibn ʿAbd Rabbih, *Kitāb al-ʿIqd*

Persians. It took issue with the idea of Arab election, based on what the movement's adherents saw as the egalitarian ideals of Islam, the ill-conceived idea of a chosen people, and the failures of Arabs generally in the realms of culture and social manners. The Shuʿūbīs belittled the Arabs as the sons of a slave, since Ishmael, their father, was born of the slave woman Hagar, whereas the Shuʿūbīs' "mother" was Sarah, Abraham's wife. Shuʿūbīs even referred to Arabs as "sons of the unclean woman" because of Hagar's lowly origins. Ibn Qutayba (d. 276/889), whose own lineage went back to Khurāsān, responded to the Shuʿūbīs by noting that not all slaves are unclean and that many great figures of Islamic history had been born of slave women. Is it allowable, he asked, for an apostate (*mulḥid*), let alone a Muslim, to describe Hagar as unclean?[70]

The idea that the Persians descend from Isaac is attested after the Shuʿūbiyya and, in the rarefied world of ʿAbbasid Baghdad, involved assertions about hierarchy, social status, and privilege, and would appear to assert the chosenness of Persians, alongside Arabs. After the fourth/tenth century, the idea of Isaac as a father persists, though it is hard to say how widely it was held. A few cases suggest that it endured in wider circles than Iranians might imagine today. Abū Nuʿaym al-Iṣfahānī (d. 430/1038), in his history of Iṣfahān and its scholars, cites a Hadith in which Abū Hurayra quotes Muḥammad as saying that "Persia is the Children of Isaac (*Fāris Banū Isḥāq*)."[71] In seventh/thirteenth-century Baghdad, Ibn Abī al-Ḥadīd (d. 656/1258) in his commentary on the *Nahj al-balāgha* – an anthology of speeches, letters, testimonials, and opinions traditionally attributed to ʿAlī b. Abī Ṭālib – cites a report in which ʿAlī puts an Arab woman belonging to the Banū Ismāʿīl on a par with a woman from the ʿAjam belonging to the Banū Isḥāq.[72] An early folio of a local history of Nīshāpūr (the *Kitāb-i Aḥvāl-i Nīshāpūr*) from the ninth/fifteenth century or later cites a Hadith in Arabic and then translated into Persian in which Ibn ʿAbbās reports that "Fāris" was mentioned in the presence of the Prophet. The Prophet stated that Fāris, that is, Persia, was "our paternal relations" and part of the *ahl al-bayt* ("people of the house," that is, the Prophet's family). When prodded

al-farīd, ed. Aḥmad Amīn, Aḥmad al-Zayn, and Ibrāhīm al-Abyārī, 7 vols. (Cairo: Lajnat al-Taʾlīf wa-l-Tarjama wa-l-Nashr, 1940–53), 3:404.

70 Ibn Qutayba, *Faḍl al-ʿArab*, 47–8.

71 Abū Nuʿaym al-Iṣfahānī, *Dhikr akhbār Iṣbahān*, ed. Sven Dedering, 2 vols. (Leiden: E. J. Brill, 1931–4), 1:11.

72 Ibn Abī al-Ḥadīd, *Sharḥ Nahj al-balāgha*, ed. Muḥammad Abū al-Faḍl Ibrāhīm, 20 vols. (Cairo: ʿĪsā al-Bābī al-Ḥalabī, 1959–63), 2:200–1.

for an explanation, the Prophet said: "Because Ishmael was the paternal uncle of the descendants of Isaac, and Isaac was the paternal uncle of the descendants of Ishmael."[73]

Still, in the long term, the theory of the Persians' descent from Isaac convinced neither al-Ṭabarī nor Iranians generally, likely because it was so thin on supporting mythology. The lineage seemed forced, as when al-Masʿūdī notes a claim that Manūshihr was the son of a man by the name of Manushkhūrnar b. Manūshkhūrnak b. Wīrak, with Wīrak being the very same person as Isaac, the son of Abraham.[74] According to the claim, Manushkhūrnar (Manūshihr's father) went to the land of Persia, where he married the Persian queen, a daughter of Īraj named Kūdak, who bore Manūshihr, whose descendants multiplied, "conquering and ruling the earth."[75] With their rise, the "ancient Persians disappeared like past nations and the original Arabs (*al-ʿArab al-ʿāriba*)."[76] Al-Masʿūdī does not bother to follow through by, for example, reconciling the relationship between Isaac's known sons and the person of Manūshkhūrnak. And although he says that Persians "are led to this" opinion and do not deny it, he admits that the genealogy was offered by Arab savants.[77] Nor does the idea have a narrative to accompany it that would explain the Persians' origins, describe the lives of exemplary forebears, and connect this history to the Persians in their own day. By comparison, Arabs, Persians, and Muslims in general knew the detailed history of the Jewish people, beginning from Isaac and Abraham.

Instead, it is probably best to view the advocates of this idea, al-Masʿūdī among them, as seeking to offer the Persians a prominent place in prophetic history in lieu of older Iranian genealogies. They were losers in an ideological contest, insofar as their model was not accepted.

[73] *The Histories of Nishapur*, ed. Richard N. Frye (Cambridge, MA: Harvard University Press, 1965), fol. 4. The *Kitāb Aḥvāl-i Nīshāpūr* is based on a lost Arabic history of Nīshāpūr by Muḥammad b. ʿAbd Allāh al-Ḥākim al-Bayyiʿ (d. 405/1014). On the manuscript, see Frye's remarks in *Histories of Nishapur*, 10–11. The manuscript has been edited and published by Muḥammad Riḍā Shafīʿī Kadkanī as Abū ʿAbd Allāh Ḥākim al-Nīsābūrī, *Tārīkh-i Nīshābūr: Tarjamah-yi Muḥammad b. Ḥusayn Khalīfah-yi Nīshābūrī* (Tehran: Āgah, 1375/1996), 64.

[74] Al-Masʿūdī, *Murūj*, 1:279 (no. 566). There are variants of these names; I follow Pellat.

[75] Ibid. The other kings feared Manūshihr's descendants "on account of their courage and horsemanship."

[76] Ibid.

[77] Most of the Arab savants from Nizār b. Maʿadd, according to al-Masʿūdī, say this and make it a foundation for genealogy; they have, he says, boasted about their kinship with the Persians, who descend from Isaac b. Abraham, against the Yemenites, who descend from Qaḥṭān (*iftakharat ʿalā al-Yaman min Qaḥṭān*). Ibid., 1:280 (no. 567).

Al-Masʿūdī was almost certainly aware of the sentiments of the Shuʿūbiyya, Ibn Qutayba, and al-Ṭabarī regarding the Persians' putative link to Isaac since he was educated in Baghdad by some of the city's most respected scholars; indeed, al-Masʿūdī listed al-Ṭabarī's *History* as one of the many sources he consulted for the *Murūj*, though he did not share his predecessor's judgment on Isaac's progeny.[78] Al-Masʿūdī traveled widely, including throughout Iran, and extensively documents more Iran-centric accounts in the *Murūj* and *Tanbīh*.[79] Still, he gives no sense of the controversies or polemics surrounding the Isaac claim. It may well be that al-Masʿūdī, an Arab of reputable stock himself, simply wished to provide the Persians with a way of viewing their history and genealogy as inseparable from those of the Arabs.[80] But in another, more fundamental sense al-Masʿūdī was part of a successful campaign to get Iranians to see themselves as part of a broader prophetic history.[81]

A Creative License

It was not just the collective category of Persians that was swept into prophetic history, but also individual localities. Consider the cases of Hamadhān and Nihāwand, two towns of ancient standing in the medieval province of Jibāl, which are located less than fifty miles apart as the crow flies. Hamadhān had been the capital of the Medes, the summer capital of the Achaemenids, and under the Seleucid, Parthian, and Sasanian dynasties, an important city on the trading route from Mesopotamia to the East. It is mentioned throughout antiquity as a wealthy city renowned for its architecture.[82] Nihāwand has a somewhat less documented and illustrious heritage, although in Sasanian times it seems to have played a role in the politics of the Sasanian state, and its Zoroastrian associations were reportedly strong.[83] By the ʿAbbasid period, however, both cities

[78] Ibid., 1:15.

[79] On al-Masʿūdī as a source for Iranian history, see esp. Michael Cooperson, "Masʿudi," in *EIr*.

[80] Biographers give him a pedigree running back to the Prophet's companion ʿAbd Allāh b. Masʿūd. On his travels, see Ahmad M. H. Shboul, *Al-Masʿūdī and His World: A Muslim Humanist and His Interest in Non-Muslims* (London: Ithaca Press, 1979), 1–28.

[81] For a fuller discussion of al-Masʿūdī's ideas, see Savant, "Genealogy and Ethnogenesis in al-Masʿudi's *Muruj al-Dhahab*," in *Genealogy and Knowledge in Muslim Societies*, ed. Savant and de Felipe.

[82] R. N. Frye, "Hamadhān," in *EI*², and Stuart C. Brown, "Ecbatana," in *EIr*.

[83] V. Minorsky, "Nihāwand," in *EI*²; al-Dīnawarī, *al-Akhbār al-ṭiwāl*, 197.

were traditionally associated with the figure of Noah. A widely cited late ninth/early tenth-century geography by Ibn al-Faqīh gives some sense of the association. In it, there is a report that Hamadhān – the possible birthplace of Ibn al-Faqīh – was named for a descendant of Noah named Hamadhān, who was a son of Peleg (in Arabic al-Falūj) b. Shem b. Noah and the brother of a certain Iṣfahān, who built his own eponymous city: "and so, each of the cities was named after its builder."[84] Nihāwand, however, was built by Noah himself and was called *Nūḥ awand* (the *awand* suffix signifying a possessive relationship).[85]

Ibn al-Faqīh also furnishes such founding fathers for other locales and peoples; the Hephthalites of Central Asia, for example, descended from a certain Hayṭal, who was a great-grandson of Noah who moved eastward after languages became confused (in Babylon, as the story goes).[86] The northwestern province of Azarbaijan provides a particularly interesting case. Throughout the Sasanian period Atropatene/Āturpātakān, as it was then known, was an important religious center and home to one of the empire's most sacred fires, that of Ādur Gushnasp, whose hearth was in the town of Shīz (see Figure 1.1). Legend has it that every newly crowned Sasanian king had to visit it on foot. There was also a royal palace in the province.[87] Muslims acknowledged this Zoroastrian heritage, with a good number believing the region to be the birthplace of Zoroaster himself.[88] However, Ibn al-Faqīh quotes Ibn al-Muqaffaʿ as tracing the name of the province back to a prophetic eponym, one Āzarbādh b. Īrān

[84] Ibn al-Faqīh here cites Abū Mundhir Hishām b. al-Sāʾib al-Kalbī. Ibn al-Faqīh (fl. second half of the third/ninth century), *Kitāb al-Buldān*, ed. Yūsuf al-Hādī (Beirut: ʿĀlam al-Kutub, 1996), 459 and 529.

[85] Ibid., 527. See also the "abridgment" of Ibn al-Faqīh's text by Abū al-Ḥasan ʿAlī b. Jaʿfar b. Aḥmad al-Shayzarī (ca. 413/1022); *Mukhtaṣar Kitāb al-Buldān*, ed. Michael J. de Goeje (Leiden: E. J. Brill, 1885), 217, 258, and 263. On Ibn al-Faqīh's text and the abridgment, see André Miquel, *La géographie humaine du monde musulman jusqu'au milieu du 11*^{e} *siècle*, 2nd ed., 3 vols. (Paris: Mouton, 1973–80), 1:153–60, and Travis Zadeh, "Of Mummies, Poets, and Water Nymphs: Tracing the Codicological Limits of Ibn Khurradādhbih's Geography," in *ʿAbbasid Studies IV: Occasional Papers of the School of ʿAbbasid Studies*, ed. Monique Bernards (forthcoming in 2013). Cf. Anas B. Khalidov, "Ebn al-Faqīh, Abū Bakr Aḥmad," in *EIr*. See also Yāqūt, *Buldān*, 5:313 and 410 (Yāqūt borrows from Ibn al-Faqīh, whose reporting he closely follows).

[86] Ibn al-Faqīh, *Kitāb al-Buldān*, 601; *Mukhtaṣar Kitāb al-Buldān*, 314. Muslim exegetes followed the myth in Genesis 11:5–9.

[87] Klaus Schippmann, "Azerbaijan iii. Pre-Islamic History," in *EIr*. See also Klaus Schippmann, *Die iranischen Feuerheiligtümer* (Berlin: de Gruyter, 1971), 309ff.

[88] C. E. Bosworth, "Azerbaijan iv. Islamic History to 1941," in *EIr*.

FIGURE 1.1. Ādur Gushnasp. Azarbaijan (Iran). Photo by Wahunam.

b. al-Aswad b. Shem b. Noah.[89] This is a bold attribution, especially since Ibn al-Muqaffaʿ was a major transmitter of Iran's pre-Islamic Sasanian heritage and seems an unlikely advocate of such an idea.

The shape and contours of the earliest history writing connected to localities are still debated among today's historians, in large measure because so few sources survive, but the problem is also partly terminological.[90] Whatever its earliest forms, starting approximately in the second half of the fourth/tenth century, we have local histories for Iranian territories that are filled with descriptions of towns and regions, geography, topography, biographies of notable residents (especially the *ʿulamāʾ*), and political history and that reflect the density of religious learning, at least among elites. Such works were composed for many of the major centers of Iranian Islam, including old cities such as Hamadhān and Iṣfahān and new ones such as Shīrāz, as well as places where wide-scale conversion

[89] Alternatively, Ibn al-Faqīh identifies the province's founder as Āzarbādh b. Bīwarāsf, Bīwarāsf (i.e., al-Ḍaḥḥāk) being a tyrant of Iranian legend. Ibn al-Faqīh, *Kitāb al-Buldān*, 581; *Mukhtaṣar Kitāb al-Buldān*, 284. See also Yāqūt al-Ḥamawī, *Buldān*, 1:128–9, s.v. "Āzarbaijān." Compare a foundation myth for Shīz relating to Jesus' nativity, which Vladimir Minorsky attributes to Christians or Zoroastrians; "Two Iranian Legends in Abū-Dulaf's Second Risālah," in *Medieval Iran and Its Neighbours* (London: Variorum Reprints, 1982), 172–5.

[90] On the question of regional schools of historiography, see Robinson, *Islamic Historiography*, 138–42. In the late second–third/ninth century, there were already works that sang the praises of particular localities such as Medina, Basra, and Kufa. For Iran, see Sezgin, *Geschichte des arabischen Schrifttums*, 1:351–4.

and Islamization appear to have occurred at a slower pace and where significant Zoroastrian communities lived on, including the provinces of Fārs in the southwest of Iran, Yazd in central Iran, and Ṭabaristān.

These works also took up ideas about the prophets, and they suggest the importance of the earlier, schematizing sources, such as those of Ibn al-Kalbī and Ibn al-Faqīh. Whatever the paths that such knowledge traveled, perhaps including transmission by Jews and Christians, the legacy of ʿAbbasid Iraq is visible in works such as the early sixth/twelfth-century *Fārs-nāmah*, which cites al-Ṭabarī as one of its authorities for Iran's earliest history. The Persian-language text is attributed to a little-known author whose ancestors hailed from Balkh and who is consequently known as Ibn al-Balkhī. The work treats Gayūmart as the first king to rule the world and faintly echoes al-Ṭabarī's reporting on theories about him as well as ideas about his kingly successor Hūshang, including that Hūshang fathered the biblical prophet Enoch, also known as the Qurʾanic Idrīs.[91] This was a well-traveled proposal and an apparently fitting way to start a text that, while containing abundant detail on Fārs, also constitutes an important source on Iran's pre-Islamic rulers.[92]

A result of this transmission of ideas was the gradual conversion of Iranian sites of great antiquity into ones with Muslim associations. In this transformation, the prophet Solomon, with his extensive travels and his association with major sites of antiquity, played an important role. Solomon was recognized as ruler over Greater Syria and associated with several sites of its antique heritage, including Jerusalem and the Temple Mount, Baalbek, and Palmyra,[93] but Iran also figured prominently in his itinerary.[94] A good example relates to the abovementioned sacred fire of Ādur Gushnasp. While the name of Azarbaijan came to be linked to Noah, the fire and its temple became folded into a set of ruins surrounding a clear

91 Ibn al-Balkhī, *The Fársnáma of Ibnu'l-Balkhí*, ed. Guy Le Strange and Reynold A. Nicholson (London: Luzac, 1921), 8–10. Cf. al-Ṭabarī, *Taʾrīkh*, esp. I:155, and Ḥamza al-Iṣfahānī, *Taʾrīkh*, 19 and 23.

92 For the text, see Ibn an-Balkhī, *Description of the Province of Fars in Persia at the Beginning of the Fourteenth Century A.D.*, trans. and ed. Guy Le Strange (London: The Royal Asiatic Society, 1912). See also Clifford Edmund Bosworth, "Ebn al-Balḵī," in *EIr*.

93 Borrut, "La Syrie de Salomon: L'appropriation du mythe salomonien dans les sources arabes," *Pallas* 63 (2003): 107–20, and *Entre mémoire et pouvoir*, 217–38.

94 On his travels in Iran, see Roy P. Mottahedeh, "The Eastern Travels of Solomon: Reimagining Persepolis and the Iranian Past," in *Law and Tradition in Classical Islamic Thought: Studies in Honor of Professor Hossein Modarressi*, ed. Michael Cook, Najam Haider, Intisar Rabb, and Asma Sayeed, 247–67 (New York: Palgrave Macmillan, 2012).

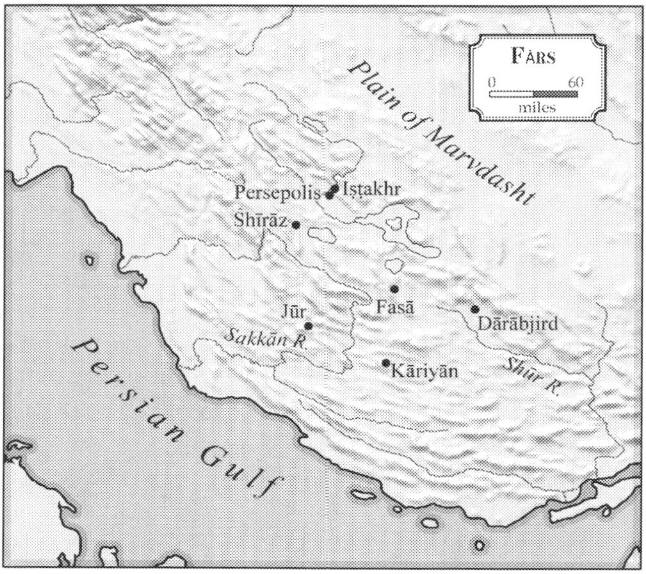

MAP 1.1. Fārs

blue lake and known as the Takht-i Sulaymān ("Throne of Solomon"). The ruins' name pointed to a belief that the buildings were a royal palace built and used by Solomon during his travels.[95]

Another case is that of Persepolis (Takht-i Jamshīd) in the province of Fārs, an enormous complex of columned halls, palaces, gates, and a treasury created by Darius the Great (r. 522–486 BCE) and his successors that covers some 125,000 square meters and was one of the five royal capitals of the Achaemenid empire. The site was founded on a promontory above the plain of Marvdasht, and the natural drama surely served it well in Achaemenid times for royal and religious occasions, as it did in the Sasanian era and in 1971, when Mohammadreza Shah Pahlavi celebrated the 2,500th anniversary of Iran's monarchy (reckoned by Iran's solar hijri calendar). The term *Takhṭ-i Jamshīd* signaled the role that the great king of Persian legend, Jamshīd, was meant to have played in the site's founding.[96] After Alexander the Great sacked Persepolis, the city of Iṣṭakhr grew up a short distance away, and the ruins of Persepolis served as a quarry for the new city. Sāsān, the eponym of the Sasanian

[95] Ibid.

[96] An important study of the site is that of Eric F. Schmidt, *Persepolis*, 3 vols. (Chicago: University of Chicago Press, 1953–70); see also A. Shapur Shahbazi, *Persepolis Illustrated* (Persepolis: Institute of Achaemenid Research, 1976), 4–6.

dynasty and sometimes remembered as the grandfather to its founder, Ardashīr, was reportedly the superintendent of the Fire Temple of the goddess Anāhīd in Iṣṭakhr. Muslims appropriated Persepolis's charisma for prophetic history through traditions that conflated it with nearby Iṣṭakhr and associated it to Solomon. The geographer Abū Isḥāq al-Fārisī al-Iṣṭakhrī (d. mid-fourth/tenth century), for example, said of the town whose name he bore:

> As for Iṣṭakhr, it is a medium-sized city, a mile in width, and among the oldest and most famous cities of Fārs. The kings of Persia dwelled in it until Ardashīr transferred rule to Gūr [also in Fārs]. It is relayed in reports that Solomon (eternal peace be his), the son of David, traveled from [the town of] Tiberias to it in a day [lit. "from morning to evening"]. In it, there is a mosque known as the "Mosque of Solomon." A group of Persian common folk claim with no proof that Jam[shīd], who preceded al-Ḍaḥḥāk, was Solomon.[97]

In his *Fārs-nāmah*, Ibn al-Balkhī vividly described a carved figure at Persepolis that he took to represent Burāq, the horse upon which Muḥammad reportedly made his night journey to heaven: "The figure is after this fashion: the face is as the face of a man with a beard and curly hair, with a crown set on the head, but the body, with the fore and hind legs, is that of a bull, and the tail is a bull's tail."[98]

The path by which such ideas about prophetic history came to be accepted among Iranian Muslims was surely complicated. In weighing evidence, though, Muslims appear to have frequently recognized as authoritative Arabic traditions from earlier centuries that wrote Iranian locales into prophetic history.

Conclusion

To sum up, genealogies were important ingredients for stories about the origins of the Persians that circulated at least from the third/ninth century

97 Abū Isḥāq al-Fārisī al-Iṣṭakhrī, *al-Masālik wa-l-mamālik*, ed. M. J. de Goeje (Leiden: E. J. Brill, 1927), 123; regarding Iṣṭakhr, see C. Barbier de Meynard, *Dictionnaire géographique, historique et littéraire de la Perse et des contrées adjacentes* (Paris: L'Imprimerie impériale, 1861), 48–50 ("Isthakhr"). The term "mile" likely refers to a distance of between roughly one-and-a-half and two kilometres; see Walther Hinz, *Islamische Masse und Gewichte: Umgerechnet ins metrische System* (Leiden: E. J. Brill, 1955), 63, and Moshe Gil, "Additions to *Islamische Masse und Gewichte*," in *Occident and Orient: A Tribute to the Memory of Alexander Scheiber*, ed. Robert Dán, 167–70 (Budapest: Akadémiai Kiadó, 1988), 169. Regarding the Sasanians' genealogy, see esp. R. N. Frye, "The Political History of Iran under the Sasanians," in *The Cambridge History of Iran*, 3(1):116–77, at 116–17.

98 Ibn al-Balkhī, *The Fársnáma of Ibnu'l-Balkhí*, 126; Le Strange, *Description of the Province of Fars*, 27.

onward. Ramón d'Abadal i de Vinyals, John Armstrong, and Anthony D. Smith have termed such stories *mythomoteurs*, and much of what they say about these stories applies to the Persian case.[99] At the center of every ethnic community and its view of the world lies a "distinctive complex of myths, memories, and symbols" that advance claims about the community's origins and lineages. These are the engines that distinguish one ethnic group from another, and much of their emotional pull is nostalgic. As they describe origins, the Persians' genealogies are schematic, positioning Persians relative to other groups and notable ancestors relative to one another. Blood ties in the remote past create filiations that explain relationships and recover and present other filiations for consideration. These bonds, in turn, inspire and encourage recognition of particular loyalties, even as they also represent antagonisms. Traditionists saw the Persians' descent in different ways, which reflects both the layering of traditions and, more profoundly, different appeals for modes of social definition. This is to be expected in a community in transition. But the divergent accounts also offer a picture of primordial continuity. Since the Persians were written into prophetic history as descendants of either Noah or Abraham, the subsequent historical trajectory that yielded the arrival of Islam in Iran represents a process of recovering the initial, collective state of *fiṭra* into which every child is born, as mentioned in the Prophetic tradition cited at the beginning of the chapter. This process also provided a license to appropriate monuments of Iran's antique history and to integrate these creatively into a narrative about Persians. And so we have a glimpse into the conflictual understandings of what it meant to be a Persian during the period of Iran's conversion to Islam.

[99] The notion of *mythomoteur* originated with d'Abadal i de Vinyals, "À propos du Legs visigothique en Espagne," *Settimane di studio del Centro italiano di studi sull'alto medioevo* 5 (1958): 541–85. See also John A. Armstrong, *Nations before Nationalism* (Chapel Hill: University of North Carolina Press, 1982), and Smith, *Ethnic Origins of Nations*. For a trenchant criticism of Smith and the school of ethnosymbolism that he represents, see Umut Özkirimli, "The Nation as an Artichoke? A Critique of Ethnosymbolist Interpretations of Nationalism," *Nations and Nationalism* 9, no. 3 (2003): 340.

2

Muḥammad's Persian Companion, Salmān al-Fārisī

Many Iranians are proud that one of their number – a man by the name of Salmān al-Fārisī, Salmān "the Persian" – was among Muḥammad's companions and played a role both in the Muslim community in Medina and afterward, when the Muslims controlled an empire. Salmān's tomb in Ctesiphon, which he governed after the Arab conquest, became a destination for travelers, who still visit it today. He is remembered as a special friend of ʿAlī and as a defender of the interests of the ʿAlids. Among the Ismāʿīlīs, Salmān has played a role in gnostic strands of thought. Recently, he has received attention in a number of popular Persian-language biographies dedicated to him.[1]

Salmān's Iranian, or Persian, identity is often emphasized today, especially in Iran. Scholars outside of Iran likewise treat him as an early Iranian representative of Islam. But was this always true? In many early texts by Muslims, including biographies of the Prophet, Salmān's Persian birthplace gives a specificity to his foreign, non-Arab origins, but

[1] In Christian polemics, Salmān has been credited with helping to compose the Qurʾan; see, for example, a writing attributed to the Byzantine emperor Leo III the Isaurian (r. 717–41) and written against ʿUmar II (r. 717–20). Much has been written about the emperor's polemic; see Arthur Jeffery, "Ghevond's Text of the Correspondence between ʿUmar II and Leo III," *Harvard Theological Review* 37, no. 4 (1944): esp. 292. For an early European iteration of the claim, see Humphrey Prideaux, *The True Nature of Imposture Fully Display'd in the Life of Mahomet, with a Discourse annex'd for the Vindication of Christianity from this Charge, Offered to the Consideration of the Deists of the Present Age*, 8th ed. (London: E. Curll, 1723), 33–4. Regarding the Ismāʿīlīs, see esp. W. Ivanow, "Notes sur l''Ummu'l-Kitab': Des Ismaëliens de l'Asie Centrale," *Revue des Études Islamiques* 6 (1932): 419–81, and Farhad Daftary, *The Ismāʿīlīs: Their History and Doctrines* (Cambridge: Cambridge University Press, 1990), 100–1 and 394.

its primary function is simply to illustrate a major theme in early Arabic writings, namely, the acceptance of Islam by diverse peoples, Persians among them. The importance of Salmān's Persian origins solidifies, however, with the emergence of the Muslim community in Iran. From the second half of the fourth/tenth century onward, Salmān's identity as an Iṣfahānī and a Persian is embraced in Arabic traditions that nostalgically recall his homeland as well as the Prophet's affection for it and its people. There were even traditions claiming special status for Salmān's descendants, possibly including those who did not convert to Islam.

Scholars have long sought to disentangle the enormous quantity of traditions attributed to and about Salmān for different purposes.[2] In this chapter, I trace the adoption of Salmān as a site of memory for Persians and particularly for the people of Iṣfahān.

Salmān in the Early Biographical Tradition

Salmān figures prominently in the Muslim biographical tradition and particularly in the second/eighth- and third/ninth-century biographies of the Prophet and the early Muslim community. A prominent story narrates how Salmān abandoned his homeland in search of a better religion. In the version repeated by Ibn Hishām and still widely known today, Salmān's yearning for a better religion compels him to overcome numerous obstacles, until at last he finds satisfaction. The story is placed amid others that show Muḥammad's arrival was anticipated, and it precedes Ibn Hishām's accounts of the revelation of the Qurʾan, the first people to accept Islam, and memorable events involving Muḥammad and the early Muslims in Mecca and Medina. The reporting begins with Salmān relating his story to Ibn ʿAbbās, the Prophet's cousin:

[2] For all the diversity of this literature, three or four purposes have chiefly been pursued: to establish Salmān as a historical person distinct from the figure of later legend, to assess the date and place of the traditions' origination, and to find evidence of the very earliest sectarian and/or Iranian ideologies. Major European studies relating to Salmān include Cl. Huart, "Selmân du Fârs," in *Mélanges Hartwig Derenbourg (1844–1908)*, 297–310 (Paris: Ernest Leroux, 1909); Leone Caetani, "Salmān al-Fārisī," in *Annali dell'Islām*, vol. 8, *Dall'anno 33. al 35 H.* (Milan: U. Hoepli, 1918); Josef Horovitz, "Salmān al-Fārisi," *Der Islam* 12, no. 3–4 (1922): 178–83; Louis Massignon, *Salmân Pâk et les prémices spirituelles de l'Islam iranien* (Tours: Arrault, 1934); and Jaakko Hämeen-Anttila, "The Corruption of Christianity: Salmān al-Fārisī's Quest as a Paradigmatic Model," *Studia Orientalia* 85 (1999): 115–26. See also G. Levi Della Vida, "Salmān al-Fārisī," in *EI*², and Parvīz Az̲kāʾī, "Salmān Fārisī," in *Dāyirat al-maʿārif-i Tashayyuʿ*, ed. Aḥmad Ṣadr Ḥājj Sayyid Javādī, Kāmrān Fānī, and Bahā al-Dīn Khorramshāhī (Tehran: Bunyād-i Islāmī-yi Tāhir, 1988–), 9:262–5.

I was a Persian man from among the people of Iṣfahān, from a village called Jayy. My father was a man from the class of the landed gentry (*dihqān*) of his village, and I was the most beloved of God's creatures to him. He loved me so much that he imprisoned me in his house, just like one imprisons a slave girl. I exerted myself in Zoroastrianism (*al-majūsiyya*), until I became the attendant of the sacred fire, who stokes it, not letting it die down for a moment.[3]

One day when Salmān's father was busy, he sent his son to check on his estate. En route, Salmān passed by a Christian church, from which he overheard the sound of prayer. He entered and, becoming engrossed by what he saw and heard, decided to forget his father's mission. "Since I had been held prisoner in my father's house, I had no idea what they were doing," he later recalled to Ibn ʿAbbās. "From where does this religion originate?" he asked. "Syria," came the reply. When he returned home, his father reprimanded him: "My son, there is no good in that religion; your religion and the religion of your fathers is better than it." Salmān naively contradicted him: "By God, no, it is better than our religion." His father, trying to put a stop to the nonsense, shackled Salmān and imprisoned him within his house.[4] Determined to find out more about this wonderful religion, Salmān escaped to Syria and entered upon a semi-itinerant existence, which first had him join up with a Christian bishop (*al-usquf*), who stole from his own church. At the bishop's death, Salmān exposed his corruption and then passed as a student through the hands of his successor and three good Christians in, sequentially, Mosul, Nisibis, and Amorium,[5] each at his death passing Salmān on to the next. At last Salmān joined a party of merchants from the tribe of Kalb, who promised to take Salmān to Arabia but instead, when they reached Wādī al-Qurā (in the northern Ḥijāz), sold him to a Jew, who sold him onward to a cousin of his from the tribe of Qurayẓa, who then brought him to Medina. Muḥammad had not yet emigrated from Mecca to Medina, but when he did, Salmān recognized him by the clues the last Christian had given. This man had promised a prophet would soon arise in Arabia, sent with the "religion of Abraham." The prophet would emigrate to a land between two lava belts, amid which grow date palms; eat food given

[3] Ibn Hishām, *Sīra*, 1:214–5; see also Ibn Hishām, *The Life of Muhammad: A Translation of Ibn Isḥāq's Sīrat Rasūl Allāh*, trans. A. Guillaume (Karachi: Oxford University Press, 1955; repr., 1978), 95–8.

[4] Ibn Hishām, *Sīra*, 1:215.

[5] Mosul and Nisibis (modern Turkish, Nusaybin) lie in upper Mesopotamia whereas Amorium was situated in Phrygia, on the Byzantine military road from Constantinople to Cilicia. Regarding the latter, see M. Canard, "ʿAmmūriya," in *EI*^{2}.

as a gift (*al-hadiyya*), but not as alms (*al-ṣadaqa*); and bear the "seal of prophecy" (*khātam al-nubuwwa*) between his shoulders.[6] Upon meeting Muḥammad, Salmān offered him alms, which the Prophet handed over to his companions, and then a gift, which Muḥammad accepted for himself. Returning on another day, Salmān came upon the Prophet, who had just attended a funeral. Ibn Hishām claims to quote Salmān in his own words, addressed still to Ibn ʿAbbās:

> [Muḥammad] was sitting with his companions. I greeted him and then went around to look at his back. Could I see the seal which my companion had described to me? When the Messenger of God saw me go around him, he recognized that I was seeking evidence for something that had been described to me, and so he threw off his cloak, laying bare his back. I looked at the seal and recognized it. I leaned over him, kissed him, and wept. The Messenger of God then said to me: "Come here." So I went and sat before him, and told him my story, just as I am telling you, O Ibn ʿAbbās.[7]

Afterward, Muḥammad told Salmān to write out an agreement with his master, with Salmān agreeing to plant three hundred date palm trees for the master and to pay forty measures of gold in order to secure his freedom. Muḥammad asked his companions to help Salmān, which they did, each bringing as many palm shoots as he could. Salmān and the companions then dug holes, and the Prophet himself planted the palms in the holes. Then the Prophet gave Salmān the gold with which to finalize his freedom.[8]

On the whole, the narrative hangs together well, as its plot unfolds with climactic moments in Medina. There are good guys (Salmān, most of the Christians, and Muḥammad) and bad guys (one Christian and the Kalbite merchants). The devices of a narrator (Salmān himself) and an audience (Ibn ʿAbbās, as well as the reader/listener) are employed. Salmān's voice is infused with emotion on his first encounter with Christianity: "By God, no, it is better than our religion!"[9]

6 Ibn Hishām, *Sīra*, 1:218.
7 Ibid., 1:220.
8 Ibid., 1:220–1.
9 Ibid., 1:215. The story, prophesying Muḥammad's coming as a prophet, has parallels elsewhere, including for the monk Baḥīrā, on which see Barbara Roggema, *The Legend of Sergius Baḥīrā: Eastern Christian Apologetics and Apocalyptic in Response to Islam* (Leiden: Brill, 2009). It also has echoes in the story of Bulūqiyā, for which see esp. Josef Horovitz, "Bulūqjā," *Zeitschrift der Deutschen Morgenländischen Gesellschaft* 55 (1901): 519–25; Stephanie Dalley, "Gilgamesh in the Arabian Nights," *Journal of the Royal Asiatic Society*, 3rd. ser., 1, no. 1 (1991): 1–17, and Dalley, "The Tale of Bulūqiyā and the *Alexander Romance* in Jewish and Sufi Mystical Circles," in *Tracing the Threads:*

The story opens onto a variety of points, none of which make much of Salmān's Persian origins. They do, however, address the succession of religions and the nature of Islam and belonging to the Muslim community. In refusing Salmān's alms, Muḥammad demonstrated his integrity, in contrast to Salmān's first patron, the corrupt bishop. This point about Muḥammad's integrity and the precedent he set is picked up in other traditions that narrow in on the gift and employ the terms *hadiyya* and *ṣadaqa*.[10] The rightness of true religion was recognized before Islam, as was the inadequacy of other religions. It was Christians who predicted the coming of Islam, but not all Christians recognized true religion. Pious Christians showed the way to Islam, but on the eve of Islam's arrival, Salmān's last Christian mentor could think of no Christian worthy of Salmān's service; this would seem to suggest that Christianity had been replaced by Islam.[11]

Salmān's instinct for true religion raises the question for Ibn Hishām of whether he should be classified as a *ḥanīf*, that is, as a follower of the original and true monotheism. Ibn Hishām seems here to grapple with a question common to religions that make their entry into environments crowded with other religions: how does one classify people who, because of the accident of their birth, could not have known the most recent revelation but were familiar with previous ones? Ibn Hishām finishes his account of Salmān with a further report, in which Salmān relates to the Prophet his journey and mentions his search for "al-Ḥanīfiyya," identified by Salmān as "the religion of Abraham." Salmān recounts that he tracked down a holy man in Syria, who was healing the sick. When questioned, the man said: "You are inquiring about something that people do not ask about today. The time has drawn near when a prophet will be sent from the people of the *ḥaram* [i.e., Mecca] with this religion. Go to him, for he will bring you to it." Hearing this account, Muḥammad says to Salmān, "O Salmān, if you have told me the truth, then you have met Jesus, the son of Mary."[12]

Studies in the Vitality of Jewish Pseudepigrapha, ed. John C. Reeves, 239–69 (Atlanta: Scholars Press, 1994).

10 E.g., Aḥmad b. Ḥanbal, *Musnad*, ed. Samīr Ṭāhā al-Majdhūb et al., 8 vols. (Beirut: al-Maktab al-Islāmī, 1993), 5:546 (no. 23717).

11 As Hämeen-Anttila notes, the story of Salmān's conversion is placed among other stories about Jews and pagans who had some preknowledge of the coming of the Prophet. On the issue of the annunciation of Muḥammad, see Hämeen-Anttila, "Corruption of Christianity," esp. 117.

12 Ibn Hishām, *Sīra*, 1:222. On the matter of salvation, see Savant, "'Persians' in Early Islam," *Annales Islamologiques* 42 (2008): 80.

It is also significant that Salmān has left behind his family, religion, and home in Jayy, suggesting that one must make a long journey – real or figurative – before being admitted into the new, Muslim community (*umma*). Salmān's travels call to mind other quests for truth, knowledge, and wisdom, as well as aspects of the more legally weighted theme of hijra – that is, the break that Muḥammad made with his past in Mecca and his emigration from the town to the more hospitable Medina, as well as the migration of the early Muslims to garrison cities in the conquered lands. Hijra marked the founding of a new life for Muḥammad and these settlers, as did Salmān's journey for him, far from his homeland.[13] Such views of Salmān and his emigration also resonate with much wider ideas in the Qurʾan and early Islamic historiography according to which Islam requires a dedication that can render problematic former commitments and loyalties. Accordingly, Salmān's origins are left behind.

Ibn Hishām's biography, composed in Egypt, is an adaptation of the work of his great predecessor Ibn Isḥāq. Ibn Isḥāq worked within a tradition of historiography that had deep roots in Iraq, although he is often regarded as a representative of Medinese historiography.[14] Ibn Isḥāq's book circulated widely in different recensions and played a large role in the shaping of memory about Muḥammad and his early community, Salmān included. The stories quoted here turn up in the works of Iraqi traditionists who cite Ibn Isḥāq as well as other authorities and paint a common picture of a man who has left his past behind.[15] Ibn Saʿd (d. 230/845), for example, was a younger contemporary of Ibn Hishām who composed in Iraq a multivolume treatment of the generations of the Muslim community. The work includes the Prophet and Salmān, to whom Ibn Saʿd dedicated a lengthy biography, with the story of the

[13] For the early concept, see Christian Décobert, *Le mendiant et le combattant: L'institution de l'islam* (Paris: Seuil, 1991), esp. 259–65; Patricia Crone, "The First-Century Concept of *Hiǧra*," *Arabica* 41, no. 3 (1994): 352–87.

[14] Ibn Hishām used a recension of Ibn Isḥāq's text transmitted by Ziyād al-Bakkāʾī (d. 183/799), who lived mostly in Kufa. Ibn Hishām may also have traveled to Iraq. W. Montgomery Watt, "Ibn Hishām," in *EI*[2]; see also Johann Fück, *Muḥammad b. Isḥāq: Literarhistorische Untersuchungen* (Frankfurt 1925), 44; and Guillaume's introduction, Ibn Hishām, *The Life of Muhammad*, xxx.

[15] E.g., Ibn Ḥanbal, whose chain of transmission runs as follows: Abū Kāmil – Isrāʾīl – Abū Isḥāq [Sabīʿī, d. 127] – Abū Qurra al-Kindī – Salmān al-Fārisī; *Musnad*, 5:545 (no. 23707). He also cites a second, longer version through Ibn Isḥāq; *Musnad*, 5:548 (no. 23732). Regarding lines of transmission (including that of Ibn Isḥāq) of the story of Salmān's journey to Muḥammad, see Massignon, *Salmân Pâk et les prémices spirituelles de l'Islam iranien*, 13–16.

journey repeated toward the start and attributed to Ibn Isḥāq.[16] Ibn Saʿd also reports another widely transmitted story, which describes a controversy that took place after Salmān's arrival in Medina at the so-called Battle of the Ditch (*al-khandaq*), when the Muslims were besieged by the Meccans and dug a deep ditch to keep the Meccans out of Medina. Amid the digging, a dispute arose among Muḥammad's followers. It centered on Salmān and on whether he, as a Muslim from neither Mecca nor Medina, belonged more with the Meccan Muhājirūn or with the Medinan Anṣār. The Muhājirūn reportedly said, "Salmān is one of us" (*Salmān minnā*), and the Medinans likewise claimed him as one of their own. Ibn Saʿd explains that the issue was which group Salmān would aid in the digging since he was strong. Muḥammad settled the matter, declaring: "Salmān is one of us, [a member of] the *ahl al-bayt*."[17]

The term *ahl al-bayt* denotes the Prophet's own family, including especially ʿAlī, his cousin who married his daughter Fāṭima, and their descendants, who include the Imams of the Shiʿa. Throughout Arabic sources, traditionists cite the report, and among the Shiʿa today, it is widely known and taught to schoolchildren, though not always in the context of the Battle of the Ditch. For Ibn Saʿd, it signals that Muḥammad had accepted Salmān as a member of his own family, and likewise that Salmān had broken ties with his past and especially with his birth family. This acceptance explains why Ibn Saʿd places his biography of Salmān, featuring the latter's journey, within a section of his book dedicated to the Banū Hāshim, the Prophet's own clan. Within the organization of the work, this is a logical place for Salmān. Ibn Saʿd quotes in the same section other traditions that underscore the replacement of Salmān's original family with the family of Muḥammad. The Prophet makes his companion Abū Dardāʾ (or, in a variant version, Ḥudhayfa) Salmān's "brother" (*ākhā bayna Salmān al-Fārisī wa-Abī Dardāʾ*), thus replacing birth with spiritual kinship. We are told that Salmān imparted wisdom about religious practice to Abū Dardāʾ.[18] In a different report, ʿAlī is asked about Salmān and replies, "That is a man who is one of us and belongs to us, the *ahl al-bayt*." ʿAlī goes on to praise Salmān's knowledge, a prominent

[16] Ibn Saʿd, *al-Ṭabaqāt al-kabīr*, ed. Eduard Sachau et al., 9 vols. (Leiden: E. J. Brill, 1904–40), vol. 4, pt. 2, 53ff. Based on evidence internal to Ibn Saʿd's book, Christopher Melchert has persuasively argued that it was not completed until a decade or more after Ibn Saʿd's death; see Melchert, "How Ḥanafism Came to Originate in Kufa and Traditionalism in Medina," *Islamic Law and Society* 6, no. 3 (1999): 324–6.

[17] Ibn Saʿd, *al-Ṭabaqāt al-kabīr*, vol. 4, pt. 1, 59.

[18] Ibid., vol. 4, pt. 1, 60–1.

theme taken up in gnostic lines of thought that make reference to Qurʾan 13:43: "Those who do not believe say: 'You are not sent as a messenger.' Say: 'God is sufficient witness between me and you, [as are] those who possess knowledge of the Scripture (*wa-man ʿindahu ʿilm al-kitāb*).'" ʿAlī says: "Salmān read the 'first scripture' (*al-kitāb al-awwal*) and the 'last scripture' (*al-kitāb al-ākhir*)."[19]

These traditions evoke another theme, that of a convert accepting Islam and consequently becoming kin with a fellow Muslim and through him with his tribe and kinsmen. Up through at least the Umayyad period, manumitted slaves and converts (Salmān was both) seem to have entered Muslim society through a practice in Islamic law known as *walāʾ* that created a bond, and rights and obligations, between the new entrants and established Muslims. Freedmen and converts became *mawālī* (sing. *mawlā*), or clients, of an agent of conversion. In public law, converts (freeborn or freed) enjoyed the same rights and duties as other Muslims, but in private law, they were dependents.[20] According to the legal thinking that underpins this mechanism, the patron and his kinsmen replace the convert's prior blood ties and affiliations (practice was another matter, as I discuss below). In medieval biographical dictionaries, the idea is reflected in the tendency for a person's lineage to begin with the ancestor who was the first to convert to Islam, a tendency that represents a fundamental assumption in Bulliet's mapping of the conversion process.[21]

This discussion of Salmān in the early biographical tradition, though by no means complete, points to a perspective within the tradition that values cultural assimilation and advertises meritocracy according to its own ideals. Ibn Saʿd also appears to show, for example, that the early Muslims valued dedication to Islam over a noble birth when he recalls that after the conquests Salmān was given a pension of four thousand dirhams, whereas ʿAbd Allāh b. ʿUmar, the son of the second caliph, ʿUmar, received 3,500 dirhams. This prompted another companion to

[19] Ibid., vol. 4, pt. 1, 61.

[20] Patricia Crone, *Roman, Provincial and Islamic Law: The Origins of the Islamic Patronate* (Cambridge: Cambridge University Press, 1987), 35–6; regarding the historical demographics of the *mawālī* ulama, see John A. Nawas, "A Profile of the *Mawālī ʿUlamāʾ*," in *Patronate and Patronage in Early and Classical Islam*, ed. Monique Bernards and John Nawas, 454–80 (Leiden: Brill, 2005) (based on research conducted jointly with Monique Bernards). Nawas finds that after 240/854–5 compilers of biographical dictionaries "scarcely made mention of whether an *ʿālim* was a *mawlā* or Arab," which illustrates the demise of this social category during the course of the third Islamic century.

[21] Bulliet, *Conversion to Islam in the Medieval Period*, 18–19 and 64ff.

ask: "How is it that this Persian gets four thousand, and the son of the Commander of the Believers receives 3,500?" To which he received the reply: "Salmān accompanied the Messenger of God to battles that resulted in martyrs, whereas ʿUmar's son did not."[22]

The Ingredients for More Satisfying Memories

The accounts of Ibn Hishām and Ibn Saʿd emerged out of the tradition of prophetic biography, but I would argue that the early Hadith collections tend to share a similar perspective on Salmān and his background. For example, one of the earliest surviving collections, by ʿAbd al-Razzāq al-Ṣanʿānī (d. 211/827), contains the following account.[23] Salmān was present at a gathering with Saʿd b. Abī Waqqāṣ, a companion of the Prophet who played a major role in the conquest of Iran. Saʿd said to one of the men present: "Give me your genealogy." The man did so; Saʿd then made the same request to others, who also complied. Reaching Salmān, Saʿd received the answer: "God favored me by means of Islam, for I am Salmān b. al-Islām." Adding to this, ʿUmar, who heard about the gathering, said: "The Quraysh had known during the *jāhiliyya* [pre-Islamic times] [my father] al-Khaṭṭāb as the most powerful of them, but verily, I am ʿUmar b. al-Islām, the brother of Salmān in Islām."[24]

On the face of it, such works of Hadith already carried reports about Salmān that could be used to value his origins more positively, the best example being a report that is generally read today as showing the Prophet's affection for Salmān's people. In Salmān's presence, Muḥammad is remembered to have declared: "If faith (*īmān*) were hung from the Pleiades, then the people of Persia (*Fāris*; in variants *abnāʾ Fāris* or *al-Furs*) would obtain it." This tradition (hereafter called the Pleiades Hadith) might attest to Muḥammad's confidence in the

[22] Ibn Saʿd, *al-Ṭabaqāt al-kabīr*, vol. 4, pt. 1, 62 (the companion in question was Maymūn). But see also the report on p. 65 to the effect that Salmān did not marry Arab women.

[23] ʿAbd al-Razzāq was a Yemeni client with likely Persian origins. Pending further investigation, it seems reasonable to follow Harald Motzki's conclusion that the work genuinely originates with ʿAbd al-Razzāq. See Harald Motzki, "The *Muṣannaf* of ʿAbd al-Razzāq al-Ṣanʿānī as a Source of Authentic *Aḥādīth* of the First Century A.H.," *Journal of Near Eastern Studies* 50, no. 1 (1991): 1–21, and Motzki, "ʿAbd al-Razzāq al-Ṣanʿānī," in *EI*^{3}.

[24] The account contains two possible phrasings of Salmān's statement, the other being: "I do not know a father in Islam; rather, I am Salmān b. al-Islām." ʿAbd al-Razzāq al-Ṣanʿānī, *al-Muṣannaf*, ed. Ḥabīb al-Raḥmān al-Aʿẓamī, 11 vols. (Beirut: al-Maktab al-Islāmī, 1970–2), 11:438–9 (no. 20942).

Persians' faith (*īmān*) or, in variants of the Hadith, their religion (*dīn*), Islam, or knowledge (*ʿilm*). It may be the most frequently cited Prophetic tradition relating to Persians, and it is nearly always cited on the authority of Muḥammad's companion Abū Hurayra. Its diffusion reflects a general confidence that the tradition goes back to Muḥammad himself.[25]

There is no consensus regarding the occasion on which the Pleiades Hadith was stated, even if the perception that it was solidly rooted in the Prophetic past appears to have facilitated its pairing with different Qurʾanic verses. Exegesis worked in both directions: the Qurʾan explaining the Hadith and it, in turn, explaining the Qurʾan. Some reporters linked the Pleiades Hadith to Qurʾan 9:39 or 47:38, which speak about the replacement of the Qurʾan's immediate listeners with another people and offer a challenge to the Qurʾan's first audience.[26] Qurʾan 47:38 states: "If you turn away, He will replace you with another people, and they will not be like you." According to al-Tirmidhī (d. 279/892), Abū Hurayra was present when some other companions asked the Prophet about the verse and the people that it mentioned. Muḥammad, who was next to Salmān, struck Salmān on the thigh and said: "This one and his companions." Then, swearing by God, he added, "If faith were hung from the Pleiades, then men of Persia (*rijāl min Fāris*) would obtain it."[27]

As one often finds with Hadith, however, the report and its meaning were not as straightforward as some Iranians might have wished. Instead of Persians specifically, versions of the report identify the people who would reach the Pleiades simply as *al-aʿājim* or, more ambiguously, as "some of these men" (*rijāl min hāʾulāʾi*). For example, some reporters thought Muḥammad's comment was meant to explain the italicized portion of Qurʾan 62:2–3, which states: "[It is] He who has sent among the

25 E.g., al-Bukhārī, *Ṣaḥīḥ*, 3:352–3 (within the section of *al-Jāmiʿ al-ṣaḥīḥ* entitled "Kitāb Tafsīr al-Qurʾān," on Qurʾan 62:2–3), and the citations below. I have not systematically traced the first appearance of this Hadith, but it is noteworthy that it does not figure in the works of Ibn Hishām and Ibn Saʿd treated earlier in this chapter, nor in the *Muṣannaf* of ʿAbd al-Razzāq.

26 Qurʾan 9:39: "If you do not come out, He will punish you severely, and will substitute another people for you. You cannot do Him any harm. God has power over everything."

27 Al-Tirmidhī, *al-Jāmiʿ al-ṣaḥīḥ*, ed. Aḥmad Muḥammad Shākir, Muḥammad Fuʾād ʿAbd al-Bāqī, and Ibrāhīm ʿAṭwa ʿAwaḍ, 5 vols. (Cairo: Muṣṭafā al-Bābī al-Ḥalabī, 1937–56), 5:384 (within the "Kitāb Tafsīr al-Qurʾān," no. 3261, on Qurʾan 47:38). See also 5:413–14 (within the "Kitāb Tafsīr al-Qurʾān," no. 3310, on Qurʾan 62:3) and 5:725–6 (within the "Kitāb al-Manāqib," no. 3933, also on 62:3).

common people a messenger from among themselves, to recite His signs to them and to purify them and to teach them the Book and the Wisdom – previously they were in manifest error – and *others of them who have not yet joined them*. He is the Mighty and the Wise." Who are these "others"? Muslim b. al-Ḥajjāj (d. 261/875), the compiler of one of the collections of *ṣaḥīḥ* ("sound") Hadith that Sunni Muslims consider most authoritative, places the report within a chapter of his collection entitled "Kitāb Faḍāʾil al-ṣaḥāba," where he reports that someone once asked Muḥammad: "O Messenger of God, who are the *others* [*of them who have not yet joined them*]?" Muḥammad did not immediately reply, but when pressed, he put his hand on Salmān and stated, "men from these [people]." Did Muḥammad mean the Persians? Our scholar hardly leads us to believe the praise was as general as that since he precedes this report with another in which the Prophet states: "If faith (*īmān*) were hung from the Pleiades, then *a man* from Persia would obtain it."[28] Given the two reports' placement among Hadith about the Prophet's companions, the Prophet's affection might belong to Salmān and a handful of Persians alone.[29]

The Shiʿa formed a special affection for Salmān centuries before Shiʿism became a defining feature of Iranian identity.[30] In the early Imāmī Shiʿi texts from the fourth/tenth and fifth/eleventh centuries, Salmān is named as a narrator, as an interlocutor to Muḥammad and ʿAlī, and as among the companions loyal to the Prophet's family. But what was the significance of his inclusion to Iranian compilers and their audiences?[31] For example, the Imāmī traditionist Ibn Bābawayh (d. 381/991) cites the eighth Imam, ʿAlī al-Riḍā, when he recalls Muḥammad's statement, "Salmān is one of us" (*Salmān minnā*) amid other prophetic Hadith

28 Or a man "from the sons of Persia" (*abnāʾ Fāris*). Muslim b. al-Ḥajjāj, *Ṣaḥīḥ*, 2nd ed., ed. Muḥammad Fuʾād ʿAbd al-Bāqī, 5 vols. (Beirut: Dār al-Fikr, 1978), 4:1972–3 (nos. 230 and 231/2546). Emphasis added.

29 It was also possible to understand the Hadith and the term Fāris differently, as Ibn Qutayba does in his tract against the Shuʿūbiyya, where he argues that the Prophet meant Khurāsān by the term Fāris. In other words, Muḥammad did not have an idea of the Persian empire in mind. Ibn Qutayba, *Faḍl al-ʿArab wa-l-tanbīh ʿalā ʿulūmihā*, 104.

30 Scholars with no discernible connection to the Shiʿa also recognized his special connection to ʿAlī. For example, see a section dedicated to Salmān (no. 598) in Sulaymān b. Aḥmad al-Ṭabarānī's (d. 360/971) biographical dictionary devoted to Hadith transmitters, *al-Muʿjam al-kabīr*, 2nd ed., ed. Ḥamdī ʿAbd al-Majīd al-Salafī, 25 vols. ([Beirut: Maktabat al-Tawʿiyya al-Islāmiyya], 1404/1983–[1410/1990]), 6:212ff.

31 On lists as a narrative device, see esp. Albrecht Noth, with Lawrence I. Conrad, *The Early Arabic Historical Tradition: A Source-Critical Study*, 2nd ed., trans. Michael Bonner (Princeton, NJ: Darwin Press, 1994), 96–108.

transmitted by the Imam.[32] Or we have another time that Ibn Bābawayh refers to Salmān as an authority on the Qur'an.[33] Or take the cases throughout Imāmī writings in which Salmān is listed among 'Alī's other loyal followers, especially Abū Dharr al-Ghifārī, al-Miqdād b. al-Aswad al-Kindī, and 'Ammār b. Yāsir. What did the various names on a list mean in their individuality, and as pieces of a whole? And what did Salmān's Persian origins signify to the producers and readers of texts? In what sense did his Shi'i and Persian identities overlap, and in what sense were they distinct? Andrew J. Newman has persuasively shown the local, Qummī perspective of three prominent Shi'i traditionists of the second half of the third/ninth and first half of the fourth/tenth centuries. In large measure, his analysis rests on analysis of networks and of the way in which ideas supported by Qummī specialists of Hadith were privileged by other scholars with ties to Qum.[34] Within such networks, it seems reasonable to expect new readings of older ideas about Salmān and the generation of new ones. But how can we discern them, and in what sense are they precisely sectarian or Persian in character, rather than demonstrative of affection for the Prophet's family generally?

Making Tradition Work for Iṣfahān

I propose that memories about Salmān are indicative of a wider pattern, which is that before the mid-third/ninth century our sources do not often speak to Persians, but rather about them. Until this time, Iranian audiences were small and the Persian identity of producers of narrative typically weak. This situation begins to change in the second half of the third/ninth century, during the lifetime of Muslim and al-Bukhārī and toward the end of what Claude Gilliot has termed the "imperial period"

32 Al-Shaykh al-Ṣadūq b. Bābawayh al-Qummī, *'Uyūn akhbār al-Riḍā*, ed. Mahdī al-Ḥusayn al-Lājūrdī, 2 vols. in 1 (Najaf: al-Maṭba'a al-Ḥaydariyya, 1970), 2:64 (no. 282).

33 Ibn Bābawayh, *A Shī'ite Creed: A Translation of I'tiqādātu 'l-Imāmiyyah (The Beliefs of the Imāmiyyah) of Abū Ja'far, Muḥammad ibn 'Alī ibn al-Ḥusayn, Ibn Bābawayh al-Qummī, known as ash-Shaykh aṣ-Ṣadūq (306/919–381/991)*, rev. ed., trans. Asaf A. A. Fyzee (Tehran: World Organization for Islamic Services, 1982), 106.

34 The works that Newman most closely examines are *al-Maḥāsin* of al-Barqī (d. 274–80/887–94), the *Baṣā'ir al-darajāt* of al-Ṣaffār al-Qummī (d. 290/902–3) – both, as he notes, assembled in Qum in the late third/ninth century – and *al-Kāfī fī 'ilm al-dīn* of al-Kulaynī (d. 329/940–1), assembled in Baghdad in the early fourth/tenth century. Andrew J. Newman, *The Formative Period of Twelver Shī'ism: Ḥadīth as Discourse between Qum and Baghdad* (Richmond: Curzon, 2000).

(*moment impérial*).[35] Sensitivity to Persians and their aspirations and concerns grows more dramatically over the course of the fourth/tenth century and into the fifth/eleventh, as evidenced particularly in the publication of works dedicated to localities and their men of learning that recognize networks of elite Muslims in centers like Qum and Iṣfahān and reveal new sensitivities to ethnicity as well as locale and lineage.[36]

As is common with Arabic and Persian historiography, the old reporting was not simply discarded, but selectively retained and rewritten, in Salmān's case with authors of local histories reframing stories about him to give prominence to Iṣfahān and Salmān's early life, selecting and emphatically reiterating reports that stress his Persianness, and introducing information of obscure origins that favors Iṣfahān. Iṣfahān and its countrymen move to the center of the story in ways that appear to belong to a wider pattern common to local histories that recycle and invent traditions so as to perpetuate and enhance the memory of the Prophetic companions, soldiers, scholars, mystics, missionaries, and merchants who made their way eastward to Iran.

In the remainder of this chapter, I will dwell on these three ways that local histories could make use of their favorite sons – reframing of content, emphatic reiteration, and the discovery of new information – through a discussion of the case of Iṣfahān. First, a few words are in order about the city and its histories. In pre-Islamic times and after the Arab conquests, the province of Iṣfahān comprised several towns or villages, districts, and rural areas. These included the walled village of Jayy, which was the main city of the province and contained a mint (the name Jayy appearing on coins minted into ʿAbbasid times), and about two miles to the west, Yahūdiyya, whose name points to Jewish inhabitants. Iṣfahān, as a geographically distinct city of the province of the same name, seems to

35 Gilliot characterizes this period – which he does not define precisely, but which seems to occupy in his thinking the end of the third/ninth century (in the lifetime of Ibn Qutayba, whom he cites) – as one of "a codification in nearly all fields: grammar, poetry, literature, criteria for accepting the prophetic traditions, exegesis, jurisprudence, theology, etc." Gilliot, "Creation of a Fixed Text," in *The Cambridge Companion to the Qurʾān*, ed. Jane Dammen McAuliffe, 41–57 (Cambridge: Cambridge University Press, 2006), at 49. Sheila S. Blair has argued that "the same regularisation took place in the field of architecture and art." Blair, "Transcribing God's Word: Qurʾan Codices in Context," *Journal of Qurʾanic Studies* 10, no. 1 (2008): 79.

36 The situation of Shiʿi-Persian loyalties is more difficult to discern, as I discuss again in Chapter 3. Regarding the "silence" of Iranian Persians in the first centuries, cf. ʿAbd al-Ḥusayn Zarrīnkūb, *Dū qarn sukūt* (Tehran: Jāmiʿah-yi Līsānsīyahā-yi Dānishsarā-yi ʿĀlī, 1330 *shamsī*/[1951]); but also, his second edition (Tehran: Amīr Kabīr, 1336 *shamsī*/[1957]).

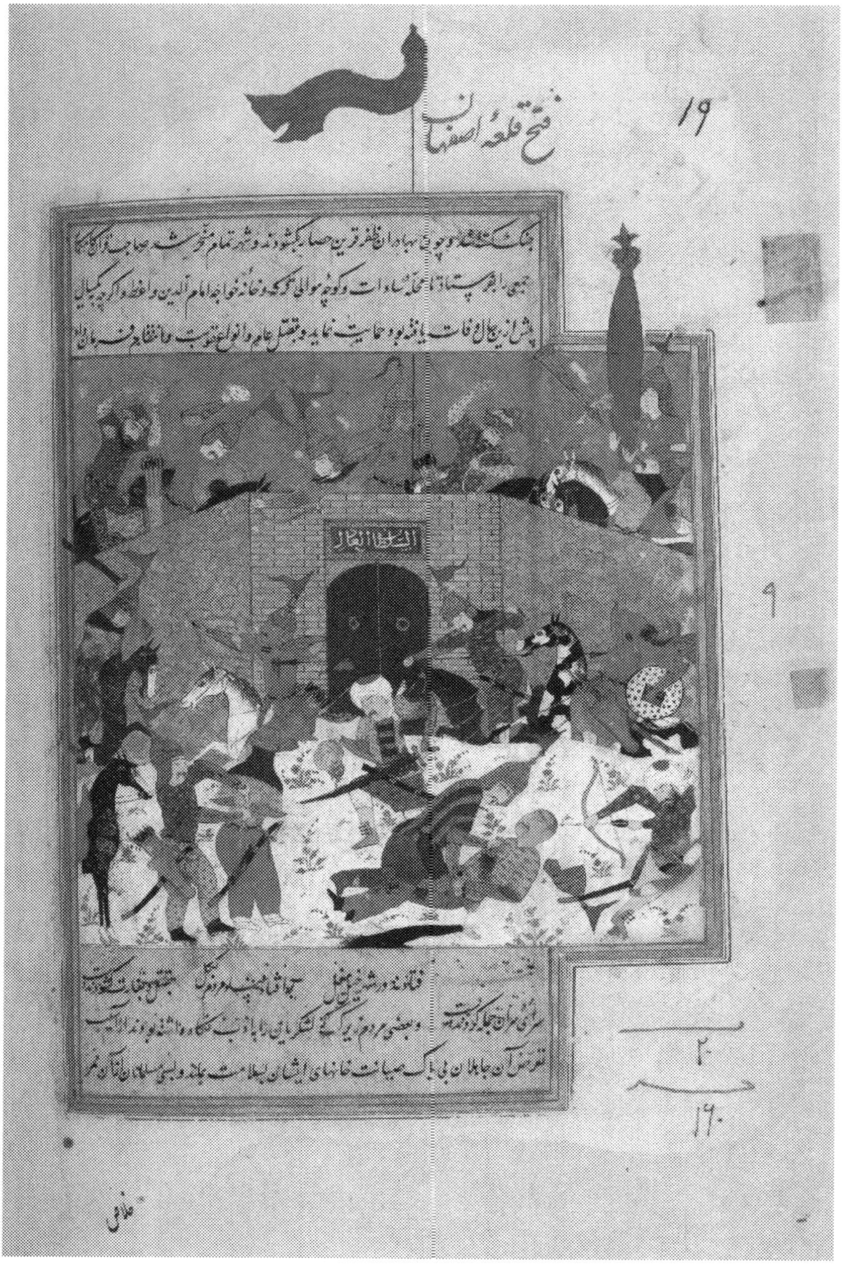

FIGURE 2.1. The capture of Iṣfahān. From a manuscript of the *Ẓafar-nāmah*, 1533. © The British Library Board.

postdate the ʿAbbasid Revolution, when it developed around Yahūdiyya and Jayy.[37] In terms of geography, history, and culture, the distance separating pre-Islamic Medina and Jayy must have been enormous – one a western Arabian desert oasis, the other a Sasanian town about a thousand miles to the east as the crow flies across desert, mountain, and valley, but much further via Syria, as Salmān was said to have traveled. But the two localities may not in fact have seemed remote, given the Christian and Jewish populations of both cities and the presumed networks of monotheists settled in Iran, Iraq, Syria, and the Ḥijāz. This is what the account of the journey would, in fact, presuppose.[38]

I rely on texts by Abū al-Shaykh al-Iṣfahānī (d. 369/979)[39] and Abū Nuʿaym al-Iṣfahānī (d. 430/1038),[40] each of whom treats Iṣfahān and the lives of its scholars and a few other men of notoriety. They wrote their biographical compilations in Iṣfahān during the period when the city was ruled in theory by the ʿAbbasids, but in practice by Buyid (r. 323–421/934 or 935–1029) and other rulers, and prior to the Seljuk conquests when that dynasty downgraded the ʿAbbasids' authority still further.[41] At that time, Iṣfahānīs were beginning to view their home as a

37 Regarding the coins, see Stephen Album, *Checklist of Islamic Coins*, 3rd ed. (Santa Rosa, CA: Stephen Album Rare Coins, 2011), 50. On Iṣfahān, its centers, and its population, see Le Strange, *Lands of the Eastern Caliphate*, 202–7; Touraj Daryaee, *Šahrestānīhā ī Ērānšahr*, 20 (no. 53) and commentary on p. 55; Hossein Kamaly, "Isfahan vi. Medieval Period," in *EIr*; A. K. S. Lambton and J. Sourdel-Thomine, "Isfahan," in *Historic Cities of the Islamic World*, ed. C. Edmund Bosworth, 167–80 (Leiden: Brill, 2007). For Eastern Syriac Christians, Jayy/Iṣfahān seems to have been a diocese through at least the early twelfth century; see "Ispahan," in Jean Maurice Fiey, *Pour un Oriens Christianus Novus: Répertoire des diocèses syriaques orientaux et occidentaux* (Beirut and Stuttgart: Franz Steiner, 1993), 96–7. Jayy is located at 32°37′50.32″N latitude and 51°42′46.12″E longitude. Hugh Kennedy, personal communication based on Google Earth, Oct. 2011.

38 Even closer ties between the Ḥijāz and Iran, involving Sasanian representatives at Medina in the sixth century CE, may also have existed; for this argument (based, however, on later Muslim sources), see Michael Lecker, "The Levying of Taxes for the Sassanians in Pre-Islamic Medina," *Jerusalem Studies in Arabic and Islam* 27 (2002): 109–26. See also M. J. Kister, "Al-Ḥīra: Some Notes on Its Relations with Arabia," *Arabica* 15, no. 2 (1968): 143–69.

39 *Ṭabaqāt al-muḥaddithīn bi-Iṣfahān wa-l-wāridīn ʿalayhā*, ed. ʿAbd al-Ghafūr ʿAbd al-Ḥaqq Ḥusayn al-Balūshī, 4 vols. (Beirut: Muʾassasat al-Risāla, 1987–92). All subsequent references to this work are to this edition, except where specified.

40 *Dhikr akhbār Iṣbahān*; on him, see Jacqueline Chabbi, "Abū Nuʿaym al-Iṣfahānī," in *EI*^{3}.

41 The name Iṣfahān appears consistently on Buyid coinage from 323/934–5 until the year 421/1029; see Treadwell, *Buyid Coinage*. After that time, control of Iṣfahān was contested by different factions, including Ghaznavid armies from Afghanistan. Clifford

second city to Baghdad and tended to face culturally westward.[42] Both books, and especially Abū Nuʿaym's, have been extensively mined in studies of Iṣfahān and the period, including by Bulliet when he formulated his periodization of Iran's conversion.[43] Nurit Tsafrir has also used these works to argue that the Ḥanafī school of law had a foothold in Iṣfahān already a decade after the death of Abū Ḥanīfa (d. 150/767), that by the beginning of the third/ninth century a "significant" Ḥanafī community had developed in Iṣfahān, and that it survived into the fourth/tenth century.[44] There were other histories of Iṣfahān that have not survived, as well as a work by a third author, al-Māfarrūkhī (written most likely in the period 464–84/1072–92), who composed what Jürgen Paul has termed "Adab-oriented local historiography" in his *Kitāb Maḥāsin Iṣfahān*. This last work, though consulted, plays a minor role in what follows because of its author's different historical circumstances and interests.[45]

Reframing Content

Abū al-Shaykh's book was probably written in the 350s/960s and likely represents the oldest surviving biographical dictionary written for an Iranian territory.[46] It consists of an edifying historical introduction that

Edmund Bosworth, *The New Islamic Dynasties: A Chronological and Genealogical Manual*, rev. ed. (New York: Columbia University Press, 1996), 154–7, 160–1, 185–8, and Kamaly, "Isfahan vi. Medieval Period," in *EIr*.

42 On which, see esp. David Durand-Guédy, *Iranian Elites and Turkish Rulers: A History of Iṣfahān in the Saljūq Period* (London: Routledge, 2010), ch. 1, "Identity."

43 Bulliet, using Abū Nuʿaym's text, *Conversion to Islam in the Medieval Period*, 16–32 and 142.

44 Nurit Tsafrir, "The Beginnings of the Ḥanafī School in Iṣfahān," *Islamic Law and Society* 5, no. 1 (1998): 1–21 and Tsafrir, *The History of an Islamic School of Law: The Early Spread of Hanafism* (Cambridge, MA: Islamic Legal Studies Program and Harvard University Press, 2004), 63–72. Among her evidence, Tsafrir cites the appointment of Ḥanafī *qāḍī*s and the transmission of Ḥanafī Hadith. She circumscribes her argument by acknowledging a rivalry between Ḥanafīs and Shāfiʿīs (the latter making inroads from the second half of the third/ninth century) and by showing that with only two exceptions, until the beginning of the fourth/tenth century none of Iṣfahān's Ḥanafī *qāḍī*s is known to have been Iṣfahānī in origin. See also the review of Tsafrir's book by Christopher Melchert in *Journal of Near Eastern Studies* 67, no. 3 (2008): 228–30.

45 Paul, "Isfahan v. Local Historiography," in *EIr*; also, his "The Histories of Isfahan: Mafarrukhi's *Kitāb maḥāsin Iṣfahān*," *Iranian Studies* 33, no. 1/2 (2000): 117–32, and Bulliet, "al-Māfarrūkhī," in *EI*^{2}. For other works on Iṣfahān, see Paul's two articles as well as Sven Dedering's analysis in Abū Nuʿaym al-Iṣfahānī, *Dhikr akhbār Iṣbahān*, 2:viii–x.

46 Paul, "The Histories of Herat," *Iranian Studies* 33, no. 1/2 (2000): 94, and Paul, "Isfahan v. Local historiography," in *EIr*.

features Iṣfahān's role in prophetic history as a supporter of Abraham and an opponent of Nimrod and as a stopping place on the itinerary of the Qurʾanic figure Dhū al-Qarnayn, the roles of Alexander the Great and Khusraw Anūshirvān in building the city of Iṣfahān and in determining its dimensions, the extent of its territory, the natural wonders and famous products of Iṣfahān, and the companions of Muḥammad involved in its conquest during the reign of ʿUmar.[47] The introduction is then followed by eleven generations (*ṭabaqāt*) of biographical entries featuring mainly Hadith transmitters and running to as late as 353/964. Salmān figures in the first generation – after short entries for the Prophet's grandson al-Ḥasan and the counter-caliph ʿAbd Allāh b. al-Zubayr, who passed through Iṣfahān en route to fight infidels in Jurjān.[48]

Salmān is the only Prophetic companion with origins in Iṣfahān, and he is honored by a longer biography than those of his peers, with accounts of his journey and conversion filling more than half of it.[49] The entry begins with statements including the Prophetic Hadith, "Salmān is one of us, [a member of] the *ahl al-bayt*" and "Salmān is the tenth of ten in Paradise," as well as a statement by ʿAlī in praise of Salmān's knowledge. Iṣfahān can be proud of him, Abū al-Shaykh states, because "among the ways in which God beautified Iṣfahān and its people was that he made Salmān al-Fārisī be from it."[50] In Chapter 1, I showed the authority that figures such as Ibn al-Kalbī garnered outside of Iraq when Iranians imagined their earliest history. Ibn Isḥāq commands here a similar respect as an authority on Salmān, as Abū al-Shaykh inserts a version of his report on Salmān's journey, containing some precise wording but also editorial changes that suggest a written text orally transmitted along the lines described by Gregor Schoeler.[51] These liven up the story and stress for audiences Salmān's foreknowledge of the coming tide of Islam. Now Salmān's father sends someone out looking for him, and Salmān answers his father: "I passed by some people who are called Christians. Their speech and supplications filled me with wonder, so I sat, watching them to see what they were doing." Salmān's father protests: "Your religion and the religion of your fathers is better than their religion." Salmān replies

[47] A treaty is subsequently quoted in the entry for ʿAbd Allāh b. ʿAbd Allāh b. ʿAtbān al-Anṣārī; Abū al-Shaykh, *Ṭabaqāt al-muḥaddithīn*, 1:291–2.

[48] Ibid., 1:191–202.

[49] Ibid., 1:203–36.

[50] Ibid., 1:203.

[51] Schoeler, *Genesis of Literature in Islam*. Abū al-Shaykh cites here a recension of Ibn Isḥāq's text from the Kufan Yūnus b. Bukayr (d. 199); on the latter, see Fück, *Muḥammad b. Isḥāq*, 44.

firmly: "By God, no, it is not better than their religion. They are a people worshipping God, supplicating him, and praying to him, whereas we only worship a fire that we light with our hands. If we leave it, it dies."[52]

When he finishes Ibn Isḥāq's account, Abū al-Shaykh moves on to two other, shorter reports that again take the reader/listener back to Salmān's first encounter with monotheism. The first features a holy man, as in Ibn Hishām's text discussed above.[53] Salmān says that he was born and grew up in Rāmhurmuz, but that his father was from Iṣfahān. His mother, a woman of means, had her son educated as a scribe, a profession at which he excelled. But one day, while passing by a mountain cave, he came across a holy man, who informed him of Jesus, a Messenger of God (*rasūl Allāh*). The man also mentioned "Aḥmad" (a variant of the name Muḥammad) as a "Messenger," who would come in the future bearing tidings of the afterlife. Salmān strayed from the path cut out for him by his mother by becoming a student of the holy man, and he learned to pronounce a forerunner to the Muslim profession of faith: "There is no God but God alone, who has no partner (*lā sharīk lahu*). Jesus, the son of Mary, is the Messenger of God and Muḥammad, God bless him and keep him, after him is the Messenger of God." Also: "Faith (*īmān*) [includes the belief in] resurrection after death." The man also gave Salmān lessons in prayer, as well as instructions that when Muḥammad appeared, Salmān should remember his teacher to Muḥammad; for according to what the teacher had heard about Jesus' sayings, he would still get the benefit of the encounter, whether he saw Muḥammad in person or not.[54] In the second report, Salmān says, "I was a man from the people of Jayy. We were worshipping speckled horses, but I knew that they did not mean anything. So I was searching for the [true] religion." The report then carries on with Salmān's arrival in Medina and his gift to the Prophet.[55]

Rather than appearing as a place abandoned, Iṣfahān, or perhaps Rāmhurmuz, takes center stage in Abū al-Shaykh's biography as the place where Salmān first learned about Jesus and Muḥammad. Abū al-Shaykh goes on to undermine Rāmhurmuz, an inconvenient possibility that does

52 Abū al-Shaykh, *Ṭabaqāt al-muḥaddithīn*, 1:211.

53 The *isnād* would suggest that Abū al-Shaykh is not relying upon Ibn Hishām (or Ibn Isḥāq at all), but rather on another telling of Salmān's story: al-Qāsim b. Fūrak from ʿAbd Allāh b. Abī Ziyād from Sayyār b. Ḥātim al-ʿAnazī from Mūsā b. Saʿīd al-Rāsibī from Abū Muʿādh from Abū Salama b. ʿAbd al-Raḥmān from Salmān; Abū al-Shaykh, *Ṭabaqāt al-muḥaddithīn*, 1:218 (and n. 1). See also Massignon, *Salmân Pâk et les prémices spirituelles de l'Islam iranien*, 13.

54 Abū al-Shaykh, *Ṭabaqāt al-muḥaddithīn*, 1:218–20.

55 Ibid., 1:222–3. See also the conclusion to the biography, which returns to Salmān's foreknowledge, 1:234–6.

not fit his Iṣfahān-focused narrative, as he returns Salmān to Iṣfahān after the Prophet's death. A witness, Abū al-Ḥajjāj al-Azdī, reports that he met Salmān in Iṣfahān, in his village, and asked him about the theological theory of *qadar* ("the divine decree," i.e., fate, destiny), which Salmān explained to him.[56] Abū al-Shaykh argues: "In this report there is evidence that Salmān came to Iṣfahān during the reign of ʿUmar b. al-Khaṭṭāb."[57]

Accounts of journeys can memorialize, through passage in space, the elimination of one past and its replacement with another, as occurred in the biographical tradition, considered above. But there is a double aspect to most journeys far from home – the pilgrimage to Mecca being a key example – where travelers not only merge with groups of fellow travelers, sharing a sense of communion, but also, through juxtaposition with them, come to appreciate the differences that distinguish them from one another. From an Iranian perspective, the early biographical tradition presented an imperfect memory, reflecting only the first aspect. Abū al-Shaykh has filled out the memory and so offered Iṣfahān's readers an image of their own double membership in an imagined Muslim community and in an imagined community centered in Iṣfahān.

Emphatic Reiteration

About a generation after Abū al-Shaykh, Abū Nuʿaym al-Iṣfahānī composed a biographical dictionary focused on Iṣfahān's religious scholars. The work consists of a historical introduction followed by biographical treatments of the Prophet's companions, and then alphabetically arranged entries for scholars with ties to Iṣfahān. Abū Nuʿaym relies heavily upon Abū al-Shaykh (to whom he refers as Abū Muḥammad b. Ḥayyān, as he claims to have heard reports directly from him), but as Jürgen Paul has noted, Abū Nuʿaym places a "perceptible stress on the good qualities of the Persians and their merits in contributing to the spread of Islam and the maintenance of its purity."[58]

This emphasis on Iṣfahān and Persians comes through in the first pages of Abū Nuʿaym's book and subsequently in his biography of Salmān.[59] He starts off by defining his book as treating the illustrious

56 Ibid., 1:228–9.

57 The reason behind this conclusion is obscure but it presumably relates to the lifespan of Abū al-Ḥajjāj al-Azdī.

58 Paul, "Isfahan v. Local Historiography," in *EIr*.

59 It is also visible in a biography for an unnamed Persian slave girl (*ama*) in Medina who was from Iṣfahān and had already converted to Islam when Salmān arrived. Abū Nuʿaym al-Iṣfahānī, *Dhikr akhbār Iṣbahān*, 1:76–7.

forebears, especially scholars, from "the people of our land, the land of Iṣfahān" (*min ahl baladinā balad Iṣfahān*). He says that he will cite Hadith reports that were transmitted regarding the excellence of the Persians, non-Arabs (*al-ʿAjam*), and *mawālī*, and goes on to cite versions of the Pleiades Hadith over the following nine pages on the authority of Abū Hurayra and, more unusually, a small number of other companions, including ʿĀʾisha and ʿAlī, who also remembered versions of the Prophet's statement.[60] As the Prophet's affection rises to higher levels on Abū Nuʿaym's pages, the term "Pleiades" becomes firmly linked to Persians, who pursued the various goals hypothetically hanging from the Pleaides: religion (*dīn*), faith (*īmān*), Islam, and knowledge (*ʿilm*). They are each singly possible goals, and collectively add up to a glowing account of the Persians. The variations create space for commentary, within which Abū Nuʿaym introduces different ideas. For example, he cites Qurʾan 62:2–3 and its reference to "others of them who have not yet joined them," as well as the statement of Qurʾan 47:38, "If you turn away, He will replace you with another people, and they will not be like you." Like Muslim, cited above, he features reports that refer to Salmān's people ambiguously as "some of these men" (*rijāl min hāʾulāʾi*, in explanation of Qurʾan 62:2–3), though now these are promptly followed by clarification: a further report has Muḥammad explain Qurʾan 47:38 by striking Salmān on the thigh and saying: "This one and his people. If religion were hung from the Pleiades, then men of Persia (*rijāl min Fāris*) would seek it."[61]

With the Persians firmly identified in the reiterations, Abū Nuʿaym takes up the theme of their displacement of the Arabs, as in the following report that he features: "The Messenger of God said: 'O you *mawālī*, hold fast to memory [of God]. Verily, the Arabs have abandoned [it]. If faith were hung from the Throne, there is someone from among you who would search for it.'"[62] In another instance, Abū Nuʿaym repeats a tradition in which the Prophet mentioned to Abū Bakr that he had a dream in which some black sheep came to him. Next some white sheep came, and then there was not a black sheep in sight. Abū Bakr offered an interpretation: "O Messenger of God! These Arabs are submitting to Islam and becoming numerous [like the black sheep]. Subsequently, the ʿAjam will convert to Islam until the Arabs cannot be perceived among them." Having heard

60 For ʿĀʾisha and ʿAlī, see ibid., 1:8.
61 Ibid., 1:2–3.
62 Ibid., 1:6.

Abū Bakr's analysis, Muḥammad verified the prediction and the passing of royal power (*mulk*) to the ʿAjam.[63]

In his reiterations of the Pleiades Hadith, Abū Nuʿaym makes more of Salmān's Persianness. He also cares more for Salmān's lineage prior to his conversion, as – unlike Ibn Hishām, Ibn Saʿd, or Abū al-Shaykh – he provides Salmān's full name prior to conversion as either Māhwayh or Mābih b. Budakhshān b. Āzarjushnas, "from among the descendants of King Manūshihr," or as a further alternative, Bahbūd b. Khushān.[64] In his *Maʿrifat al-ṣaḥāba*, Abū Nuʿaym displays a similarly complex sense of Salmān's identity as an Iṣfahānī, a Persian, and a man with roots sunk in Iran's pre-Islamic past, implicitly arguing that Salmān's ancestry is worth remembering. He begins with his *kunya* (agnomen):

> Abū ʿAbd Allāh. He traced his genealogy to Islam (*intasaba ilā al-Islām*), and so he said "Salmān b. al-Islām." He was one of the first of the people of Persia and Iṣfahān to convert to Islam (*sābiq ahl Fāris wa-Iṣfahān ilā al-Islām*). And it is said his name before Islam was Mābih b. Būdakhshān b. Mūrsilān b. Bahbūdhān b. Fayrūz b. Shahrak, from the descendants of Āb al-Malik. He was a Zoroastrian (*majūsī*), attendant of the fire (*qāṭin al-nār*). He converted to Islam at the arrival of the Messenger of God in Medina. And it is said he converted in Mecca before the hijra.[65]

The detail regarding Mecca is unusual in reporting on Salmān and would likely give Salmān further credit as an early believer in and interlocutor of Muḥammad.

What can we make of the fact that Persians, as such, seem to command the interest and loyalty of Abū Nuʿaym in a way that they do not for Abū al-Shaykh, who makes no mention of the Pleiades Hadith in his book? Written half a century after its predecessor, Abū Nuʿaym's text generally seems to reflect a different stage in the development of Iṣfahān and its scholars, when Persian Muslims were more confident in themselves and conscious of their shared history. The comparative maturity and integration of this community is also reflected in Abū Nuʿaym's choice of format, an integrated, alphabetically arranged work, which subordinates chronology and allowed readers in his day to "look someone up."[66]

63 Ibid., 1:10.
64 Ibid., 1:48.
65 Abū Nuʿaym al-Iṣfahānī, *Maʿrifat al-ṣaḥāba*, ed. ʿĀdil b. Yūsuf al-ʿAzzāzī, 7 vols. (Riyadh: Dār al-Waṭan li-l-Nashr, 1998), 3:1327.
66 On the difference between works arranged by *ṭabaqāt* versus biographical dictionaries, see Robinson, *Islamic Historiography*, 66–74.

Discovering New Information

So far, we have seen how, by reframing content and by emphatic reiteration, Abū al-Shaykh and Abū Nuʿaym raised the profile of aspects of Salmān's identity – his Iṣfahānī origins and Persian ethnicity. Each traditionist changed the forms and meaning of the historiographical tradition, but not its substance. In a third case, which concerns Salmān's lineage, we have an apparent attempt to add to the store of memory. Two intriguing but little studied legal "documents" seem to have entered the Arabic historiographical tradition in Iṣfahān and to bear signs of their generation in Iran, the circulation of traditions between Iranian cities, and the establishment of networks of Salmān's descendants.[67] They are a document of clientship (*walāʾ*) and a testament (*waṣiyya*). I will summarize their contents based on our earliest source, Abū al-Shaykh.

Shortly after Abū al-Shaykh reports on Salmān's journey and conversion, he returns to the moment in the story in which Muḥammad purchased Salmān's freedom. Abū al-Shaykh includes a report claiming that Muḥammad dictated a "writing" (*kitāb*) to ʿAlī b. Abī Ṭālib on the second day of the month of Jumādā al-Ūlā[68] and that it was witnessed by Muḥammad's companions, listed as Abū Bakr al-Ṣiddīq, ʿUmar b. al-Khaṭṭāb, ʿAlī b. Abī Ṭālib,[69] Ḥudhayfa b. [Saʿd] al-Yamān, Abū Dharr al-Ghifārī, al-Miqdād b. al-Aswad, Bilāl "the *mawlā* of Abū Bakr," and ʿAbd al-Raḥmān b. ʿAwf. Abū al-Shaykh identifies generations of transmitters running back to Salmān: ʿAbd Allāh b. Muḥammad b. al-Ḥajjāj, ʿAbd al-Raḥmān b. Aḥmad b. ʿAbbād ʿAbdūs, and Qaṭn b. Ibrāhīm al-Nīsābūrī, the last of whom obtained the document from Salmān's descendants, named as Wahb; Wahb's mother and his father, Kathīr; Kathīr's father, ʿAbd al-Raḥmān; and ʿAbd al-Raḥmān's grandfather, Salmān himself.

The document buys Salmān's freedom from his owner and establishes a new legal relationship:

Muḥammad b. ʿAbd Allāh, the Messenger of God, redeems Salmān al-Fārisī by this ransom from ʿUthmān b. al-Ashhal al-Yahūdī ["the Jew"] and the man

[67] For lack of an alternative, I employ the term "documents," while recognizing that it is problematic for the authority it carries, whereas we are discussing a very likely case of pseudepigraphy, or the forgery of texts and their ascription to early authorities.

[68] "Kataba ʿAlī b. Abī Ṭālib yawm al-ithnayn fī jumādā al-ūlā muhājar Muḥammad." The Arabic is clarified by subsequent reporters as indicating that the agreement was dictated in the first year of the hijra; see al-Khaṭīb al-Baghdādī, *Taʾrīkh Baghdād*, 1:170. On *muhājar*, see Crone, "First-Century Concept of *Hiǧra*," 356, 362.

[69] It is unusual that ʿAlī is listed as both scribe and witness.

from Qurayẓa,[70] by planting three hundred date palms and [paying] forty ounces (*ūqiyya*) of gold.[71] Therefore Muḥammad b. ʿAbd Allāh, the Messenger of God, has absolved the cost of Salmān al-Fārisī. Muḥammad b. ʿAbd Allāh, the Messenger of God, and the *ahl al-bayt* are his patrons[72] and no one [else] has any claim on Salmān.[73]

Abū al-Shaykh follows this report with another line through which it was transmitted, and then a further report to the effect that Salmān had three daughters: one in Iṣfahān – "and a group claims to be her descendants" – and two in Egypt.[74]

The second document, a testament, follows shortly afterward in Abū al-Shaykh's text. Here the claim seems to be that Salmān had sought to safeguard the interests of his brother and his brother's offspring and that sometime in the past a man in Shīrāz named Ghassān had come forward stating that he was the great-great grandson of the brother, whose name was Māhādharfarrūkh.[75] This Ghassān, the leader of the brother's descendants in Shīrāz, claimed that a document on bleached leather in his possession bore the handwriting of ʿAlī and the seals of Muḥammad, Abū Bakr, and ʿAlī.[76] While Abū al-Shaykh states his source for the information about Ghassān and the document as "someone concerned with this affair," Abū Nuʿaym supplies a chain of authorities leading back to Ghassān.[77]

The text of the testament establishes privileges for the offspring. It begins with the *basmala* ("In the name of God, the Almighty, the Merciful"); the statement that "this is a writing (*kitāb*) from Muḥammad, the

70 Recall the story, narrated above by Ibn Hishām; see also Abū al-Shaykh, *Ṭabaqāt al-muḥaddithīn*, 1:213. It is not clear, in legal terms, why the document names ʿUthmān b. al-Ashhal al-Yahūdī since the man from Qurayẓa was Salmān's last owner according to the various versions of the story.

71 For possible conversions (they vary regionally), see Hinz, *Islamische Masse und Gewichte*, 34–5.

72 *Walāʾuhu li-Muḥammad b. ʿAbd Allāh rasūl Allāh wa-ahl baytihi.*

73 Abū al-Shaykh, *Ṭabaqāt al-muḥaddithīn*, 1:224–6. Also, Abū Nuʿaym al-Iṣfahānī, *Dhikr akhbār Iṣbahān*, 1:52.

74 He cites ʿAbd Allāh [b. Muḥammad b. al-Ḥajjāj], mentioned above, as well an Abū Bakr b. Abī Dāwūd. Regarding the daughters, see Massignon, *Salmân Pâk et les prémices spirituelles de l'Islam iranien*, 10, n. 5.

75 Abū Nuʿaym: Mābandādhfarrūkh; *Dhikr akhbār Iṣbahān*, 1:52.

76 Abū al-Shaykh, *Ṭabaqāt al-muḥaddithīn*, 1:230–4.

77 According to Abū Nuʿaym: al-Ḥasan b. Ibrāhīm b. Isḥāq al-Burjī al-Mustamlī from Muḥammad b. Aḥmad b. ʿAbd al-Raḥmān from Abū ʿAlī al-Ḥusayn b. Muḥammad b. ʿAmr al-Waththābī. Al-Waththābī says that he saw the record (*sijill*) – which he specifies as the Prophet's agreement (*ʿahd*) granted to Salmān al-Fārisī – in Shīrāz in the hand of one of Ghassān's grandchildren. Abū Nuʿaym, *Dhikr akhbār Iṣbahān*, 1:52–3.

Messenger of God;" and clarification that Salmān had asked Muḥammad for a testament (*waṣiyya*) for his brother, Māhādharfarrūkh, the people of his house (*ahl baytihi*), and his subsequent progeny – those who had converted to Islam and maintained their religion (*man aslama minhum wa-aqāma ʿalā dīnihi*).[78] "Muḥammad then continues with a doxology of five lines, praising the unicity of God, His creation of the world, His singular role in it, the finitude of life, and the heavenly rewards. Muḥammad emphasizes that "there is no compulsion in religion" (Qurʾan 2:256): "he who stays in his own religion, we leave him." The testament states:

This is a writing (*kitāb*) for the people of the house of Salmān (*ahl bayt Salmān*). They have God's protection (*dhimmat Allāh*) and my protection of their blood and property where they reside: their plains, mountains, pastures, and springs will not be treated unjustly nor will they have difficulty imposed on them. For to whomever, believing men or women, this writing of mine is read, it is obligatory that he maintain, honor, and treat them [Salmān's family] with reverence, and that he not oppose them with harm or anything reprehensible. I have removed from them [the obligation] to shear the forelocks, the *jizya*, the *ḥashr*, the *ʿushr*, and the rest of the burdens and payments [imposed on non-Muslims]. In addition, if they ask of you [something], give it to them. If they seek aid from you, aid them. If they seek protection from you, protect them. If they misbehave, forgive them, but if misdeeds are committed against them, defend them. Each year, in the month of Rajab, they should receive from the public treasury (*bayt māl al-Muslimīn*) two hundred garments[79] and one hundred slaughtered animals. Verily, Salmān deserves that from us because God, blessed and exalted, has given Salmān precedence over a great many of the believers. He [God] revealed to me:[80] "Paradise longs for Salmān more than Salmān longs for Paradise." He is a man in whom I put my trust and faith, pious, pure, and a sincere advisor to the Messenger of God (Peace be upon him!) and the believers. Salmān is one of us, [a member of] the *ahl al-bayt*. Let no one oppose this testament (*waṣiyya*) regarding what I have ordered regarding the maintenance and reverence for the people of Salmān's house and their descendants, including he who converted to

[78] Abū al-Shaykh, *Ṭabaqāt al-muḥaddithīn*, 1:231; also in a different edition of Abū al-Shaykh's text, edited by ʿAbd al-Ghaffār Sulaymān al-Bindārī and Sayyid Kasrawī Ḥasan, 2 vols. (Beirut: Dār al-Kutub al-ʿIlmiyya, 1989), 1:59. Versus Abū Nuʿaym: Mābandādhfarrūkh and *man aslama minhum aw aqāma ʿalā dīnihi*. *Dhikr akhbār Iṣbahān*, 1:52.

[79] Arabic, *ḥilla*; see Abū al-Shaykh, *Ṭabaqāt al-muḥaddithīn*, 1:232, n. 7. Abū Nuʿaym's version stipulates two hundred garments in the month of Rajab and a hundred garments in the month of Dhū al-Ḥijja. *Dhikr akhbār Iṣbahān*, 1:53.

[80] Abū al-Shaykh: *Anzala ʿalayya fī al-waḥī anna*. On the phenomenon of extra-Qurʾanic revelation, see William A. Graham, *Divine Word and Prophetic Word in Early Islam: A Reconsideration of the Sources, with Special Reference to the Divine Saying or Ḥadîth Qudsî* (The Hague: Mouton, 1977).

Islam or maintained his religion (*man aslama minhum aw aqāma ʿalā dīnihi*).[81] Whosoever opposes this testimony has opposed God and his Messenger, and will continue to be cursed all the way up to the Day of Reckoning. Whosoever honors them has honored me, and will be rewarded by God. And whosoever harms them has harmed me, and I will be his adversary on the Day of Resurrection: the Fires of Gehenna will repay him, and I will remove my protection (*dhimmatī*) from him.

Peace,

[Muḥammad, the Messenger of God]

The text states that it had been written at the command of the Prophet in the month of Rajab in the ninth year of the hijra (i.e., 630 CE) in the presence of Abū Bakr, ʿUmar, ʿUthmān, Ṭalḥa [b. ʿUbayd Allāh], al-Zubayr [b. al-ʿAwwām], ʿAbd al-Raḥmān, Saʿd [b. Abī Waqqāṣ], Saʿīd [b. Zayd?], Salmān, Abū Dharr, ʿAmmār, Suhayb [al-Rūmī], Bilāl, al-Miqdād, "and a group of other believers."[82]

Such documents are hardly a rarity in Arabic historiography, and they are almost always dismissed as forgeries by modern scholars.[83] These two are also likely forgeries, as neither appears to be attested in an earlier source and they contain manifest anachronisms, including references to a hijri dating system in the lifetime of the Prophet (i.e., the statement that the first document was dictated by Muḥammad on the second day of the month of Jumādā al-Ūlā), whereas the tradition widely holds that this system was introduced during ʿUmar's reign.[84] The first document reflects classical Islamic law and its notion of *walāʾ al-ʿitq* as a tie between a manumitter and a freedman that arises upon manumission and that entails rights and obligations for each party.[85] It refers to the *ahl al-bayt* as Salmān's patrons. Judging by Abū al-Shaykh's antipathy to the Shiʿa elsewhere in his book, it is possible, but unlikely, that he has

81 Abū al-Shaykh, *Ṭabaqāt al-muḥaddithīn*. 1:233; the Bindārī/Ḥasan edition has here *man aslama minhum wa-aqāma ʿalā dīnihi*; 1:59 (as in the first instance, mentioned above). Abū Nuʿaym has here *man aslama minhum aw aqāma ʿalā dīnihi*; *Dhikr akhbār Iṣbahān*, 1:53.

82 Abū al-Shaykh, *Ṭabaqāt al-muḥaddithīn*, 1:233–4.

83 For a more credulous view that does not, however, include these documents, see Muhammad Hamidullah, *Majmūʿat al-wathāʾiq al-siyāsiyya li-l-ʿahd al-nabawī wa-l-khilāfa al-rāshida*, 3rd ed. (Beirut: Dār al-Irshād li-l-Ṭibāʿa wa-l-Nashr wa-l-Tawzīʿ, 1969).

84 As noted by Balūshī for both documents, *Ṭabaqāt al-muḥaddithīn*, 1:227 and 233–4; and regarding the first, al-Khaṭīb al-Baghdādī, *Taʾrīkh Baghdād*, 1:170–1.

85 Crone, *Roman, Provincial and Islamic Law*, 35–40. On *walāʾ*, see also Ulrike Mitter, "Origin and Development of the Islamic Patronate," in *Patronate and Patronage*, ed. Bernards and Nawas, 70–133.

included a document of sectarian origins.[86] Its author might have sympathies consistent with what Teresa Bernheimer has termed "ʿAlidism," that is, "a non-sectarian reverence and support for the family, as distinct from 'Shīʿism,' the political and religious claims of some of its members or others on their behalf."[87] The second document also contains anachronisms of a legal nature, with its references to "burdens and payments" imposed on non-Muslims and gifts to be funded from the public treasury that seem to anticipate the financial arrangements of the conquest period and afterward (I consider a story about the origins of hereditary pensions in Chapter 3).[88]

Forgery makes the documents no less – and in fact more – informative of the situation of Salmān's Iranian descendants (or those who claimed to be such), at least until Abū al-Shaykh's day and likely into that of Abū Nuʿaym, who also elects to transmit both of these reports. Even if it is hard to believe that Salmān's purported family, centered on Iṣfahān and Shīrāz, gained all of the privileges stipulated in the second document, the text lays claims to respect and maintenance on the basis of Salmān's family's adjunct membership in the *ahl al-bayt*. The identity of the forgers is likely lost to history, although they surely included the beneficiaries; the analysis of the chains of transmission undertaken by the modern editor, Balūshī, has yielded no more specific fruit.[89] Still, Abū al-Shaykh's decision to include the documents might well reflect the spirit of the Buyid era and

[86] See, for example, in *Ṭabaqāt al-muḥaddithīn*, 2:329, Abū al-Shaykh's description of a Hadith transmitter who took up with the "Rāfiḍa," denying the legitimacy of Abū Bakr's caliphate, and 2:278–9 relating to the error of Shiʿi ideas about ʿAlī. Abū al-Shaykh's legal affiliation, if he had one, is not known. Though treating Abū al-Shaykh, Tsafrir lists no *madhhab* for him. My own light search has been unsuccessful. Regarding the formation of the classical legal schools and their development, see esp. Christopher Melchert, *The Formation of the Sunni Schools of Law, 9th–10th Centuries C.E.* (Leiden: Brill, 1997) and George Makdisi, "*Ṭabaqāt*-Biography: Law and Orthodoxy in Classical Islam," *Islamic Studies* (Islamabad) 32, no. 4 (1993): 379–83.

[87] Teresa Bernheimer, "Genealogy, Marriage, and the Drawing of Boundaries among the ʿAlids (Eighth–Twelfth Centuries)," in *Sayyids and Sharifs in Muslim Societies: The Living Links to the Prophet*, ed. Kazuo Morimoto, 75–91 (Abingdon: Routledge, 2012), at 75–6. ʿAlī's quietist son, al-Ḥasan, for example, figures prominently as a subject in both works. Abū al-Shaykh, *Ṭabaqāt al-muḥaddithīn*, 1:191–4; Abū Nuʿaym, *Dhikr akhbār Iṣbahān*, 1:44–6, citing Abū al-Shaykh, among others.

[88] Though first-century forms of *walāʾ* may have included non-Muslims (i.e., there may be a "kernel of truth" in the agreement); see Mitter, "Origin and Development of the Islamic Patronate," 80.

[89] See esp. *Ṭabaqāt al-muḥaddithīn*, 227 and 234.

ʿAlidist sympathies and ideas about Muḥammad and his companions that favored Iranian interests.[90]

Even Salmān's non-Muslim descendants might fare surprisingly well in the arrangements. Our evidence is admittedly not vast – here just the second document. It relieves Salmān's family of the burdens and payments imposed on non-Muslims; it presumably therefore has in mind his non-Muslim descendants. Who should be protected also hinges on how one reads the Arabic, and this is not straightforward, since in Abū al-Shaykh's book, there are references to "he who converted to Islam *and* maintained his religion" (*man aslama minhum wa-aqāma ʿalā dīnihi*), as well as to "he who converted to Islam *or* maintained his religion" (*man aslama minhum aw aqāma ʿalā dīnihi*). In the second case, one could read the Arabic as relating to persons who converted to Islam as well as to others who kept their prior, non-Muslim faith. Abū Nuʿaym appears to be satisfied with "or," and that the brother's descendants would be treated well whether or not they have converted to Islam.[91] Whereas, in principle, *walāʾ* entailed breaking former ties, now they might be strengthened, legitimized, and rewarded with payments, along the lines of those extended to the Prophet's companions and their descendants.

The question that must remain open is whether contemporaries believed the documents to be authentic and whether Salmān's descendants did enjoy the material and social benefits demanded on their behalf. Only a short while later in Baghdad, al-Khaṭīb al-Baghdādī (d. 463/1071) uses Abū Nuʿaym's reporting on Salmān. While expressing doubts about the document of manumission, he transmits a version of it; the testament allegedly written for Salmān's family, however, must have seemed too far-fetched, as he leaves it out.[92] In Damascus, Ibn ʿAsākir (d. 571/1176), who also uses Abū Nuʿaym as a source, makes the same choice.[93] While al-Khaṭīb and Ibn ʿAsākir generally lavish attention on Salmān, Salmān's

90 Regarding Buyid pretensions, see esp. Wilferd Madelung, "The Assumption of the Title Shāhānshāh by the Būyids and the 'Reign of the Daylam (Dawlat Al-Daylam),'" *Journal of Near Eastern Studies* 28, no. 2 (1969): 84–108.

91 In texts generally, *wa* and *aw* are easily exchanged by scribes. The oral dimensions of such reports often favored minor changes. The text refers to a written form (as a *kitāb*) and its oral circulation ("To whomever . . . this writing of mine is read . . . ").

92 Al-Khaṭīb al-Baghdādī, *Taʾrīkh Baghdād*, 1:170–1 (no. 12, "Salmān al-Fārisī," at 163–71).

93 Ibn ʿAsākir keeps any doubts he may have about the document of manumission to himself; *Taʾrīkh Madīnat Dimashq*, ed. ʿUmar al-ʿAmrawī, 80 vols. (Beirut: Dār al-Fikr, 1995–8), 21:403–4 (no. 2599, "Salmān b. al-Islām," at 373–460).

brother and his descendants seem to fare poorly here as well as in the main arteries of Muslim tradition, judging by my searches of electronic databases of Arabic texts.[94]

Conclusion

Beginning with prophetic biography and the account of Ibn Hishām, we have seen how Muslim traditionists found the life and experiences of Salmān meaningful for relating the history of the Muslim community, its nature, and its requirements. They presented this community as superseding those of Christianity and of the *ḥanīfiyya*, with annunciation of Muḥammad's prophethood as a dominant theme, along with the idea that the Muslim community is a family that commands an exclusive loyalty. As Salmān passed through the hands of numerous monks en route to Muḥammad, his Persian homeland receded, and likewise, when in Medina, he joined himself to the Prophet as a devoted follower and left behind his family.

As a site of memory, Salmān also comes to appear as a mediator between Iran's pre-Islamic past and Islamic present, and between Persians and Arabs. Salmān proved useful for Iranians, who inherited much historical knowledge about him, such as versions of Ibn Isḥāq's text, but reworked it by methods that involved putting Iṣfahān at the center of the story, emphatic citation of the Pleiades Hadith, and extension of past memory. One is particularly struck by the forging of a corporate identity for Salmān's descendants in Iran, referred to collectively in the testament as *ahl bayt Salmān*, and the sympathies of Salmān's descendants for ʿAlī and his family in Abū al-Shaykh's day and likely also in Abū Nuʿaym's. Iranians, and Iṣfahānīs in particular, are offered an antique image that establishes greater continuity between their pre- and post-Islamic pasts, an image that also seems to deny rupture within Salmān's own family, which might hypothetically reap the rewards of Muslim rule.

I have proposed a periodization and a shift in perspective from the second half of the third/ninth century onward. Investigations of memory

[94] Especially al-Maktaba al-shāmila and al-Jāmiʿ al-kabīr li-kutub al-turāth (for details on both, see the bibliography). In 1925, however, what seems to be a version of the testament was published along with two other documents by Gushtasp Kaikhusru Nariman; see the discussion of Jamshedji Maneckji Unvala in his preface to his English translation of Massignon's *Salmân Pâk et les prémices spirituelles de l'Islam iranien; Salmān Pāk and the Spiritual Beginnings of Iranian Islām* (Bombay: n.p., 1955), i–ii (the book says that it was published by Unvala himself).

of different topics and texts – courtly traditions, for example – might yield refinements, though it is likely, and logical enough, that in other cases the meaning of a Persian identity and Persian origins also changed with the development of a Persian Muslim society. There were also most probably disputes on the way to the new views, as the cases of the *dīwān* and a Persian princess, considered in Chapter 3, suggest.

3

Finding Meaning in the Past

In the generations after Salmān al-Fārisī, a small number of high-profile Iranians were remembered fondly for their early adherence to Islam, the stalwartness of their faith, and the extent of their accomplishments. A notable example is al-Ḥasan al-Baṣrī (d. 110/728), a famous preacher in Umayyad Basra who was reckoned a member of the "successors" (*tābiʿūn*), the generation that came after Salmān and Muḥammad's other companions. Ibn Saʿd (d. 230/845), himself of Basran origins, wrote the earliest surviving substantial biographical notice on al-Ḥasan, in which he mentions stories about al-Ḥasan's parents and youth, including that his father was a man by the name of Yasār who came to Medina as a captive. Al-Ḥasan was born during the caliphate of ʿUmar, and one witness quoted by Ibn Saʿd avers that in his generation, al-Ḥasan was the person who, on matters of judgment, most resembled ʿUmar. His practice of ritual is reported, as are his associations with Muḥammad's companions and members of his own generation. But Ibn Saʿd gives very little sense of al-Ḥasan as an Iranian.[1] By contrast, al-Ḥasan turns up in local histories, where he appears as a mediator between two worlds, much like Salmān. For example, Qazwīn, northwest of modern Tehran, was an important crossroads and a barrier against frontier territories to

[1] Ibn Saʿd, *al-Ṭabaqāt al-kabīr*, vol. 7, pt. 1, 114–29; Christopher Melchert, "Ḥasan Baṣri," in *EIr* (esp. the first para.). Al-Ḥasan is also called "al-Ḥasan, the son of the father of al-Ḥasan" (al-Ḥasan b. Abī al-Ḥasan), reflecting the uncertainty of his lineage (this forms part of the section's heading). For an insightful consideration of the shaping of al-Ḥasan's image (that gives light attention to its Persian dimensions), see Suleiman Ali Mourad, *Early Islam between Myth and History: Al-Ḥasan al-Baṣrī (d. 110H/728CE) and the Formation of His Legacy in Classical Islamic Scholarship* (Leiden: Brill, 2006).

the north at several key junctures of the caliphate's history. The author of a late twelfth/early thirteenth-century local history calls on the memory of al-Ḥasan in an act of boundary maintenance as he cites a report in which al-Ḥasan explains that Qurʾan 9:123, which directs believers to fight against those "unbelievers who are near you," was revealed for the people of Qazwīn.[2]

As one of the most dramatic events in human history, the conquests gave rise to a creative mythology that long afterward continued to inspire generations of traditionists, who recalled the events of the conquests as they negotiated their own loyalties to the ʿAbbasid state and its successors, to sect and family, and to region, town, and neighborhood. In this chapter, I accordingly consider changing perceptions of Iranians from different vantage points, beginning with a view of the conquests in early Islamic narratives fashioned mostly in Iraq, and the proposal that memory of the role played by Iranians began to change in roughly the second half of the third/ninth century. Then, I get out of Iraq and move on to the fourth/tenth and fifth/eleventh centuries to consider closely two local histories, of Jurjān and Sīstān, and their far more profound shaping of memory to address local Iranian sensibilities.

Conquest and Kerygma

Much of the history written by Muslims in the third/ninth and fourth/tenth centuries is deeply kerygmatic in character.[3] In these writings, details serve to historicize theological ideas, as observed a generation ago by John Wansbrough.[4] The conquests, in Arabic *futūḥ* (literally "openings"), represent perhaps the most important proof of Islam as the true religion, and they formed part of Muslims' visions of salvation history already in the early phases of history writing.[5] In narratives about the

[2] ʿAbd al-Karīm b. Muḥammad al-Rāfiʿī, *al-Tadwīn fī akhbār Qazwīn*, ed. ʿAzīz Allāh ʿUṭāridī, 4 vols. (Beirut: Dār al-Kutub al-ʿIlmiyya, 1987), 1:34. The narrator also features Salmān and his Iranian genealogy; see 1:70ff.

[3] By which I mean to point to its theological, didactic character.

[4] Wansbrough, *The Sectarian Milieu: Content and Composition of Islamic Salvation History* (Oxford: Oxford University Press, 1978), esp. 1–49.

[5] Regarding the *futūḥ* in early Islamic thought, see esp. Donner, *Narratives of Islamic Origins*, 174–82 (where Donner treats the *futūḥ* as a theme addressing the inception of Muslim hegemony over non-Muslims and dates the first books discussing the *futūḥ* to the very end of the first and the beginning of the second century AH); Donner, "Arabic *fatḥ* as 'Conquest'" (unpublished manuscript); and his recent theory about the origins of Islam in a "Believers" movement as a form of militant monotheism, *Muhammad and the*

conquests, one often finds arguments "retrojected into the historical past in narrative form," as, for example, in the letters reportedly sent by the Prophet to invite contemporary rulers, including Heraclius (r. 610–41), the Negus of Abyssinia, and Khusraw Parvīz (r. 591–628), to embrace Islam.[6] Christian traditionists appear to have been familiar with at least some such narratives, and they formed their own interpretations of the meanings behind the conquests, which can often help shed light on the ways in which the early Muslim community chose to recall its conquest past.[7]

Regarding Iran, although narratives were often composed with significant recourse to Sasanian-era historiography, their very structures are frequently kerygmatic, like accounts of the *futūḥ* generally; they serve to explain the rapid success of the Arab conquerors as divinely inspired and as the most logical outcome of the disastrous final years of the Sasanian Empire. Modern historians have surprisingly often adopted this perspective, with only a passing glance at the kerygmatic interpretive motives of traditionists.[8] By way of example from an earlier generation, T. W. Arnold argued that the reigns of the last Sasanian rulers were marked by "terrible anarchy," which left Persians ready for a change. Above all, they were impressed and swayed by Muslim law, which granted them "toleration." Christians and Jews – but also "Sabæans" and followers of "numerous sects in which the speculations of Gnostics, Manichæans,

Believers: At the Origins of Islam (Cambridge, MA: Belknap Press of Harvard University Press, 2010), esp. ch. 3, "The Expansion of the Community of Believers."

6 Lawrence I. Conrad, "Heraclius in Early Islamic Kerygma," in *The Reign of Heraclius (610–641): Crisis and Confrontation*, ed. Gerrit J. Reinink and Bernard H. Stolte, 113–56 (Leuven: Peeters, 2002), at 114–17.

7 See esp. Thomas Sizgorich, "'Do Prophets Come with a Sword?' Conquest, Empire, and Historical Narrative in the Early Islamic World," *American Historical Review* 112, no. 4 (2007): 992–1015. For the issue of intercultural transmission, see esp. Robert Hoyland, "Arabic, Syriac and Greek Historiography in the First Abbasid Century: An Inquiry into Inter-Cultural Traffic," *ARAM Periodical* 3, no. 1 (1991): 211–33, esp. 223–33; Conrad, "Theophanes and the Arabic Historical Tradition: Some Indications of Intercultural Transmission," *Byzantinische Forschungen* 15 (1990): 1–44 and "The Conquest of Arwād: A Source-Critical Study in the Historiography of the Early Medieval Near East," in *The Byzantine and Early Islamic Near East*, vol. 1, *Problems in the Literary Source Material*, ed. Averil Cameron and Conrad, 317–401 (Princeton, NJ: Darwin Press, 1992); Borrut, *Entre mémoire et pouvoir*, 140ff.

8 See Wansbrough's comments on positivism and literary analysis, which, for Iran, do not strike me as dated; *Sectarian Milieu*, esp. 2. This is not to deny the impressive results that have been achieved by sensitive mining of our sources regarding Iran; see esp. Parvaneh Pourshariati, *Decline and Fall of the Sasanian Empire: The Sasanian–Parthian Confederacy and the Arab Conquest of Iran* (London: I. B. Tauris, 2008).

and Buddhists found expression" – could enjoy "religious freedom" and exemption from military service simply by paying a light tribute. Compare this situation to the old days, when non-Zoroastrians had suffered under "the persecuting policy of the state religion."[9] Arnold's interpretation thus emphasizes the smoothness of Iran's transition and the material interests of Persians. He refutes the views of many earlier scholars that emphasized conquest violence and the role that coercion played in bringing Iranians over to Islam.

The dramatic collapse of the Sasanian Empire demanded explanation, which our sources provide by depicting the Arabs as ending a failed Sasanian state in ways that often support Arnold's views. They frequently portray a centrally planned and coordinated Arab assault in the name of Islam,[10] extol the benefits of the caliphate and stable government, and highlight the bonds of blood and affection between members of the new and old regimes. Sasanian Iran appears in serious decline, worn down by its long wars with Byzantium, rebellious populations on its frontiers, conflict within its ruling house, and the strategic and moral failings of its rulers. Events were rushing toward the empire's extinction, which was written in the stars, predicted by angels, foretold by omens, and even admitted by Persian kings and generals themselves. The chaotic period beginning with the death of Khusraw Parvīz in 628 CE and ending in 632 receives special attention. As many as ten rulers came and went in this period, with several simultaneous claims to power being advanced until 637, when Yazdagird III had already been on the throne for some years.[11]

[9] T. W. Arnold, *The Preaching of Islam: A History of the Propagation of the Muslim Faith*, 2nd ed. (Delhi: Low Price Publications, 2001), 206–10. On the in fact more complicated issue of tolerance, see Yohanan Friedmann, *Tolerance and Coercion in Islam: Interfaith Relations in the Muslim Tradition* (Cambridge: Cambridge University Press, 2003), 87–120 ("Is there no compulsion in religion?"). For an explanation that emphasizes the "material and spiritual bankruptcy of the ruling class" of Iran, see ʿAbd al-Ḥusain Zarrīnkūb, "The Arab Conquest of Iran and Its Aftermath," in *The Cambridge History of Iran*, 4:1–56, esp. 17.

[10] On this view, see especially the skeptical views of Albrecht Noth, "Der Charakter der ersten großen Sammlungen von Nachrichten zur frühen Kalifenzeit," *Der Islam* 47 (1971): 168–99, and Donner, "Centralized Authority and Military Autonomy in the Early Islamic Conquests," in *The Byzantine and Early Islamic Near East*, vol. 3, *States, Resources and Armies*, ed. Averil Cameron, 337–60 (Princeton, NJ: Darwin Press, 1995).

[11] Regarding this period, see Frye, "Political History of Iran under the Sasanians," 170–2; Robert Göbl, *Sasanian Numismatics*, trans. Paul Severin (Braunschweig: Klinkhardt & Biermann, 1971), 54–5 (showing that only five rulers minted coins between Khusraw II and Yazdagird III); and Touraj Daryaee, *Sasanian Persia: The Rise and Fall of an Empire* (London: I. B. Tauris, 2009), 34–8.

A central figure of blame was Shīrawayh (Shīroe), who participated in a revolt against his father, Khusraw Parvīz, and afterward agreed to the latter's execution. Christian sources, albeit from their own perspectives, could go surprisingly easy on him.[12] Not so Muslim ones, which say he killed every brother he could lay his hands on, seventeen "men of good education, bravery, and manly virtues," in al-Ṭabarī's account.[13] After a short time, Shīrawayh fell sick, with some traditionists specifying that he, along with the nobles and great men of Persia, suffered death from the plague (*al-ṭāʿūn*).[14] The third/ninth-century historian al-Yaʿqūbī sums up his just deserts: "When Shīrawayh came to power, he freed all the prisoners and married his father's women [i.e., wives and concubines]. He killed seventeen of his brothers unjustly and with wanton aggression. But his reign did not go well, nor did he enjoy good health. He became severely ill and died after eight months [in power]."[15] Al-Ṭabarī – having considered all of Shīrawayh's actions – makes what seems like a serious understatement: "He was an inauspicious figure for the house of Sāsān."[16]

This kerygmatic and teleological perspective was hardwired into many narratives, even when they made abundant use of Sasanian-era sources. A particularly striking example is the account of Abū Ḥanīfa al-Dīnawarī (d. ca. 281 or 282/894–5), whose *Akhbār al-ṭiwāl* is a history covering the span from the origins of humanity to the third/ninth century. Al-Dīnawarī gives scant attention to the Prophet's life or to the early days of Islam in Arabia, but he pays extensive attention to Sasanian history. The Prophet's virtual absence has puzzled some of al-Dīnawarī's modern readers, but it can at least partly be explained by his belief that the

12 See Ignazio Guidi, ed., *Chronicon anonymum*, in *Chronica Minora*, Corpus Scriptorum Christianorum Orientalium 1–2, Scr. Syri 1–2 (Paris: Imprimerie nationale, 1903), 1:15–39 (Syriac text), 2:15–32 (Latin trans.); I rely on an unpublished English translation of this text by Sebastian Brock. But see also Theophanes, *The Chronicle of Theophanes Confessor: Byzantine and Near Eastern History, AD 284–813*, trans. Cyril Mango and Roger Scott (Oxford: Clarendon, 1997), 28–30.

13 Al-Ṭabarī, *Taʾrīkh*, I:1060–1; *The History of al-Ṭabarī*, vol. 5, *The Sāsānids, the Byzantines, the Lakhmids, and Yemen*, trans. C. E. Bosworth (Albany: State University of New York Press, 1999), 398.

14 E.g., Muḥammad b. Ḥabīb, *al-Muḥabbar*, ed. Ilse Lichtenstädter (Hyderabad: Maṭbaʿat Jamʿiyyat Dāʾirat al-Maʿārif al-ʿUthmāniyya, 1942), 363 (through the transmission of Abū Saʿīd al-Ḥasan b. al-Ḥusayn al-Sukkarī, d. 275/888); Ibn Qutayba, *al-Maʿārif*, ed. Tharwat ʿUkāsha (Cairo, 1960; repr., Cairo: al-Hayʾa al-Miṣriyya li-l-Kitāb, 1992), 665; al-Ṭabarī, *Taʾrīkh*, I:1061, *History of al-Ṭabarī*, 5:399.

15 Al-Yaʿqūbī, *Taʾrīkh*, 1:172.

16 Al-Ṭabarī, *Taʾrīkh*, I:1061; *History of al-Ṭabarī*, 5:399.

failures of the Sasanians played a large role in Iran's rapid conquest.[17] In his account, the devastation wrought by Shīrawayh is immediately followed by thirty-five pages of conquests and city building. The Prophet's life gets only the briefest of mentions during al-Dīnawarī's discussion of Anūshirvān, during whose reign Muḥammad was born.[18] Al-Dīnawarī summarizes the linkage of events along the following lines: Shīrawayh killed fifteen of his brothers out of jealous fear before illness overtook him. He left behind a vacuum at the top of the Sasanian hierarchy that was filled by children and women, among the latter a daughter of Khusraw Parvīz named Būrān. As a result, Persia's authority deteriorated: "When sovereignty came to Būrān, the daughter of Kisrā b. Hurmuz, it got out in all corners of the world that the land of Persia no longer had a king." The grab for the Persians' land then began, led by men from the Arab tribe of Bakr b. Wāʾil.[19] The Sasanian women bear a large portion of the blame. Yazdagird, the last Sasanian king, comes to power when the Persians, now ruled by another woman, Āzarmīdukht, recognize their losses: "We have come to this because of the domination of women over us!"[20]

The Dīwān *of ʿUmar*

This kerygmatic vision also recognized Persians as participants on the winning side that changed Iran; traditionists such as Ibn Isḥāq, al-Wāqidī (d. 207/822), Ibn Hishām, Ibn Saʿd, and al-Ṭabarī exploited Salmān especially for this purpose.[21] As I discuss in more detail in Chapter 6, our sources often preserve a record of the Arabs' allies and opponents. But as with Salmān, we should ask questions of a mnemohistorical nature: when and in what ways were such narratives adapted to speak to Iranian Muslims, rather than about them? Who recognized Persians, and possibly

17 On Iranian aspects of al-Dīnawarī's book, see esp. Pourshariati, "The *Akhbār al-Ṭiwāl* of Abū Ḥanīfa Dīnawarī: A *Shuʿūbī* Treatise on Late Antique Iran," in *Sources for the History of Sasanian and Post-Sasanian Iran*, ed. Rika Gyselen, 201–89 (Bures-sur-Yvette: Groupe pour l'Étude de la Civilisation du Moyen-Orient, 2010).

18 Al-Dīnawarī, *al-Akhbār al-ṭiwāl*, 124–5.

19 Ibid., 161–3.

20 Ibid., 173. See Chapter 5, where I continue my discussion of Būrān in early Islamic kerygma.

21 E.g., Muḥammad predicts to Salmān at the so-called Battle of the Ditch the Muslims' future conquest of Syria, the Yemen, and the "White Palace of Kisrā" in al-Madāʾin; al-Wāqidī, *al-Maghāzī*, ed. Marsden Jones, 3 vols. (London: Oxford University Press, 1966), 2:449–50 (al-Wāqidī's *al-Maghāzī* survives in the recension of Muḥammad b. al-ʿAbbās b. Ḥayyawayh [d. 382/992], on which see S. Leder, "al-Wāḳidī," in *EI*²).

why? What might narrative choices and differences reveal about shifts in perspective? The next two cases – those of ʿUmar's registry and of Yazdagird's daughter – give some sense of the complex developments of memory, particularly in Iraq from the second half of the third/ninth century onward.

When modern historians trace the origins of administrative practice in the Muslim territories, they frequently begin with the military register of the second caliph ʿUmar, which recorded the names of those who had fought in the conquests in order to facilitate the distribution of pensions and to regulate the flow of money to and within the military settlements. The idea was that rather than living off the land, the conquerors would become a hereditary pensioned class that would survive on tax revenues.[22] The origins of ʿUmar's idea are murky. The term *dīwān* is a Persian loan word attested in Zoroastrian Middle Persian in the spellings *dpywʾn* and *dywʾn*.[23] We also know that the Sasanians had a well-developed administrative apparatus, which ʿUmar could have adapted to serve his purposes.[24] Still, Gerd-Rüdiger Puin has persuasively argued that the register in its origins is more an Arab than a Persian institution, and so too much may be made of the etymology and Sasanians and too little of the particular circumstances of the Arabs.[25] Moreover, the register also surely benefited from Byzantine precedents, especially when the caliphate moved to Syria.[26]

There are a few milestones in the development of memory concerning ʿUmar's conception of the *dīwān*. To start, we have a work dealing with financial administration of the caliphate by one of the founders of the

[22] On the workings of the *dīwān*, see esp. Hugh Kennedy, "The Financing of the Military in the Early Islamic State," in *The Byzantine and Early Islamic Near East*, 3:361–78.

[23] François de Blois, "Dīvān i. The Term," in *EIr*. See also Jamāl al-Dīn ʿAbd Allāh b. Aḥmad al-Bashbīshī, *Jāmiʿ al-taʿrīb bi-l-ṭarīq al-qarīb*, ed. Nuṣūhī Ūnāl Qarah Arslān (Cairo: Markaz al-Dirāsāt al-Sharqiyya, Kulliyyat al-Ādāb, Jāmiʿat al-Qāhira, 1995), 134. On other early *dīwān*s (e.g., *dīwān al-khātam*), see also A. A. Duri, "Dīwān i. The Caliphate," in *EI*^{2}.

[24] This is also an object of memory; see, e.g., al-Yaʿqūbī on Khusraw Anūshirvān in *Taʾrīkh*, 1:164–5. On the survival of Sasanian administrative theory and practice, see esp. Michael G. Morony, *Iraq after the Muslim Conquest* (Princeton, NJ: Princeton University Press, 1984), 27ff.

[25] Gerd-Rüdiger Puin, "Der Dīwān von ʿUmar ibn al-Ḫaṭṭāb: Ein Beitrag zur frühislamischen Verwaltungeschichte" (Ph.D. diss., Rheinische Friedrich-Wilhelms-Universität, 1970). Cf. M. Sprengling, "From Persian to Arabic," *American Journal of Semitic Languages and Literatures* 56, no. 2 (1939): 175–224. The *dīwān* is also described in Noth's discussion of "administration" as a primary theme of the early Arabic historical tradition; Noth, *Early Arabic Historical Tradition*, 35–6.

[26] C. Edmund Bosworth, "Dīvān ii. Government Office," in *EIr*.

Ḥanafī school of law, Abū Yūsuf (d. 182/798), in which he treats pensions awarded to the early Muslims from the spoils of war. There he cites the companion Abū Hurayra, who reports that when he came back from the fighting in Baḥrayn, he brought with him five hundred thousand dirhams, about which he informed the caliph, ʿUmar.[27] ʿUmar, apparently doubting the high figure, sent him away to get some rest, and told him to return the next day. When Abū Hurayra returned, ʿUmar asked him whether the money had been acquired in an honest way. Abū Hurayra assured him that it had been, whereupon ʿUmar addressed those present, informing them of the spoils and asking them whether they wished it to be distributed by measuring, counting, or weighing the shares to be allotted. "One of those present" (*rajul min al-qawm*) suggested that *dīwān*s should be established for dealing with pensions (*dawwana li-l-nās dawāwīn yuʿṭūna ʿalayhā*). ʿUmar liked this idea and granted to each of the Muhājirūn five thousand dirhams, to each of the Anṣār three thousand, and to each of the wives of the Prophet twelve thousand. Abū Hurayra then proceeds to relate how the Prophet's wife, Zaynab, redistributed her share.[28] The reports on either side of this one make clear that Abū Yūsuf had no more interest than Abū Hurayra in the identity of "one of those present" but rather was addressing the relative merits of the recipients of pensions. Another report, for example, mentions that ʿUmar granted the wives ten thousand dirhams each, but ʿĀʾisha twelve thousand.[29]

By the start of the third/ninth century, if not earlier, we have an etymology for the term *dīwān* that gave it the root meaning of "devil" (*shayṭān*) – from the Persian word *dīv*, "demon" – due, we are told, to the shrewdness with which the Persian court secretaries conducted their affairs.[30] This theory is attribted to the philologist and courtier al-Aṣmaʿī (d. 213/828) and his teacher, Abū ʿAmr b. al-ʿAlāʾ (d. 154/770–1), but was widely cited, including by Ibn Qutayba, whose highlighting of this theory is hardly surprising, given his general reservations about Persian

27 For historical Baḥrayn, see Hugh Kennedy, *An Historical Atlas of Islam/Atlas historique de l'Islam*. 2nd ed. (Leiden: Brill, 2002), 16b.

28 Abū Yusūf, *Kitāb al-Kharāj* (Bulaq: al-Maṭbaʿa al-Mīriyya, 1302/[1884–5]), 26. Loosely translated by A. Ben Shemesh in *Taxation in Islam*, vol. 3, *Abū Yūsuf's Kitāb al-Kharāj* (Leiden: E. J. Brill, 1969), 71.

29 Shemesh, *Taxation in Islam*, 3:25. But for a case of Abū Yusūf giving credit to the Sasanian king Kavādh for ʿAbd al-Malik's tax policies, see Abū Yusūf, *Kitāb al-Kharāj*, 49, cited by S. D. Goitein in "A Turning Point in the History of the Muslim State," in *Studies in Islamic History and Institutions* (Leiden: E. J. Brill, 1966), 165.

30 On the term, see Mahmoud Omidsalar, "Dīv," in *EIr*.

cultural values in ʿAbbasid society.[31] While Ibn Qutayba also quoted translations of various pieces of Iran's cultural heritage (especially wisdom sayings and stories), his attitude toward it was ambivalent and complicated. One will not find, for example, Sasanian models discussed in any detail in his manual for court secretaries, written during the caliphate of al-Mutawakkil (r. 232–47/847–61) and dedicated to the latter's vizier, Fatḥ b. Khāqān; in the work, Ibn Qutayba lectures his readers on Arabic pronunciation, Arab food and drink, and the correct names of the date palms, horses, and plants of Arabia, but he says nothing about the Persian administrative or courtly tradition, though one might expect such lessons in an educational work for courtiers, and we indeed find them in a subsequent commentary on his manual.[32] His book against the Shuʿūbiyya, *Faḍl al-ʿArab* (The superiority of the Arabs), and a little-studied text that survives with it, known as the *Tanbīh ʿalā ʿulūmihā* (An exposition of their learning), likewise support Franz Rosenthal's characterization of Ibn Qutayba as "an eloquent spokesman for Arab civilization and in intellectual makeup [someone] totally committed and assimilated to it."[33]

So far, in discussions of the *dīwān*, there is little sensitivity to or express pride in a Persian history of administrative expertise.[34] Moving forward in time, we find a version of the Abū Hurayra report repeated, but hardly in a more satisfying manner. According to the historian al-Balādhurī (d. ca. 279/892), "someone" said to ʿUmar: "O Commander of the Believers, I have seen these Persians keeping a *dīwān* according to which they pay the men." Inspired, ʿUmar had such a register created, and assigned

[31] Ibn Qutayba, *ʿUyūn al-akhbār*, 4 vols. (Cairo: Maṭbaʿat Dār al-Kutub al-Miṣriyya, 1925–30), 1:50. See also Mawhūb b. Aḥmad al-Jawālīqī, *al-Muʿarrab min al-kalām al-aʿjamī ʿalā ḥurūf al-muʿjam*, ed. Aḥmad Muḥammad Shākir ([Cairo]: Dār al-Kutub, 1969), 202, and Ibn al-Sīd al-Baṭalyawsī, *al-Iqtiḍāb fī sharḥ Adab al-kuttāb*, ed. Muḥammad Bāsil 'Uyūn al-Sūd, 3 vols. (Beirut: Dār al-Kutub al-'Ilmiyya, 1999), 1:139–40.

[32] Ibn Qutayba, *Adab al-kātib*, ed. Max Grünert (Leiden: E. J. Brill, 1900). The commentary, treating the Persian origins of the institution, is that of Ibn al-Sīd, *al-Iqtiḍāb*, 1:139–40.

[33] Rosenthal, "Ebn Qotayba, Abū Moḥammad ʿAbd-Allāh," in *EIr*; Ibn Qutayba, *Faḍl al-ʿArab wa-l-tanbīh ʿalā ʿulūmihā*. See also a translation of this work from the Library of Arabic Literature, *The Superiority of the Arabs and an Exposition of Their Learning: A Translation of Ibn Qutaybah's Faḍl al-ʿArab wa l-tanbīh ʿalā ʿulūmihā*, ed. Riḍā al-ʿArabī, trans. Sarah Bowen Savant and Peter Webb, reviewed by James E. Montgomery (New York: New York University Press, forthcoming).

[34] Similarly, see the section of ʿAbd al-Razzāq al-Ṣanʿānī's *Muṣannaf* dedicated to the *dīwān*, 11:99–106 (nos. 20036–49).

to the Muhājirūn payments of five thousand dirhams, to the other companions four thousand, and to the wives of the Prophet twelve thousand. But a few pages further on in the text, al-Balādhurī quotes another report that raises a problem with the pensions. When the register was established, the Arab Abū Sufyān b. Ḥarb asked: "Is it a *dīwān* like that of the Byzantines (*Banū Aṣfar*)? If you assign pensions to the people, they will eat by the *dīwān* and neglect business." ʿUmar responded, "There is no way out of it, for the booty of the Muslims is abundant."[35]

From the fourth/tenth century onward, however, Abū Hurayra's report got new legs.[36] The vivid recollection of the ʿAbbasid courtier al-Ṣūlī (d. 335/947) – whose lineage originated in the territory of Jurjān and who played a major role in recording the courtly poetic tradition – puts the report into a wider context with additional details. According to al-Ṣūlī, money had begun to flow into the state's coffers under Abū Bakr (r. 632–4) with the conquest of Baḥrayn. At that time, Abū Bakr decided to give ten dirhams to each free man and woman as well as to each slave. When revenues increased the following year, he increased the allowance to twenty dirhams. The Anṣār complained that this system did not recognize merit (*faḍl*), but Abū Bakr put them off by asking whether they had exerted themselves for God and religion, or merely for this world.[37] By ʿUmar's reign, the revenues from Baḥrayn had risen further, with Abū Hurayra bringing ʿUmar large sums of money: eight hundred thousand dirhams in one fetching, five hundred thousand in another. ʿUmar then asked the people whether he should distribute the money by weighing it or counting it. Al-Ṣūlī continues: "Al-Fayrūzān [a Persian secretary from Sasanian Iraq] said to him (though it may have been someone else): 'Verily, the ʿAjam have created a *dīwān* for themselves in which they write names and what is owed to each one of them.' So [ʿUmar] authorized the adoption of the register."[38]

35 Al-Balādhurī, *al-Buldān wa-futūḥuhā wa-aḥkāmuhā*, ed. Suhayl Zakkār (Beirut: Dār al-Fikr, 1992), 496–7 and 501; al-Balādhurī, *The Origins of the Islamic State*, vol. 2, trans. Francis Clark Murgotten (New York: Columbia University, 1924), 246 and 51.

36 In addition to al-Ṣūlī's account, see Ibn ʿAbdūs al-Jahshiyārī, *Kitāb al-Wuzarāʾ wa-l-kuttāb*, ed. Muṣṭafā al-Saqqā, Ibrāhīm al-Abyārī, and ʿAbd al-Ḥafīẓ Shalabī (Cairo: Muṣṭafā al-Bābī al-Ḥalabī, 1938), 16–17 (and the notes therein), and Sprengling, "From Persian to Arabic," 177–8.

37 Al-Ṣūlī, *Adab al-kuttāb*, ed. Muḥammad Bahjat al-Atharī (Cairo: al-Maṭbaʿa al-Salafiyya, 1341/[1922–3]), 189–90.

38 Ibid., 190.

Having identified the idea's origin, al-Ṣūlī presses on with more information regarding its implementation. He cites a further report according to which al-Fayrūzān saw ʿUmar dispatch an expeditionary force and expressed surprise about ʿUmar's poor record keeping. He showed ʿUmar the Persians' register for recording names and payments, and ʿUmar subsequently set one up for the Muslims with the agreement of the Prophet's companions. ʿUmar recorded the recipients' names, along with annual payments due to them, beginning with twelve thousand dirhams for ʿĀʾisha and ten thousand for the Prophet's other wives, and five thousand dirhams for ʿAlī, members of the Banū Hāshim, and their *mawālī* who had participated in the battle of Badr, as well as for ʿUthmān, the Banū Umayya, and their *mawālī*, and for the family of Abū Bakr, including Ṭalḥa b. ʿUbayd Allāh (one of his kinsmen) and Bilāl (one of his *mawālī*). For himself and for members of the other lineages of Quraysh who fought at Badr he likewise awarded five thousand dirhams, and for the Anṣār who participated at Badr, four thousand. When this last group objected, he answered them by quoting the Qurʾan (59:8): "For the poor Emigrants who were driven from their homes and their possessions while seeking merit (*faḍl*) and approval from God, and who help God and His messenger. These are the truthful ones." After the Anṣār, the names of persons with less merit were entered, including those who only joined up at the time of the battle of Uḥud (three thousand dirhams) and those who fought only at the conquest of Mecca (two thousand dirhams).[39]

In this account, Persians provided the expertise required to recognize merit, but by al-Ṣūlī's day, the registries in fact no longer played a role in ʿAbbasid administration, having fallen out of use during the reign of al-Muʿtaṣim (r. 218–27/833–42), when the caliph recruited peoples from the fringes of the empire for his army and built a new capital in Samarra about eighty miles north of Baghdad on the Tigris. This initiated what Hugh Kennedy has appropriately called the "divorce of the military élite from the rest of society, by origin, language and custom."[40] Still, memory of the old days remained, and with the ʿAbbasids' debt to the Sasanians generally accepted, two realities likely informed al-Ṣūlī's presentation. First, there was the power of the elite secretarial class (*kuttāb*) and

[39] Al-Ṣūlī's account continues with the transfer of the *dīwān* into Arabic during the time of al-Ḥajjāj and ʿAbd al-Malik by the Sijistānī Abū al-Walīd Ṣāliḥ b. al-ʿAbd al-Raḥmān al-Baṣrī in Iraq and by Sirjūn b. Manṣūr in Syria. Ibid., 198–200.

[40] Hugh Kennedy, *The Prophet and the Age of the Caliphates: The Islamic Near East from the Sixth to the Eleventh Century* (London: Longman, 1986), 160.

palace servants, many Iranians among them, upon whom the caliphs often depended when faced with military elites dominated by Turkish groups. This need for a counterbalance may well have fostered appreciation for the illustrious Persian origins and character of institutions even among courtiers of Turkish descent, such as al-Ṣūlī.[41] But this had been the case already in Ibn Qutayba's day. More crucially, there was the growing power of Iranian governorates, such as the Samanids and the Saffarids, which likely made the ʿAbbasids and their court in Iraq more eager to claim an Iranian heritage themselves.[42] And so, because Persians such as al-Fayrūzān had always provided advice for caliphs, the ʿAbbasid caliphate had authentic Iranian roots. Al-Fayrūzān was an appropriate enough agent, as traditionists knew him in different roles as a servant of the Sasanian state.[43]

The case of the *dīwān* might suggest a wider pattern whereby appreciation for and recognition of the Persian heritage and character of the caliphate and its institutions increased over time, regardless of what the realities may have been.[44] A more obvious example might be the vizierate, the historical development of which overlaps with my chronological framework.[45] Ibn Qutayba, whose career coincided with the increasing strength of the military classes, may well have been dismayed by challenges to the caliph; surrounded by Persian courtiers, he could urge the bureaucracy to recognize an Arabic heritage, but he had little clout with the Turkish soldiers who, within his lifetime, toppled the caliph al-Mutawakkil (r. 232–47/847–61) and his successors. But his were still relatively early days in the sufferings of the caliphate, whereas by al-Ṣūlī's time, power had devolved to a considerably greater extent, so it became

41 "The Disastrous Reigns of al-Muqtadir and His Successors," in Kennedy, *The Prophet and the Age of the Caliphates*; Dominique Sourdel, *Le vizirat ʿabbāside de 749 à 936 (132 à 324 de l'hégire)*, 2 vols. (Damascus: Institut français de Damas, 1959–60), 1:9–10.

42 Clifford Edmund Bosworth, "The Heritage of Rulership in Early Islamic Iran and the Search for Dynastic Connections with the Past," *Iran* 11 (1973): 51–62.

43 On al-Fayrūzān (or al-Fīrūzān), see the index in Parvaneh Pourshariati, *Decline and Fall of the Sasanian Empire*. As Sprengling noted, "the better-known and more vivid figure of *Hurmuzān* the Mihrjānite" was also proposed; Sprengling, "From Persian to Arabic," 177–9. On al-Hurmuzān, see Chapter 6; for his portrayal as the source of the information, see al-Māwardī, *Kitāb al-Aḥkām al-sulṭāniyya wa-l-wilāyāt al-dīniyya*, ed. Samīr Muṣṭafā Rubāb (Sidon and Beirut: al-Maktaba al-ʿAṣriyya, 2000), 220, and *al-Ahkam as-Sultaniyyah: The Laws of Islamic Governance*, trans. Asadullah Yate (London: Ta-Ha, 1996), 282.

44 Morony has made this argument; see *Iraq after the Muslim Conquest*, esp. 27.

45 I am planning a study on this institution from a history of memory perspective. As narratives about the conquests do not focus on it, I do not treat it in the present chapter.

more attractive to envision an institution running back to a distant Sasanian past and, al-Ṣūlī likely hoped, into a distant future.

Yazdagird's Daughter

Another case for mnemohistory involves a daughter, or even daughters, of Yazdagird. This case, I believe, is one of contest, where an ostensibly Iranian site of memory was of interest not just to Iranians. Moreover, it was likely only meaningful to some Iranians – and to others not at all.

In the second half of the third/ninth century, Ibn Qutayba argued in his polemic against the Shuʿūbiyya, mentioned above, that a mother's ancestry is unimportant in determining nobility: a slave woman can give birth to a caliph just as well as a wife can. His argument reflected common ʿAbbasid practice ever since the days of the caliph al-Mahdī (r. 158–69/775–85) and his beloved al-Khayzurān (a former slave of Yemeni origins), who bore his heirs, the caliphs al-Hādī (r. 169–70/785–6) and Hārūn al-Rashīd (r. 170–93/786–809). The Shuʿūbīs had maligned the Arabs – believed to be the descendants of Hagar, Abraham's slave – as "sons of the unclean woman" (*Banū al-lakhnāʾ*). In their defense, Ibn Qutayba mentions the renowned figures ʿAlī b. al-Ḥusayn b. ʿAlī b. Abī Ṭālib, al-Qāsim b. Muḥammad b. Abī Bakr al-Ṣiddīq, and Sālim b. ʿAbd Allāh b. ʿUmar b. al-Khaṭṭāb, all of whom were born of slaves.[46] Each of the three men has a noble lineage reckoned through the male line, as their names indicate: each is the grandson of a successor to Muḥammad, and the father of each is also well known. They are noble regardless of who their mothers were.

The first name that Ibn Qutayba mentions, ʿAlī b. al-Ḥusayn b. ʿAlī b. Abī Ṭālib, is the fourth Imam of the Shiʿa, also known as ʿAlī Zayn al-ʿĀbidīn ("Ornament of the Worshippers," d. ca. 95/713), and here we have another case of sharpening memory for Persians. In a Shiʿi biographical dictionary composed in Ibn Qutayba's day, the Imam's mother is a nameless slave (*umm walad*), and this is also how he depicts her.[47] But other sources from his time know her as a daughter of Yazdagird III who married the Prophet's grandson al-Ḥusayn, although her name and

[46] Ibn Qutayba, *Faḍl al-ʿArab wa-l-tanbīh ʿalā ʿulūmihā*, 48; see also his *al-Maʿārif*, 214–15, where Ibn Qutayba identifies ʿAlī b. al-Ḥusayn's mother as a woman from Sind named either Sulāfa or Ghazāla.

[47] Yaḥyā b. al-Ḥasan al-Madanī al-ʿAqīqī (d. 277/891), *Kitāb al-Muʿaqqibīn min wuld al-Imām Amīr al-Muʾminīn*, ed. Muḥammad al-Kāẓim (Qum: Maktabat Āyat Allāh al-ʿUẓmā al-Marʿashī al-Najafī, 2001), 75–9; Ibn Qutayba, *Faḍl al-ʿArab wa-l-tanbīh ʿalā ʿulūmihā*, 48.

FIGURE 3.1. Shahrbānū. Photo by Wahunam.

the circumstances of her union were in question then and long afterward. Today it is commonly (though not universally) held among the Shiʿa that the mother of al-Ḥusayn's son ʿAlī Zayn al-ʿĀbidīn was a daughter of Yazdagird's named Shahrbānū, whose shrine lies at Mount Ṭabarak at Rayy in central Iran (see Figure 3.1).

As Mohammad Ali Amir-Moezzi has shown, the legend likely began to take form in the third/ninth century.[48] One of the earliest Shiʿi sources to mention the idea is al-Yaʿqūbī, who presents Zayn al-ʿĀbidīn as a man of nobility and serious character and as a trailblazer because his example made slave women (*imāʾ*) popular as mothers. ʿUmar had procured two daughters of Yazdagird as captives and gave one of them to al-Ḥusayn, who named her Ghazāla (of the other we hear nothing). She bore Zayn

[48] On the development of her legend and her absence from sources that would likely know her, see esp. Amir-Moezzi, "Shahrbānū, Dame du pays d'Iran et Mère des Imams: Entre l'Iran préislamique et le Shiisme Imamite," *Jerusalem Studies in Arabic and Islam* 27 (2002): 497–549; abridged version: "Shahrbānū, princesse sassanide et épouse de l'imam Ḥusayn: De l'Iran préislamique à l'Islam shiite," *Comptes rendus de l'Académie des Inscriptions et Belles-Lettres*, Jan.–Mar. 2002, 255–85; and Amir-Moezzi, "Šahrbānu," in *EIr*.

al-ʿĀbidīn, after which everyone wished to have their children borne by slaves.[49]

By the late third/ninth century, a few other noteworthy stories had also developed. We have an account by al-Ṣaffār al-Qummī (d. 290/902–3), attributed to the fifth Imam of the Shiʿa, Abū Jaʿfar Muḥammad al-Bāqir (the son of Zayn al-ʿĀbidīn). During ʿUmar's reign as caliph, a daughter of Yazdagird was brought as a captive to Medina. Light radiated from her face, illuminating the Prophet's mosque. She upset the caliph with a Persian expression as she covered her face (thus blocking the light), but ʿAlī intervened on her behalf, instructing the caliph to let her choose one of the Muslim men and to make her his booty. ʿUmar agreed and told her to choose a man, whereupon she put her hand upon the head of al-Ḥusayn. ʿAlī then asked her for her name, and she replied "Jahān-shāh" ("King of the World"). He responded, "No, [let us call you] Shahrbānawayh" ("Lady of the Land"). He then announced that she would be the mother of al-Ḥusayn's child, who would be "the best person in the world" (*khayr ahl al-arḍ*).[50] As Amir-Moezzi noted, this story is reported among Imāmī Shiʿi narratives about the divine light because from Shahrbānū's son onward the Imams were "bearers of a twofold light," that of the sacred transmission (*walāya*) from ʿAlī and Fāṭima and that of transmission from Persia's kings through Shahrbānū.[51]

At some stage, the fourth Imam acquired a nickname to reflect his parentage: he was the "offspring of the two elect" (*dhū al-khiyaratayn*), because of the nobility of both sides of his family. The name derives from a Prophetic statement that among God's creatures there are two elect (*li-llāh min khalqihi* [or *ʿibādihi*] *khiyaratān*), the first being the Quraysh, the elect of the Arabs, and the second being the Persians, the

49 Al-Yaʿqūbī also recognizes voices that do not seem to attribute Sasanian ancestry to her, as he states that it is also said that Zayn al-ʿĀbidīn's mother was taken captive in Kābul. Al-Yaʿqūbī, *Taʾrīkh*, 2:303. Cf. Ibn Saʿd, *al-Ṭabaqāt al-kabīr*, 5:156 (where Ghazāla is identified as a slave and mother of ʿAlī b. al-Ḥusayn, without any mention of Sasanian ancestry).

50 Abū Jaʿfar al-Ṣaffār al-Qummī, *Baṣāʾir al-darajāt fī faḍāʾil Āl Muḥammad* (Qum: Ṭalīʿat al-Nūr, 1384 *shamsī*/[2005]), 439 (no. 8).

51 Shahrbānawayh is a variant of Shahrbānū (containing the -wayh ending). Amir-Moezzi has written extensively on this light; see esp. *The Divine Guide in Early Shiʿism: The Sources of Esotericism in Islam*, trans. David Streight (Albany: State University of New York Press, 1994), 29ff. On the special sense of *walāya* among the Shiʿa as pertaining to a sacred transmission, see Mawil Y. Izzi Dien and P. E. Walker, "Wilāya," in *EI*². For the full connotations of *walāya* in early Shiʿi thought, see Maria Massi Dakake, *The Charismatic Community: Shiʿite Identity in Early Islam* (Albany: State University of New York Press, 2007).

elect of the ʿAjam ("non-Arabs"). The nickname was transmitted widely, not just by partisans of the Shiʿa. The Basran philologist al-Mubarrad (d. ca. 286/900) explains the name and then reports that one of Yazdagird's daughters came to ʿAlī amid a hundred other slave girls. ʿAlī ordered his companions to show her respect and then instructed her to marry his son al-Ḥusayn. The woman suggested that instead she should marry ʿAlī himself, but ʿAlī replied that al-Ḥusayn was a youth and therefore more deserving of the marriage. The woman accepted, though with some grumbling. Al-Mubarrad then cites a statement by ʿUmar praising the children of concubines since they possess both the mightiness of the Arabs (*ʿizz al-ʿArab*) and the administrative expertise of the non-Arabs (i.e., Persians, *tadbīr al-ʿAjam*).[52]

Why did some Muslims want to believe that al-Ḥusayn married a Sasanian princess, and what might the union have meant to those who wrote about it? Following Amir-Moezzi, I am inclined to see the germs of a Persian Shiʿi historical consciousness in the first iterations of the story.[53] But whereas Amir-Moezzi hypothesizes the importance of the court of al-Maʾmūn (r. 198–218/813–33) and the Shuʿūbiyya as the primary early setting for the claim, I would put more emphasis on the later crystallization of memory and its diffuse set of discursive contexts, a conclusion that Amir-Moezzi's own evidence in fact supports (especially regarding its earliest attestation in the late third/ninth century, after al-Maʾmūn's day, and his citation of widely variant reports as late as the sixth/twelfth century).[54] I would also note that Ibn Qutayba, in his polemic against the Shuʿūbiyya, addresses many a Shuʿūbī claim but has nothing to say about a Sasanian princess, though he certainly could have raised the subject when discussing Zayn al-ʿĀbidīn's mother.

Indeed, meaningful details of the legend differ long after al-Maʾmūn and the Shuʿūbiyya, among them the name of Zayn al-ʿĀbidīn's mother, the ruler during whose reign she was taken captive (ʿUmar, ʿUthmān, or ʿAlī), whether she was a slave or a free woman (probably a slave),

52 He cites as his source al-Aṣmaʿī. An explanation of the term "half-breed" (*al-hajīn*) follows. Al-Mubarrad, *al-Fāḍil*, ed. ʿAbd al-ʿAzīz al-Maymanī (Cairo: Dār al-Kutub al-Miṣriyya, 1956), 106.

53 Amir-Moezzi writes ("Šahrbānu," in *EIr*): "The story is obviously highly charged in doctrinal, ethnical and political terms. These two pro-Shiʿite and pro-Persian tendencies are introduced in such a manner that they seem indisociable. One might even say more precisely that the legend, in its Shiʿism pertains to the Ḥosaynid movement and that in its 'Persianism,' the most popular version seems to have emerged from radical milieu. All of this sounds very much like a challenge to a kind of Sunnite arabo-centrist 'orthodoxy.'"

54 Amir-Moezzi, "Shahrbānū, Dame du pays d'Iran," esp. 509–11.

and whether she remarried after the death of al-Ḥusayn (unlikely). Well past the third/ninth century, Ibn Funduq (d. ca. 565/1169) offers us, in a lengthy section of his genealogical work treating descendants of the Prophet's family, possible answers to these questions, including that she was a daughter of Yazdagird named Shahrbānawayh, Sulāfa, Ghazāla, Jadā (or Judā?), Ḥalwa, Salāma, Shāh-Āfarīd, or Shahrbānū.[55] In the seventh/thirteenth century, Ibrāhīm Muḥammad b. Abī Bakr al-Anṣārī al-Burrī (d. 690/1291) writes:

> ʿAlī [Zayn al-ʿĀbidīn] was the best of the Banū Hāshim after ʿAlī and al-Ḥusayn. His mother was a Persian of known genealogy. Her name was Sulāfa bt. Yazdagird b. Shahriyār b. Kisrā Anūshirvān b. Qubādh. Sulāfa was among the best of women. It is said that she was the aunt of the mother of Yazīd al-Nāqiṣ[56] or her sister. ʿAlī b. al-Ḥusayn showed the greatest filial piety to his mother, Sulāfa. He would never eat with her from the same platter. When he was asked about that, he said: "I would hate for my hand to take anything her eye had first sought, and so I be undutiful to her." He was called Ibn al-Khiyaratayn on account of the statement of the Messenger of God, "Among God's servants there are two elect." Among the Arabs, His elect are the Quraysh, and among the non-Arabs, the Persians.[57]

The surfeit of contradictory details suggests a diffused, not consolidated, image of Zayn al-ʿĀbidīn's mother. It also indicates how attractive she was as a site for a wide variety of ideas, not limited to sectarian loyalties. Stories that use Yazdagird's daughters to link al-Ḥusayn by marriage

55 Abū al-Ḥasan ʿAlī b. Zayd al-Bayhaqī, commonly known as Ibn Funduq, *Lubāb al-ansāb wa-l-alqāb wa-l-aʿqāb*, ed. Mahdī Rajāʾī and Maḥmūd Marʿashī (Qum: Maktabat Āyat Allāh al-ʿUẓmā al-Marʿashī al-Najafī al-ʿĀmma, 1410/[1989–90]), 346–52. He also considers possibilities for the identity of Yazdagird's daughter's mother. On this work, see Kazuo Morimoto, "Putting the *Lubāb al-ansāb* in Context: *Sayyids* and *Naqībs* in Late Saljuq Khurasan," *Studia Iranica* 36, no. 2 (2007): 163–83. Ibn Funduq is better known for his *Tārīkh-i Bayhaq*.

56 According to one version of this theory, Qutayba b. Muslim captured in Khurāsān a granddaughter of Yazdagird, whom he presented to the caliph al-Walīd I (b. ʿAbd al-Malik, r. 86–96/705–15). She bore Yazīd III, who became caliph in 126/744. Yazīd's ancestry was illustrious because he was the descendant of Persian, Byzantine, Turkish, and Muslim-Arab kings (the significance of his name, al-Nāqiṣ, the "Depriver" or "Deficient," is another matter). See esp. the explanation of Muḥammad b. Ḥabīb (d. 245/860), *al-Muḥabbar*, 31–2. On this work, see Ilse Lichtenstädter, "Muḥammad b. Ḥabīb and His Kitâb al-Muḥabbar," *Journal of the Royal Asiatic Society*, n.s., 71, no. 1 (1939): 1–27. Muḥammad b. Ḥabīb was a student of the genealogist Hishām b. Muḥammad al-Kalbī. On Yazīd's mother, see also Garth Fowden, *Quṣayr ʿAmra: Art and the Umayyad Elite in Late Antique Syria* (Berkeley: University of California Press, 2004), 243–7.

57 Ibrāhīm b. Abī Bakr al-Burrī, *al-Jawhara fī nasab al-nabī wa-aṣḥābuhu al-ʿashara*, ed. Muḥammad al-Tūnjī, 2 vols. (al-ʿAyn: Markaz Zāyid li-l-Turāth wa-l-Taʾrīkh, 2001), 2:233.

to the sons of the early caliphs are particularly intriguing and might be suggestive of the ways in which the Shiʿa developed ideas about the legitimacy of the caliphate and its early history.[58] The Shiʿi biographer Shaykh al-Mufīd (d. 413/1022), for example, recalls that ʿAlī had appointed one Ḥurayth b. Jābir al-Ḥanafī in charge of part of the eastern provinces. The latter then sent two daughters of Yazdagird to him as captives. ʿAlī gave one daughter, Shahzanān (Shaykh al-Mufīd notes the name Shahrbānū as a variant), to al-Ḥusayn, and she bore him Zayn al-ʿĀbidīn. He gave the other daughter, who is not named, to Muḥammad b. Abī Bakr, and she bore him al-Qāsim b. Muḥammad b. Abī Bakr, who was therefore a maternal cousin of Zayn al-ʿĀbidīn.[59] For Shaykh al-Mufīd, this union may have made sense as uniting by marriage ʿAlī's descendants to a line of Abū Bakr that had reportedly sympathized with ʿAlī in the first *fitna*.[60] By contrast, another story linking ʿAlī, Abū Bakr, and ʿUmar through their progeny would seem to fit more comfortably in a Sunni milieu, and it is reported by al-Zamakhsharī (d. 538/1144). Here, we learn that during the caliphate of ʿUmar, *three* daughters of Yazdagird were taken prisoner and brought to Medina. ʿAlī saved them from the marketplace and presented them to al-Ḥusayn, Abū Bakr's son Muḥammad, and ʿUmar's son ʿAbd Allāh. The daughters (who are not named) bore Zayn al-ʿĀbidīn, al-Qāsim, and Sālim b. ʿAbd Allāh b. ʿUmar.[61]

The discursive context for many of these legends does likely relate to the earliest germs of a Persian Shiʿi historical consciousness, as Amir-Moezzi argues, although given the other possible ways of interpreting the union, its specifically ethnic (much less "Iranian") dimension is somewhat hard to pin down. Al-Dīnawarī relates a report that seems to discourage visions of the marriage of Yazdagird's daughter into the Prophet's family – and also, perhaps, of the ʿAjam (his preferred term) to the Shiʿa. In his version, during the reign of ʿAlī, the people of Nīshāpūr rebelled and took

58 Regarding Shiʿi attitudes toward the companions, see Etan Kohlberg, "Some Imāmī Shīʿī Views on the Ṣaḥāba," *Jerusalem Studies in Arabic and Islam* 5 (1984): 143–75.

59 Al-Shaykh al-Mufīd, *al-Irshād fī maʿrifat ḥujaj Allāh ʿalā al-ʿibād*, ed. Muʾassasat Āl al-Bayt li-Iḥyāʾ al-Turāth, 2 vols. (Beirut: al-Muʾassasa, 1995), 2:137; Shaykh al-Mufīd, *Kitāb al-Irshād: The Book of Guidance into the Lives of the Twelve Imams*, trans. I. K. A. Howard (London: Balagha Books, 1981), 380.

60 See G. R. Hawting, "Muḥammad b. Abī Bakr," in *EI*^{2}.

61 The three men mentioned by Ibn Qutayba, quoted above. Al-Zamakhsharī, *Rabīʿ al-abrār wa-nuṣūṣ al-akhbār*, ed. ʿAbd al-Amīr Muhannā, 5 vols. (Beirut: Muʾassasat al-Aʿlamī, 1992), 3: 350–1 (no. 32); also, citing al-Zamakhsharī, Ibn Khallikān, *Wafayāt al-aʿyān*, ed. Iḥsān ʿAbbās, 8 vols. (Beirut: Dār al-Thaqāfa, 1968–72), 3:266–9, at 267 (no. 422, "Zayn al-ʿĀbidīn"; but cf. his other reports).

as their leader an unnamed daughter of Kisrā from Kābul. The governor of Khurāsān put down the rebellion and sent her to ʿAlī. ʿAlī proposed that she marry his son al-Ḥasan, but she refused, suggesting she marry ʿAlī instead. This he refused on the grounds that he was an old man. Noting that he was socially on a par with her (*anā qurābatuhā*), one of the leading members of the land-owning class of Iraq (*dihqāns*) offered to marry her, but ʿAlī decided to let her choose for herself. Al-Dīnawarī does not report her decision.[62]

Views from the "Edge": Making the Conquests Meaningful at Home

So far, the perspectives we have considered in this chapter belong to what Richard Bulliet has helpfully termed "the center," that is, a view of history in which the caliphate plays a central part in the narrative.[63] They largely originate in the formative periods of Muslim historiography and reflect the broad historiographical questions and interests of the major Iraq-based traditionists. Traditionists assigned meaningful roles to Persians, though only after the passage of some time and then with some ambiguity. The cases discussed so far – those of the *dīwān* and of Yazdagird's daughter – suggest the second half of the third/ninth century as the start of a new phase. Ideas about the origins of the *dīwān* evolved within the ʿAbbasid court and among courtiers with strong ties to Iran, whereas given the widely discrepant versions of the Shahrbānū legend, I am reluctant to accept the importance of an original ʿAbbasid courtly context. Instead, I think that we have a more complicated negotiation of her memory that began in the late third/ninth century and continued over the course of several centuries. In other words, the metaphorical marriage of the family of ʿAlī to the Persians was not negotiated in al-Maʾmūn's reign but far more gradually, with its final form taking shape after the period of this study.

As time passed and the composition of reading publics changed to include more Iranians, works began to take greater account of them. In the first/seventh and second/eighth centuries, traditionists may have composed histories focused on localities, but their fourth/tenth- and fifth/

62 Al-Dīnawarī, *al-Akhbār al-ṭiwāl*, 222.

63 As Bulliet wrote, "The view from the center portrays Islamic history as an outgrowth from a single nucleus, a spreading inkblot labeled the caliphate." Richard W. Bulliet, *Islam: The View from the Edge* (New York: Columbia University Press, 1994), 8.

eleventh-century counterparts were writing in completely different settings following the amalgamation of the conquering to the conquered, conversion, and the development of legal, sectarian, and pietistic affiliations and institutions.[64] In an empire, a group requires a small place to feel at home. Local histories provided such places in more modest and localized narratives.

The following two cases are selected for their local perspectives, their different forms (biographical vs. annalistic), and contrasting attitudes toward violence – a will to forget versus a will to remember.[65] In both cases, one sees the importance of the conquests to local memory, the necessity of coming to terms with defeat, and the ways in which memory served the broader interpretive aims of the traditionist recording the event. In Bulliet's terms, they represent "views from the edge," where for the traditionists themselves, home was central.

Violence Forgotten: Our Shared History Dating from the Conquests

Located on the southeastern coast of the Caspian Sea, Jurjān (classical Hyrcania) played an important role in antiquity as a frontier and a shield against nomadic populations to the north, as shown by an extensive defensive wall known, inaccurately, as the Sadd-i Iskandar, or Barrier of Alexander, which runs eastward from the southeastern corner of the Caspian Sea for almost 200 km, marked at intervals by forts.[66] It took the Muslims some time in the first/seventh and second/eighth centuries to subjugate the territory, and in the centuries that followed, it was overshadowed by Ṭabaristān in the west and Khurāsān in the east. In the first part of the fourth/tenth century, a rebel from the royal clan of

64 Even the vision of universal histories had grown narrower since al-Ṭabarī; see "ii. Local history," in Robinson, *Islamic Historiography*, 138–42.

65 There is already considerable scholarship on local Iranian historiography, although still no monograph that considers the myriad issues in its analysis. See the special issue of *Iranian Studies*, vol. 33, no. 1/2 (2000), especially Jürgen Paul, "Histories of Isfahan" and "Histories of Herat."

66 The wall's origins are debated; compare Muhammad Yusof Kiani, "Excavations on the Defensive Wall of the Gurgān Plain: A Preliminary Report," *Iran* 20 (1982): 73–9, with James Howard-Johnston, "The Two Great Powers in Late Antiquity: A Comparison," in *The Byzantine and Early Islamic Near East*, 3:157–226, at 192–4, and again, Kiani, "Gorgān iv. Archaeology," in *EIr*; but see also now Eberhard W. Sauer et al., *Persia's Imperial Power in Late Antiquity: The Great Wall of Gorgān and Frontier Landscapes of Sasanian Iran* (Oxford: Oxbow Books, 2013). The authors find that the wall was built in the fifth or possibly early sixth century CE. They also propose that a sizable section in the west is buried under marine sediment.

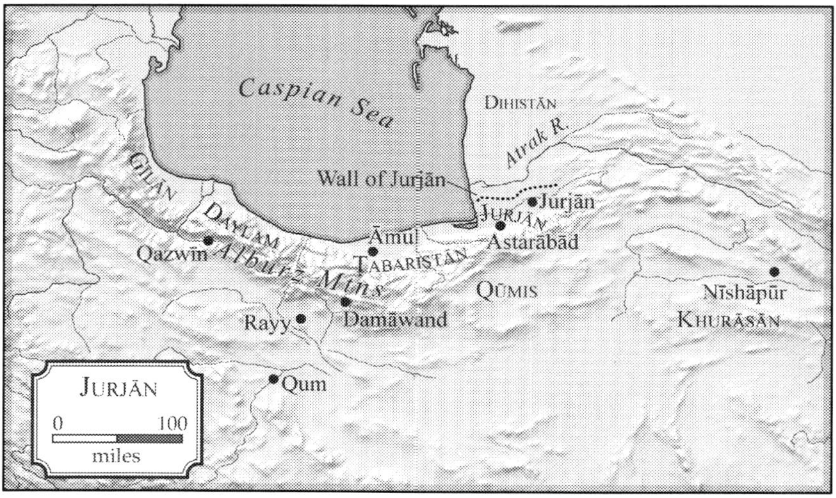

MAP 3.1. Jurjān

Gīlān by the name of Mardāvīj b. Ziyār (d. 323/935) had a throne of gold and a crown decorated like Khusraw's made for himself, and he set out, seeking to conquer Iraq as well as the buildings of al-Madāʾin and the dwellings and homes of Kisrā. Victorious, he would henceforth be addressed by the Sasanian era title *shāhān-shāh* and rule a kingdom that would survive off and on in Jurjān and Ṭabaristān until ca. 483/1090. After his death, power passed to his brother Wushmgīr and the latter's descendants, the Ziyarids, who in the ensuing decades were involved in the struggles between the Buyid and Samanid dynasties in northern Iran, lingering on as tributaries to the Ghaznavids.[67]

In the first part of the fifth/eleventh century, as the Ghaznavids were extending their control over the region, a traditionist named Abū al-Qāsim Ḥamza b. Yūsuf b. Ibrāhīm al-Sahmī (d. 427/1038) composed a *Taʾrīkh Jurjān*, which consists of a short historical introduction followed by an alphabetized collection of biographies of scholars totaling about 450 pages in the Hyderabad printed edition.[68] Al-Sahmī says he

[67] Wilferd Madelung, "Assumption of the Title Shāhānshāh by the Būyids," 87–8; Bosworth, *New Islamic Dynasties*, 166–7.

[68] The book is also known as *Kitāb Maʿrifat ʿulamāʾ ahl Jurjān*, with the printed edition based on a single manuscript, housed at Oxford's Bodleian Library. Al-Sahmī's book was transmitted through oral and written means, and each part of the book carries its own colophon. These colophons name a transmitter as late as four or five generations after al-Sahmī, in the sixth/twelfth century. See the introduction by ʿAbd al-Raḥmān b. Yaḥyā

perceived a need to safeguard memory after seeing how scholars of other regions did so: "I did not see any of our senior scholars composing works in remembrance of the *ʿulamāʾ* of Jurjān or recording histories about them," he notes.[69] The scholars are shown in a variety of lights: as the companions of caliphs, as *qāḍī*s (judges) and ascetics, and as dreamers and travelers. Jurjān emerges as a hub of knowledge, with reports about the Prophet and the early generations of Muslims being repeated on its scholars' authority.

From the entries, one gets a picture of many microcommunities within Jurjān with their own separate memories, as al-Sahmī speaks of Jurjān's villages, markets, and streets and their associations. Take the case of Sufyān b. Saʿīd b. Masrūq al-Thawrī (d. 161/778) as an example. In al-Sahmī's book, one of Jurjān's villages is said to have strong connections to al-Thawrī and his lineage (in other works he is more closely associated with Kufa).[70] A Jurjānī source attests that al-Thawrī was born in Jurjān, moved to Kufa, and then came back to Jurjān, where he transmitted Hadith.[71] Among those who transmitted reports from him was Saʿd b. Saʿīd, "known as Saʿdwayh," for whom a mosque was built adjacent to Jurjān's congregational mosque.[72] One Abū Nuʿaym ʿAbd al-Malik b. ʿAbd Allāh al-Dihistānī al-Bābānī is said to have followed the *madhhab*, or legal school, of Sufyān al-Thawrī, suggesting the success of al-Thawrī's legal views in Jurjān.[73] The reputation of another scholar might be considered in question when al-Sahmī quotes Sufyān al-Thawrī as saying: "I passed by Jurjān when Jawāb al-Taymī was there, so I did not enter it."[74] More probably, however, as Christopher Melchert suggests, Sufyān al-Thawrī did not enter because, with Jawāb al-Taymī in it, the town had no need of his knowledge.[75]

In terms of affiliations (legal, sectarian, and otherwise), the scholars of Jurjān were a diverse lot. Many illustrious members of the Shāfiʿī

al-Yamānī in al-Sahmī, *Taʾrīkh Jurjān* (Hyderabad: Osmania Oriental Publications, 1950), alif-kāf-ḥāʾ. Whether al-Sahmī can bear credit for the unity of his manuscript is an open question.

69 Al-Sahmī, *Taʾrīkh Jurjān*, 4.

70 H. P. Raddatz, "Sufyān al-Thawrī," in *EI*[2].

71 Al-Sahmī, *Taʾrīkh Jurjān*, 174–6 (no. 338).

72 Ibid., 176 (no. 340).

73 Ibid., 236–7 (no. 469). On the nascent *madhhab* of al-Thawrī, its followers, and its presence in the biographical tradition, see Steven C. Judd, "Competitive Hagiography in Biographies of al-Awzāʿī and Sufyān al-Thawrī," *Journal of the American Oriental Society* 122, no. 1 (2002): 25–37.

74 Al-Sahmī, *Taʾrīkh Jurjān*, 131–2 (no. 221).

75 Oral communication, Oct. 2011.

school are mentioned, including a transmitter of al-Sahmī's book (ʿAbd al-Raḥmān b. al-Ḥusayn b. ʿAbd al-Raḥmān al-Shāfiʿī). When the caliph Hārūn al-Rashīd came to Jurjān, he brought with him Abū Yūsuf. We are told that Shujāʿ b. Ṣabīḥ al-Jurjānī, Jurjān's *muḥtasib* – a legal official whose jurisdiction included the markets – prayed behind Abū Yūsuf and praised his practice of the ritual, which pleased the jurist. Another Jurjānī posed him a question about Abū Ḥanīfa.[76] The partisans of Hadith as sources of law (*aṣḥāb al-ḥadīth*, juxtaposed with the *aṣḥāb al-raʾy*, or "proponents of opinion") are also mentioned, though the *aṣḥāb al-raʾy* are more prominent, likely signifying followers of Abū Ḥanīfa.[77] A Jurjānī traveled with Aḥmad b. Ḥanbal in the Yemen and was the first person to bring the Ḥanbalī legal tradition to Jurjān (*aẓhara madhhab al-ḥadīth bi-Jurjān*).[78] Numerous ʿAlids made their way to Jurjān, although it is hard to tell from al-Sahmī's text what, if any, sectarian or political designs they had. A descendant of ʿAlī and al-Ḥusayn reports that ʿĀʾisha, the Prophet's wife, was asked whom the Prophet had loved best (the Jurjānī connection here seems to be merely that al-Sahmī heard the report in Jurjān). She replied: "Among the men, ʿAlī. As for the women, it was Fāṭima."[79] She thus recognized the Prophet's affection for his family, the *ahl al-bayt*.[80] In another case, we are told that a descendant of ʿAlī named Muḥammad b. Jaʿfar came to Jurjān with the caliph al-Maʾmūn (r. 198–218/813–33) in 203 and died there in the same year; he figures in long chains of authorities backing up several reports about the Prophet and ʿAlī.[81]

The first generations of Jurjānīs spawned elite descendants. A certain settler named Ṭayfūr is named as a *mawlā* of the caliph al-Manṣūr (r. 136–58/754–75), and the *Taʾrīkh Jurjān* lists several of his children and his own *mawālī* who became landowners.[82] Scholarship ran particularly deep in certain families. Al-Sahmī went on the pilgrimage to Mecca twice with an Abū Saʿd from the Ismāʿīlī family, which adhered to the Shāfiʿī interpretation of Islamic law and features prominently in the

76 Al-Sahmī, *Taʾrīkh Jurjān*, 177 (no. 341) and 187–8 (no. 367).
77 Jeanette Wakin and A. Zysow, "Raʾy," in *EI*²; Bulliet, *View from the Edge*, 110–1.
78 Al-Sahmī, *Taʾrīkh Jurjān*, 334 (no. 627).
79 Ibid., 171–2 (no. 329).
80 On ʿĀʾisha and her memory among the Shiʿa, see D. A. Spellberg, *Politics, Gender, and the Islamic Past: The Legacy of ʿAʾisha bint Abi Bakr* (New York: Columbia University Press, 1994).
81 Al-Sahmī, *Taʾrīkh Jurjān*, 317–29 (no. 620).
82 Ibid., 193–4 (no. 380).

Ta'rīkh with twenty biographies of its members.[83] A picture of scholarly vibrancy and connection is maintained right up to al-Sahmī's own day. As might be expected, al-Sahmī's information on recent scholars is especially detailed. A jurist (*faqīh*) named Abū al-ʿAlāʾ al-Sirrī (b. 360/970–1), for example, was still evidently alive. His father had brought him to Mecca in 384/994–5, and he studied under teachers in Baghdad, Rayy, Hamadhān and Jurjān.[84]

As a whole, then, the book integrates many communities and their distinct experiences into a single account. There is virtually no sense of conflict between the different groups. Rather, al-Sahmī's picture is one of improbable equilibrium and concord.[85] The introduction to the book sets the stage by portraying Jurjān as ready and waiting for Islam and Muslim rule. History starts with prophetic genealogy: al-Sahmī states that the name Jurjān derives from a descendant of Noah who established settlements in the area (one Jurjān b. Lud b. Shem b. Noah). He says nothing more of its history before Islam and moves swiftly on to describe its conquest in the time of the caliph ʿUmar by Suwayd b. Muqarrin, who conquered Rayy, Qūmis, and then Jurjān (presumably in the late 630s and early 640s). The ruler of Jurjān, one Ruzbān Ṣūl (ancestor to al-Ṣūlī, the abovementioned courtier), made an agreement with Suwayd, according to which the Arabs would receive the *jizya* and war would end. Al-Sahmī provides a copy of the treaty[86] along with verses regarding Ṣūl's payment and then lists several companions of the Prophet who came to Jurjān afterward, among them major protagonists in the conflicts of the early community: ʿUmar's son ʿAbd Allāh; ʿAbd Allāh b. al-Zubayr, whose claims to the caliphate were remarkably successful in Arabia and Iraq but who was ultimately defeated by the Umayyad ʿAbd al-Malik in 73/692; and ʿAlī's two sons, al-Ḥusayn and al-Ḥasan.[87]

We learn that there was a second conquest in the year 98/716–17 during the rule of ʿAbd al-Malik's son Sulaymān (r. 96–9/715–17), but al-Sahmī does not explain why it was necessary to resubjugate the region. The effort this time was led by Yazīd b. al-Muhallab, who stayed for a

[83] On the Ismāʿīlī family, see Bulliet, *View from the Edge*, 102ff.

[84] Al-Sahmī, *Ta'rīkh Jurjān*, 185 (no. 360).

[85] There are cracks; for an example, see Bulliet, *View from the Edge*, 111.

[86] The treaty mentions Ruzbān Ṣūl and "the people of Dihistān and all those of Jurjān." Al-Sahmī, *Ta'rīkh Jurjān*, 4–6 (Sayf b. ʿUmar is named as a source). The text appears nearly verbatim in al-Ṭabarī's reporting, also citing Sayf b. ʿUmar as a source; al-Ṭabarī does not pass on the poem. Al-Ṭabarī, *Ta'rīkh*, I:2658–9.

[87] Al-Sahmī, *Ta'rīkh Jurjān*, 6–8.

year until ʿUmar b. ʿAbd al-ʿAzīz, Sulaymān's successor upon his death, recalled him from Jurjān. During this year, al-Sahmī reports, Yazīd undertook extensive urban projects, building the city wall and marking out the boundaries for approximately forty mosques.[88] Some pages later, the locations of Jurjān's mosques, as established in Umayyad times, are given in detail. Their names connect their origins especially to the Arab tribes that played a leading role in the settlement of Jurjān; in cases where a mosque had acquired a different name in his day, al-Sahmī makes a note of it.[89] As Parvaneh Pourshariati has observed, "the historical memory of al-Sahmī of the Arab conquest and the short rule of the Umayyads over Gurgān was extremely vivid" nearly four hundred years afterward.[90]

But despite the smooth image that al-Sahmī gives of the conquests, we have every reason to believe that Jurjān was not easily conquered, nor was it always the epitome of social equilibrium. Rather, al-Sahmī has carefully collected reports from his predecessors, Sayf b. ʿUmar included, to stress the orderliness and continuity of the conquests and the government that followed. Regarding the "second" conquest, for example, al-Sahmī features, well into his book, a biography of a grandson of Ṣūl that contains a story about how Ṣūl surrendered to Yazīd b. al-Muhallab and asked to be brought to Sulaymān b. ʿAbd al-Malik so that he might convert to Islam. As an account of Ṣūl's conversion, this report was valuable to his family, but since it placed the conquest nearly eighty years later than Sayf b. ʿUmar, al-Sahmī omitted it from the book's introduction.[91] What is more, al-Sahmī leaves out the violence, rebellions, and conflict that other sources report. So, for example, he does not feature the widely reported bloody subjugation of the region by Yazīd b. al-Muhallab.[92] Yazīd and the Muhallabid clan were servants of the Umayyad state and reportedly involved in its complex politics, including disputes with the notorious governor al-Ḥajjāj over the revenues of the provinces, especially Khurāsān. Yazīd had a staunch enemy in al-Ḥajjāj and a rival in Qutayba b. Muslim, who played a leading role in the consolidation and

88 Ibid., 9.

89 Ibid., 16–17.

90 Parvaneh Pourshariati, "Local Histories of Khurāsān and the Pattern of Arab Settlement," *Studia Iranica* 27, no. 1 (1998): 54–7.

91 See al-Sahmī, *Taʾrīkh Jurjān*, 194 (no. 381) for al-Ṭayyib b. Muḥammad b. Ṣūl al-Jurjānī. Cf. Bulliet, *View from the Edge*, 43–4 and 214, n. 10. Al-Sahmī cites in this entry a work by the Samanid historian al-Sallāmī (fl. mid-fourth/tenth c.). Al-Sallāmī's works are quoted by other historians but do not survive as independent texts. Bosworth, "al-Sallamī," in *EI²*.

92 E.g., al-Ṭabarī, *Taʾrīkh*, II:1317ff. Also noted by Pourshariati in "Local Histories of Khurāsān," 54–5.

expansion of Muslim rule in Khurāsān and Central Asia.[93] The ʿAbbasid era traditionists, al-Ṭabarī included, report extensively on the Muhallabids, as do later traditionists, such as Ibn Isfandiyār in his history of neighboring Ṭabaristān.[94]

Al-Sahmī's picture, by contrast, is innocent of conflict, presenting Yazīd b. al-Muhallab as a noble, uncomplicated man who undertook building projects for Jurjān. Al-Sahmī's reports stress Yazīd's generosity and lack of greed – as if to protest against claims that he seized taxes for his own benefit. As military ruler (*amīr*), for example, he was visited by ʿIkrima, an elderly member of the second generation of Muslims, who appealed for help and was presented with a handsome payment.

Given the challenges that Jurjān must have faced in al-Sahmī's own day – both from its neighbors and from the various groups residing within its borders – his reaching into the past for a common history seems entirely reasonable. For the chaotic world in which he lived, a simple beginning was preferable. The region's illustrious early history probably did seem, as he says, increasingly remote and subject to forgetfulness. The people of Jurjān needed a reminder of the lineages that held them together and gave them a sense of membership in and belonging to Jurjān. The inclusion of so many different groups within the biographical entries accomplishes this, as does the account of the generations of settlers and visitors who followed Yazīd. And so, following his account of the second conquest, al-Sahmī details members of the generation that succeeded the Prophet's companions who came to Jurjān, the lineage of Yazīd, a Hadith transmitted on his authority, his good deeds, the names of the Umayyads' governors and the lengths of their stays in Jurjān, the demarcation of Jurjān's mosques in Umayyad times, the ʿAbbasids who came to Jurjān, and the reigns of their governors.

While depicting common origins and minimizing conflict, al-Sahmī has also provided a picture that confirms his readers' manifestly different identities. With the pre-Islamic past effaced, they belong to communities that are defined not only by shared Muslim origins but also by common lineages that include family, scholarship, and locality from region down to town, village, and even street and alleyway. Jurjān's scholars traveled widely, receiving knowledge from far-flung locales; equally, knowledge traveled from afar to Jurjān. In this way, very particular identities, as

93 See P. Crone, "Muhallabids," in *EI*[2]; Borrut, *Entre mémoire et pouvoir*, 260ff.

94 Ibn Isfandiyār, *Tārīkh-i Ṭabaristān*, ed. ʿAbbās Iqbāl, 2 vols. in 1 (Tehran: Majlis, [1941]), 1:161ff.; *An Abridged Translation of the History of Ṭabaristán Compiled about A.H. 613 (A.D. 1216) by Muḥammad b. al-Ḥasan b. Isfandiyár*, trans. Edward G. Browne (Leiden: E. J. Brill, 1905), 105–9.

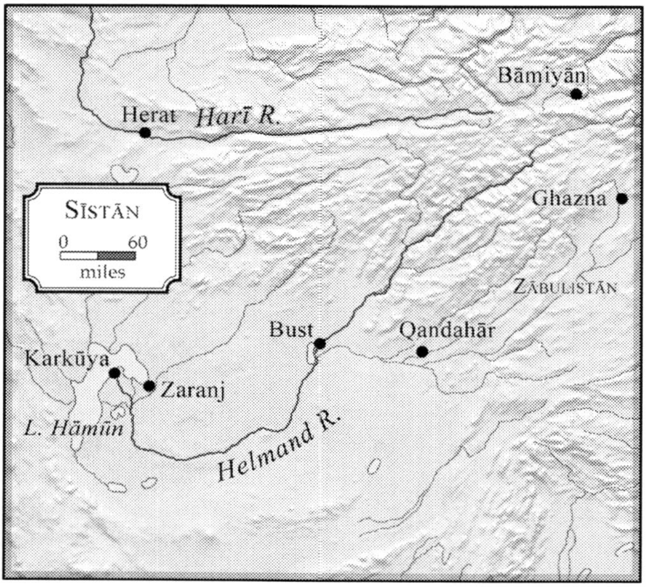

MAP 3.2. Sīstān

small places in a big world, are shown to go hand in hand with a Muslim identity. This emphasis on the particular and the local also helps explain why al-Sahmī makes little of ethnicity – Arab, Persian, or Turkish – as a common bond.[95] In troubled times, al-Sahmī has therefore negotiated a vision of the past that unites the Jurjānīs.

Violence Remembered: A Plea for Good Rulers

The story of a locality's conquest often helps explain its subsequent history. This history may take on a nostalgic hue, as with Jurjān, but the conquest may also shed light on a troubled history that follows it. In this next case, a traditionist shows his region's destiny for Islam and early devotion to the cause but also depicts the conquests' ambivalent outcome, describing how the region's residents suffered under Umayyad and ʿAbbasid governors. His audience likely included its present ruling classes.

95 The same may probably be said for other local histories. The prestige of the Arabs that persisted even in al-Sahmī's day is reflected, however, by a Hadith that al-Sahmī quotes in his entry for Aḥmad b. Abī Aḥmad al-Jurjānī, who transmitted his book (*Taʾrīkh Jurjān*, 25, no. 10): "The Prophet spoke Arabic well and treated the half-blood with scorn."

The region of Sijistān (Middle Persian Sakastān/Sakistān, "Land of the Sakas," then in new Persian Sīstān) lies south of Khurāsān and straddles the modern border between Iran and Afghanistan. It was the setting for some of the most dramatic moments in Persian epic tradition, featuring the legendary noble warrior Rustam, who tragically slew his son Sohrab in ignorance.[96] During the reign of the caliph ʿUthmān, the Arabs pushed from neighboring Kirmān across the southern part of the desert known as the Dasht-i Lūṭ and entered Sīstān, in 31/651–2 taking the town of Zaranj. In early Umayyad times, ʿAbd Allāh b. al-Zubayr found support in Sīstān for his claims to the caliphate, and in 72/691–2, a Zubayrid governor of Sīstān minted drachms featuring the Muslim *shahāda*, or statement of faith, in Pahlavi script – this five years prior to the coinage reform of the Umayyad caliph ʿAbd al-Malik, which began in 77/696–7.[97] Under the Umayyads and ʿAbbasids, Muslim armies passed through Sīstān en route to the virtuous fight against non-Muslims. It was also a notorious home to Khārijite rebellions and a challenge to govern. The Saffarid autonomous governate emerged in Sīstān in the second half of the third/ninth century and subsequently ruled a military empire that lasted for nearly 150 years. In 393/1003, Sīstān was folded into the Ghaznavid empire, though a local line of amirs, known as the Maliks of Nīmrūz (Nīmrūz being an ancient name for Sīstān), continued to rule into Seljuk times.[98]

Arabic sources composed outside of the region depict the conquest of Zaranj as bloody. Under the leadership of al-Rabīʿ b. Ziyād al-Ḥārithī the Arabs fought the townspeople for some time and then besieged them. Finally, the governor overseeing the area's defense (*marzubān*),[99] known

[96] Yarshater, "Iranian National History," 453–7.

[97] On the coins, see Malek Iradj Mochiri, "A Pahlavi Forerunner of the Umayyad Reformed Coinage," *Journal of the Royal Asiatic Society*, n.s., 113, no. 2 (1981): 168–72 and Stefan Heidemann, "Numismatics," in *The New Cambridge History of Islam*, vol. 1, *The Formation of the Islamic World, Sixth to Eleventh Centuries*, edited by Chase F. Robinson, 648–63, 775–9, and plates (Cambridge: Cambridge University Press, 2010), 654–5. On classes of early Muslim coins in Sīstān, see Stuart D. Sears, "The Sasanian Style Drachms of Sistan," *Yarmouk Numismatics* 11 (1999): 18–28.

[98] Bosworth, *New Islamic Dynasties*, 172–3; Hugh Kennedy, *The Great Arab Conquests: How the Spread of Islam Changed the World We Live In* (London: Weidenfeld & Nicolson, 2007), 185–7; see also Bosworth, *Sīstān under the Arabs: From the Islamic Conquest to the Rise of the Ṣaffārids (30–250/651–864)* (Rome: Istituto italiano per il Medio ed Estremo Oriente, Centro studi e scavi archeologici in Asia, 1968), 16–18, for what follows.

[99] The title has different senses in the Arabic sources, but it broadly refers to a Sasanian regional governor with responsibilities that varied at different times and locales, often including those of a military character; see J. H. Kramers and M. Morony, "Marzpān,"

as Aparvīz (Persian for "victorious," "glorious"), sought a guarantee of safety so that he might negotiate a peace agreement. Al-Rabīʿ – a "dark complexioned, broad-mouthed and tall" man – made a chair for himself out of the bodies of two slain men, and his companions did likewise. When the *marzubān* saw al-Rabīʿ, seated in this way, he was terrified and agreed to turn over one thousand servants, each one bearing a vessel of gold.[100]

This story was told in Sīstān itself, but the anonymous fifth/eleventh-century *Tārīkh-i Sīstān* provides a richer account. This Persian-language work narrates the history of the region from the earliest of times, as a caliphal province, and then as a subject of the different empires that ruled Sīstān afterward.[101] The largest part of the text runs to 448/1062 – about a generation after the *Taʾrīkh Jurjān* – ending during the reign of the first of the Maliks of Nīmrūz (Tāj al-Dīn Abū al-Faḍl Naṣr b. Aḥmad [r. 429–65/1038–73]). Its author worked in a literary environment, and his book, an early example of Persian prose, mentions a variety of sources. These include, among others, the Zoroastrian *Bundahishn*; a now-lost *Kitāb-i Garshāsp* by Abū al-Muʾayyad Balkhī (fl. second half of the fourth/tenth century);[102] a work entitled *Siyar mulūk al-ʿAjam* by Ibn al-Muqaffaʿ (presumably his version of the *Xwadāy-nāmag*); Qudāma b. Jaʿfar's (d. 337/948) *Kitāb al-Kharāj*;[103] a *Kitāb Anbiyā* by one ʿAlī b. Muḥammad Ṭabarī;[104] and the *Shāh-nāmah* of Firdawsī. The

in *EI*², and Ph. Gignoux, "L'organisation administrative sasanide: Le cas du *marzbān*," *Jerusalem Studies in Arabic and Islam* 4 (1984): 1–29.

100 The story traveled. See esp. al-Balādhurī, *al-Buldān wa-futūḥuhā*, 439; Qudāma b. Jaʿfar, *Kitāb al-Kharāj wa-ṣināʿat al-kitāba*, ed. Muḥammad Ḥusayn al-Zubaydī (Baghdad: Dār al-Rashīd, 1981), 393; and Ibn al-Athīr, *al-Kāmil fī al-taʾrīkh*, 3:100–2. However, compare with, among others, Khalīfa b. Khayyāṭ al-ʿUṣfurī, *Taʾrīkh*, ed. Suhayl Zakkār, 2 vols. (Damascus: Wizārat al-Thaqāfa wa-l-Siyāḥa wa-l-Irshād al-Qawmī, 1967–8), 197.

101 At one point, the author says of his apparent contemporary, the Seljuk Ṭughril (d. 455/1063), "May God perpetuate his rule!" *Tārīkh-i Sīstān*, ed. Malik al-Shuʿarā Bahār (Tehran: Khāvar, 1935), 373. Throughout this chapter, I also cite Milton Gold's translation (Rome: Istituto italiano per il Medio ed Estremo Oriente, 1976) (here p. 305), which I have lightly edited.

102 He is also credited with a prose *Shāh-nāmah*, and scholars of Persian literature have assumed that the book mentioned in the *Tārīkh-i Sīstān* represented a part of it. See G. Lazard, "Abu'l-Moʾayyad Balk̲ī," in *EIr*.

103 That is, the *Kitāb al-Kharāj wa-ṣināʿat al-kitāba*, cited above. On this work, see Paul L. Heck, *The Construction of Knowledge in Islamic Civilization: Qudāma b. Jaʿfar and his Kitāb al-kharāj wa-ṣināʿat al-kitāba* (Leiden: Brill, 2002).

104 Identification uncertain; the editor, Bahār, does not incline to Muḥammad b. Jarīr al-Ṭabarī and introduces other possibilities. *Tārīkh-i Sīstān*, 9, n. 3.

work provides a detailed picture of Khārijites in Sīstān as well as of the rise and fall of the Saffarids, including the reigns of Yaʿqūb b. al-Layth al-Ṣaffār (r. 247–65/861–79) and ʿAmr b. al-Layth (r. 265–87/879–900). As a source, the book has been extensively mined for histories of these rulers, of the region, and also of Persian letters.[105]

The book says that al-Rabīʿ was sent to Sīstān (here meaning Zaranj)[106] by ʿAbd Allāh b. ʿĀmir, who was a key player in the early empire's administration.[107] En route, al-Rabīʿ demanded of a local ruler, "You must show me the road to Sīstān." The ruler replied: "Behold! This is the way. After you ford the Helmand River, you will see the desert. After crossing the desert, you will come upon the gravelly area; and from there, the fortress and outlying districts of the city are visible."[108] Al-Rabīʿ followed these directions and, once across the river, engaged in a furious battle with many casualties suffered by both the Muslims and the Sīstānīs, but more by the Muslims. The Muslims charged again, whereupon the Sīstānīs retreated into the city. At this point, the "Shāh of Sīstān," named by the *Tārīkh* as Īrān b. Rustam b. Āzādkhū b. Bakhtiyār (rather than Aparvīz), summoned the chief Zoroastrian priest (*mūʾbad-i mūʾbadān*) and the nobles of Sīstān and said:

> This is not a matter that will pass in a day, or a year, or even a thousand years: this much is clear from our books. [On the contrary] their religion and their earthly power will last unto eternity. And there is nothing to be gained by killing and waging war, for no one can alter what is Heaven's decree. So our solution is to make peace.[109]

105 Julie Scott Meisami, *Persian Historiography to the End of the Twelfth Century* (Edinburgh: Edinburgh University Press, 1999), 108–40; C. Edmund Bosworth, "Sistan and Its Local Histories," *Iranian Studies* 33, no. 1/2 (2000): 34–5. Bosworth concludes that the author of the *Tārīkh* was "apparently unaware of the standard, general" sources for "Eastern Islamic history, such as Ṭabari, Ṭabari-Balʿami, Masʿūdi, Sallami, etc., or of near-contemporary and contemporary Ghaznavid authors like ʿOtbi, Gardizi, and Abu'l-Fażl Bayhaqi." Bosworth, "Tāri̱k-e Sistān," in *EIr*. Several studies have drawn on the book; see especially Bosworth, *The History of the Saffarids of Sistan and the Maliks of Nimruz (247/861 to 949/1542–3)* (Costa Mesa, CA: Mazda Publishers, 1994); Bosworth, *Sīstān under the Arabs*; Deborah G. Tor, "Historical Representations of Ya'qūb b. al-Layth: A Reappraisal," *Journal of the Royal Asiatic Society*, 3rd ser., 12, no. 3 (2002): 247–75; and Tor, "A Numismatic History of the First Saffarid Dynasty (AH 247–300/AD 861–911)," *Numismatic Chronicle*, 7th ser., 162 (2002): 293–314.

106 The *Tārīkh* consistently refers to Zaranj as Sīstān.

107 H. A. R. Gibb, "ʿAbd Allāh b. ʿĀmir," in *EI*².

108 *Tārīkh-i Sīstān*, 80; Gold, 63–4.

109 *Tārīkh-i Sīstān*, 81; Gold, 64.

The Sīstānīs agreed with their Shāh, who sent an envoy to al-Rabīʿ with the following message:

> We are not powerless to wage war, for this is a land of brave men and warriors (*pahlavāns*). But [for all that], we cannot fight against the Almighty (*khudā-yi ta ʿallā*), and yours is the army of God. We have read in our books about your appearance and that of Muḥammad and thus we know that this reign [of yours, *dawlat*] will endure for a long time. So the proper thing to do is to make peace in order that the killing on both sides will cease.[110]

Al-Rabīʿ agreed to make peace and ordered his army to desist. He gave orders for the slain to be covered with garments and for a mound to be made of their bodies, with a place to sit, also composed of bodies, atop it. Once this was done, al-Rabīʿ climbed upon the mound and sat down. Īrān b. Rustam arrived with his nobles and the chief *mobadh*. They dismounted from their horses and stood, watching al-Rabīʿ, "a tall, swarthy man, with large teeth and thick lips." Beholding the gory scene, Īrān said to his companions, invoking the devil of Zoroastrian cosmology: "It is said that Ahriman is not visible in the daytime. Behold, Ahriman became visible, there is no doubt about it!" When an interpreter informed al-Rabīʿ about the Persian's remarks, al-Rabīʿ "laughed heartily." Then, Īrān greeted al-Rabīʿ but refused to come close to his "dais" (*ṣadr*) because it was "unclean" (*na-pākīzih*). Instead, he and his companions spread out some pieces of cloth on the ground, sat down, and proceeded to work out a deal with al-Rabīʿ that involved Īrān promising to pay one million dirhams annually to the caliph on behalf of the people of Sīstān, and in the current year to buy a thousand slave girls and in the hands of each place a golden goblet as a gift for the caliph. This deal was put in writing, after which al-Rabīʿ climbed down and entered Sīstān in complete safety.[111] From there, he moved on to Bust, where he was more forcefully resisted.

With the added dialogue and details, the *Tārīkh-i Sīstān* presents the locals' defeat as foreseen. The Sīstānīs fight but know the fruitlessness of their struggle against Muslim occupation. They even make peace because the invading armies represent the religion that they have been awaiting.

110 Ibid.

111 *Tārīkh-i Sīstān*, 82; Gold, 65. Although he discusses the conquest under al-Rabīʿ and cites the *Tārīkh-i Sīstān* as one of his main sources (al-Balādhurī being another), Bosworth omits this scene from his account. Bosworth, *Sīstān under the Arabs*, 16–17.

Such a teleology on a local scale is apparent in the first pages of the text, in which the author describes the merits (*faḍā'il*) of Sīstān. Sīstān's greatest claim to superiority derives from the fact that it was the first province in Persia where Muḥammad's "name and his message were talked about by all, notables and common people alike (*khāṣṣ wa-ʿāmm*)."[112] A teleological vision also underpins the report that Sīstān's founder, Garshāsp – aware of what history would deliver for his region – laid the foundation stone and orders were given that the city should be constructed to last for four thousand years.[113] Reaching even further back in search of portents of Sīstān's fate, the *Tārīkh* finds the province singled out already in prophetic history. When Adam left the island of Ceylon in search of Eve, he stopped in Sīstān.[114] When Noah sailed the earth in his ark, he moored his ship at Sīstān, where the dove brought news that the waters were receding; in the ark, a grateful Noah prayed for Sīstān.[115] When Solomon ordered the wind to carry him and his army around the world, he paused for a meal in Sīstān, where he said: "Of all the various places to which we have traveled, here is the most pleasant. The world today rests on justice and not on injustice because the people of the world have become equal through religion."[116]

The first eighty or so pages of the Persian text, which cover events up to and including the conquest, thus provide an overarching prophetic and Islamic framework for the province's history. Garshāsp, a figure of eastern Iranian legend, is identified in Adam's lineage[117] and so is given a place in prophetic genealogy – whereas in roughly the same period, ʿAlī b. Aḥmad Asadī Ṭūsī (d. ca. 465/1072–3) completed his *Garshāsp-nāmah*, an epic poem complementary to Firdawsī's *Shāh-nāmah* that places Garshāsp in an Iranian lineage.[118] In the *Tārīkh-i Sīstān*, Adam's descendants,

[112] Or perhaps the first place anywhere. *Tārīkh-i Sīstān*, 3; Gold, 2.

[113] Ibid.

[114] *Tārīkh-i Sīstān*, 9; Gold, 6 (citing ʿAlī b. Muḥammad Ṭabarī). Cf. al-Ṭabarī, *Ta'rīkh*, I:119ff.

[115] *Tārīkh-i Sīstān*, 9–10; Gold, 7.

[116] *Tārīkh-i Sīstān*, 10; Gold, 7. After mentioning Solomon's visit, the *Tārīkh* notes: "It was from this that the Khārijites conceived the difference between 'the abode of injustice' (*dār-i jawr*) and the 'abode of justice' (*dār-i ʿadl*)."

[117] "Garshāsp b. Asrat b. Shahr b. Kūrang b. Bīdāsb b. Tūr b. King Jamshīd b. Nūnjahān b. Īnjad b. Ūshang (Hūshang) b. Farāwak b. Siyāmak b. Mūsā b. Kayūmarth (Gayūmart), and Kayūmarth was Adam." *Tārīkh-i Sīstān*, 2 and n. 3; Gold, 1.

[118] ʿAlī b. Aḥmad Asadī Ṭūsī, *Garshāsp-nāmah*, ed. Ḥabīb Yaghmā'ī (Tehran: Kitābkhānah-i Ṭahūrī, 1975). Asadī says in the epilogue to the poem that he completed it in

including Garshāsp, followed the faith of their father, praying "at dawn, at sunset, and at night"; among them, adultery, sodomy, theft, and unjust killing were forbidden. They knew the right way to slaughter animals for eating, gave of their wealth liberally, and were hospitable to guests. And they did not "marry daughter, sister, or mother." But the birth of Muḥammad represented the most important event for the history of Sīstān, with many of the most important scholars of Islam hailing from this region. The *Tārīkh* provides a generous list of such scholars, with its author apologizing that space constraints prevent him from elaborating on it.[119]

As for the story about al-Rabīʿ and the mound of bodies, the *Tārīkh* describes the Sīstānīs' terror and also presents their perspective: although the conquering army brought Islam, the imposing and heartless figure of al-Rabīʿ seemed a lot like Ahriman, the demon adversary in the cosmology of the "Good Religion," as Zoroastrians know their faith. The Sīstānīs, we are led to believe, saw events through two lenses simultaneously. On the one hand, given the region's deep, antique connections to Islam, they understood the macrocosmic forces at work. On the other hand, as Zoroastrians, they perceived the Muslims, by their grotesque behavior, as taking the place of Ahriman. They stood their ground as Zoroastrians, avoiding the unclean "dais," but they surrendered due to their knowledge of and sympathy for Islam. In effect, although the author does not refer here to the Sīstānīs as Muslims, he depicts them as having appreciated its internal core.[120] With al-Rabīʿ atop the mound of bodies, he has also presented a moving image of their subjugation.

Immediately after the conquests, the *Tārīkh* shows Sīstān to have been home to a dynamic and principled community that included many *ʿulamāʾ*, such as the abovementioned al-Ḥasan al-Baṣrī. During Muʿāwiya's days, Sīstān's governor was a man who administered with "justice and equity" and promoted the teaching of the Qurʾan and exegesis. Because of his virtuous example, many Zoroastrians converted to Islam. With al-Ḥasan, the governor set up a treasury with secretaries, accountants, a collector of taxes, regulators of accounts, inspectors, and other trustworthy officials, and he also waged war in Bust and Rukhad (a

458/1066. He does have material relating to Adam and prophetic history in his work. On Asadī's text, see the summaries of scholarship by François de Blois, "Garšāsp-nāma," in *EIr* and by Bosworth, "Sistan and Its Local Histories," 33 and 35–6.

119 *Tārīkh-i Sīstān*, 18–21; Gold, 14–15.

120 See where the author refers to the Sīstānīs' Islam before the appearance of Muḥammad; *Tārīkh-i Sīstān*, 38; Gold, 27.

territory in southeastern Afghanistan, around the later city of Qandahār) against recalcitrant rulers who refused to submit to Muslim rule.[121] When the governor's successor arrived with orders to kill the Zoroastrians' chief priest and to stamp out their fires, the Sistānīs successfully defended the Zoroastrians to imperial authorities in Damascus on the basis of the toleration of the Prophet and the first four caliphs.[122] During the struggle between ʿAlī and Muʿāwiya, they debated in the company of al-Ḥasan how to correctly conduct the Friday prayer and the *khuṭba*, or sermon, in which the ruler is acknowledged.[123]

By contrast, the *Tārīkh-i Sīstān* portrays Muslims from outside Sīstān as consistently failing to live up to the ideals of the faith. The internal problems of the early caliphate are elaborated and the murder of the Prophet's grandson al-Ḥusayn and members of his entourage at Karbala movingly recalled. As his head is carried back to Syria, the Umayyad party stays overnight with a Christian monk who reprimands them: "You are an evil band because if Jesus had had a son, we would have revered him." The monk pays a large sum to keep the head in his possession overnight; he cleanses it and pours a mixture of rosewater, musk, and camphor through its passages, kisses it, and weeps until morning, whereupon he professes Islam and becomes a client (*mawlā*) of al-Ḥusayn.[124] The Sīstānīs experience much violence at the hands of rulers from outside the territory, as well as treachery and extortion. They are shown to be surprisingly forbearing, as Sīstān is placed under the control of different governors. While a few are virtuous, many squeeze the province for its revenues. The reign of al-Ḥajjāj is particularly trying. For the author of the *Tārīkh*, the failures of Muḥammad's successors seem to explain the origin of the Khārijites in general and in Sīstān in particular. With empathy, he explains the Khārijites' case, as he says of them:

> The battles that took place among the Muslims, and the things that happened for which no justification could be found in the Qurʾan or in the traditions of Muḥammad, shocked these people. Yet there were more things each day. First, there was what happened to the Commander of the Believers, ʿUthmān, when the intimates [of the Prophet] gathered together and denounced him, and matters

121 Bosworth, "al-Rukhkhadj," in *EI*²; *Tārīkh-i Sīstān*, 91–2; Gold, 73–4. Regarding al-Ḥasan in the *Tārīkh-i Sīstān*, see Mourad, *Early Islam between Myth and History*, 115, and Bosworth, *Sīstān under the Arabs*, 22–3, 25–6 (emphasizing al-Ḥasan's Persianness).

122 *Tārīkh-i Sīstān*, 92–3; Gold, 74–5.

123 *Tārīkh-i Sīstān*, 89; Gold, 71–2.

124 *Tārīkh-i Sīstān*, 98–9; Gold, 78–80.

> arrived at such a state that he was assassinated. Then the Battle of the Camel and the killing of Ṭalḥa and Zubayr, and the killing of other notables on both sides; then the opposition of Muʿāwiya, the battle of Ṣiffīn, the matter of the two arbitrations, the simple-mindedness of Abū Mūsā Ashʿarī, the duplicity of ʿAmr b. al-ʿĀṣ, and the assassination of the Commander of the Believers, ʿAlī b. Abī Ṭālib; the rallying of the mob around Muʿāwiya and the deposal of [Ḥasan b. ʿAlī and the killing of][125] Ḥusayn b. ʿAlī and all the children and descendants of Muṣṭafā [i.e., Muḥammad] during the reign of Yazīd b. Muʿāwiya; followed by the cutting off of the head of Ḥusayn and the transporting of the womenfolk of Muṣṭafā, unveiled, to Syria, and the striking with a rod of Ḥusayn's mouth and teeth, which Muṣṭafā had covered with thousands of kisses... and other such things which, were we to mention them all, would prolong the story.[126]

The Khārijites, we learn, deserted the rulers, having judged that there should be a limit to such evildoing. The people of Sīstān rallied to their cause when a powerful man by the name of Qaṭarī b. al-Fujāʾa, an Arab noble and prince (*az sādāt wa-ṣanādīd-i ʿArab*), sent agents to Sīstān explaining "what evils were being introduced into Islam."[127]

The *Tārīkh*'s account of al-Rabīʿ's conquest, occurring at the very beginning of what Clifford Edmund Bosworth termed the "historical" part of the text, thus lays the groundwork for a picture of the early Islamic state and the way that its rulers dominated the principled people of Sīstān. Accordingly, the well-documented unruliness of Sīstān as the home of the Khārijites is traced to outside causes. The tone of the book changes correspondingly when the author turns to Sīstān's homegrown governors, the Saffarids, who reigned in the region from 247/861 to 393/1003. Their route to power is paved by the Khārijite Ḥamza b. ʿAbd Allāh, "a man of learning" (*ʿālim*), who stopped the province's tax payments to Baghdad once and for all. In an exchange of letters with Hārūn al-Rashīd, Ḥamza appears as a religiously principled man who accepts no authority save God and the Qurʾan and accuses the caliph's servants: "They have taken lives, confiscated property, and committed debauchery, and other acts which God prohibits man from doing."[128] Yaʿqūb b. al-Layth

125 The bracketed text was added by Bahār.

126 *Tārīkh-i Sīstān*, 109–10; Gold, 87–8.

127 *Tārīkh-i Sīstān*, 109–10; Gold, 88.

128 Ḥamza decides against fighting the people of the city of Sīstān (Zaranj) when he hears their morning prayers. He challenges Hārūn al-Rashīd's governor to a fight, but the latter goes into hiding. Ḥamza then summons the people and says: "Do not give another dirham in taxes and goods to the governor, because he will not be able to see to your safety. I don't want anything from you, and I shall not take anything from you, because I shall not remain in any one place." The *Tārīkh-i Sīstān* then states: "And from that day to the present, no longer would revenue and tribute arrive in Baghdad from Sīstān.

then emerges somewhat further along in the narrative out of a rebellion born in Bust. His Iranian genealogy shows his illustrious descent from the Sasanian line and runs all the way back to Gayūmart.[129] The ʿAbbasid rulers are expelled, and then Yaʿqūb turns on the Khārijites and various other enemies who are plundering Sīstān. A golden era follows as Yaʿqūb levies taxes, establishes governorships, and sets up an administration for the welfare of the Sīstānīs. He distributes money to the poor. But most notably, he fights on behalf of Sīstān and Islam, extending the dominion of Sīstān far and wide.[130] He receives envoys from throughout the world, including from Ethiopia and Byzantium.[131] The first post-conquest Persian poetry is recited because Yaʿqūb could not understand an Arabic poem in his honor. A poet praised him after he killed a Khārijite rebel named ʿAmmār:

> Eve gave birth to no one, and Adam sired no one, with a lion's heart and a majestic nature such as yours.
>
> You are the miracle of the Prophet of Mecca in deed, in thought, and in word.
>
> And the great day will come when ʿAmmār will proclaim: "I am the one who was killed by Yaʿqūb.[132]

Within the book as a whole, Yaʿqūb, and to a lesser extent his brother ʿAmr, stand out as the only rulers who rule with justice, protect, and enforce the state's administration with "the word, the whip, and the sword."[133] Yaʿqūb, the text affirms, prayed devoutly, gave alms generously, never cast a licentious glance at women or youths, protected women

Eventually, an agreement was reached whereby the people of the city remained under the caliph Rashīd; the *khuṭba* continued to be said [in his name], and the *khuṭba* still continued to be said in the name of the Banū ʿAbbās. However, the flow of revenue was cut off." *Tārīkh-i Sīstān*, 156–8 and 166; Gold, 123–5 and 133.

129 *Tārīkh-i Sīstān*, 200–2; Gold, 159–60.

130 The caliph al-Muʿtamid (r. 256–79/870–92) recognizes Yaʿqūb's authority with patents. When the people of Nīshāpūr complain that he has no such patent for Nīshāpūr, he asks its notables: "Has not this sword established the caliph in Baghdad?" When they reply affirmatively, he continues: "This same sword has also established me here, thus my patent and that of the caliph are one and the same." *Tārīkh-i Sīstān*, 216–23; Gold, 171–7.

131 *Tārīkh-i Sīstān*, 231; Gold, 182–3.

132 *Tārīkh-i Sīstān*, 212; Gold, 168. On this moment in the *Tārīkh*, see Jerome W. Clinton, "A Sketch of Translation and the Formation of New Persian Literature," in *Iran and Iranian Studies: Essays in Honor of Iraj Afshar*, ed. Kambiz Eslami, 288–305 (Princeton, NJ: Zagros, 1998), at 292, esp. n. 10.

133 *Tārīkh-i Sīstān*, 279; Gold, 223.

from his soldiers, and was attentive to economic prosperity, social peace, and the relationship of government officials to the people.[134]

Seen in the context of the book as a whole, then, the story of al-Rabīʿ's conquest functions as an originary metaphor through which the author shows the receptivity of the Sīstānīs to Islam and critiques the virtues of those who came from outside the region. Sīstān appears as an ideal place for Islam to flourish, as acknowledged by the prophets and as evidenced by its early history. The ʿAbbasid state is "founded upon treachery and deceit," says Yaʿqūb.[135] For the *Tārīkh* the great tragedy is that the heirs of Yaʿqūb and ʿAmr failed to live up to the Saffarid legacy in every measurable dimension. The governate's fall to the "Turks" (i.e., the Ghaznavids and the Seljuks) is movingly related and follows a fractious period. The *Tārīkh*'s author laments: "The people fell upon evil days, and so things have remained, and only Almighty God knows when things will change."[136]

We do not know who wrote the *Tārīkh-i Sīstān*, and internal evidence suggests that the text includes additions by later hands. Still, the part of the book that covers the period from Sīstān's pre-Islamic history until at least the late 1040s–early 1050s seems to be a single-authored work, as the text repeats annalistically and with painstaking detail the political history of the province, especially the comings and goings of its Umayyad and ʿAbbasid governors, the various revolts, and antagonisms internal to Sīstān.[137] The author himself is clearly wearying of the wars Sīstān has suffered.[138] It seems that he had in mind an audience knowledgeable about and interested in such elaborate detail; that is, he was addressing first and foremost Sīstān's present ruling classes, including the Maliks of Nīmrūz. Like dynastic histories and the genre of "mirrors for princes," then, the text demonstrates the benefits that come to virtuous

[134] See especially a separate section praising the virtues of Yaʿqub in *Tārīkh-i Sīstān*, 263–8; Gold, 209–14. Bosworth's description of the *Tārīkh-i Sīstān* as "essentially a secular history" underestimates the book's prophetic framework as well as this picture, satisfying to Sīstān, of the virtues of Yaʿqūb. Bosworth, "Sistan and Its Local Histories," 37. Cf. Tor, "Historical Representations of Yaʿqūb b. al-Layth al-Ṣaffār."

[135] "Do you not see what these people [the ʿAbbasids] have done to Abū Salama, Abū Muslim, the Barmakid clan, and Faḍl b. Sahl, despite the fact that these men served them well? One should not trust this dynasty!" *Tārīkh-i Sīstān*, 267–8; Gold, 213.

[136] *Tārīkh-i Sīstān*, 354; Gold, 289.

[137] On the text's composition, see Meisami, *Persian Historiography*, esp. 131–4. Meisami identifies three separate authors, distinguished by style and thematic interests, the second and third continuing the work from 445/1053 on. Cf. Bosworth, "Tārik̲-e Sistān," and Bosworth, "Sistan and Its Local Histories," 34–5.

[138] Cf. Gold, xxvi–xxvii.

administration and the cooperation of the Sīstānīs with good governance, and it makes a plea that its current rulers not exploit Sīstān. Although pride is a major factor in the composition of the work, its ends are also practical: protecting the people of Sīstān from rapacious government.[139]

Comparing our two local histories, there are many points of difference. The *History of Jurjān* is written in Arabic and structured largely by the generations of Jurjān's *ʿulamāʾ*; the *History of Sīstān* is written in Persian, as a chronography attentive to Sīstān's political and military rulers. In form, the former more resembles biographical dictionaries (the entries are arranged alphabetically by name), whereas the latter belongs with annalistic histories. In Jurjān, one sees space up close – the book's sense of locality is fine-grained, a good example being the various street names it provides. In Sīstān, the subjects of the book seem to be constantly on the move, flitting across a landscape dominated by the cities of Zaranj and Bust. As for the Arab-Islamic conquests, for Jurjān history begins with them, whereas for Sīstān history runs deep into the pre-Islamic past. Al-Sahmī favors a picture of easy conquest; our Sīstānī author emphasizes scenes of brutality. While both works contain detailed information, neither portrayal of the conquests appears more "realistic" than the other – to use a term sometimes applied to local histories.

Still, there is something common and peculiarly local about these works. History is read through a lens that places value on early and enduring loyalty to Islam, that looks for what made a locality special and unlike its neighbors, that picks out key moments – the conquests being one – when the locality was transformed in character and in form, and that acknowledges tensions and conflicts known to readers on the ground, such as the revolts of the Khārijites in Sīstān. There is social solidarity across neighborhoods and juristic schools and a search for a less conflictual political order. The way in which each author structures his work and emplots anecdotes within it does not seem to be accidental, but rather guided by broader values and ideas – including the ideals of Islam and the *ʿulamāʾ* in the case of Jurjān and fair administration in Sīstān – with the result that the works were likely able to appeal to their readers' sentiments. As examples of what Bulliet has termed "views from the edge" (as distinct from the center, focused on the caliphate), both works attest to memories whose perspective is shaped by the complexity

139 Cf. esp. S. M. Stern, "Yaʿqūb the Coppersmith and Persian National Sentiment," in *Iran and Islam: In Memory of the Late Vladimir Minorsky*, ed. C. E. Bosworth, 535–55 (Edinburgh: Edinburgh University Press, 1971).

of local circumstances, in which the conquests serve as a meaningful *lieu de mémoire*. The edge becomes the center here, with Jurjān and Sīstān depicted as centers of true Islam as opposed to their many peripheries where Islam is under threat.

Conclusion

For mnemohistory, the conquests provide a particularly good subject because they transformed Iran and were remembered for that. Many particular memories about the Sasanians and their empire, administrative practices, and family history had the conquests as an ending point, but they were also a starting point for Muslim Iranians, their heritage, families, and local history. Virtually all genres of Arabic letters treated them in some regard, although some in more focused fashion. And so one witnesses particular small reports and their repetition across genres, but also fresh treatments as integral parts of both the grand narratives of Muslim history and the specific narratives of localities.

The approach of mnemohistory has its limitations, which bear acknowledging in more detail at this juncture. Reading narrative sources for their peculiarities can seem a lot like eavesdropping on one side of a phone conversation, with the other party unknown, and possibly not listening. The size of the pool of speakers would fail to meet any modern scientific standards meant to minimize margins of error, and it was generated by, and quite often for, elites, whether in Iraq or in eastern Iran. Arguments about the chronological development of memory are often based on the silence of our earliest sources on matters such as Salmān's Persianness, the identity of ʿUmar's informant on the *dīwān*, or the mother of the fourth Imam. We have a bare fraction of the earliest writings, and far more for later periods – so it is always possible that third/ninth-century memories were not inventions. In addition to all of the other normal problems inherent in interpreting premodern sources composed in languages not one's own, there are also important issues relating to texts and their transmission in the period, which can make assigning agency to a traditionist, as an author, difficult: the loss of the earliest layers of historiography, especially from the first/seventh century; the "publication" of books, with lightly noted changes, by a traditionist's students, often unrecognized by modern scholars; the passing on of earlier texts in later texts, where the interests of the later compiler can be hard to know; and the peculiarities of genres, which require some approaches but do not allow others to be considered. All of these necessitate some caution when dating and interpreting individual narratives.

These difficulties acknowledged, if we examine the development of traditions on a case-by-case basis, we find adjustments to narratives that appear to take more notice of Iranians over time, sometimes in dramatic increments, and, in the case of local histories in particular, to rewrite history to give more texture to the subjective experience and concerns of Iranian readers and audiences. In Jurjān, the conquests retained a kerygmatic dimension and teleological perspective, with al-Sahmī deftly presenting his readers with a picture of continuity before and after the conquests and of improbable equilibrium and concord among its present population. A comparison with other Arabic sources treating Jurjān's conquest suggests that he has chosen to remember events in a particular way, or alternatively, to forget the violence and discord that historians such as al-Ṭabarī recall. The account in the *Tārīkh-i Sīstān*, by contrast, reflects poorly on the Arab conquerors and justifies the territory's reputation for rebellion. Here, too, comparison suggests that its author was up to something, namely, dramatizing the sufferings of Sīstān as an admonition for its present ruling classes.

In each of the cases considered, memory was not revised overnight and never conclusively. Rather, it was gradually renegotiated, the product of many shifts, and always subject to revision in light of contemporary circumstances. Sometimes, it was built on strong probabilities, as with the *dīwān*; at other times on what was likely fancy, as with Shahrbānū. Individual traditionists played an important role, but their works and particular perspectives should be seen as part of a wider process. Both grand narratives with their kerygmatic perspectives and local histories represented and likely shaped collective agreements about the past and the ways in which Iranians conceived of themselves in relation to the Muslim community to which they belonged.

PART II

TRADITIONS FOR FORGETTING

In Part II, we turn our attention to the strategies through which a variety of traditionists in the third/ninth to the fifth/eleventh centuries shaped memory of Iran's past and the immediate concerns their efforts reflected. As modern scholars have often noted, there is much evidence that Muslims of this period sought to preserve a record of Iran's royal heritage by translating Middle Persian works featuring Iran's kings into Arabic or by including excerpts of such works in their own writings. With the Sasanian dynasty gone, these Muslim traditionists became the most important custodians of its historical and ethico-didactic literature, while also taking some interest in the ruling house's Zoroastrian faith and scriptures, including the Avesta. ʿAbbasid courtly circles transmitted significant quantities of this material, which was developed still further in the following centuries in Baghdad for the benefit of Buyid and Seljuk rulers and ruling classes, and in centers of power to the east, such as Samanid Khurāsān and Transoxiana.[1] But while much of the historiographic tradition reflects the success of a "Persian" humanities crystallized around

[1] The issue of transmission of Sasanian era materials has been investigated from many angles. To works already cited in this study, I would add M. Inostranzev, *Iranian Influence on Moslem Literature*, pt. 1, trans. G. K. Nariman (Bombay: D. B. Taraporevala Sons, 1918); Sh. Shaked, *From Zoroastrian Iran to Islam: Studies in Religious History and Intercultural Contacts* (Aldershot: Variorum, 1995); Muḥammad Muḥammadī-Malāyirī, *Tārīkh va farhang-i Īrān dar dawrān-i intiqāl az ʿaṣr-i sāsānī bih ʿaṣr-i islāmī*, vols. 1 and 2 (Tehran, 1996–7), translated by Shahrokh Mohammadi-Malayeri as *Iranian Civilization and Culture: Before Islam and Its Impact on Islamic Civilization and Arab Literature* (New Delhi: Manohar, 2012); Aḥmad Tafażżulī, *Tārīkh-i adabiyāt-i Īrān pīsh az Islām*, ed. Zhāla Āmūzigār (Tehran: Intishārāt-i Sukhan, 1997).

the figure of the king and royal ethics[2] as well as a variety of social, political, and linguistic revivalist sentiments, there is also substantial evidence of more complex stances toward Iran's heritage, including a considerable degree of ambivalence and anxiety.

The Issue of Perspective

To set the tone for the chapters that follow, it will be useful to consider a couple of reports passed on late in our period by a man of Arabic letters and friend of eastern Iranian ruling elites, Abū Manṣūr al-Thaʿālibī (d. 429/1038). The reports were transmitted in his lexicon of memorable two-word phrases and clichés, the *Thimār al-qulūb fī al-muḍāf wa-l-mansūb* (Fruits of the heart among nouns in construct form), a work dedicated to reminding readers, or more likely bringing them into the know, about a variety of topics.[3] In an entry for the expression "the justice of Anūshirvān" (*ʿadl Anūshirwān*), he reports that Muḥammad was born during the reign of Khusraw Anūshirvān (r. 531–79 CE), and he quotes a Hadith in which the Prophet states: "I was born in the time of the Just King (*al-malik al-ʿādil*). As for the rest of the Kisrās, they were unjust and wicked."[4] Al-Thaʿālibī then explains with a sprinkling of rhymed prose:

[2] Amir-Moezzi, "Shahrbānū, Dame du pays d'Iran," 517. For the phrase, see a "note by Professor H.A.R. Gibb" in Arnold J. Toynbee, *A Study of History*, 2nd ed., 12 vols. (London: Oxford University Press, 1935), 1:400–2, at 402 (Annex I to I.C (i) (b)). Gibb wrote about Shiʿism in opposition to "the Persian 'humanities.'" I thank Dan Sheffield for suggesting the origin of the expression.

[3] Al-Thaʿālibī wrote in Arabic, not Persian, although given his locale and appointments, he would have been well aware of the development of Persian letters and composed macaronic poetry with Persian words inserted in the Arabic. Regarding al-Thaʿālibī's life and works, see esp. Bosworth's introduction to another of his books, *The Laṭāʾif al-maʿārif of Thaʿālibī (The Book of Curious and Entertaining Information)*, trans. Bosworth (Edinburgh: Edinburgh University Press, 1968), 1–31; Maḥmūd ʿAbd Allāh al-Jādir, "al-Thaʿālibī: Nāqidan wa-adīban" (M.A. thesis, Baghdad University, 1974), esp. pt. 1, "Ḥayātuhu wa-thaqāfatuhu"; and Bilal Walid Orfali, "The Art of Anthology: Al-Thaʿālibī and His *Yatīmat al-dahr*" (Ph.D. diss., Yale University, 2009), esp. ch. 1, "The Life of Abū Manṣūr al-Thaʿālibī," and ch. 2, "The Works of al-Thaʿālibī."

[4] Abū Manṣūr al-Thaʿālibī, *Thimār al-qulūb fī al-muḍāf wa-l-mansūb*, ed. Muḥammad Abū al-Faḍl Ibrāhīm (Cairo: Dār Nahḍat Miṣr, 1965), 178–9 (no. 255). Al-Thaʿālibī also cites the Hadith in his anthology of poetry in Arabic, *Yatīmat al-dahr fī maḥāsin ahl al-ʿaṣr*, ed. Muḥammad Muḥyī al-Dīn ʿAbd al-Ḥamīd, 4 vols. in 2 (Cairo: Maṭbaʿat Ḥijāzī, 1947), 4:437 ("Abū al-ʿAbbās al-Faḍl b. ʿAlī al-Isfirāʾīnī"). Other reporters are more critical of this Hadith's authenticity; e.g., see Aḥmad b. al-Ḥusayn al-Bayhaqī, *Shuʿab al-īmān*, ed. Abū Hājar Muḥammad al-Saʿīd b. Basyūnī Zaghlūl, 9 vols. (Beirut: Dār al-Kutub al-ʿIlmiyya, 2000), 4:305–6 (no. 5195). Balʿamī quotes the first, but not the

They would enslave free men and treat their subjects like bondmen, slaves, or servants; they would treat them as if they were of no consequence. They would appropriate for themselves the choicest of food, fine clothes, mounts, beautiful women, choice dwellings, and the advantages of culture. None of their subjects would dare to cook [the fine dish of] *sikbāj*,[5] to dress in silk brocade, to trot proudly on their horses (*yarkab himlāj*),[6] to marry a beautiful woman, to build a spacious house, to instill learning in his children, or to attempt manly virtues.[7]

By al-Thaʿālibī's lifetime, nearly four centuries had passed since the Sasanians ruled, but their reputation as supporters of an elitist culture lived on. The entry actually said little that was meaningful about Anūshirvān's justice or even about the Sasanians themselves, but far more, by inference, about the more egalitarian values of the Muslim empire and society that superseded them.

Al-Thaʿālibī began his career under the last Samanids; he worked at the court of the Maʾmūnid Khwārizm-Shāhs, who reigned for twenty-two years (385–408/995–1017) in the region of Khwārizm on the lower Oxus and in whose court at Gurgānj al-Thaʿālibī seems to have made frequent appearances; and he finished his very productive literary life under the Ghaznavids. It was during their reign that he dedicated the *Thimār* to a notable from Nīshāpūr named Abū al-Faḍl ʿUbayd Allāh b. Aḥmad al-Mīkālī (d. 436/1044–5).[8] Despite his eastern locale, placement within its ruling circles, and possible attention elsewhere to the Persians' pre-Islamic history, he was no simple romantic for Iran's history or legacy, as the preceding story reveals.[9] Nor do I think it accurate to describe him

second, half of the report ("I was born in the time of the Just King"); *Tārīkh-i Balʿamī* (ed. Taqī Bahār and Gunābādī), 2:1053.

5 Or *sakbāj* (Middle Persian, *sik*, vinegar; *bāg*, stew). This luxury meat dish of Persian origin was popular in ʿAbbasid times and featured a vinegar sauce containing aromatics, including fresh and dry coriander, cinnamon bark, white onions, and Syrian leeks (a variant was made with fish); Maxime Rodinson, A. J. Arberry, and Charles Perry, *Medieval Arab Cookery* (Blackawton, Devon: Prospect Books, 2001), 40, 139, 151–2, 305–6, 482.

6 For the Persian origin of the term *himlāj* (the rhyme and Persian origins of *himlāj* being the likely reasons for al-Thaʿālibī's choice of this horse), see Ibn Manẓūr, *Lisān al-ʿArab*, 15 vols. (Beirut: Dār Ṣādir, [1955–6]), 2: 393–4.

7 Al-Thaʿālibī, *Thimār al-qulūb*, 178–9.

8 On the Mīkālī family, see esp. C. E. Bosworth, "Mīkālīs," in *EI*[2], and idem., *The Ghaznavids: Their Empire in Afghanistan and Eastern Iran, 994–1040* (Edinburgh: Edinburgh University Press, 1963), 176 and 179–85.

9 See esp. his *Yatīmat al-dahr*, which displays an intense consciousness of regional poetic traditions in Arabic, including volume 4 (featuring Jurjān, Ṭabaristān, Khurāsān, Transoxiana, and Khwārizm, as well as special treatment of Bukhārā, Bust, and Nīshāpūr). There has been a long-standing debate about whether another work, featuring Persia's ancient kings – the *Ghurar akhbār mulūk al-Furs wa-siyarihim*, ed. and trans. H. Zotenberg (Paris: Imprimerie nationale, 1900) – can securely be attributed to

as simply following the "well-trodden Arabo-Islamic ways" of figures such as Ibn Qutayba.[10] Instead – like many Iranians from the third/ninth century onward – he found himself adjudicating at the trial of a past empire and its civilization, sympathetic in some regards but critical in others, and he expressed this in the way he remembered its legacy.

A further report suggests the complexity of cultural and historical consciousness among brokers of Iran's past such as al-Thaʿālibī. The report concerns "the Cypress of Bust" (*sarwa Bust*) and evokes shades of tragedy. It runs like this: in Khurāsān, within the boundaries of the rural district of Bust,[11] there was an enormous cypress tree of unprecedented height and width that had been planted in the time of King Yustāsif (the ruler in Zoroaster's lifetime).[12] It cast a shadow a *farsakh* (about 6 km) long and was one of the major points of pride of Khurāsān. More than once, the ʿAbbasid caliph al-Mutawakkil heard about it, and this made him want to see it; but he was not able to visit it, so he wrote to his governor Ṭāhir b. ʿAbd Allāh ordering him to cut it down, to package the pieces of its trunk and branches in padding, preserving its leaves, and to transport the tree on camels to Iraq so that it might be re-erected in his presence. The caliph's companions told him of the bad luck that would result from cutting down the tree, but this only tempted him more. No intercessor could help the cypress, nor could Ṭāhir see any option other than following the order. When the woodcutters arrived to fell the tree, along with the camels to carry it, the people of the district pledged a large quantity of money for them to spare it, still to no avail. In refusing

him. Regarding the question, see esp. Brockelmann, *Geschichte der arabischen Litteratur*, Suppl., 3 vols. (Leiden: E. J. Brill, 1937–42), 1:581–2; Rosenthal, "From Arabic Books and Manuscripts III: The Author of the *Ġurar as-siyar*," *Journal of the American Oriental Society* 70, no. 3 (1950): 181–2; Bosworth, "al-Thaʿālibī, Abū Manṣūr," in *EI*²; and al-Jādir, "al-Thaʿālibī," 114–9 (no. 22). Disputing his authorship on the grounds of the *Ghurar*'s Persian contents or al-Thaʿālibī's prominence in Arabic literary circles seems to me unsound and based on an overly narrow understanding of al-Thaʿālibī's cultural profile.

10 Cf. Bosworth, *The Laṭāʾif al-maʿārif of Thaʿālibī*, 11–12. Bosworth's characterization here of Ibn Qutayba's corpus and cultural profile underrates his engagement with Iranian sources, particularly in his *ʿUyūn al-akhbār*.

11 This is the rural district (*rustāq*) of Bust, near Nīshāpūr, which is not to be confused with the city of Bust in Sīstān, mentioned in Chapter 3. Al-Thaʿālibī specifies the locale in Bust more precisely as a village named Kashmīr. *Thimār al-qulūb*, 590 (no. 977).

12 Regarding Zoroaster's mysterious history, much has been written; for a relevant summary, see W. W. Malandra, "Zoroaster," in *EIr*. Regarding the philology behind the name of Yustāsif (Gushtāsp in the *Shāh-nāmah*), see A. Shapur Shabazi, "Goštāsp," in *EIr*. For another linking of Yustāsif (as such) and Zoroaster, see, e.g., al-Masʿūdī, *Murūj*, 2: 398–9 (no. 1402).

the plea, Ṭāhir said that he would not be willing to acquiesce under any conditions, since he could not oppose the order of the Commander of the Believers.[13]

The calamity of the loss of the cypress hit the people of the area hard. They raised a hue and cry, but the trunk was nonetheless wrapped in padding and transported on three hundred camels to the caliph. A court poet and onetime companion of the caliph, ʿAlī b. al-Jahm (d. 249/863), regarded the event as an ill omen for al-Mutawakkil and recited:

An omen for al-Mutawakkil departed by night on its way;
The cypress is traveling, and fate on its way.
It is wrapped only because our Imam [al-Mutawakkil]
Is wrapped with a sword against his children.[14]

We then hear the conclusion: matters passed as the poet had foreseen, with al-Mutawakkil dead (his offspring partly to blame) before the cypress reached him and the poem recited afterward as a reminder of his folly.[15]

Al-Mutawakkil coveted a great object of Iranian pride, one whose roots, literally, were sunk in its mythic Zoroastrian past. The consequences were predicted, but this did not stop the vain caliph or his Iranian protégé. The result was tragic for the people of Khurāsān as well as for al-Mutawakkil. He may have uprooted the cypress, but he thereby sealed his own fate and never actually saw the tree. The story provides an apt metaphor for the failures of the ʿAbbasids to co-opt Iran's aristocratic past for their purposes and a literary example of the futile efforts of post-conquest rulers to take down and dismantle the material remains of Iran's heritage. Just as in Egypt, with the pyramids, or in Iraq, with Ctesiphon, a ruler sought to eliminate the vestiges of a past empire at his own peril.[16] The story may have appealed especially to Khurāsānian audiences

[13] Al-Thaʿālibī, *Thimār al-qulūb*, 590–1.

[14] See also *Dīwān ʿAlī b. al-Jahm*, ed. Khalīl Mardam Bey, 2nd ed. (Beirut: Committee of Arab Manuscripts, n.d.), 167 (no. 76). At one point in time, the poet fell out of the caliph's favor and was imprisoned for a year before being released and sent to Khurāsān. Regarding him, see H. A. R. Gibb, "ʿAlī b. al-Djahm," in *EI*².

[15] Palace intrigues regarding succession preceded al-Mutawakkil's assassination by Turkish soldiers; his son, al-Muntaṣir (r. 247–8/861–2), played a role in his downfall. See esp. H. Kennedy, "al-Mutawakkil ʿAlā 'llāh, Abū 'l-Faḍl Djaʿfar b. Muḥammad," in *EI*².

[16] Regarding Egypt, see Michael Cooperson, "Al-Maʾmūn, the Pyramids, and the Hieroglyphs," in *ʿAbbasid Studies II: Occasional Papers of the School of ʿAbbasid Studies, Leuven, 28 June–1 July 2004*, ed. John Nawas, 165–90 (Leuven: Peeters, 2010). For an anecdote about the efforts of the ʿAbbasid caliph al-Manṣūr (r. 136–58/754–75) to take down the *īwān* of Kisrā (or the White Palace) at al-Madāʾin, see Savant, "Forgetting Ctesiphon," 177–8.

because it showed the punishment for exploitation by the caliph in Iraq; it is noteworthy, however, that the tree was in fact felled.

What Lies Ahead

In the first part of this study, especially in Chapters 2 and 3, my methodology has been largely stratigraphic, as I have sought to decipher the gradual process by which Iranians, and Persians in particular, were written into a historiographical tradition that was kerygmatic in character and profoundly shaped by the concerns of its first reporters and audiences. The past, as imagined, was typically not a new invention, but an incrementally adjusted recreation that in a variety of ways engaged with the expectations of a reading and listening public. Such reformulations began while Iranian Muslim audiences were small and were well under way by the mid-third/ninth century, but they continued in different ways afterward, shaping the possibilities for all later generations' remembrance.

My goal in Part I was to identify the emergence of an affective past. In Part II, by contrast, my focus is on varieties of disaffection and methods for the destruction of memory. Returning to a point I made in the Introduction, oblivion is often the product not just of omission but of superimposition. To repeat Eco, "mnemonic additions" foster forgetfulness of the past "not by cancellation but by superimposition, not by producing absence but by multiplying presences."[17] While in Part II I continue to identify the historical contexts in which traditionists operated and make some general observations about the chronological development of ideas about the past, my main concern is structural: I seek to consider superimpositions as they occur in narrative form, to describe and classify the strategies underlying them, and to identify the subjects of erasure. I therefore seek to discern patterns in the corpus of traditions, while giving some consideration to their particular contexts.

[17] Eco, "An *Ars Oblivionalis*? Forget It!" 254–61.

4

Reforming Iranians' Memories of Pre-Islamic Times

History prior to the rise of Islam provided a wide canvas on which traditionists could introduce and develop ideas about Persians and their past, as well as to press for realignments of loyalties. As a focus of positive knowledge, these earlier times came with a lighter burden of proof than subsequent periods, particularly that of the Prophet's lifetime, in part because the field was less crowded with scholars and therefore less encumbered by competing views and demands. As material, it was rich, as the most antique history generally is, for the choices it offered in time periods, geographical focus, and themes, and the comparative liberty that distance in time allowed.

Traditionists approached antique history in a variety of ways. They chose their material, gave it structure, and inserted it into wider accounts of the origin and progress of humanity in ways that diminished the autonomy of Persia's history. They omitted past knowledge, but also reduced its autonomy through editorial choices that restructured and reframed their material. And, through literary devices, they urged their readers/listeners to respond with sentiments that ranged from affectionate nostalgia to distrust and anxiety. This chapter identifies three such editorial choices, paying attention to the historical sensibilities and approaches that underpin them, as well as to the loyalties they reflect and advocate. These editorial strategies took shape in the third/ninth to fifth/eleventh centuries, providing patterns for Arabic and Persian historiography afterward, and they consist of (1) rewriting a Persian past as a purely local past, (2) replacing a Persian past with a Muslim past, and (3) raising doubts about the past. While in some cases reporters might employ the three techniques simultaneously, for analytical purposes it is useful to consider them separately.

Creating a Local Past

In Chapter 1, I sketched the ways in which al-Ṭabarī wove Persians into his *History of Prophets and Kings*; demonstrated the importance that he attached to prophets, especially Noah; and discussed the potential challenge that Iranian views of the past posed in his attempt to place Muḥammad and the Muslim community at the center. To illustrate the respect al-Ṭabarī granted to Iranian sources but the priority he accorded to Muslim ones, I mentioned his treatment of Gayūmart's possible identities: as father to humanity as a whole, as Adam, as one of Adam's sons, or as a descendant of Noah. I noted that without committing to any one view, al-Ṭabarī shapes his account to show that Persians are born early, whether at humanity's inception (with Gayūmart) or more likely afterward, among Noah's offspring. Al-Ṭabarī's treatment of this first, early stage serves as a central point of his reconciliation of two possible historical visions: one pre-Islamic and Iranian, the other Islamic.

For al-Ṭabarī and other traditionists of the period, the problems that Gayūmart presented mirrored those of Iranian pre-Islamic history as a whole. Not only did narratives about him flatly contradict those otherwise known by Muslims, but he came with strong Zoroastrian associations as well.[1] The Pahlavi *Bundahishn* was completed in the third/ninth century CE and gives some sense of the ideas that were current among Zoroastrians at the time: Ahura Mazdā created Gayūmart as the sixth creation, "shining as the sun" and measuring the same in height as in width;[2] Gayūmart's offspring, Masya and Masyānī, grew from the earth, fertilized by his sperm, as a single stalk of a *rīvās* (Middle Persian *rēbāh/rēbās*,

1 Gayūmart has been treated frequently in modern scholarship. Regarding Muslim legends about Gayūmart, see esp. "Sources islamiques" in Sven S. Hartman, *Gayōmart: Étude sur le syncrétisme dans l'ancien Iran* (Uppsala: Almqvist & Wiksells Boktryckeri, 1953), 130ff.; Shaul Shaked, "First Man, First King: Notes on Semitic-Iranian Syncretism and Iranian Mythical Transformations," in *Gilgul: Essays on Transformation, Revolution and Permanence in the History of Religions; Dedicated to R. J. Zwi Werblowsky*, ed. S. Shaked, D. Shulman, and G. G. Stroumsa, 238–56 (Leiden: E. J. Brill, 1987); Mohamad Tavakoli-Targhi, "Contested Memories: Narrative Structures and Allegorical Meanings of Iran's Pre-Islamic History," *Iranian Studies* 29, no. 1/2 (1996): 152ff.; Subtelny, "Between Persian Legend and Samanid Orthodoxy"; and the other sources that follow.

2 *Zand-Ākāsīh: Iranian or Greater Bundahišn*, trans. Behramgore Tehmuras Anklesaria (Bombay: Rahnumae Mazdayasnan Sabha, 1956), ch. 1a:13 (pp. 24–7).

i.e., rhubarb) plant, before being separated to become a human couple.[3] Nine months after they copulated, they produced a male and female pair, but owing to the "sweetness" of the children, the parents ate them. Then Ahura Mazdā removed the sweetness of the children, after which Masya and Masyānī produced six more pairs.[4] Given the variance of this account with Islamic ideas, it is no wonder that many traditionists wished to forget Gayūmart altogether and begin human history simply with Adam.[5] The concerns of Muslim scholars are reflected in their identification and description of an Iranian sect bearing Gayūmart's name, the Kayūmarthiyya, whether or not such a group existed in reality.[6]

One common way of dealing with Gayūmart and the challenges of Iranian historiography more generally was to present them as history for Persia and not for humanity as a whole. According to this view, Iranian history was simply a body of knowledge running parallel to those of other localities such as the Yemen, Egypt, Syria, and the Maghreb, all ultimately, if implicitly, offering only partial contributions to a universal narrative of Islam. This relativizing effort could be achieved in a variety of ways: by giving Persian ideas structural significance and prominence in wider narratives that synchronized different histories, as al-Ṭabarī does; by anthologizing Persian history among other histories; and/or by treating it separately – but stressing its characterization as specifically "Persian" or, some time after the rise of Persian letters, "Iranian" history. In all three cases, the strategy's appeal lay in the ways it seemed to respect and preserve Persian views, lessen the traditionists' burden of achieving consistency, and create space for narrative development. As

[3] *Zand-Ākāsīh*, ch. 14:5–10 (pp. 126–9). On this passage, see Ehsan Yarshater, "Iranian Common Beliefs and World-View," in *The Cambridge History of Iran*, 3(1):343–58, at 353.

[4] *Zand-Ākāsīh*, ch. 14:31–2 (pp. 132–3) and Hartman, *Gayōmart*, 45ff.

[5] Eventually, even some Zoroastrians came to mention Adam in their accounts of human origins. See esp. Alan Williams's *The Zoroastrian Myth of Migration from Iran and Settlement in the Indian Diaspora: Text, Translation and Analysis of the 16th Century Qeṣṣe-ye Sanjān 'The Story of Sanjan'* (Leiden: Brill, 2009), 56–61 (verses 11–31), 149–50 (commentary).

[6] Abū al-Fatḥ Muḥammad al-Shahrastānī (d. 548/1153) mentions the sect in *Kitāb al-Milal wa-l-niḥal*, ed. ʿAbd al-ʿAzīz Muḥammad al-Wakīl, 3 vols. in 1 (Cairo: Muʾassasat al-Ḥalabī, 1968), 2:38–9. For skeptical views on the existence of the sect, see Richard Reitzenstein and Hans Heinrich Schaeder, *Studien zum antiken Synkretismus aus Iran und Griechenland* (Leipzig: B. G. Teubner, 1926), 237ff., and Shaul Shaked, "Some Islamic Reports concerning Zoroastrianism," 45. Cf. Hartman, *Gayōmart*, 30–1, and Touraj Daryaee, "The Mazdean Sect of Gayōmartiya," in *Ātaš-e Dorun: The Fire Within, Jamshid Soroush Soroushian Commemorative Volume*, ed. Carlo G. Cereti and Farrokh Vajifdar, 131–7 ([United States]: 1st Books, 2003).

a way of remembering, however, it introduced perspective to Persian history, replacing past views that regarded Iranian history as the entire truth rather than one among several.

Many Muslim scholars showed a keen interest in "comparative chronology" and sought to synchronize different views of the pre-Islamic past, often giving priority to the Persian view.[7] Typically, Persia's history is royal history, as in al-Ṭabarī's *History of Prophets and Kings*, where, as I noted in Chapter 1, the traditionist asserts that "a history based upon the lives of the Persian kings has the soundest sources and the best and clearest data."[8] His narrative moves in fits and starts because of his dutiful citation of his sources and his introduction and consideration of detail, including genealogies; apart from these elements, it is otherwise tentative because of his acknowledgment of uncertainty regarding chronology.

Al-Ṭabarī faced a large issue: what was to be the measure of time before the adoption of the hijri calendar? At the turn of the fifth/eleventh century, much further to the east and after Muslims had devoted centuries of thought to Iran's pre-Islamic heritage, the problem continued. This is when the traditionist al-Bīrūnī (d. 440/1048) wrote up his own profound analysis of history, dating, and periodization that showed the past as linked to the memories of particular communities, including the Persians. He writes, "Each one of the various peoples in the [world's] regions has its own dating system (*ta'rīkh*) by which it reckons, beginning with its kings, prophets, state reigns, or [other] events that I have already mentioned [including natural disasters, such as floods and earthquakes]."[9] Al-Bīrūnī's knowledge of different dating systems is vast and detailed, and it includes points such as that the birth of "Jesus, the son of Mary" occurred in the year 304 of Alexander's calendar and his ascension in the year 336.[10] He gives generous attention to Persians as one of the world's

[7] Roy Mottahedeh, "Some Islamic Views of the Pre-Islamic Past," *Harvard Middle Eastern and Islamic Review* 1, no. 1 (1994): 20.

[8] Al-Ṭabarī, *Ta'rīkh*, I:148; for discussion of some Armenian Christian authors' use of the regnal years of the Sasanian kings as guideposts, see *The Armenian History Attributed to Sebeos*, trans. R. W. Thomson with commentary by James Howard-Johnston, 2 vols. (Liverpool: Liverpool University Press, 1999), 1:lviii and lxx–lxxi.

[9] Abū al-Rayḥān al-Bīrūnī, *Chronologie orientalischer Völker*, ed. C. Eduard Sachau (Leipzig: F. A. Brockhaus, 1878), 13; see also the English translation by Sachau (with the Arabic pages in the margins): *The Chronology of Ancient Nations* (London: W. H. Allen, 1879; repr., Whitefish, MT: Kessinger Legacy Reprints, n.d.).

[10] Al-Bīrūnī, *Chronologie*, 17. As Muriel Debié notes (personal communication, May 2013), al-Bīrūnī likely relies upon a Syriac source, since Syriac authors refer to the Seleucid era as that of Alexander. The dates, however, are not the usual ones, so it is

great peoples with strong ideas about history before the "reign of Islam" (*dawlat al-Islām*).[11] Regarding their ideas about the origins of humanity, he notes that "they have made many strange statements" and launches into a discussion of Gayūmart and Ahriman, the latter of whom he identifies with "Iblīs," the term used by Muslims to refer to the devil and arch-opponent to Adam and humanity. He seems skeptical as he reports a view that Gayūmart, a first man of sorts, came into existence from the sweat of God's brow. Gayūmart's children were born, meanwhile, in an equally mythical event: Ahriman devoured Gayūmart, but just as he reached his testicles, two drops of Gayūmart's semen fell, fertilizing the earth, from which two rhubarb (*rībās*) plants grew, producing Mīshī and Mīshānah, who are for the Persians "in the position of Adam and Eve" (see Figure 4.1). The offspring are also called Malhā and Malhayāna, whereas the Zoroastrians of Khwārizm call them Mard and Mardāna.[12] Al-Bīrūnī also reports at length a different view he says he had read in the *Shāh-nāmah* of Abū ʿAlī Muḥammad b. Aḥmad al-Balkhī, the sources of which he lists.[13] In this version, Gayūmart's children came into existence when God killed him following Gayūmart's conflict with Ahriman; at his death, Gayūmart dripped sperm onto Mount Damdādh in Iṣṭakhr. From this spot grew two *rībās* bushes, which sprouted branches that, after nine months, yielded Mīshī and Mīshiyānah (the names as rendered). What follows is a Zoroastrian version of the Garden of Eden tale, featuring the couple's temptation by Ahriman. Al-Bīrūnī concludes by mentioning briefly their children, whose names, he says, occur in the Avesta.[14]

Histories could be juxtaposed for many different reasons. Consider the example of the second part of the Persian *Naṣīḥat al-mulūk* (Counsel for Kings), attributed to the great Seljuk-era Muslim scholar al-Ghazālī (d. 505/1111), which presents Persian and prophetic history as distinct but complementary accounts of the past in its treatment of the art of government.[15] Patricia Crone has persuasively argued that while the first

probable that either al-Bīrūnī used a source other than the known Syriac chronicles or the date was corrupted during the transmission process.

11 Al-Bīrūnī, *Chronologie*, 102.

12 Ibid.

13 Al-Bīrūnī's list is important for the history of Persian epic. On this al-Balkhī, see Abolfazl Khatibi and John Cooper, "Abū ʿAlī Balkhī," in *Encyclopaedia Islamica* (online ed.; Leiden: Brill, 2008).

14 Al-Bīrūnī, *Chronologie*, 99–100.

15 There is no critical edition of the *Naṣīḥa*. F. R. C. Bagley has provided what he described as a provisional English translation based primarily on a Persian edition by Jalāl al-Dīn Humāʾī (Tehran: Majlis, 1315–17 *shamsī*/[1936–9]), to which he gives priority, and

FIGURE 4.1. *Ahriman tempts Mishyana.* Edinburgh University Library, Special Collections Department.

part of the *Naṣīḥa*, "a treatise of the faith," can safely be attributed to al-Ghazālī, the second part – a *Fürstenspiegel* (guide for princes) – cannot. Crone's argument is based on an examination of the manuscript tradition as well as a comparison of the two parts, which reveals the second part's different outlook, spirit, style, and ways of referring to its author and reader. As Crone shows, however, the two parts must have been joined together as early as the second half of the sixth/twelfth century, since the Arabic translation from that time (*al-Tibr al-masbūk fī naṣīḥat al-mulūk*) contains both of them.[16] If she is correct (as it seems she is),[17] a forgery nonetheless suggests the contested nature of Iran's past and the benefits of attaching ideas about it to a Sunni luminary. At the start of the second part, the author – for lack of an alternative I will call him pseudo-Ghazālī – advises his reader that God has honored two classes of the "sons of Adam" with superiority over the rest of humanity, the first being prophets and the second being kings. Whereas prophets were sent to guide men to God, kings were sent to protect men from one another. To dispute with kings is improper, and to hate them is wrong.[18] As Qur'an 4:59 states: "Obey God and obey the Messenger and those of you who have authority." This means that "everybody to whom God has given religion must therefore love and obey kings and recognize that their kingship is granted by God, and given by Him to whom He wills."[19]

an Arabic edition prepared by H. D. Isaacs (M.A. thesis, University of Manchester, 1956); the first three paragraphs of part 2 (pp. 45–7 in Bagley's text) are based firstly on pp. 39–41 of Humāʾī's edition, whereas the portion treating Persian kings – pages 47–53 in Bagley's text – derives from Isaacs's text (which is based on a manuscript held by Oxford's Bodleian Library). Bagley supplemented Isaac's text with a Cambridge Arabic manuscript (Qq. 231); see *Ghazālī's Book of Counsel for Kings (Naṣīḥat al-mulūk)* (London: Oxford University Press, 1964), xxvi–xxvii and 47, n. 2, for Bagley's explanation of his method. Humāʾī subsequently published a second, revised edition; *Naṣīḥat al-mulūk*, 2nd ed. (Tehran: Anjuman-i Āsār-i Millī, 1351 *shamsī*/[1972]), 81ff. for part 2 of the *Naṣīḥa* (see also 71ff. of his introduction, where he entertains the question of the second part's attribution to al-Ghazālī).

16 Crone, "Did al-Ghazālī Write a Mirror for Princes? On the Authorship of *Naṣīḥat al-mulūk*," in *From Kavād to al-Ghazālī: Religion, Law and Political Thought in the Near East, c.600–c.1100* (Aldershot: Ashgate Variorum, 2005), 167–92 (see especially the chapter's postscript). Regarding *al-Tibr al-masbūk fī naṣīḥat al-mulūk*, see the edition of Muḥammad Aḥmad Damaj (Beirut: al-Muʾassasa al-Jāmiʿiyya li-l-Dirāsāt wa-l-Nashr wa-l-Tawzīʿ, 1987), esp. 171ff. (he relies on different Arabic manuscripts than did Bagley/Isaacs). Judging by a comparison of Bagley's text with those of Humāʾī and Damaj, I believe that the conclusions I draw are reasonable because they pertain to structure rather than detail.

17 But cf. Naṣr Allāh Pūrjavādī, *Dū mujaddid: Pazhūhishhā-yi dar bārah-yi Muḥammad Ghazzālī va Fakhr al-Rāzī* (Markaz-i Nashr-i Dānishgāhī, 1381/[2002 or 2003]), 414–8.

18 *Ghazālī's Book of Counsel*, 45; see also Humāʾī, *Naṣīḥa*, 2nd ed., 81–2.

19 *Ghazālī's Book of Counsel*, 45–6; Humāʾī, *Naṣīḥa*, 2nd ed., 82.

A little further on in his text, pseudo-Ghazālī advises that there are lessons to be learned from the thousands of years during which the "Magi" ruled, and he then launches into a more detailed discussion of Persia's kings. Adam, the first human, gave birth to two sons, Seth and Gayūmart. Adam charged Seth with "the preservation of religion and [the affairs of] the next world," whereas he charged Gayūmart with the "affairs of this world and kingship."[20] Pseudo-Ghazālī then enumerates the names of the Persian kings, beginning with Gayūmart and ending with Yazdagird, the last Sasanian, and the lengths of their reigns, their qualities, and major achievements.[21] When he has finished with Yazdagird, he states: "After him there was no other king of their community; the Muslims were victorious and took kingship out of their hands. Power and dominion passed to the Muslims, through the benediction of the Prophet."[22]

Gayūmart, who once embodied a specifically Zoroastrian, Persian kingship, thus provides the author a respected point of departure for history, a history with pedagogical and moral value.[23] A generally positive valuation of this history, and of its continuity with the history of Islam, is reflected in a Hadith cited by pseudo-Ghazālī toward the start of the second part of his book, according to which the Prophet recalled that God instructed the prophet David, himself a king: "O David, tell your nation not to speak ill of the ʿAjam (*ahl-i ʿAjam*) for it is they who developed the universe so that My slaves might live in it."[24] But if in moral and political terms there is continuity, with the caliphs taking over from Persia's kings, the past is otherwise discontinuous, as kingship no longer belongs to the Magi.

Anthologizing, or preserving Iranian ideas in collections of related ideas, was perhaps a more common way to give perspective to Persian views of history. In Chapter 1, I mentioned al-Masʿūdī's reporting on Persians, Isaac's children, as an ethnic elect, and I noted that the attempts he cited were unconvincing at the level of detail and lacked a narrative to support them. His anthologizing is extensive, perhaps even grasping all that one *could* possibly say about the claim. Similarly, but generally

[20] *Ghazālī's Book of Counsel*, 47. Regarding the manuscripts and their treatment of these sentences and what immediately follows, see also the detailed notes of Humāʾī, *Naṣīḥa*, 2nd ed., 84ff.

[21] *Ghazālī's Book of Counsel*, 47–53; *al-Tibr al-masbūk*, 175–80.

[22] *Ghazālī's Book of Counsel*, 53; *al-Tibr al-masbūk*, 180.

[23] For the lessons to be learned from the lives of Persia's kings, see especially the anecdotes that follow pseudo-Ghazālī's listing of Persia's kings.

[24] *Ghazālī's Book of Counsel*, 46 and n. 9 on the same page (Bagley translates *ʿAjam* as "the people of Persia"); Humāʾī, *Naṣīḥa*, 2nd ed., 82–3.

with less air of controversy, he reports on the world's peoples, their geographies, dynastic histories, internal divisions, religions, bits of wisdom, and the opinions they held on these subjects, including in his purview the Persians as well as the Chinese, the Turks, the Greeks, the Byzantines, the Yemenis, the Arabs, and others. He starts his account of Persian dynastic history with Gayūmart, noting that although Persians held many views on his identity, the bottom line is that he should be considered "the greatest person of his age," who summoned the people of that age to establish kingship, since the masses were given to hating and envying one another, and to wickedness and enmity. He proceeds to give an account of "Persia's first kings" (*mulūk al-Furs al-ūlā*), their genealogies, the lengths and chronologies of their reigns, their achievements and inventions, and their relations with other peoples, especially the Children of Israel. Throughout one gains a rather generous view into one people's history and the narrative elements that supported it. Still, it is a history that unfolds in a particular time, in a particular place, and in relation to other, particular peoples. In a word, it is not universal.[25]

Such anthologizing occurs often, if normally less systematically, across Arabic historiography when traditionists relate competing views on the origins of humanity. Its signal characteristic is an apparent detachment on the traditionists' part, expressed in the comparative framework into which Persian history is slotted, citation of sources that do surprisingly little to support the truthfulness of particular accounts, and occasional comments indicating the traditionists' own doubts.

The most emotionally powerful and enduring way to rewrite Persia's past as a local one occurs when it is separated out, labeled "Persian" or, sometimes after the fourth/tenth century in Persian letters, "Iranian," and treated as the past of a particular, albeit very special, place. What Iranians once saw as *the* account of history becomes *their* history. The very effort to translate Pahlavi works into Arabic in late Umayyad and early ʿAbbasid times already placed Iran's history in perspective as it was made available to Muslims at large. Iran's pre-conquest history appears notably as the chief subject of five Arabic histories first identified by Sayyid Ḥasan Taqīzadeh, as well as of the better-known Persian prose and verse accounts, most famously that of Firdawsī.[26]

25 Al-Masʿūdī, *Murūj*, 1:262–3 (nos. 530–1). See also his *Tanbīh*, 85, and the discussion of Gayūmart.

26 Regarding the Arabic histories, see Sayyid Ḥasan Taqīzadeh, "Shāh-nāmah va Firdawsī," in *Hazārah-yi Firdawsī* (Tehran: Dunyā-yi Kitāb, 1362 *shamsī*), 43–107 (where his 1920 and 1921 articles on the matter are reprinted); also, V. Minorsky, "The Older Preface to the *Shāh-nāma*," 2:160–2.

The way Firdawsī introduces his work is particularly telling: he refers to his efforts to recover a body of Persian legend from oblivion. He describes how he came upon his source material through the assistance of a dear friend who provided him with a Pahlavi book whose author had ransacked the earth for legends of ages past.[27] He thus asserts the value of but also the potential loss of and limitations to the knowledge he relates. Dick Davis has pointed to Firdawsī's employment here of a topos – the helpful, unnamed friend – and has argued that the poet was motivated by a need for authentic references that could establish his own credibility as the best man available to tell Iran's story at a time when the new culture of the conquerors seemed to make the survival of his people's pre-conquest history doubtful. Davis has also repeated doubts regarding Firdawsī's employment of a Pahlavi text.[28] If Davis is correct, one can say that citing the unnamed friend and claiming Pahlavi evidence provided Firdawsī with credentials that showed his account to be a genuinely Iranian one.

The first pages of the narrative then place Iran and its traditions of kingship at the center.[29] The first human worthy of mention, an Iranian, is also the world's first king, Gayūmart, who "invented crown and throne." The objectionable details of his birth are omitted, as are his twin offspring. Siyāmak is presented as his son, with no mention of incest, and the same goes for Siyāmak's son Hūshang.[30] Gayūmart, who wore leopard skins and under whom "the arts of life began," ruled the earth for thirty years and initiated a line running from his son Siyāmak through the heroes Jamshīd, Farīdūn, Manūshihr, and beyond.[31]

As Firdawsī draws attention to the religious acceptability of his account – with, for example, statements of praise for Muḥammad and ʿAlī and pious declarations about the one true God[32] – he also reveals the

[27] Abū al-Qāsim Firdawsī, *Shāh-nāmah*, ed. Djalal Khaleghi-Motlagh, 8 vols. plus 2 note vols. (New York: Bibliotheca Persica Press, 1988–2008), 1:13–14.

[28] Davis, "Problem of Ferdowsî's Sources," 48–51. See Chapter 1 for references to further works treating Firdawsī's sources.

[29] Regarding the *Shāh-nāmah*'s complex picture of kingship, see esp. the sensitive interpretation of Dick Davis, *Epic and Sedition: The Case of Ferdowsi's Shāhnāmeh* (Fayetteville: University of Arkansas Press, 1992).

[30] Firdawsī, *Shāh-nāmah*, 1:21ff.

[31] Ibid., 1:21–22; *The Sháhnáma of Firdausí*, trans. Arthur George Warner and Edmond Warner, 9 vols. (London: Kegan Paul, Trench, Trübner & Co., 1905–25), 1:118–19.

[32] Firdawsī, *Shāh-nāmah*, 1:9–11. Regarding Firdawsī's likely Shīʿī orientation, see Khaleghi-Motlagh, "Ferdowsi, Abuʾl-Qāsem, i. Life," in *EIr*. Cf. Nöldeke, *Das Iranische Nationalepos*, 36–40 (no. 25 in the text).

insufficiency of his account as a world history along Islamic lines. It neglects too much to serve such a purpose, including detailed explanation of the origins of humanity, all of prophetic history, Arabia's own history (treatment of the Yemen notwithstanding), and the lifetimes of the Prophet and ʿAlī.

The sources with which Firdawsī worked may well have viewed their account as comprehensive. Still, Firdawsī doesn't show things that way. Instead, he has nested Iran's history within a broader, though unexplored narrative framework that begins with human creation and continues after the Arab conquests, where his account ends. It is notable that he has composed his text in such a manner, whatever his choice of material may have been. While some Zoroastrian ideas may have been carried over,[33] the framework through which they were filtered is important. The result is the identification of his account as a specifically "Persian" or even "Iranian" one, given his terminology, within the bounds of Islamic orthodoxy.[34] A Buyid ruler once understandably defined the *Shāh-nāmah* as a history of the Persians, versus al-Ṭabarī's history of Islam.[35]

In each of these ways, Iran's history is most often given a positive valuation: as a matter of chronological certainty, for its pedagogical lessons, as a point of curiosity for filling out the history of the world's peoples, and/or as a source of nostalgic pride. At the same time, this history is put into perspective as that of only a particular people. When inserted into longer texts, for example, it is accordingly abridged. The result is a diminution of a universal vision of Iranian, pre-Islamic historiography. With regard to Gayūmart, memory is reduced to that of kingship, Gayūmart being the first king, reflecting the widely held view of Iranian prehistory as the history of royalty. This royal history is contained within, and limited by, a wider history of humanity, beginning with Adam and ending with the arrival of Islam – marking the end of Persian history as a separate point of study. The views represented are labeled Persian, Iranian, or, often enough, "Magian" or Zoroastrian. Even when the latter descriptor is used, substantive traces of Zoroastrian belief are erased – Gayūmart's

33 Including in some form, with regard to creation of the world, in Firdawsī's introduction.

34 Firdawsī, *Shāh-nāmah*, 1:13–14. The term *Īrān* is employed far more extensively in the *Shāh-nāmah*; this is consistent with my point, in the introduction, that the term *Īrān* is employed with reference to what, following Nöldeke, Christensen, and Yarshater, is now commonly labeled Iran's "national" past; for the scale of usage, see Fritz Wolff, *Glossar zu Firdosis Schahname* (Hildesheim: Georg Olms, 1965), and compare "Ērān" and "Ērānī" (pp. 89–91) with "Pārs" and "Pārsī" (p. 177).

35 Ibn al-Athīr, *al-Kāmil fī al-Taʾrīkh*, 9:261.

case, I propose, being exemplary of traditions as a whole – or, at most, reported as unbelievable, mythical possibilities.

Making a Muslim Past

In writing about Iran's earliest history, traditionists had the choice of where to draw the boundary lines. The previous cases involved a strong demarcation, distinguishing Iran's history from others, and so introducing perspective that allowed readers to view Iranian history from the outside and promoted awareness of other potentially valid chronologies, geographical centers, dominant narratives, and lessons to be learned.

Traditionists could also remove such boundary lines, arguing that Persians, as such, had little or no separate past. This occurred most commonly when Iran was featured on the wider canvas of Muslim history as a whole, although it could also happen in other ways that submerged Iranian history. Either way, such narratives emphasize Iran's involvement in the dramas of a prophetic past that is shared with other peoples and that leads directly into a history of Islam and the Muslim community. From this perspective, the prophetic framework is sufficient for encompassing the history of Iranians, and knowledge about the latter is accordingly limited by the scope, literary devices, and arrangement and structure of the narrative. This could result in extensive omissions as well as the definition and restriction of themes to those associated with Islam, but at the same time it could create a vehicle for the surprising survival and validation of some kinds of historical knowledge, as well as unusual fusions of vision where traditionists sought to reconcile contradictions.

The best example of this strategy is found in the earliest pages of Abū Ḥanīfa al-Dīnawarī's *al-Akhbār al-ṭiwāl*. The author's scope here is limited to a chronology beginning with Adam, in which prophetic history provides the scaffolding for the histories of other peoples, among them Arab and Yemeni tribes, Persians (or more precisely, the ʿAjam), the Children of Israel, Egyptians, Kurds, and Turks. Although told in unusual ways, the role of antiquity in these first pages is generally to fill out the prophetic past by supplying further details regarding its key figures and especially their genealogies, their relations with one another, their languages, and their geographical settings; by inserting and completely absorbing episodes from a Persian past into that of the prophets (and likewise for Yemeni, Arab, and other histories); and by developing narratives, their motifs, and their morals to illustrate Islamic lessons about obedience to God, the results of self-aggrandizing and tyrannical rule, and the moral questionableness of practices such as astrology.[36]

In genealogical terms, this strategy relies strongly on notions of shared descent: Persians share the same history as other Muslims because, biologically, they have a respectable share in human origins from Adam. The same, of course, can be said of the other peoples that al-Dīnawarī mentions, such as the Yemenis. Noah and his genealogy play an important role in linking Persians to the overall framework: history begins with Adam, about whom little is said, but it branches out after the Flood, when Noah's descendants populate the planet. In these early pages of al-Dīnawarī's book, anyone of note is linked to Noah, with representatives of the various peoples filling each generation of his descendants. In this scheme, Jamshīd – who stays behind in Babylon (*arḍ Bābil*) after Noah's children fan out – becomes a grandson of Arpachshad b. Shem b. Noah, and Noah's descendants settle Iranian and other regions that come to carry their names: Khurāsān (Khurāsān b. ʿĀlam), Fārs (Fāris b. al-Aswar), Byzantium (al-Rūm b. al-Yafar), Armenia (Irmīn b. Nawraj), and Kirmān (Karmān b. Tāraḥ), as well as the "country of the Hephthalites" (Hayṭal b. ʿĀlam).[37] Through the genealogical details al-Dīnawarī provides, one can readily see the generations of Noah's descendants, their interactions, and their conflicts. For example, he shows that Moses was a contemporary of the ʿĀdite al-Walīd b. Muṣʿab, the Yemenite al-Milṭāṭ, the Persian Kay Qubādh, and the prophet Shuʿayb.[38]

While Iranians, and the Sasanians in particular, play a major role in al-Dīnawarī's account as an independent object of knowledge, their earliest history and its chronologies, genealogies, narratives, and themes are significantly diminished. Gayūmart is absent. The tale of Persian epic about Jamshīd, al-Ḍaḥḥāk, and the tyranny suffered by Iran is related as one of many stories concerning Noah's descendants. In the story, Jamshīd – the first, after Noah's son Shem, to consolidate the power of rule and to "raise the beacon of kingship" – falls at the hand of al-Ḍaḥḥāk, who is identified as a descendant of the Arab branch of ʿĀd, a tribe the Qurʾan mentions as being destroyed for its rejection of the prophet Hūd, and whose eponymous ancestor in al-Dīnawarī's account was a great-grandson of Noah.[39] Al-Dīnawarī relates that after the ʿĀdites multiplied

[36] Regarding astrology, see al-Dīnawarī, *al-Akhbār al-ṭiwāl*, 42.
[37] Ibid., 32–3 and 35–6. The names are vocalized following the editor, ʿIṣām Muḥammad al-Ḥājj ʿAlī.
[38] Ibid., 37 and 47–9.
[39] Ibid., 32 and 36.

in the Yemen, they behaved haughtily and insolently like tyrants and were unruly. The ʿĀdites were ruled by Shadīd b. ʿImlīq b. ʿĀd b. Aram b. Shem b. Noah, who dispatched his "nephew" (*ibn akhīhi*) al-Ḍaḥḥāk b. ʿUlwān b. ʿImlīq b. ʿĀd to Shem's descendants in Babylon. When al-Ḍaḥḥāk arrived, King Jamshīd fled from Babylon, but al-Ḍaḥḥāk pursued him until he caught him, whereupon al-Ḍaḥḥāk seized him and killed him with a saw, gaining mastery over his dominion.[40] As al-Dīnawarī subsequently recounts al-Ḍaḥḥāk's cruelty to the children of "Arpachshad," he gives an unusual version of an etiology common to Persian epic tradition, explaining the origin of the Kurds among the refugees and thus linking them as Arpachshad's children, also, to prophetic history and to Noah.[41]

The result of al-Dīnawarī's approach is the reconfiguration in peculiar ways of assorted Near Eastern materials, including genealogies, narratives, and their motifs. For a reader familiar with the Bible or with Firdawsī's *Shāh-nāmah*, identities are highly confused: the biblical Nimrod becomes Farīdūn, and his descent from Jamshīd is specified along with his rule over Noah's descendants, his defeat of al-Ḍaḥḥāk, and his subsequent reign, during which he (rather than Farīdūn as such) parceled out his territory among his sons, who also ruled over Noah's descendants.[42] The drama spans a similarly perplexing territory, including Arabia, Syria, Iraq, Babylonia, and Mount Damāwand, and echoes vaguely a variety of ancient Near Eastern and Iranian legends. One passage of the text therefore states that after God destroyed the disobedient people of ʿĀd and their ruler Shaddād (the brother of and successor to Shadīd, mentioned above), al-Ḍaḥḥāk's support became weak, his rule atrophied, "Arpachshad b. Shem's descendants" became emboldened against him, and plague befell his army and those who were with him.[43] Al-Ḍaḥḥāk went out, seeking aid from his brother Ghānam b. ʿUlwān, whom Shadīd had "made king over the descendants of Japheth."[44] Al-Ḍaḥḥāk's subjects, identified again as "Arpachshad b. Shem's descendants," seized on his departure and sent a message to "Nimrod b. Kanʿān b. Jamshīd, the king."[45] Al-Dīnawarī continues, including details found in the Persian epic tradition relating to Farīdūn's and Kāvah's (rather than Nimrod's) conquest of al-Ḍaḥḥāk, telling his readers that Nimrod and his father

40 Ibid., 36.
41 Ibid., 37–8. Cf. Firdawsī, *Shāh-nāmah*, 1:57.
42 Al-Dīnawarī, *al-Akhbār al-ṭiwāl*, 39–40, 42, and 44.
43 Ibid., 39.
44 Ibid.
45 Ibid.

were hidden throughout al-Ḍaḥḥāk's reign at Mount Damāwand. Nimrod came to Arpachshad's descendants, and they made him king over them. He then betook himself to Babylonia, where he slew al-Ḍaḥḥāk's supporters and gained mastery over the latter's dominion. This news reached al-Ḍaḥḥāk, who advanced toward his opponents, but Nimrod overcame him and struck him on the head with an iron rod. Having heavily wounded him, Nimrod bound him firmly and locked him up in a cave in Mount Damāwand. Al-Dīnawarī concludes the passage on an upbeat note with the observation that things started then to go well for Nimrod and the clarification that it is Nimrod whom "the ʿAjam call Farīdūn."[46]

Subsequently, al-Dīnawarī replaces the world's division among Noah's progeny with a division based on the descendants of Farīdūn (Nimrod). It is Nimrod, rather than Farīdūn, his alter ego, who is credited with fathering Īraj, Salm, and Tūr. Nimrod appointed Salm over "Ham's descendants" and Tūr over "Japheth's descendants." Salm and Tūr envied their brother Īraj, whom their father assigned authority over them and to whom he gave his own dominion, since he was younger than they were. So, according to al-Dīnawarī, they seized him unawares and killed him. After this, Nimrod assigned Īraj's dominion to Manūshihr, Īraj's son, and took it away from Salm and Tūr. Then, al-Dīnawarī writes, Nimrod died.[47]

With origins in the medieval province of Jibāl, it is easy to imagine al-Dīnawarī having access to a wide variety of material from which to fashion his history, including sources on Nimrod. Dīnawar, his hometown, in which he seems to have spent at least some part of his life, had strong conquest-era links to Kufa, as well as to other cities within Jibāl, most notably the commercial center of Hamadhān, also treated in Chapter 1.[48] As a whole, Jibāl (which in Arabic signifies "the mountains") – including Dīnawar as well as Iṣfahān, Qum, Hamadhān, and Rayy – was well-traveled. The major road from Iraq to Khurāsān passed just

46 Ibid., 39–40.

47 Ibid., 44.

48 On al-Dīnawarī's little-documented life, see Yāqūt, *Muʿjam al-udabāʾ (Irshād al-arīb ilā maʿrifat al-adīb)*, ed. D. S. Margoliouth, 7 vols. (London: Luzac, 1907–13), 1:123–7 (entry for "Aḥmad b. Dāwūd b. Wanand"); Parvaneh Pourshariati, "The *Akhbār al-Ṭiwāl* of Abū Ḥanīfa Dīnawarī: A *Shuʿūbī* Treatise on Late Antique Iran," in *Sources for the History of Sasanian and Post-Sasanian Iran*, ed. Rika Gyselen, 201–89 (Leuven: Peeters, 2010), at 201–8; Charles Pellat, "Dīnavarī, Abū Ḥanīfa Aḥmad," in *EIr*; B. Lewin, "al-Dīnawarī," in *EI*^{2}.

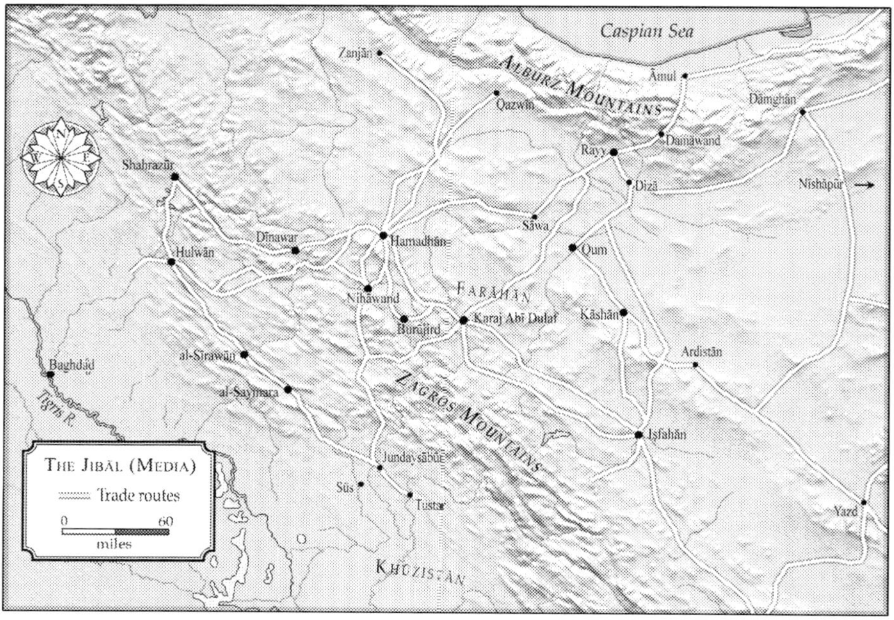

MAP 4.1. Jibāl (Media), adapted from Georgette Cornu, *Atlas du monde Arabo-islamique à l'époque classique: IXe–Xe siècles*, 2 vols. (Leiden: E. J. Brill, 1983–5), 1:V.

south of Dīnawar, which served as a stopping point, and then, crossing through Hamadhān and Rayy, carried on eastward – skirting mountain and desert – to Nīshāpūr and Ṭūs.[49]

Al-Dīnawarī was well respected by his contemporaries in Iraq, and elements in his biography and book support grouping him with Iraqi historians of his period.[50] But the unusual mixing of identities in this portion of his text suggests the formation of a historical vision not within the confines of Baghdad but outside of it, namely, along routes such as the one described above. The biblical Nimrod was known here, but so were perhaps other remnants of ancient Near Eastern legend, as suggested

[49] W. Barthold, *An Historical Geography of Iran*, trans. Svat Soucek, ed. C. E. Bosworth (Princeton, NJ: Princeton University Press, 1984), 207–8; Le Strange, *Lands of the Eastern Caliphate*, maps 1 and 5; Hugh Kennedy, *The Early Abbasid Caliphate: A Political History* (London: Croom Helm, 1981), 26–7.

[50] Abū Ḥayyān al-Tawḥīdī (d. 414/1023), a man of letters himself, reportedly compared al-Dīnawarī's literary expression and achievements to those of the luminary al-Jāḥiẓ and the geographer and philosopher Abū Zayd al-Balkhī (d. 322/934); quoted by Yāqūt, *Mu'jam al-udabā'*, 1:123–7. See also Lewin, "al-Dīnawarī," in *EI*^{2}.

by Nimrod's descent in al-Dīnawarī's account from Shem, rather than from Ham as in the Bible.[51] Many sites in Iraq and Jibāl already had their own associations with the most antique periods of history, reflecting centuries of local knowledge about major biblical and Persian epic figures. This knowledge was atomistically captured in works of geography and their reports on pre-Islamic associations. Read together, the books present possibilities, for example, relating to the episode in the Qurʾan in which Abraham is saved from a fire (Qurʾan 21:51–70). It was in Bābil (Babylon), in Iraq – a Canaanite city – that Abraham was thrown into the fire. Other suggested locations were on a hill, near Abarqwayh in Fārs, or perhaps in the town of Kūthā Rabbā, in the vicinity of al-Madāʾin (Ibn Ḥawqal, fl. fourth/tenth century, seems to favor the city of Bābil).[52]

Why has al-Dīnawarī composed his account in this way? The answer likely lies, first, in a moralizing appeal to an Iranian Muslim audience that stakes out through narrative means two possible types of rulership and, more broadly, two ways of being in the world: one of obedience to God and the other of disobedience. Iran's rulers and Iranians collectively have abided both ways, with the implication that both possibilities remain open. The potential for obedience is demonstrated by the strong leadership of Jamshīd. The negative potential is demonstrated by Nimrod, who behaved poorly toward the end of his life, his crime apparently being that he became devoted to astrology and brought astrologers from the far ends of the earth, rewarding them with wealth.[53] It is also demonstrated by Nebuchadnezzar, who is given a Persian genealogy among the mythical Kayanids. It was Nebuchadnezzar who undid all of the great deeds of King Solomon, a true supporter of monotheism, who ruled throughout the lands of Shem's descendants, including in Iraq and Khurāsān, and who completed the "mosque" begun by his father, David, in Jerusalem.[54]

[51] See Genesis 10:6–8 and 1 Chronicles 1:8–10. On the legends and their ancient and post-biblical contexts, see esp. Yigal Levin, "Nimrod the Mighty, King of Kish, King of Sumer and Akkad," *Vetus Testamentum* 52, no. 3 (2002): esp. 354–6; K. van der Toorn and P. W. van der Horst, "Nimrod before and after the Bible," *Harvard Theological Review* 83, no. 1 (1990): 1–29.

[52] Ibn Ḥawqal, *Kitāb Ṣūrat al-arḍ* (Beirut: Dār Maktabat al-Ḥayā, 1979), 219 and 259–60. For consideration of other narratives about Nimrod and the relation between Jewish and Muslim traditions (without, however, taking al-Dīnawarī into account), see Shari L. Lowin, "Narratives of Villainy: Titus, Nebuchadnezzar, and Nimrod in the *Ḥadīth* and *Midrash Aggadah*," in *The Lineaments of Islam: Studies in Honor of Fred McGraw Donner*, ed. Paul M. Cobb, 261–96 (Leiden: Brill, 2012).

[53] Al-Dīnawarī, *al-Akhbār al-ṭiwāl*, 42.

[54] Ibid., 60.

After building the mosque, Solomon visited the Kaʿba in Mecca, where he circumambulated the Kaʿba, clothed it with the traditional cloth known as the *kiswā*, sacrificed at it, and remained there for seven days.[55] But Nebuchadnezzar destroyed the mosque (i.e., temple) of Jerusalem, as "he raised his sword against the Children of Israel, took captive the sons of its kings and its great men, and tore down the city of Jerusalem." In his conquest, "he did not leave a house standing, took to pieces the mosque, and carried away its gold, silver, and jewels, and likewise the throne of Solomon."[56]

Al-Dīnawarī's identification of Nebuchadnezzar as being of Persian origin is remarkable, not least because the biblical figure has been traced in modern scholarship to Babylonia of the late seventh/early sixth century BCE (r. 605–562) and identified as the second Chaldean dynast. Far from being Persian, the Chaldean dynasty perished in the second half of the sixth century BCE with the success of an up-and-coming rival, Achaemenid Persia. Moreover, whereas in the biblical story (2 Chronicles) one sees God punish the Israelites, a rebellious people, through Nebuchadnezzar, al-Dīnawarī's Israelites are innocent victims of a military official in the service of a tyrant. Here, as on many other occasions, al-Dīnawarī compresses the generations, since – unlike in the biblical tradition – the events in question are but one generation removed from Solomon himself. Al-Dīnawarī thus draws the contrast all the more sharply between righteous Solomon and the Persians, including Nebuchadnezzar.[57]

Al-Dīnawarī develops this theme of disobedience to and falling away from God throughout his sections on pre-Islamic history, including in his depiction of the foundations of Zoroastrianism as representing a fundamental break with monotheism that ruined Iran's ancient ties to true religion. As patrons, Iran's kings are blamed. Employing phrasing that is common to prophetic history and that supports the narrative's critique of Zoroastrianism as a whole, al-Dīnawarī tells the story of how Zoroaster, the "leader of the Magi" (*ṣāḥib al-Majūs*), came to a Kayanid king, Bishtāsif, as a true heretic, proclaiming, "I am the messenger of God [sent] to you (*innī rasūl Allāh ilayka*)," and bringing Bishtāsif "the book (*al-kitāb*), which is [still] in the hands of the Magi," that is, the Avesta.[58]

55 Ibid.
56 Ibid., 63–4.
57 Al-Dīnawarī shares this Persian and Kayanid identification of Nebuchadnezzar with other Muslim sources, including al-Ṭabarī.
58 Al-Dīnawarī, *al-Akhbār al-ṭiwāl*, 65.

Bishtāsif believed in him (*āmana lahu*), followed the religion of the Magi, and brought the people of his kingdom to it, willingly or not. Bishtāsif's governor over Sijistān and Khurāsān, the legendary noble warrior Rustam al-Shadīd, was a fellow Kayanid and lamented Bishtāsif's conversion: "He left the religion of our fathers, which they inherited the last from the first, and yearned for a newly created religion."[59] In the events that followed, Iranians fought among themselves. A grandson of Bishtāsif by the name of Bahmān, who was married to a descendant of David, "entered into the religion of the Children of Israel"; he led an effort to rebuild Jerusalem and returned the throne of Solomon to the city.[60] Bahmān's reversion to Zoroastrianism afterward, however, speaks volumes about Iran's potential for reversion, as he married his own daughter, Khumānī, who became pregnant with a child prior to his death.[61]

It is also worth noting that al-Dīnawarī's approach diminishes doubts regarding the legitimacy of the extensive material he covers afterward in the *Akhbār*, especially regarding the Sasanians. In these later pages, he draws on an extensive corpus of Iranian historiography regarding the regime and its rulers, suggesting familiarity with a version of the *Xwadāy-nāmag* and Sasanian historiography. This focus on kingship might lead one to read the pre-Islamic sections of al-Dīnawarī's material, as a whole, as a work primarily on kingship and politics. But while al-Dīnawarī does have a lot to say about these matters, the pre-Islamic sections are not of one cloth, and were it not for the text's first pages, his treatment of the Sasanians might raise greater doubts about his own loyalties. Sasanian historiography becomes more respectable, in other words, through careful pruning and manipulation of its own mythic accounts of origins and frank admissions of the errors of its forebears. The anxiety he likely feels toward the pre-Islamic legends of Sasanian Iran comes through in a story he relates much further on in his narrative, in which a spy for the Sasanian king, Khusraw Parvīz, witnesses the rebel Bahrām Chūbīn reading the book of animal fables known as *Kalīla wa-Dimna*. The king states that he was not afraid of Bahrām until he heard about his devotion to this book, since the guidance of *Kalīla wa-Dimna* could make a man like Bahrām clever and dangerous.[62]

59 Ibid., 66.
60 Ibid., 68.
61 Ibid., 68–9.
62 Ibid., 136–7.

Through his insertion of Iranian figures onto the canvas of prophetic history, al-Dīnawarī therefore fashions a narrative in which local heroes and villains are just so many figures in a drama common to all Muslims. Iranians are not authochthons, but rather one branch of a human family whose earliest history was determined by major events, including the Flood, the dispersal and intermingling of the world's peoples, and the periodic appearance of true religion and righteous government. All peoples are on the move in this fast-paced account, which, although told from "an Iranian point of view,"[63] does not see Iran in its own, independent terms, nor present it in a nostalgic or uncritical way. Denying the specificity of an Iranian history in these ways serves forgetfulness well. By making his readers forget for the moment that their history and interests were once distinct from those of other Muslims, al-Dīnawarī urges conformity in the realm of religious practice and obedience to a single God.

Justifying the Manipulation of History

Rewriting Iran's past as Muslim history naturally brought traditionists into conflict with those of their sources whose original authors had no knowledge of Islam. A work of uncertain authorship, the *Nihāyat al-arab fī akhbār al-Furs wa-l-ʿArab*, exemplifies this conflict at work. It also exemplifies, through its rationalization of its authorship, a tendency, discussed in the first chapters of this book, to heavily filter Iran's history and to give pride of place to Iraqi authorities and their interpretations of Iran's history.

Mario Grignaschi, who studied the *Nihāya* extensively, dated it to the third/ninth century, after the lifetime of its supposed author, al-Aṣmaʿī (d. 213/828). Grignaschi believed that its real author used a source shared by al-Dīnawarī.[64] He was neither the first nor the last to question the origins of the *Nihāya*.[65] The text itself claims origins in the reign of Hārūn al-Rashīd (170–93/786–809) from materials of even older provenance

[63] Lewin, "al-Dīnawarī," in *EI*².

[64] Mario Grignaschi, "La Nihāyatu-l-ʾArab fī Aḫbāri-l-Furs wa-l-ʿArab," pt. 1, *Bulletin d'études orientales* 22 (1969): 15–67; also, "La *Nihāyatu-l-ʾArab fī Aḫbāri-l-Furs wa-l-ʿArab* et les *Siyaru Mulūki-l-ʿAǧam* du Ps. Ibn-al-Muqaffaʿ," *Bulletin d'études orientales* 26 (1973): 83–184.

[65] Theodor Nöldeke believed it to be a poorly executed recension of al-Dīnawarī's *Akhbār*; *Geschichte der Perser und Araber*, 475–6. See also Browne, "Niháyatu'l-irab"; Franz Rosenthal, "From Arabic Books and Manuscripts I: Pseudo-Aṣmaʿî on the Pre-Islamic Arab Kings," *Journal of the American Oriental Society* 69, no. 2 (1949): 90–1; and Muḥammad Javād Mashkūr, *Tārīkh-i siyāsī-yi Sāsāniyān* (Tehran: Dunyā-yi Kitāb, 1987), 21.

dating to the days of ʿAbd al-Malik (r. 65–86/685–705). Al-Aṣmaʿī is made to explain that he used to entertain Hārūn with accounts of past nations and ages. One night, the caliph expressed a desire to see a copy of a book, the *Siyar al-mulūk*; it was brought to him, and al-Aṣmaʿī read out loud to him the first six sections, which began with Noah's son Shem. Unsatisfied, Hārūn sent al-Aṣmaʿī off with the following instructions:

O Aṣmaʿī, see what was before Shem the son of Noah by way of legends and events, and set them in their right order, and make mention therein of all such as ruled from the time of Adam until it came to Shem the son of Noah, which is the beginning of this book as it is [here] written, king by king and episode by episode.[66]

Al-Aṣmaʿī dutifully visited the jurisconsultant Abū al-Bakhtarī and through him received a copy of Ibn Isḥāq's *Kitāb al-Mubtadaʿ*, that is, the first part of his biography of Muḥammad, covering the beginnings of pre-Islamic prophetic history.[67] Al-Aṣmaʿī explains that he then wrote a book using the *Kitāb al-Mubtadaʿ* as a source for all events prior to and including Noah's death:

[The material concerning Adam, Seth, Enoch (Idrīs), Noah, and the Flood] was added at the beginning of the *Siyar al-mulūk* . . . and we kept it separate therefrom and constituted it as an introduction to that book (it comprising some ten leaves), in such a way that the two form a continuous narrative.[68]

Subsequently, two figures of Umayyad times – ʿĀmir al-Shaʿbī and Ayyūb b. al-Qirriyya – are identified as the authors of the *Siyar al-mulūk* portion of the *Nihāya*, with the explanation that they completed their work under the supervision of ʿAbd al-Malik in the year 85 of the hijra (704 CE) with the aid of Ibn al-Muqaffaʿ, who is identified as "one of the ulama of the ʿAjam [Persians] who knew the histories of their kings (*siyar mulūkihim*), and was profoundly versed in the knowledge of their affairs, the fruits of their culture, and the most signal achievements of their wisdom."[69]

66 Al-Aṣmaʿī [attr.], *Nihāyat al-arab fī akhbār al-Furs wa-l-ʿArab*, ed. Muḥammad Taqī Dānish-Pazhūh (Tehran: Anjuman-i Āsār va Mafākhir-i Farhangī, 1996), 1; Browne, "Niháyatu'l-irab," 197.

67 Gordon Darnell Newby has sought, somewhat controversially, to reconstruct this part of Ibn Isḥāq's work using quotations in later sources; see *The Making of the Last Prophet: A Reconstruction of the Earliest Biography of Muhammad* (Columbia: University of South Carolina Press, 1989); cf. Lawrence I. Conrad, "Recovering Lost Texts: Some Methodological Issues," *Journal of the American Oriental Society* 113, no. 2 (1993): 258–63.

68 *Nihāya*, 2; also, Browne, "Niháyatu'l-irab," 198.

69 *Nihāya*, 16–17; Browne, "Niháyatu'l-irab," 199–200.

In this convoluted story, al-Aṣmaʿī maintains that Persian history could be inserted into prophetic history while remaining intact as a non-conflictual account. Nonetheless, we have knowledge of Persian history only indirectly, through multiple mediators vetting it along the way: Ibn al-Muqaffaʿ, ʿĀmir al-Shaʿbī and Ayyūb b. al-Qirriyya, al-Aṣmaʿī, and finally the *Nihāya*, the finished product. We are asked to believe that a book treating Sasanian era historiography – the term *siyar al-mulūk* here and generally having such associations – began with Noah's son Shem – in other words, that prophetic history was part of Persian history before Islam. Never mind that Ibn al-Muqaffaʿ thrived a half-century after ʿAbd al-Malik and so could not have served as a consultant to the caliph.[70]

However implausible in hindsight, the work's author must have supposed that his account was believable enough and likewise that he had explained the provenance of his material in a way that would satisfy his readers. Hārūn al-Rashīd's role is vaguely reminiscent of his role in the *Arabian Nights*, suggesting another dimension to the work and, together with its anachronism, the possibility that it represented a more "popular" sort of text than al-Dīnawarī's *Akhbār*, aimed at a learned public less hung up on the strictures of dating but impressed by the lineage that the author cites as well as, he must have hoped, the contents of the book itself. In any case, what one sees here are different phases of writing collapsed and, likewise, the downplaying of difference, as Iran's pre-Islamic heritage became part of a Muslim past – a development more probable in the third/ninth century or later than in the first or second/seventh or eighth.

Raising Doubts about the Past

The previous two strategies involved attempts to place the Iranian past within larger frameworks or to reformulate it in ways that diminish its significance as an independent focus of loyalty. The heritage of kingship receives special attention: kings and their dramas define the arc of history and link it to the emergence of Zoroastrianism, which was supported by royal patronage. Yet even when they are unsympathetic, traditionists using these strategies address Iranian history in ways that acknowledge local knowledge, even if it must be represented as having been vetted by the caliph in Baghdad.

Nevertheless, there are also many traditions that reflect less engagement with and respect for Iran's past, projecting instead a wholesale

[70] As noted by Browne, "Niháyatu'l-irab," 200.

distrust of its legacy, particularly with regard to kingship. These challenge the moral bases of royal authority, which are presented as being at odds with those of the caliphs and Islam. They also address the foundations and practices of Zoroastrianism in terms that present little or nothing of this heritage as salvageable. In this type of "genealogical thinking," antique periods of history become a canvas for expressing concerns about the past, gratitude for its finitude, and a wish to banish it and the examples it provides from memory.

Returning to Gayūmart, for example, one sees anxieties expressed in traditions that depict him as a morally corrupt forefather who, while responsible for actions typical of world-ruling kings, namely, constructing cities and protecting their populations, fell away from virtue and obedience to God. In one tradition that al-Ṭabarī attributes to non-Persians, this theme is developed by means of an explanation for how Persians could possibly think that Gayūmart had originated humanity when he was father only to the Persians themselves. By this account, Gayūmart first took control of the mountains of Ṭabaristān and ruled there and in Fārs; subsequently, his power grew, and he commanded his children to take control of Babylon. For various (brief) periods, they ruled over all of the regions of the earth. Gayūmart built cities and castles, populated them, and made them prosperous. He also assembled weapons and established a cavalry. At the end of his life, however, Gayūmart behaved haughtily and pretended to be Adam, saying: "If someone calls me by any other name, I shall cut off his head."[71] Also according to al-Ṭabarī's sources, Gayūmart married thirty women who produced many offspring, among them his son Mārī and daughter Māriyāna, parents to Persia's later kings. The upshot of the story, reflecting cynical appraisals of Zoroastrian cosmogony, is that Persia's kings came into the world through a delusional and corrupt father.[72]

This case is indicative of wider efforts by traditionists to write over Persia's past by embedding in their narratives negative associations and incriminating details, along with labels, iconic images, homologies, and other devices that represented Iran's past as potentially deeply antagonistic to Islam. Versions of such traditions circulated widely, crossing genres and geography, becoming cultural knowledge that was

[71] Al-Ṭabarī, *Ta'rīkh*, I:147–8; *History of al-Ṭabarī*, 1:318–19.

[72] Al-Ṭabarī states that non-Persian scholars believe that Gayūmart was not Adam, but rather Gomer b. Japheth b. Noah; ibid. Compare a similar passage cited by al-Bīrūnī (not discussed above): al-Bīrūnī, *Chronologie*, 24.

continuously reproduced, even if an individual traditionist transmitting such reports had other narrative goals in mind.

Two further examples demonstrate the ways in which negative associations and incriminating details were passed on by traditionists even though they were, in hindsight, ridiculous. They illustrate the deep and pervasive distrust in some quarters of Iran's past and particularly its royal and Zoroastrian heritage.

In the first case, the Qurʾan's "Pharaoh" was identified as a Persian. This identification, made by Qurʾan exegetes, reflects how such traditions could originate and be deemed just credible enough to be passed on. It also suggests the special capacity of Qurʾan commentary, with its atomistic structure, to preserve and pass on insinuations.

Exegetes ostensibly addressed the following questions: who was the Pharaoh mentioned by the Qurʾan and who were his people? Especially important passages regarding Pharaoh and his family are found in Qurʾan 28. Here the term Pharaoh (*firʿawn*) occurs in reference to the opponent of Moses and the Children of Israel. In Qurʾan 28:7–8, it is the family of Pharaoh (*āl firʿawn*) that takes in Moses, after his mother, at God's command, puts him out. In Qurʾan 28:15, Moses enters an unnamed city and finds two people fighting, one from his own party (*shīʿatihi*) and the other from his enemies. The man from his party appeals to Moses for help against his opponent. The Qurʾan states that Moses struck the opponent and made an end of him. Then he (Moses) said: "This is of Satan's doing. He is an enemy who clearly leads astray."[73]

The twenty-eighth chapter of the Qurʾan does not specify Egypt (*Miṣr*) as the location of Pharaoh but otherwise reflects Jewish and Christian traditions regarding Moses and Pharaoh and their biblical Egyptian context.[74] Most exegetes have placed the chapter in an Egyptian context and identified Moses's enemies within it. For example, Qurʾan 28:5–6 states: "We wished to show favor to those who had been treated as weaklings in the land, and to make them examples and to make them the inheritors, and to give them a place in the land, and to show Pharaoh and Hāmān and their hosts what they feared from them." Muqātil

[73] Regarding Pharaoh in the Qurʾan, see Reuven Firestone, "Pharaoh," in *Encyclopaedia of the Qurʾān*, ed. Jane Dammen McAuliffe, 6 vols., 4:66–8 (Leiden: Brill, 2001–6).

[74] Elsewhere in the Qurʾan, the association of Pharaoh with Egypt is strong; see esp. Qurʾan 10:87–8 and 43:51. See also A. J. Wensinck and G. Vajda ("Firʿawn," in *EI*^{2}), who treat this idea of Persian origins as "isolated," even though the sources would suggest it circulated more widely than one might expect, in good measure because of the general strength of the commentarial traditions of Mujāhid and al-Ṭabarī.

b. Sulaymān (d. 150/767) explained that "the land" in the passage refers to "the land of Egypt," whereas "their hosts" refers to "the Copts." The Copts were taking precautions because the soothsayers (*kāhins*) had told Pharaoh that in that year, a child from the Children of Israel would be born who would later destroy him.[75]

As early as the end of the first Islamic century, Mujāhid b. Jabr al-Makkī (d. between 100/718 and 104/722), in commenting on Qur'an 28:15, identified the party of Moses (*shī'atihi*) as the Children of Israel. Unlike Muqātil, he does not directly identify the opponent, instead offering the information that "Pharaoh was from Iṣṭakhr in Fārs." Mujāhid's statement is known from a recension of his commentary edited by 'Abd al-Raḥmān al-Ṭāhir b. Muḥammad al-Sūratī (the origins of this recension have been debated extensively by modern scholars, who view it as an important case study regarding the possibilities for dating the development of early Muslim tradition).[76] Mujāhid's statement is also recorded by al-Ṭabarī, who treats it as a possibility but gives preference in his commentary to other traditions that situate Pharaoh in Egypt. Al-Ṭabarī reproduces Mujāhid's statement, *wa-kāna fir'awn min Fāris min Iṣṭakhr*,

[75] Regarding Qur'an 28:15, Muqātil identifies the two fighters as unbelievers, with the party of Moses referring to the Children of Israel and the enemies to the Copts (*al-Qibṭ*); *Tafsīr*, ed. 'Abd Allāh Maḥmūd Shiḥāta, 5 vols. ([Cairo]: al-Hay'a al-Miṣriyya al-'Āmma li-l-Kitab, 1979–89), 3:335–6. Regarding the dating of his *tafsīr*, see esp. M. Plessner and A. Rippin, "Muḳātil b. Sulaymān," in *EI*^{2}.

[76] The chain of authorities for this report is as follows: 'Abd al-Raḥmān – Ibrāhīm – Ādam [b. Abī Iyās] (d. 220 or 221/835–7) – Warqā' – Ibn Abī Najīḥ (d. 130 or 131/747–9) – Mujāhid. *Tafsīr Mujāhid*, ed. 'Abd al-Raḥmān al-Ṭāhir b. Muḥammad al-Sūratī (Doha: Maṭābi' al-Dawḥa al-Ḥadītha, 1976), 482, on Qur'an 28:15. For the debate, see esp. Georg Stauth, "Die Überlieferung des Korankommentars Muǧāhid b. Ǧabrs: Zur Frage der Rekonstruktion der in den Sammelwerken des 3. Jh. d. H. benutzten frühislamischen Quellenwerke" (Ph.D. diss., Universität Giessen, 1969); Fred Leemhuis, "Ms. 1075 Tafsīr of the Cairene Dār al-Kutub and Muǧāhid's *Tafsīr*," in *Proceedings of the Ninth Congress of the Union Européenne des Arabisants et Islamisants* (Amsterdam, Sept. 1–7, 1978), ed. Rudolph Peters, 169–77 (Leiden: E. J. Brill, 1981), and the notes therein (including on p. 171, pertaining to the chain of authorities I cite here), and by the same author, "Origins and Early Development of the *Tafsīr* Tradition," in *Approaches to the History of the Interpretation of the Qur'ān*, ed. Andrew Rippin, 13–30 (Oxford: Clarendon, 1988); Herbert Berg, *The Development of Exegesis in Early Islam: The Authenticity of Muslim Literature from the Formative Period* (Richmond: Curzon, 2000), esp. 73–8 and 115–18, as well as "Competing Paradigms in the Study of Islamic Origins: Qur'ān 15:89–91 and the Value of *Isnāds*," in *Method and Theory in the Study of Islamic Origins*, ed. Berg, 259–90 (Leiden: Brill, 2003); and Harald Motzki with Nicolet Boekhoff-Van Der Voort and Sean W. Anthony, *Analysing Muslim Traditions: Studies in Legal, Exegetical and Maghāzī Ḥadīth* (Leiden: Brill, 2010), esp. 249–53.

verbatim, but not his authorities; he knows the first transmitters from Mujāhid but credits different traditionists afterward. This is interesting insofar as it suggests the likelihood that the tradition was picked up by different transmitters of Mujāhid's work.[77] In other words, it had a certain currency among Qurʾan exegetes, who, as current research broadly suggests, had at least some latitude to pick and choose from Mujāhid's corpus.

The significance of the Persian identification of Pharaoh lies in his association with all manner of corruptness, an idea that has long and enduring roots among Muslims. In Iran, when in 1971 ʿAlī Sharīʿatī wished to insult the last Shah of Iran, he labeled him a pharaoh; Sayyid Qutb (d. 1966) did likewise for Egypt's president Gamal Abdel Nasser. In the revolution of 2011 in Egypt, Hosni Mubarak's regime was labeled a "pharaonic dictatorship" by the opposition figure Mohamad al-Baradei.[78] The identification of Pharaoh as a Persian makes Persia into the sort of place that could produce a Pharaoh, and it also insinuates a link between Iran's ancient rulers and the ruling house of Pharaoh, the choice of Iṣṭakhr being significant as both the Sasanian homeland and a historic center of Zoroastrianism. It was the fire of Iṣṭakhr that was said to have died out for the first time in a thousand years on the night of Muḥammad's birth. Pharaoh, an opponent of monotheism, would then hail from a city widely known to have historic associations with Iran's last ruling dynasty and with Zoroastrianism as well.[79]

Mujāhid's tradition traveled widely. It was displaced from the Qurʾan verse it originally explained, disconnected from Mujāhid as the source to whom it was credited, and joined together with other traditions that originally contradicted it. Whereas in al-Ṭabarī's text it is presented as a

[77] Muḥammad b. ʿAmr – Abū ʿĀṣim – ʿĪsā – al-Ḥārith – al-Ḥasan – Warqāʾ (*jamīʿan*) – Ibn Abī Najīḥ – Mujāhid; al-Ṭabarī, *Jāmiʿ al-bayān ʿan taʾwīl āy al-Qurʾān*, ed. Aḥmad ʿAbd al-Rāziq al-Bakrī et al., 10 vols. (Cairo: Dār al-Salām, 2007), 8:6359 (on Qurʾan 28:15).

[78] See "Elbaradei urges Mubarak to quit," *al-Jazeera*, Jan. 29, 2011; http://www.aljazeera.com/news/middleeast/2011/01/201112919263354 2354.html.

[79] Regarding Pharaonic Egypt and its complex legacy, much has been said; see esp. Ulrich Haarmann, "Regional Sentiment in Medieval Islamic Egypt," *Bulletin of the School of Oriental and African Studies* 43, no. 1 (1980): 55–66, and his "Medieval Muslim Perceptions of Pharaonic Egypt," in *Ancient Egyptian Literature: History and Forms*, ed. Antonio Loprieno, 605–27 (Leiden: E. J. Brill, 1996); Michael Cook, "Pharaonic History in Medieval Egypt," *Studia Islamica*, no. 57 (1983): 67–103, and the Ph.D. dissertation of Mark Fraser Pettigrew, "The Wonders of the Ancients: Arab-Islamic Representations of Ancient Egypt" (University of California, Berkeley, 2004).

marginal possibility, for at least some exegetes it came to have a respected status as a variant opinion or even as the only information offered.[80] In the fifth/eleventh century, al-Māwardī (d. 450/1058), while discussing a reference to Pharaoh in Qur'an 50:13, rather neutrally states that there was a difference of opinion as to who Pharaoh was, and he gives Mujāhid's view first.[81] Ibn Kathīr (d. 774/1373) – admittedly beyond the purview of my time period – reports amid an explanation of Qur'an 2:49–50[82] that Pharaoh was from Iṣṭakhr, and he offers two genealogies for, as he puts it, "Pharaoh, who was in the time of Moses": either he was al-Walīd b. Muṣʿab b. al-Rayyān, or he was Muṣʿab b. al-Rayyān himself. Either way, he was a descendant of Noah through ʿImlīq b. Lud b. Aram b. Shem, and his roots were Persian from Iṣṭakhr (*aṣluhu Fārisī min Iṣṭakhr*).[83]

Ancient history generally allowed far greater liberties for invention than the history of, for example, the early Muslim community. Qur'an commentaries could provide a particularly good vehicle for passing on such views, since traditionists had the burden of searching for details that could shed light on the allusive history related by the Qur'an, and they had recourse to a body of shared tradition that was frequently recycled. Their labors were circumscribed by the many and rigorous demands of their genre, whose typically atomistic structure, in which each verse is explained in turn, could result in an equally atomistic presentation of historical knowledge. Although the narratives in histories are also often fragmented by citations of sources, their chronological structure arguably puts greater emphasis on narrative consistency, and therefore plausibility, than do the commentaries.[84] By comparison,

80 E.g., Ibn Abī Ḥātim cites Mujāhid for Pharaoh's origins in Iṣṭakhr in *Tafsīr al-Qur'ān al-ʿaẓīm: Musnadan ʿan al-Rasūl Allāh wa-l-ṣaḥāba wa-l-tābiʿīn*, 14 vols. (Sidon and Beirut: al-Maktaba al-ʿAṣriyya, 2003), 5:1531 (no. 8787, on Qur'an 7:103), 1537 (no. 8813, on Qur'an 7:121–2), 6:1972–3 (no. 10504, on Qur'an 10:75), and 2080 (no. 11189, on Qur'an 11:97); but see also 9:2953–5 (on Qur'an 28:15).

81 Al-Māwardī, *al-Nukat wa-l-ʿuyūn: Tafsīr al-Māwardī*, ed. Khiḍr Muḥammad Khiḍr, 4 vols. (Kuwait: Wizārat al-Awqāf wa-l-Shuʾūn al-Islāmiyya, 1982), 4:83 (on Qur'an 50:13).

82 Qur'an 2:49–50: "And [recall] when We delivered you from the family of Pharaoh who were afflicting you with evil torment, slaughtering your sons, but sparing your women. In that there was a great trial for you from your Lord; And when We divided the sea for you and saved you and drowned the family of Pharaoh as you watched."

83 Ibn Kathīr, *Tafsīr al-Qur'ān al-ʿaẓīm*, 7 vols. (Beirut: Dār al-Andalus, 1966), 1:157.

84 See the critique of al-Maqdisī (fl. 355/966), *al-Badʾ wa-l-taʾrīkh*, ed. and trans. Clément Huart, 6 vols. (Paris: Ernest Leroux, 1899–1919; repr., without the translation, Baghdad: Maktabat al-Muthannā, n.d.), 3:81–2.

with a less focused narrative thread, exegetes could – arguably – introduce new material more freely.[85]

In its association of Pharaoh with Persia, the tradition reflects general distrust of Iran's heritage of kingship. Ibn Kathīr indiscriminately casts doubt on the heritage of all Persians when he declares Pharaoh to have Persian origins. There is also a way in which particular Iranian cities are assigned a negative heritage. For example, one can read in this light the commentary of al-Samʿānī (d. 489/1096), who, in the fifth/eleventh century, chose to cite an unspecified "some of them" (*ʿan baʿḍihim*, or "one of them") as the source for his assertion that Pharaoh came from Iṣṭakhr. Similarly, other traditions put forward Iṣfahān or Hamadhān as Pharaoh's home.[86] The tradition was also helpful to Egyptians. As Ulrich Haarmann has noted, the Qurʾanic Pharaoh represented the epitome of tyranny and disbelief, and this posed a problem for Egyptians, requiring strategies to salvage Egyptian regional pride. And so a host of antique Egyptian virtues (*faḍāʾil*) were elaborated, monotheistic sites such as Joseph's prison and granary and Jacob's mosque were identified, and Pharaoh and his line were even given Iranian, not Egyptian, origins. Haarmann surmises: "One cannot help suspecting a certain envy directed towards the lucky Iranians who had so much less difficulty in accommodating their own past within the framework of Islamic doctrine."[87]

Contra Haarmann, while the Qurʾan may not have singled out Kisrā as it did Pharaoh, Iran's past clearly vexed traditionists, as is also evident in a second case, in which they passed on negative associations in a fantasy that associated Zoroastrian fire worship to murder, jealousy, and the occult. In this case, an incriminating detail gained a foothold in prophetic history, as featured in Qurʾan commentaries, because it helped to explain a common theme, that of Adam's sons and their sacrifices, and drew a connection between a narrative element in it – sacrificial fire – and Zoroastrian practice. It was presented as simply one of many details

[85] Such innovations might be noticed by specialists in *tafsīr*, but once they entered the body of exegetical works, they would have staying power; see Walid A. Saleh's discussion of the "genealogical" character of Qurʾan commentary in *The Formation of the Classical* Tafsīr *Tradition: The Qurʾān Commentary of al-Thaʿlabī (d. 427/1035)* (Leiden: Brill, 2004), esp. 14–16.

[86] Manṣūr b. Muḥammad al-Samʿānī, *Tafsīr al-Qurʾān*, ed. Abū Tamīm Yāsir b. Ibrāhīm and Abū Bilāl Ghanīm b. ʿAbbās b. Ghanīm, 6 vols. (Riyadh: Dār al-Waṭan, 1997), 5:237–8 (on Qurʾan 50:13) and 6:150 (on 79:17–24).

[87] Haarmann, "Regional Sentiment," esp. 56–7.

clarifying ambiguous points in prophetic history, connecting elements within it, and otherwise producing narrative unity and coherence.

Adam's son Cain is known by Muslims to have been the first to commit murder. The Qur'an refers to the two sons of Adam, their sacrifices, and God's acceptance of only one sacrifice. The text joins the two sons' sacrifices to the murder of one son by the other, without naming either son, spelling out precisely the relationship between the sacrifice and the murder, or specifying who murdered whom.[88] Traditionists filled out the narrative: Cain committed the murder out of jealousy for the success of Abel. Some then extended the story, making Cain the first to worship fire after his sacrifice failed. According to one report cited by al-Ṭabarī in his *Ta'rīkh*, after Cain killed Abel, he fled to the Yemen. Iblīs came to him there and explained that Abel's sacrifice had been consumed by the fire because Abel had worshipped and ministered to it. He then instructed Cain to set up a fire for himself and his progeny, which Cain did, building a fire temple (*bayt nār*), and so Cain "was the first to set up and worship it."[89] Aḥmad b. Muḥammad al-Thaʿlabī (d. 427/1035) furnishes another story according to which a blind son of Cain pelted Cain with a stone, killing him (and then his own son, by an overhard slap).[90] Al-Thaʿlabī goes on to note the sinful, merrymaking ways of Cain's descendants, who dedicated themselves to music, wine, fire worship, adultery, and other abominations. For all these sins, Cain's descendants perished in the Flood.[91]

The idea's originators may well have been Iranian. Accordingly, they did not need to specify fire worship as a distinctively Zoroastrian practice. In eighth/fourteenth-century Egypt (again, admittedly beyond the purview of this study), al-Nuwayrī (d. 733/1333) knows the traditions about Cain and fire worship; he uses phrasing that is similar to that of al-Thaʿlabī but

88 Qur'an 5:27–32, on which see Heribert Busse, "Cain and Abel," in *Encyclopaedia of the Qur'ān*, 1:270–2. Compare with the biblical account of the murder in Genesis 4: 1–16 (including 4–5: God "had regard for Abel and his offering, but for Cain and his offering he had no regard").

89 Al-Ṭabarī does not name sources for this tradition, choosing instead the formula: "It has been mentioned that . . . "; al-Ṭabarī, *Ta'rīkh*, I:166–7. He does not mention fire temples or Zoroastrians in his commentary on Qur'an 5:27–32 (nor does he employ the phrase *bayt nār* or *bayt al-nār* anywhere in his *tafsīr*). Cf. Balʿamī, *Tārīkh-i Balʿamī*, 1:110–11.

90 Al-Thaʿlabī, *al-Kashf wa-l-bayān*, ed. Abū Muḥammad b. ʿĀshūr, 10 vols. (Beirut: Dār Iḥyā' al-Turāth al-ʿArabī, 2002), 4:52–3 (on Qur'an 5:27–32). He introduces the story with "They said . . . "

91 Ibid. Al-Thaʿlabī cites Mujāhid here. On Muslim legends about Cain and Abel generally, see Roberto Tottoli, "Cain and Abel (Qābīl wa Hābīl)," in *EI*[3].

clarifies the Persian and Zoroastrian connection for readers less familiar with the cultural context of fire worship. He recounts that after Cain, Jamshīd was the first of the Persian kings to worship fire; the practice then spread to Iraq, Fārs, Kirmān, Sijistān, Khurāsān, Ṭabaristān, Jibāl, Azarbaijan, Arrān, and the lands of Hind, Sind, and China. In all of these lands, fire temples were built. In his day, al-Nuwayrī reports, fire worship had died out in most of these places, except for Hind.[92]

While Muslims may have been familiar with some details about Zoroastrian cosmogony, their general ignorance made it possible for them to entertain such a damning tradition, which inserted a Zoroastrian practice into prophetic history and washed out alternative earlier Iranian ideas about fire. Among modern academics, the history of fire worship in general and the worship of particular fires among Zoroastrians has been the subject of long, enduring, and perhaps irresolvable debates.[93] Whatever the origins of or later Zoroastrian ideas about the practice (in the Avesta, for example, or the *Bundahishn*), these Muslims traditionists took significant liberties.[94]

Within prophetic history, Cain was available as a strongly defined, even wooden, figure suitable as a focus for narrative expansion. Traditionists appear to have put Cain to work committing other transgressions (from a Muslim point of view) of a particularly Zoroastrian character, mentioning his wish to marry his own twin sister, rather than his brother's sister, evoking, for some traditionists at least, consanguineous marriage.[95] In these traditions, Cain also exposes the body of Abel, "not knowing about burials." God sends two crow brothers who fight, the one killing the other and then covering his dead brother with soil. From this, Cain learns to bury his brother. Qurʾan 5:31 also mentions a crow, sent to show

92 He does not name his sources. Aḥmad b. ʿAbd al-Wahhāb al-Nuwayrī, *Nihāyat al-arab fī funūn al-adab*, 33 vols. (Cairo: Maṭbaʿat Dār al-Kutub al-Miṣriyya, 1923–2002), 1:105–6.

93 Among the several treatments of this topic, see Mary Boyce, "On the Zoroastrian Temple Cult of Fire," *Journal of the American Oriental Society* 95, no. 3 (1975), 454–65, and Mark Garrison, "Fire Altars," in *EIr*.

94 Compare, for example, the cosmogony in the eighteenth chapter of the *Bundahishn* where the text speaks about the fires of Farnbāg, Gushnasp, and Būrzīn-mitrō, which have existed since the original creation when they were formed by Ahura Mazdā; *Zand-Ākāsīh*, ch. 18:8–9 (pp. 158–9).

95 E.g., reported on different authorities by al-Ṭabarī, *Taʾrīkh*, I:137–40, 144. On such practices and perceptions of them, see esp. Bodil Hjerrild, *Studies in Zoroastrian Family Law: A Comparative Analysis* (Copenhagen: Museum Tusculanum Press, 2003), 167–203, and Geert Jan van Gelder, *Close Relationships: Incest and Inbreeding in Classical Arabic Literature* (London: I. B. Tauris, 2005), 36–9.

the murderer how to bury his brother's naked corpse, and quotes the murderer: "Woe is me. Am I unable to be like this crow, and hide the corpse of my brother?"[96] While the Qur'anic text does not spell out Cain's ignorance, the traditionists do. Their emphasis might suggest an intention to parody the Zoroastrian practice of exposing the dead. Such traditions depict Zoroastrian practices in incorrect or distorted ways that seem mean-spirited because their reporters make little or no contact with the historical ideas, doctrines, and institutions of Zoroastrianism that supported them.

In a parallel strategy, when Zoroaster is mentioned, he is made the author of reprehensible practices. Al-Jāḥiẓ reportedly claimed that Zoroaster required from his companions certain practices, which al-Jāḥiẓ named as ritual ablution with urine, sexual relations with mothers, and glorification of fires with revolting substances.[97] Whatever Zoroastrians' actual practices, the list suggests al-Jāḥiẓ's disgust, and a similarly phrased list is also cited by al-Māwardī in an argument against the law of Zoroaster, who prescribed practices that the traditionist finds objectionable.[98]

In promoting such reports, traditionists establish negative genealogies for Iranian, and especially Zoroastrian, institutions, belief systems, and practices that pay little heed to indigenous ideas on the same subjects. Instead, they transport them to foreign narrative contexts. Iranian Muslim readers may never have subscribed to the ideas that Gayūmart usurped the role of Adam, Pharaoh was a Persian, or Cain initiated fire worship, but hearing these reports from some of the most highly respected traditionists likely created negative associations. One may also wonder at the spirit in which traditionists traded in such ridiculous claims. Was al-Jāḥīẓ expressing his distaste for Zoroastrianism by speaking off the cuff, whereas Ibn al-Jawzī took such statements literally when he quoted him? In any case, the reporter excluded any substantial knowledge about the custom in

[96] Al-Ṭabarī, *Ta'rīkh*, I:138–39 and 141.

[97] Al-Jāḥiẓ is quoted by Ibn al-Jawzī (d. 597/1201) in his great work of Ḥanbalī polemic, *Talbīs Iblīs* (The Devil's delusion), ed. Muḥammad Munīr al-Dimashqī et al. (Beirut: Dār al-Rā'id al-'Arabī, n.d. [198?]), 62; he is also cited by Ibn al-Jawzī in *al-Muntaẓam fī ta'rīkh al-mulūk wa-l-umam*, ed. Muḥammad 'Abd al-Qādir 'Aṭā and Muṣṭafā 'Abd al-Qādir 'Aṭā, 18 vols. (Beirut: Dār al-Kutub al-'Ilmiyya, 1992), 1:412–3. On the use of bull's urine (*gūmīz*) for ritual purity as part of Zoroastrian religious praxis, see Boyce "Cleansing i. In Zoroastrianism," in *EIr*, and "Gōmēz," in *EIr*.

[98] Al-Māwardī, *A'lām al-nubuwwa*, ed. Muḥammad al-Mu'taṣim bi-llāh al-Baghdādī (Beirut: Dār al-Kitāb al-'Arabī, 1987), 61.

question, and such unforgettable reports chipped away at residual fondness and loyalty for Iran's royal and Zoroastrian heritage.

Conclusion

The adoption of Islam by Iranians initiated the formation of a set of conflicting loyalties that raised doubts about the ruling institutions of pre-Islamic times and their supporting ideologies, belief systems, and religious practices, many of which continued to play important roles in the realms of politics, culture, and society.[99] As a result, traditionists were highly selective in their references and allusions to Iran's pre-Islamic past and developed ways of reporting that promoted conformity with their ideas about a common Muslim society.

The past does not exist on its own terms but rather must be assembled, this occurring as an act of representation. Representation takes place within a social framework encompassing agents and their audiences, and it is made to an audience on behalf of a social entity, its most blatant forms appearing as propaganda. But Muslims could not write history however they pleased. The past was not infinitely flexible, but it could be reworked within certain boundaries. Consensus of this sort generally heavily circumscribes the work of traditionists. To rephrase Foucault's radical statement about authors: culture is the principle of thrift that constrains the proliferation of meanings.[100]

Traditions made good use of the pre-Islamic past as they sought to shape broader understandings about Persians and their history. Details of this history mattered and were meaningful because they gave Persians a sense of their own history in relation to that of other Muslims. Editorial choices on questions such as how humanity began were not accidental, but rather reflected broader ideas and sentiments. These sentiments were sometimes nostalgic, but often reflected reservation, anxiety, and distrust.

In working with their materials, traditionists were ingenious in devising ways to maintain, preserve, and value as "authentic" aspects of Iran's past that served their agendas while omitting, reformulating, maligning, and otherwise suppressing those that troubled them. One way in which they did this was to represent Iran's past specifically as "Persian" history, and

[99] See, e.g., Dimitri Gutas, *Greek Thought, Arabic Culture: The Graeco-Arabic Translation Movement in Baghdad and Early ʿAbbāsid Society (2nd–4th/8th–10th Centuries)* (New York: Routledge, 1998), esp. Part 2, "Translation and Society," 107ff.

[100] As nicely rephrased by Steven Kemper, *The Presence of the Past: Chronicles, Politics and Culture in Sinhala Life* (Ithaca, NY: Cornell University Press, 1991), 17–18.

to give it structural significance alongside other histories, anthologize it among them, or treat it separately, but as only part of a wider history of humanity. In such ways, Iran's history became neither unique nor sufficient. For Iranians who thought they had their own separate history even if only one among others, traditionists showed otherwise, submerging it in the broader history leading to Islam. In al-Dīnawarī's case, the extensive citation of Iranian details draws attention to Iran's place in that history. Traditionists also chipped away at Iranians' confidence in a heritage of kingship and Zoroastrianism by circulating ridiculous associations and details that fared surprisingly well against the critical apparatuses of exegetical and historical studies.

What made these strategies possible, at root, was the common understanding that traditionists, in whatever genre they worked, were responsible for creating narrative coherence by clarifying details, drawing connections in history, acknowledging and, where possible, showing ways to resolve contradictions – all of these commentatorial tasks giving them liberty to shape what Muslims knew about the past. To these issues of narrative coherence, memory, and forgetfulness we turn in greater depth in Chapter 5, with a discussion of narrative filters and a whole body of traditions that, as in our third category in this chapter, raised doubts about the past.

5

The Unhappy Prophet

The internal logic of most great narratives is oppositional and features conflicts. In the Iliad, we have Achilles versus Hector; in the Sanskrit Ramayana, the princely Rama versus Ravana; and in the Bible, Moses versus Pharaoh. Early Muslim narratives were no different and were structured around profound oppositions: the Prophet versus Abū Jahl or Abū Lahab; Muḥammad's stalwart companion, a slave of Abyssinian background called Bilāl, versus a pagan Meccan named Umayya b. Khalaf; in the first *fitna*, the Prophet's beloved wife ʿĀʾisha and the Meccan aristocrats Ṭalḥa and al-Zubayr versus ʿAlī, and subsequently ʿAlī versus Muʿāwiya; and in the second *fitna*, al-Ḥusayn versus Muʿāwiya's son Yazīd, and the Umayyads and their supporters versus Zubayr's son ʿAbd Allāh. In narratives about later times, such oppositions continue: most grandly, the Umayyads versus the ʿAbbasids, but also, on a smaller stage in ʿAbbasid times, al-Amīn vs. al-Maʾmūn, and the latter versus Aḥmad b. Ḥanbal. Such oppositions, as rooted in historical realities as they may have been, form part of the spine of all accounts of the first centuries of Islam. They represent the narrative means by which the earliest traditionists explained the Islamic kerygma as the bright light of Islam conquering the forces of darkness, and why – because of the oppositions among the earliest Muslims – Utopia did not follow.

When they situated Islam on the vast screen of world history, traditionists of the first centuries saw the past in imperial and equally oppositional terms, with late Sasanian Persia and its rulers cast opposite Muḥammad and a small coterie of companions who sought to win Persia over to Islam and, failing that, to conquer it (or in more theological terms, to "open" it). The opposition of Muḥammad's community to late Sasanian

Persia became part of the Muslim community's shared imagination and of a metanarrative underlying and informing numerous tellings and retellings of the past, whereby the unfolding of a meaningful history could be plumbed by Qurʾan exegetes and scholars of Hadith, collectors of poetry, genealogies, and anecdotes, and creators of Prophetic biography and conquest accounts. This opposition added a historical dimension and depth to the appearance of Islam in history, and through the greatness of Muḥammad's Iranian opponents, it showcased the power of his message and his early community.

The memory of late Sasanian Persia often fared poorly, to put it mildly, in this metanarrative, as I have already discussed in Chapter 3. In what follows, I argue that when traditionists up through the third/ninth and fourth/tenth centuries created an image of late Sasanian Persia in opposition to Muḥammad and Islam, they restricted future generations' capacity for memory as they raised profound doubts about its past. This restriction can be understood in cultural terms as negatively conditioning the expectations of Muslims for knowledge about Iran's past, especially its late Sasanian history. It worked through the application of narrative "filters," which I identify as (1) labeling, (2) creating homologies, (3) fashioning icons, and (4) gendering. For each of these filters, I consider narratives, their oppositions, and the operation of the filter on past memory.

Like this book more broadly, this chapter seeks to put memory of Iran's past into a broader context so as to show that it did not arise on its own, but rather was part of wider developments in which Muslims took measure of the past and sought to preserve it or, alternatively, to banish it to oblivion. In either case, the past came into being only insofar as Muslims molded it. Whereas elsewhere in this study I consider issues of textual transmission and authority for the same purpose (especially the importance of memory generated in Iraq to traditionists in later times in Iran), my efforts here are more structural, as I try to outline a logic to memory that was primary in the sense of its early development, but more precisely primary in its impact and importance. In order to suggest something of the strength and endurance of this metanarrative, I also touch on how some Muslims today have drawn on surprisingly unnuanced views of late Sasanian Persia in conflict with the Prophet.

Labeling

I begin with the first narrative filter, "labeling," and an example that illustrates an opposition between Qurʾanic history sanctioned by Muḥammad and that sanctioned by Iranian sources. In all cultures, labels can serve as important memory aids around which ideas cluster. But equally, by narrowing down the past to a set of associations, they promote oblivion. The Qurʾanic term *jāhiliyya* (the era of "ignorance," *jahl*) has at various points in history fulfilled the latter function, obliterating for many of its audiences the complexities of pre-Islamic Arabian (especially Ḥijāzī) culture and society. It also became a signifier that served constructive purposes in the late Umayyad and early ʿAbbasid periods. As Rina Drory persuasively argued, images of a distant, *jāhilī* pre-Islamic past played a prominent role in power struggles in the cultural arena and belonged to an overall project of constructing Arab ethnicity. She noted that in such struggles, "the pre-Islamic past becomes an icon of 'Arab' ethnic identity. Pre-Islamic poetry, which in classical Arab literature was long assigned the function of authentically representing the past, becomes a central prop for that icon, and consequently, a focus of literary attention and activity."[1] Drory argued that the function of the pre-Islamic past changed from late Umayyad to early ʿAbbasid times, with attitudes shifting from its condemnation "as an age of wrong belief, dominated by conflicting tribal interests and rivalries" to a view of it as a "unified Arab past, in which the 'true' values of Arab ethnic identity were manifested, and even emphasized as against Persian values."[2]

At roughly the same time, other pasts took shape, including Persia's. In this process, traditionists applied two labels derived from the Qurʾan to Persian epic: *asāṭīr al-awwalīn* ("fables of the ancients") and *lahw al-ḥadīth* ("diverting tales"). The association of the former with Persia is traced to a dispute between Muḥammad and a Meccan named al-Naḍr b. al-Ḥārith. In today's polemics against Islam, the Prophet's decision to execute a small number of prisoners after the battle of Badr (2/624) is cited as evidence of the intolerance of Islam and its Prophet. As one web writer has asked: "How can Muhammad preach that there is to be *no compulsion in religion* [Qurʾan 2:256] and then he puts to death those who do not obey and believe in him but resist him strongly with eloquent words?"[3] On the other side, defenders of Islam and the Prophet, when they mention the executions at all, tend to emphasize the Prophet's benevolent treatment of nearly all of the prisoners. Those few who were killed

[1] Rina Drory, "The Abbasid Construction of the Jahiliyya: Cultural Authority in the Making," *Studia Islamica*, no. 83 (1996): 34.
[2] Ibid., 35.
[3] See answering-islam.org/Muhammad/Enemies/nadr.html (accessed May 8, 2013).

are depicted as an exception, executed for their "unrelenting hostility towards the Muslims."[4]

Al-Naḍr, a Meccan trader opposed to Muḥammad, was reportedly among those killed.[5] When Ibn Hishām transmitted his biography of Muḥammad around the first part of the third/ninth century, based on the work of his predecessor, Ibn Isḥāq, he mentioned al-Naḍr's knowledge of Persia's past amid a longer discussion of the Prophet's opponents among the Quraysh. He relates that the Prophet would sit in an assembly and recite the Qurʾan, warning his audience of what had happened to former peoples. Al-Naḍr followed him, speaking about Rustam, Isfandiyār, and the kings of Persia, and he challenged Muḥammad to tell a better story: Muḥammad's tales, al-Naḍr charged, were nothing but "fables of the ancients" (*asāṭīr al-awwalīn*), copied down as were those of al-Naḍr himself.[6] Ibn Hishām tells us that God revealed Qurʾan 25:5–6 in response to this challenge: "And they say, 'Fables of the ancients that he has copied down; and they are dictated to him morning and evening.' Say, 'He who knows the secret in the heavens and the earth sent it down. He is Forgiving and Compassionate.'" God also revealed 68:15: "When Our signs are related to him, he says, 'Fables of the ancients,'" as well as 45:7–8: "Woe to every sinful liar, Who hears God's signs recited to Him, and then persists in being haughty as though he had not heard them. Give him the tidings of painful torment." Ibn Hishām, taking measure of al-Naḍr's challenge to Muḥammad, exclaims: "The liar! The liar!" (*al-affāk al-kadhdhāb*).[7]

With such reporting in mind, the twentieth-century Orientalist D. S. Margoliouth (d. 1940) and a host of later interpreters, including our web polemicist, concluded that Muḥammad had al-Naḍr executed as punishment for his challenge.[8] In criticism of Margoliouth, Muhammad

4 http://islamicresponse.blogspot.com/2008/07/allegation-that-muhammad-killed-poet-al.html (accessed May 8, 2013).

5 On him, see esp. Ch. Pellat, "al-Naḍr b. al-Ḥāri<u>th</u>," in *EI*[2], and Claude Gilliot, "Muḥammad, le Coran et les 'contraintes de l'histoire,'" in *The Qurʾan as Text*, ed. Stefan Wild, 3–26 (Leiden: E. J. Brill, 1996), at 23–4 (and the notes therein).

6 Ibn Hishām, *Sīra*, 1:358. Regarding this term, which has been intensely discussed by scholars, see esp. F. Rosenthal, "Asāṭīr al-Awwalīn," in *EI*[2].

7 Ibn Hishām, *Sīra*, 1:358. Guillaume lists this exclamation among Ibn Hishām's "notes"; see Ibn Hishām, *Life of Muhammad*, 722 (no. 206).

8 According to Margoliouth, al-Naḍr accepted the challenge to match the Qurʾan in eloquence and either versified or put into rhyme the tales of the Persian kings (or perhaps those of the kings of al-Ḥīra). Margoliouth writes: "These 'surahs' he read out at séances similar to those in which the Prophet published the Koran. The effect of this criticism

Mohar Ali – in a book printed in 1997 in Saudi Arabia by the King Fahd Complex for the Printing of the Holy Qurʾan in collaboration with the Centre for the Service of Sunnah and Sîrah – argued that while al-Naḍr "did indeed versify the stories of the Persian kings and recite them at gatherings to distract the people from listening to the Qurʾân," al-Naḍr's composition was far inferior to the Qurʾan: "We do not hear of anyone falling away from Islam or even relapsing into skepticism about the Prophet on account of Al-Naḍr's exhibitions as we hear in connection with some other incidents like *isrâʾ* and *miʿrâj* [the Prophet's miraculous journey to Jerusalem and ascension to Heaven]."[9] The Prophet could never have viewed al-Naḍr as a serious rival or executed him for his storytelling. Had a composition about Persia's past been at all comparable to the Qurʾan, Ali surmises, "the Quraysh would have made a hill out of that mole and would have preserved and transmitted it as a continuing challenge to the Prophet's claim." Rather, "he along with at least another prisoner were condemned to death for offences other than his alleged success as a rival composer."[10]

Third/ninth- and fourth/tenth-century sources, however, better support Margoliouth's view that al-Naḍr was killed for the challenge – however feeble – he posed to the Prophet and the Qurʾan, much like the false prophet Musaylima (also commonly labeled *al-kadhdhāb*), who was killed during Abū Bakr's reign.[11] Al-Naḍr's tales become "fables of the ancients," versus the Qurʾan recited by Muḥammad. In electronic databases, one can readily see the strong association among the words *asāṭīr al-awwalīn*, al-Naḍr, and Rustam as an indicator of the pervasiveness of the label and its application to Persian epic – as in the case of Ibn Hishām's text – even if the association is not exclusive.[12] By way of

must have been very damaging; for when the Prophet at the battle of Badr got the man into his power, he executed him at once, while he allowed the other prisoners to be ransomed." Margoliouth, *Mohammed and the Rise of Islam*, 3rd ed. (New York: G. P. Putnam's Sons, 1905), 135. Ibn Hishām's reporting has al-Naḍr taken prisoner at Badr and killed by ʿAlī without direct explanation; *Sīra*, 1:643 and 710.

9 Ali, *Sîrat al-Nabî and the Orientalists, with Special Reference to the Writings of William Muir, D. S. Margoliouth and W. Montgomery Watt*, vol. 1B, *From the Early Phase of the Prophet's Mission to His Migration to Madinah* (Medina: King Fahd Complex for the Printing of the Holy Qurʾan and Centre for the Service of Sunnah and Sîrah, 1417/1997), 772.

10 Ibid. Ali does not identify the offense here, although on pp. 873–4 he names al-Naḍr among the assassins who tried to ambush the Prophet before his migration to Medina.

11 Claude Gilliot, "Muḥammad, le Coran et les 'contraintes de l'histoire,'" 23–4.

12 For a list of such databases, see the bibliography. The term *asāṭīr al-awwalīn* has also featured in discussions concerning literacy in Mecca during the lifetime of the Prophet

further example, al-Ṭabarī, in his commentary on Qurʾan 8:31,[13] cites reports that lay out the possible nature of al-Naḍr's challenge to the Qurʾan.[14] According to one report, the Prophet's companion al-Miqdād captured al-Naḍr at Badr and was upset that the Prophet planned to kill him (thus depriving al-Miqdād of the ransom he would otherwise receive). Muḥammad justified his order to execute al-Naḍr: "He was saying about the Book of God what he was saying."[15]

Traditionists also frequently identify al-Naḍr's materials by a second label: "diverting tales" (*lahw al-ḥadīth*), derived from Qurʾan 31:6: "Among the people are those who buy diverting tales to lead [people] away from the path of God without any knowledge and to take it in mockery. Those will have a humiliating punishment." A connection of this term to Persia's epic past also appears at a relatively early stage. In commenting on this verse and on the words *lahw al-ḥadīth*, Muqātil notes that al-Naḍr is also the person who applied the term "fables of the ancients" to the Qurʾan. Al-Naḍr had been to the Lakhmid capital al-Ḥīra and discovered there the story of Rustam and Isfandiyār. He brought this to Mecca, where he told the people that the Qurʾanic story of ʿĀd and Thamūd was no more remarkable than the story of Rustam and Isfandiyār.[16] Based on such a body of traditions, the modern translator and commentator ʿAbdullah Yūsuf ʿAlī commented on the verse:

> Life is taken seriously by men who realise the issues that hang upon it. But there are men of a frivolous turn of mind who prefer idle tales [*lahw al-ḥadīth*] to true Realities and they are justly rebuked here. In the time of the Holy Prophet there was a pagan Naḍr ibn al-Ḥārith who preferred Persian romance to the Message of Allah, and turned away ignorant men from the preaching of Allah's word.[17]

and the Prophet's own illiteracy; see Sebastian Günther, "Illiteracy," in *Encyclopaedia of the Qurʾān*, 2:492–500.

13 Qurʾan 8: 31: "When Our signs are recited to them, they say, 'We have heard. Were we to wish, we could say something like this. These are merely the fables of the ancients (*asāṭīr al-awwalīn*).'"

14 These may also have concerned assertions that the Qurʾan sounded like the Christian Gospels recited in Persia, or the rhymed prose of the people of al-Ḥīra, the capital of the Persian client state of the Lakhmids, located in Iraq to the southeast of present-day Najaf. Al-Ṭabarī, *Jāmiʿ al-bayān*, 5:3828–9 (nos. 16030 and 16031, on Qurʾan 8:31).

15 Ibid., 5:3829 (no. 16032, on Qurʾan 8:31).

16 Muqātil, *Tafsīr*, 3:431–2 (on Qurʾan 31:6).

17 *The Meaning of the Holy Qurʾān*, trans. ʿAbdullah Yūsuf ʿAlī, 7th ed. (Beltsville, MD: Amana Publications, 1995), 1034 (on Qurʾan 31:6), n. 3584.

This picture of al-Naḍr giving the lie to the Qurʾan also made its way into the bank of reports upon which poet-traditionists in ʿAbbasid times drew, suggesting the interpenetration of genres of Arabic letters and the persistence of the memory of al-Naḍr and his audacity. One finds, for example, ruminations on the fate of a woman named Qutayla, who the traditionists reckoned was either a daughter or a sister of al-Naḍr. Ibn Hishām identifies Qutayla as his sister and attributes to her a poem lamenting his death, which begins:

> O Rider, you should hit al-Uthayl
>   At dawn on the fifth night[18] if you are lucky.
> Greet a dead man there for me
>   If noble camels still rush there.
> "Greetings from me to you," and a tear shed,
>   Some tears flowing, while others are choked up.
> Does al-Naḍr hear me when I call him?
>   How can a dead man, who cannot speak, hear?[19]

The ʿAbbasid poet Abū Tammām (d. 231–2/845–6) features these verses (with some differences) in his *al-Ḥamāsa*, and they also passed into that text's commentarial tradition.[20] In his comment on Abu Tammām's corpus, al-Marzūqī (d. 421/1030) explains that Uthayl – a spot close to Medina, between Badr and Wadī al-Ṣafrāʾ[21] – is the locale of al-Naḍr's grave. He also spells out that Muḥammad, who had suffered on account of al-Naḍr, killed him when he was a prisoner. Al-Naḍr had recited the accounts of the ʿAjam (*akhbār al-ʿAjam*), including accounts of the Kisrās and Caesars, to the Arabs as a challenge to Muḥammad's prophethood. Al-Marzūqī also credits Ibn ʿAbbās with the insight that Qurʾan 31:6 – "Among the people are those who buy diverting tales" – was sent down

18 The Islamic calendar is based on the moon's cycles, with a new "day" starting with the rising of the moon. Dawn marks not the beginning of a "day" but the middle of one.

19 Ibn Hishām, *Sīra*, 2:42–3; *Life of Muhammad*, trans. Guillaume, 360 (I use Guillaume's translation only loosely). The Arabic editors as well as Guillaume note that some manuscripts make Ibn Hishām, rather than Ibn Isḥāq, responsible for the verses' inclusion in the *Sīra*. I thank Peter Webb for suggestions regarding these lines.

20 Abū Tammām, *Dīwān al-Ḥamāsa*, ed. Muḥammad ʿAbd al-Munʿim Khafājī, 2 vols. (Cairo: Maktabat Muḥammad ʿAlī Ṣubayḥ, 1955), 1:562–4 (no. 71). Regarding the verses, see also Th. Noeldeke, *Delectus veterum carminum arabicorum* (Berlin: H. Reuther, 1890), 67–8.

21 For more on this spot, see "al-Uthayl," in Yāqūt, *Buldān*, 1:121–2; Yāqūt cites Qutayla's verses here.

by God from Heaven with respect to al-Naḍr and his purchase of books (*kutub*) of the Persians, the Byzantines, and the people of al-Ḥīra.[22]

With al-Naḍr, we have found a literary counterpart and even opposite to Salmān, al-Naḍr being someone who brought a source of corruption to Mecca. A reconciliation between al-Naḍr and the Prophet, or between a Persian version of history and a Qurʾanic one, seems impossible, whereas Salmān does successfully bridge a gap between western Arabia and Persia, especially Iṣfahān. In contrast to the redemption of the *jāhiliyya* in ʿAbbasid times outlined by Drory, we find ourselves with a significantly different situation here, as the opposition between Muḥammad and al-Naḍr, or between Qurʾanic history and Persian history, becomes fixed in the commentarial tradition, in Prophetic biography, and in belles-lettres in the formative periods of these genres, thereby becoming part of the literary capital of ʿAbbasid and, indeed, all future Muslim societies. The stark opposition between these two forms of historical memory – Qurʾanic and Persian – was disseminated in ʿAbbasid era Iraq, where we know that translations of Persian epic materials circulated. It likely reflects the perspective of religious elites, exemplified by Ibn Hishām, who, in the late second/eighth and early third/ninth centuries, could hardly imagine the creative syntheses of scholars such as Abū Ḥanīfa al-Dīnawarī or al-Ṭabarī two or three generations later. It is also possible to speculate that when Iranians such as Firdawsī came to generate works that actually treated Rustam and Isfandiyār, they ran the risk of being viewed as latter-day al-Naḍrs by their contemporaries, and that this possibility may have generated a degree of caution on their part.

Creating Homologies

Homology represents one of the most potent tools of social and cultural classification through which equivalencies are presented and relationships created.[23] It begins with an orderly correspondence, such as between the animal world and social groups or between types of positions (pope and caliph). The nature of the correspondence is structural, although a genealogy might be provided, as when Vedic tradition speaks about the origins of the caste system by reference to vivisection of a primeval

[22] Al-Marzūqī, *Sharḥ dīwān al-Ḥamāsa*, ed. Aḥmad Amīn and ʿAbd al-Salām Hārūn, 4 vols. (Cairo: Lajnat al-Taʾlīf wa-l-Tarjama wa-l-Nashr, 1951–3), 2:963–8 (no. 332); see esp. 963, n. 1, for a list of further sources in which Qutayla's poem appears.

[23] Regarding homology, see esp. Bruce Lincoln, *Death, War, and Sacrifice: Studies in Ideology and Practice* (Chicago: University of Chicago Press, 1991), 7–12.

man. Homologies are not literally believed nor are they merely comparative; rather, by classification, they exaggerate similarity in pursuit of a point. Muslim traditionists knew many homologies. The Qur'an posits a homology between all monotheisms. The Prophet was the new Moses or Jesus, and Mecca the new Jerusalem. Similarly, throughout history various groups have styled themselves, or been styled by others, as Muhājirūn and Anṣār, corresponding to the immigrants to Medina and those who helped them on their arrival.

Up until the advent of the Crusades at the end of the fifth/eleventh century, Muslim traditionists thought that the Prophet recognized two other homologies. On the one hand, there were the Muslims, who were monotheists, as were the Byzantines.[24] On the other hand, there were his Meccan opponents, who were polytheists, as were the Persians. The main point of the homologies was originally to ennoble the Muslims and downgrade the Meccan polytheists. With time, however, two shifts in attitudes changed the nature of the homologies. First, enmity to the Byzantines grew, so the link between Muslims and Byzantines was broken. Second, as awareness of Iran's past grew among Muslims, they began to give more attention in the second homology to the Persians; although the pre-Islamic Meccans were by no means forgotten, the legacy of the Persians lived on throughout Iran as a vibrant force, whereas the Meccan polytheists were subjects of the past.

In her historical sketch of reader reactions to the Qur'an, Nadia Maria El Cheikh has persuasively shown how the first homology worked based on a careful reading of a variety of exegetical genres and major commentators from various schools and sects: Sunni, Twelver Shiʿi, Muʿtazilite, and Sufi.[25] Early Muslim sources constructed an image of the Roman emperor Heraclius (r. 610–41) in their efforts to legitimate the prophetic mission of Muḥammad and the new Muslim state. Heraclius became an "ideal 'witness' to the prophet Muḥammad and to the emerging *umma*."[26] He was depicted as pious, politically astute, and upright and as acknowledging the new faith and the excellence of the Muslim

[24] As discussed by Nadia Maria El Cheikh, "*Sūrat al-Rūm*: A Study of the Exegetical Literature," *Journal of the American Oriental Society* 118, no. 3 (1998): 356–64; see also El Cheikh, *Byzantium Viewed by the Arabs* (Cambridge, MA: Harvard University Press, 2004), 24–33, and her "Byzantines, Exegetical Explanations," in *Encyclopaedia of the Qur'ān*, 1:66–9.

[25] Regarding the history of "reader reaction" to the Qur'an, see Andrew Rippin, "Introduction," in *Approaches*, ed. Rippin, 1–9.

[26] El Cheikh, "Muḥammad and Heraclius: A Study in Legitimacy," *Studia Islamica*, no. 89 (1999): 5.

community. As he was placed on a pedestal, Heraclius was detached from his unjust and treacherous Byzantine following. Ultimately, however, though Heraclius knew the truth of Islam, he could not abandon his privileges, nor withstand the opposition to Islam by Byzantine patricians and dignitaries. The sources maintained a remarkably durable image of him as recognizing Islam and nearly converting to it himself.[27] And so when traditionists interpreted the Qurʾan, they discovered that the Qurʾan had predicted the military success of Heraclius and the Byzantines, as attested in Qurʾan 30:1–5:

(1) Alif, Lām, Mīm. (2) The Byzantines (*al-Rūm*) have been vanquished (3) in the nearer part of the land; and, after their vanquishing, they shall be victors (4) in a few years. To God belongs the Command before and after, and on that day the believers shall rejoice (5) in God's help; God helps whomsoever He will; and He is All-mighty, the All-compassionate.

From an early date, exegetes traditionally classified these verses as belonging to the Meccan phase of the revelation[28] and as *āyāt bayyināt*, "a sign that the Qurʾān is God-sent because of the effective accomplishment of the prophecy."[29] Traditionists explained that the verses were revealed in Mecca and referred to the wars between Persia and Byzantium, including the Byzantines' defeats, beginning in 611 CE, at the start of Muḥammad's mission, and their later victories, after the hijra to Medina. Commentators up to the fifth/eleventh century, aware in varying degrees of these events, generally understood there to be an ideological alliance between the Muslims and the Byzantines. They thus stressed the Byzantines' monotheism, the monotheism of the Muslim Meccans, and the preference of the latter for the Byzantines over the Persians.[30] As El Cheikh notes, in the commentaries "the believers are taken to be the followers of the Prophet. This reading reflects a positive outlook toward the Byzantines in the expectation of a later Byzantine victory that will give the believers reason to rejoice."[31] Over time, changes in attitudes

[27] See also, building on El Cheikh's work, Conrad, "Heraclius in Early Islamic Kerygma," 113–56. Also, Stefan Leder, "Heraklios erkennt den Propheten: Ein Beispiel für Form und Entstehungsweise narrativer Geschichtskonstruktionen," *Zeitschrift der Deutschen Morgenländischen Gesellschaft* 151 (2001): 1–42.

[28] Cf. Richard Bell, *A Commentary on the Qurʾān*, vol. 2, *Surahs XXV–CXIV* (Manchester: University of Manchester, 1991), 69–70.

[29] El Cheikh, "*Sūrat al-Rūm*," 357. See also Choksy's discussion of these verses amid "Islamic auguries" in *Conflict and Cooperation*, 49.

[30] El Cheikh, "*Sūrat al-Rūm*," 360–1.

[31] Ibid., 359–60.

toward the Byzantines were reflected in the way Muslim commentators vocalized the verses' verbs, and the homology was undone. The early commentators read the verb "to vanquish" in the second verse predominantly in the passive voice (the Byzantines were vanquished, *ghulibat al-Rūm*), while in the third verse, they read it in the active voice (they shall be victors, *sa-yaghlibūn*; both as cited above). This view was dominant until the fifth/eleventh century, when a formerly variant reading gained in prominence.[32] In the variant, which went back to several early authorities, including ʿAbd Allāh b. ʿUmar (son of the second caliph; d. 73/693), the first verb was read in the active voice (the Byzantines were victors, *ghalabat al-Rūm*, which by 628 they were), while in the third verse, the verb was read in the passive voice (they will be vanquished, *sa-yughlabūn*). The variant produced a very different meaning: the Qurʾan was now interpreted as predicting the Muslims' victory over the Byzantines, rather than the latter's victory over the Persians.[33] Most importantly, the commentators now denied any "ideological affiliation between Islam and Byzantium." Rather than being seen as "People of the Book," the Byzantines came to be labeled as polytheists (sing. *mushrik*, pl. *mushrikūn/mushrikīn*),[34] and several reasons were advanced for why the Qurʾan states in the fourth and fifth verses that the believers shall rejoice ("and on that day, the believers shall rejoice in God's help"). One of these explanations attributed the rejoicing to the fact that two factions of polytheists – the Persians and the Byzantines – were battling one another. Importantly, adjustments made in the fifth/eleventh to the seventh/thirteenth centuries to this commentarial tradition followed on, and coincided with, the Muslims' military weakness and losses of Muslim territory to the Byzantines and then to the Crusaders.[35]

Like the homology of Muslims and Byzantines, upon which El Cheikh focused, that between Persians and Meccans also seems to have developed as the commentarial tradition evolved, though without the sort of reversal

[32] "It is true, however, that the variant reading never stands on its own, but is always juxtaposed side by side with the traditional one. Working as they were within a tradition, the commentators reiterated the traditional reading and interpretation. . . . It is because of this entrenched tradition that the exegetical literature took so long to turn the Byzantines into an enemy." Ibid., 363–4.

[33] Ibid., 361.

[34] For a useful analysis of the term *mushrik* that addresses its polemical dimensions in the Qurʾan, see G. R. Hawting, *The Idea of Idolatry and the Emergence of Islam: From Polemic to History* (Cambridge: Cambridge University Press, 1999), 45–66.

[35] El Cheikh, "*Sūrat al-Rūm*," 362–3; also, *Byzantium Viewed by the Arabs*, 30–3.

she described in the case of the former. Early on the Persians were homologized to Meccan unbelievers as opponents of monotheism. Mujāhid explains in his exegesis that the Qurʾan predicted the eventual success of Byzantium (*al-Rūm*) over Persia and the rejoicing of the believers (*al-muʾminīn*) when God rendered the "People of the Book" (i.e., the Byzantines) victorious over the "People of Idols" (*ahl al-awthān*).[36] Muqātil b. Sulaymān reports that when Persia initially defeated al-Rūm, the news reached Mecca, and the unbelievers (*al-kuffār*) rejoiced, taunting the Prophet's companions by saying: "Verily, the Persians do not have a book, and we are on their side (*inna Fāris laysa lahum kitāb wa-naḥnu minhum*). They have vanquished the Byzantines, who are a people with a book like you. We will vanquish you just as Persia vanquished Byzantium."[37]

In one widely circulating tradition, Abū Bakr explains the companions' sympathies in the conflict between Byzantium and Persia to Muḥammad. As Aḥmad b. Ḥanbal reports, Abū Bakr notified the Prophet that the Muslims felt sympathy for the Byzantines (described as *ahl al-kitāb*), whereas the Meccan "polytheists" sympathized with the Persian "idolators" (*ahl al-awthān*). The Prophet assured Abū Bakr that the Byzantines would be victorious, a message that Abū Bakr passed on to the Muslims, who then made a wager with Mecca's polytheists that their side would be victorious in five years. When the five years had passed, and there was still no victory, Abū Bakr went back to the Prophet, who told Abū Bakr to make it ten years. Within this time period, the Persian idolators were finally defeated.[38]

Over time, the Meccan-Persian homology held, but the description of the nature of the Persians' unbelief seems to have become more nuanced. This is in large measure due to the generally accretive nature of the exegetical tradition and the tendency for exegetes to add layers of explanation, including those of a historical nature. As El Cheikh noted, al-Ṭabarī features two and a half centuries of Muslim exegesis, citing material of standard earlier authorities as well as insignificant variants.[39] The additions expand the possible ways of interpreting the Qurʾan, including the history that lies behind it. For the report about Abū Bakr's wager, Ibn

36 Mujāhid, *Tafsīr*, 499 (on Qurʾan 30:1–2).
37 Muqātil, *Tafsīr*, 3:406 (on Qurʾan 30:1–2).
38 Ibn Ḥanbal traces the report back to Ibn ʿAbbās. He also cites Saʿīd b. al-Jubayr (d. 94 or 95/711 or 712), who clarifies that the Qurʾan's phrasing, "in a few years" (*fī biḍʿi sinīn*), indicates a number below ten (proving the Qurʾan was not wrong – victory was on the way). Ibn Ḥanbal, *Musnad*, 4:168 (no. 2495).
39 El Cheikh, "*Sūrat al-Rūm*," 358–60.

Ḥanbal cites Ibn ʿAbbās, and so does al-Ṭabarī, but the latter also cites another version of it on the authority of ʿIkrima (d. 105/723–4), in which the Persians remain "idolators" but are also labeled with a technical term signifying someone who "did not know a scripture" (*ummiyyūn*).[40] They are also called, more simply, Zoroastrians (*Majūs*). The report states that the Byzantines and the Persians met in battle in the "nearer part of the land," meaning Adhriʿāt, a town south of Damascus, where the Byzantines were defeated. When the news reached Muḥammad and his companions in Mecca, they were troubled, since the Prophet hated for the fact that the People of the Book from Byzantium (*ahl al-kitāb min al-Rūm*) had been defeated by Zoroastrians who did not have a scripture (*al-ummiyyūn min ahl al-Majūs*). The unbelievers (*kuffār*) of Mecca rejoiced and said to the Muslims: "Verily, you are People of the Book, and the Christians are People of the Book. We are a people who do not know a scripture (*ummiyyūn*), and our brethren (*ikhwān*) from the people of Persia have been victorious over your brethren from the People of the Book. If you fight with us, then we will triumph over you." Then God sent down Qurʾan 30:1–5.[41] Such phrasing moved the Persians close to the Meccans, without asserting polytheism. The traditionists do not trouble themselves with specifying which Persians they had in mind, although ostensibly the homology relates to imperial Persians, that is, those who were engaged in fighting the Byzantines. What we seem to have here, then, is a homology between two original oppositions – Muslims versus Meccan polytheists, Byzantines versus Persians – that becomes strained because the Byzantines, from the fifth/eleventh century onward, cannot be reckoned the Muslims' allies. Given the accretive nature of the exegetical tradition, the Persian side gets elaborated.[42] But it also might be the case that over the centuries, as more Iranians became

[40] The core meaning of *ummī* in the Qurʾan is problematic. For this sense (which the interpretive context I examine supports), see Sebastian Günther, "Ummī," in *Encyclopaedia of the Qurʾān*, 5:399–403, and E. Geoffroy, "Ummī," in *EI*². ʿIkrima is generally identified as one of the main transmitters from Ibn ʿAbbās, but he does not list him as a source here. On him, see J. Schacht, "ʿIkrima," in *EI*².

[41] Al-Ṭabarī, *Jāmiʿ al-bayān*, 8:6501 (no. 27697).

[42] For a few further examples illustrating how context softens the homology (all on 30:1–5), see al-Wāḥidī, *Asbāb al-nuzūl wa-yalīhi al-Nāsikh wa-l-mansūkh* (Cairo: Maktabat al-Mutanabbī, n.d.), 194–5 and his *al-Wajīz fī tafsīr al-Kitāb al-ʿAzīz*, ed. Ṣafwān ʿAdnān Dāwūdī, 2 vols. (Damascus: Dār al-Qalam, 1995), 2:838; al-Qurṭubī, *al-Jāmiʿ li-aḥkām al-Qurʾān*, vol. 14 (Cairo: Dār al-Kutub al-Miṣriyya, 1945), 1–7, and Abū Ḥayyān al-Gharnāṭī, *al-Baḥr al-muḥīt fī tafsīr*, vol. 7 (Beirut: Dār al-Fikr, 1983), 160–2.

Muslims, it became harder to speak of Persians in the simplistic terms of earlier days.

Fashioning Icons

Both labels and homologies can serve as catalysts for memory, insofar as they provide ways of conceiving of phenomena, but they can equally restrict memory, when a large body of historical lore, such as that of Persian epic, is summed up prejudicially in a few words, or when the religious convictions of a territory, Persia, are amalgamated to those of another, pre-Islamic Mecca. In both cases, the filter limits significations, and insofar as a traditionist's text gained credibility as a normative account, it creates an obstacle to later generations, who may write from different and more positive perspectives but are forced to reckon with the past as their predecessors knew it. In the next case, we consider a different type of filter in stories that set the Prophet in opposition to Sasanian Iran's Khusraw Parvīz. These stories appear to juxtapose the Prophet's authority, underwritten by Islam, with Kisrā's kingship, or *mulk*, as an inferior authority.

In a narrow sense, the term "icon" refers to religious images, but more broadly the term can connote anything visually memorable. Religious icons, such as the infant Jesus and his mother, evoke sentiments of reverence, admiration, and longing for a past and its saints, heroes, and reformers. The Epiphany and the three kings who recognized the baby Christ were memorialized in the Gospel of Matthew, and from Roman times onward they have been vividly portrayed in art and celebrated in Christian liturgy.[43] The kings also became the focus of legends in Syriac and Arabic.[44] For Muslims, Muḥammad's ascension (*miʿrāj*) to the heavens, where he reportedly met with past prophets, lived on in iconic images.

An image can be reckoned iconic if it is visually memorable, but icons do not require artistic expression nor must they evoke reverence. Stories

[43] See Rolf M. Schneider, "Orientalism in Late Antiquity: The Oriental in Imperial and Christian Imagery," in *Ērān ud Anērān: Studien zu den Beziehungen zwischen dem Sasanidenreich und der Mittelmeerwelt*, ed. Josef Wiesehöfer and Philip Huyse, 241–78 (Munich: Franz Steiner, 2006), at 247–52.

[44] See *La Caverne des trésors: Les deux recensions syriaques*, ed. and trans. Su-Min Ri, 2 vols., Corpus Scriptorum Christianorum Orientalium (Leuven: E. Peeters, 1987), 2:140–9 (chs. 45–6), and Minorsky, "Two Iranian Legends in Abū-Dulaf's Second *Risālah*," 172–5.

often create icons that become part of a society's visual memory rendered in words. The image can evoke any variety of thoughts or emotions. Think of the story of Sisyphus and his rock in Greek myth, iconic for the modern philosophy of existentialism with its tragic sense of absurdity. The image (Greek, *ikon*) evokes a conceptual framework that resonates with a modern audience. Along similar lines, the body of mostly third/ninth- and early fourth/tenth-century traditions discussed below furnished generations of Muslims, Iranians included, with memorable images of a prophet unhappy with the Persians, their kings, and their rejection of Islam.

Moustapha Akkad's 1977 film, *The Message: The Story of Islam*, opens with three men on horseback riding across a vast expanse of empty desert. The men, barely visible as the film begins, come into view, their faces and bodies concealed by white robes and scarves. As day turns to night turns to day, the horses gallop on. The tempo of the music quickens. The riders emerge from the sand dunes, each raises a hand into the sky in a farewell, and they part in three directions. The camera follows one rider across the desert to a court, that of Caesar (Heraclius). He strides into the court as dozens of silent courtiers clear a path for him and move close to hear him. Before this audience, the rider unfurls a scroll and reads to a bejeweled Caesar:

> In the name of God, the Most Gracious, the Most Merciful
> From Muḥammad, the Messenger of God, to Heraclius, the emperor of Byzantium:
> Greetings to him who is the follower of righteous guidance. I bid you to hear the divine call. I am the Messenger of God to the people. Accept Islam for your salvation.

An advisor pulls close to the emperor and states: "He speaks of a new prophet in Arabia." Before taking the scroll to see it for himself, Heraclius says sarcastically out of the corner of his mouth: "Was it like this when John the Baptist came to King Herod? Out of the desert, crying about salvation?"

The camera dwells briefly on the second rider, who gallops past pyramids to the Patriarch of Alexandria. Then the camera turns to the third rider, who travels along a shoreline to arrive at a third court. The rider strides in and reads:

> Kisrā, emperor of Persia:
> Muḥammad calls to you with the call of God. Accept Islam for your salvation. Embrace Islam.

Kisrā – a burning fire on his left and a partially clad slave to either side – bends down, waves a finger at the rider, and hisses: "You come out of the desert, smelling of camel and goat, to Persia, where he should kneel?" Kisrā then rips the letter in two and throws it at the rider.

The camera returns to Heraclius, who says to his visitor: "Muḥammad, 'Messenger of God'? Who gave him this authority?" The visitor explains: "God sent Muḥammad as a mercy to mankind." A view of the desert follows, announcing the film's title in bright red lettering, naming the leading members of its cast and production team, and certifying its intellectual vetting by the University of al-Azhar in Cairo and by the High Islamic Congress of the Shiat in Lebanon, which have "approved the accuracy and fidelity of this film."

For Akkad's movie, Muḥammad's message is a central metaphor. Heraclius receives it with puzzlement and doubt, Kisrā with scorn. Kisrā's reaction anticipates the obstacles to the Prophet's message shown subsequently in the film and, metaphorically, those occurring through all times.

For nearly all of Islam's long history, Muslims have believed that their Prophet envisioned Islam beyond Arabia's borders, and that the Prophet undertook missions to summon the leaders of the empires of his day to Islam. As part of early Islamic kerygma, Muḥammad's messengers bear witness to Islam as a world religion, much as Jesus sent forth his apostles to spread the Christian message in new lands.[45] As Arnold aptly summarized: "Islam was not to be confined to the Arab race."[46] Old pieces of parchment and seals have been identified as documentary evidence, generating considerable public excitement.[47] This seems an overly optimistic reaction given the general state of first/seventh-century sources, contradictions in the later literary record, letters as a commonplace literary form in the early Islamic historical tradition,[48] and a wider Near Eastern pattern in late antiquity of major Roman and Byzantine historians

[45] On which see esp. Conrad, "Heraclius in Early Islamic Kerygma," 114–17; as Conrad notes, Ibn Hishām has Muḥammad discuss Jesus' use of his disciplines as messengers amid an account of Muḥammad's own messengers; *Sīra*, 2:606–7.

[46] Arnold, *Preaching of Islam*, 29–30.

[47] Muhammad Hamidullah has published extensively on the letters; see esp. "La lettre du Prophète à Héraclius et le sort de l'original," *Arabica* 2, no. 1 (1955): 97–110; "Original de la lettre du Prophète à Kisrà," *Rivista degli Studi orientali* 40 (1965): 57–69 (including discussion of publicity around the letter in the 1960s); *Le Prophète de l'Islam*, 2 vols. (Paris: J. Vrin, 1959), 1:241–5; *Majmūʿat al-wathāʾiq*, 109–12 (no. 53); *Six originaux des lettres du Prophète de l'islam: Étude paléographique et historique des lettres du Prophète* (Paris: Tougui, 1985).

[48] Noth, *Early Arabic Historical Tradition*, 76–87.

using letters in dramatic ways.[49] Still, whatever the truth, the accounts create an iconic site of memory that has been rethought many times and from many different vantage points. The letters have been cited in discussions of whether the Prophet was illiterate, as most Muslims believe. They have been cited as establishing a legal precedent: one must summon one's enemies to Islam before fighting them. Muḥammad's messengers are today viewed as diplomats, as they were in Akkad's film: "The spirit of sympathy, tact and judgment governed the Prophet's standing instructions to his envoys who were accredited to numerous cities, communities and countries to convey his message," wrote Afzal Iqbal, a twentieth-century Pakistani diplomat-scholar. "Their directions were to work with patience and avoid severity, to give good tidings to the people and not to incite hostility towards their mission."[50] Whatever the vantage point, Kisrā's response displeases the Prophet and suggests the inferiority of his government versus that of the Prophet in Medina.[51]

Across traditions and genres of Arabic writing, one finds the letters episode and the stylized response of Kisrā. Traditionists produced reports that identified a list of companions of the Prophet and the rulers to whom they were sent with a letter from him. The ruler of Persia was included as one of two, three, six, or more recipients. In the rather long narrative account of Ibn Saʿd, on a day in the month of Muḥarram in the seventh year of the hijra, Muḥammad sent out six messengers to kings, including Persia's, summoning them to Islam with texts that bore his own seal in three lines:

Muḥammad
rasūl
Allāh

[49] Averil Cameron, *Procopius and the Sixth Century* (London: Duckworth, 1985), 148–9; Conrad, "Heraclius in Early Islamic Kerygma," 125. For an important early skeptical consideration of Muḥammad's letters, see Leone Caetani, *Annali dell'Islām*, 10 vols. (Milan: U. Hoepli, 1905–26), 1:725ff; see also R. B. Serjeant, "Early Arabic Prose," in *Arabic Literature to the End of the Umayyad Period*, ed. A. F. L. Beeston et al., 114–53 (Cambridge: Cambridge University Press, 1983), at 141–2.

[50] Iqbal, *The Prophet's Diplomacy: The Art of Negotiation as Conceived and Developed by the Prophet of Islam* (Cape Cod, MA: Claude Stark, 1975), 75–81. See also Afzalur Rahman, *Muhammad: Encyclopædia of Seerah*, 7 vols. (London: Muslim Schools Trust, 1981), 1:845–51("The Letters of the Prophet") and 885–909 ("A Short List of Letters of the Prophet").

[51] Regarding the letter to Heraclius, by comparison, see Suliman Bashear, "The Mission of Diḥya al-Kalbī and the Situation in Syria," *Der Islam* 74, no. 1 (1997): 64–91, and Conrad, "Heraclius in Early Islamic Kerygma," 125–30.

Each of the messengers had the ability to speak the language of the people to whom he was sent. The first three addressees were "the Negus" (the ruler of Abyssinia), "Caesar" (Emperor Heraclius of Byzantium), and "Kisrā" (Khusraw Parvīz of Persia). The Negus placed Muḥammad's invitation over his eyes, descended from his throne, and sat down on the earth, humbling himself. Then he "surrendered to Islam and bore witness to the truth" (*aslama wa-shahida shahādat al-ḥaqq*), stating, "If I were able to go to him, I would do so." Afterward, he wrote to the Prophet confirming his acceptance of Islam.[52] Caesar received Muḥammad's letter while in Homs fulfilling an oath he had made – namely, to march barefoot from Constantinople to Jerusalem should his armies be victorious over Persia. Caesar sought to persuade his people to embrace Islam, but he was unsuccessful. When Muḥammad's letter was read to Kisrā, the latter tore it up (*mazzaqahu*). On hearing this, Muḥammad said, "May God tear up his kingdom (*mazziq mulkahu*)."[53]

These traditionists connect the Prophet's statement about Persia to Qur'an 34:19: "They said, 'Our Lord, make the stages of our journey longer.' They wronged themselves; and so We made them tales (*aḥādīth*) and tore them completely to pieces (*wa-mazzaqnāhum kulla mumazzaq*). In that there are signs for everyone who is truly steadfast and grateful." In the traditionists' accounts, the episode and the Qur'anic rephrasing typically show that Muḥammad knew that Kisrā and his kingdom would be punished for the ruler's actions. Ibn Sa'd's version thus continues with Kisrā writing to Bādhān, his governor (*'āmil*) in the Yemen, and instructing him to send two men to Muḥammad so that they might gather information. Muḥammad received the men, invited them to Islam, and then told them to return to him the next day. When they returned the next day, Muḥammad clairvoyantly informed them that God, his lord, had killed the previous night Bādhān's lord, Kisrā, and given power to Kisrā's son, Shīrawayh (Ibn Sa'd specifies the time and day of the killing

[52] Ibn Sa'd, *al-Ṭabaqāt al-kabīr*, vol. 1, pt. 2, 15ff. (I provide only the barest outline of his account). Ibn Sa'd identifies three other recipients among the six: al-Muqawqis, the ruler of the Copts in Alexandria (regarding whom see K. Öhrnberg, "al-Muḳawḳis," in *EI*^{2}); the Ghassanid ruler al-Ḥārith b. Abī Shamir (before Islam, the Ghassanids were Arab Christian clients of the Byzantines); and, finally, Hawdha b. 'Alī al-Ḥanafī, chief of the Banū Ḥanīfa in the Arabian region of Yamāma (Ibn Sa'd follows these letters with accounts of the Prophet's correspondence with Arab tribes). Regarding al-Ḥārith and Hawdha, see *The History of al-Ṭabarī*, vol. 8, *The Victory of Islam*, trans. Michael Fishbein (Albany: State University of New York Press, 1997), 98–9.

[53] Ibn Sa'd, *al-Ṭabaqāt al-kabīr*, vol. 1, pt. 2, 16.

according to the hijri calendar). Astonished, Bādhān's spies returned home with the news, whereupon Bādhān and the Persian settlers (*al-anbā'*) in the Yemen, impressed by Muḥammad's foreknowledge, converted to Islam.[54]

As in Akkad's film, a comparison, however implicit, is often made between Caesar and Kisrā, with Kisrā acting as a foil to Caesar. Not surprisingly, Kisrā's ripping up of the letter features somewhat in commentaries on the opening verses of Sūrat al-Rūm (Qur'an 30), and here, if anywhere, one can see the way in which traditions interlock and support an enduring memory about the Byzantines and the Sasanians and their respective fates. For example, the Shi'i exegete Abū al-Ḥasan 'Alī b. Ibrāhīm al-Qummī (d. 328/939) begins his commentary on the Sūra with an exchange between Abū 'Ubayda (al-Hadhdha') and Abū Ja'far (Muḥammad al-Bāqir, the fifth Imam of the Shi'a), in which the former asks the latter about the meaning of the verses. The latter explains that for these verses there is an interpretation (*ta'wīl*) known only to God and to those of the Imams who are deeply versed in knowledge (*al-rāsikhūn fī al-'ilm min al-a'imma*)." The Imam mentions that after the Prophet's hijra to Medina, he wrote to the kings of Byzantium and Persia inviting them to Islam. He recounts the respectful way in which Caesar received his letter and messenger, in contrast to Kisrā, who tore up his letter and disdained the messenger. The Imam then launches into an interpretation: the verses indicate that the Persians defeated the Byzantines, and they – the Persians – would subsequently be defeated by the Byzantines (as they were).[55]

The centrality of Caesar, and by implication Byzantium, in all of these accounts seems to suggest that the earliest reporting originated in Umayyad-era Syria, since the rulers' different reactions to Muḥammad's invitation helped to explain the outcome of the conquests there and in Byzantium more broadly.[56] For example, in a section of his *al-Amwāl* dealing with revenue from the conquered territories (*al-fay' wa-wujūhuhu*

[54] Ibid., vol. 1, pt. 2, 16; cf. ibid., vol. 4, pt. 1, 139 (this is an entry for 'Abd Allāh b. Ḥudhāfa, the messenger; here 'Abd Allāh delivers the letter to Kisrā via a governor in Baḥrayn).

[55] Al-Qummī, *Tafsīr*, ed. Ṭayyib al-Mūsawī al-Jazā'irī, 2 vols. (Najaf: Maktabat al-Hudā, 1387/1967–8), 2:152 (on Qur'an 30:1–4).

[56] For other recent arguments around Umayyad-era origins, see esp. Serjeant, "Early Arabic Prose," 142, and regarding Heraclius, Conrad, "Heraclius in Early Islamic Kerygma," esp. 116–7 and 130. Both Serjeant and Conrad give priority to Muslim–Byzantine/Christian encounters as the original context for reports about the letters.

wa-subuluhu), Abū ʿUbayd al-Qāsim b. Sallām (d. 224/838) treats the *jizya* tax and passes on several reports about Muḥammad's letters through which he explains the tax's original context in Muḥammad's day. As in other reports, Kisrā's refusal is blunt. One report that Abū ʿUbayd cites states:

> The Messenger of God wrote to Kisrā and to Caesar. As for Kisrā, when he read the text (*al-kitāb*), he tore it up (*mazzaqahu*). As for Caesar, when he read the text, he folded it, then he put it down. When this reached the Messenger of God, he said, "As for these [meaning Kisrā], they will be torn up (*fa-yumazziqūna*). As for these [the Byzantines], a remnant of them will remain."[57]

The different political and fiscal fates of Byzantine and Persian territories would be linked to the actions of their rulers with respect to Muḥammad's letters.

Dating the origins of any such reporting is a problem, but it does seem a safe conclusion that by the second half of the third/ninth century Muslims were confident that their Prophet had written to Kisrā, Caesar, the Negus, and a handful of other contemporary rulers. It also seems reasonably clear that the third/ninth century represented a period of narrative crystallization. Khalīfa b. Khayyāṭ al-ʿUṣfurī (d. 240/854) lists a variety of messengers (*rusul*) sent by Muḥammad but does not provide narrative elaboration or treat the messages sent to Caesar and Kisrā as distinct from, for example, ʿUthmān's mission to the people of Mecca in the year of al-Ḥudaybiya (6/628).[58] Such reporting could lead one to suspect that traditionists added narrative details to an early list of messengers;[59] it is also possible that Ibn Khayyāṭ may have extracted names from an existing body of narrative. In any case, after the third/ninth century, reports about the letters formed part of the bedrock of Arabic historiography. Notably, this crystallization took shape before most Iranians – who, hypothetically, could have nurtured fonder memories of Kisrā's reaction – likely had converted to Islam.

[57] Abū ʿUbayd al-Qāsim b. Sallām, *al-Amwāl*, 2nd ed., ed. Muḥammad Khalīl Harrās (Cairo: Dār al-Fikr, 1975), 31 (no. 58); see also Abū ʿUbayd, *The Book of Revenue (Kitāb al-Amwāl)*, trans. Imran Ahsan Khan Nyazee (Reading: Garnet, 2002), 18–22. Other reports that he cites supply texts of Muḥammad's letters.

[58] Ibn Khayyāṭ al-ʿUṣfurī, *Taʾrīkh*, 1:74. Regarding ʿUthmān at the Muslims' expedition to al-Ḥudaybiya, see W. Montgomery Watt, "al-Ḥudaybiya," in EI^2.

[59] In support of the existence of such a list, see Ibn Hishām, *Sīra*, 2:607; al-Ṭabarī, *Taʾrīkh*, I:1560.

When it is recalled, the text of Muḥammad's letter to Kisrā speaks in rather general terms of a warning. The contents are reported with remarkable consistency. The third/ninth-century historian al-Yaʿqūbī provides an early version of the text of the letter:

> In the name of God, the Merciful and Compassionate
>
> From Muḥammad, the Messenger of God, to Kisrā, the ruler of Persia (*ʿaẓīm Fāris*). Peace be upon him who follows the Guidance (*al-hudā*), believes in God and His Messenger, and bears witness that there is no god but God alone, Who has no partner, and that Muḥammad is His servant and His Messenger to all mankind *to warn those who are alive, and that the word may be proved true against the unbelievers.*[60] So convert to Islam and you shall be safe. If you refuse, the sins of the Magians (*al-Majūs*) will be held against you.[61]

In some traditions, Kisrā is made to tear up the letter and then exclaim: "He writes this to me, when he is my servant!"[62]

There are some differences in the reporters' traditions, for example, surrounding whether Muḥammad's messenger delivered the letter to Kisrā directly or through one of Kisrā's governors. After hearing of Kisrā's reaction, Muḥammad states that his kingdom (*mulk*) would be ripped up, or, alternatively, his *umma*.[63] The differences do not, however, detract from the iconic image. The constancy of the reported outcome, despite the variations, suggests the wider significance of the letters episode as foreboding and justifying the oblivion of Kisrā and his kingdom. The condemnation is not applied to Kisrā's people, the Persians, for whom redemption is still theoretically possible. Whereas in our previous examples, of al-Naḍr and Sūrat al-Rūm, blame falls on a space – Persia – and its past, here the traditions single out a single political ruler, Kisrā (and the late Sasanian dynasty that he embodies) who memorably is the ruler most directly opposed to Muḥammad.

Gendering

The traditions discussed above belong, I argue, to a metanarrative that explained the success of Muḥammad, the early community, and Islam

[60] See Qurʾan 36:70.

[61] Al-Yaʿqūbī, *Taʾrīkh*, 2:77. For a list of other sources that provide the text of the letter and for comparisons, see Hamidullah, *Six originaux des lettres du Prophète*, 178–80.

[62] Al-Ṭabarī, *Taʾrīkh*, I:1572; *History of al-Ṭabarī*, 8:111.

[63] Ibn Abī Shayba, *Muṣannaf*, ed. Mukhtār Aḥmad al-Nadwī, 15 vols. (Karachi: Idārat al-Qurʾān wa-l-ʿUlūm al-Islāmiyya, 1987), 14:337–8 (no. 18476). Here we seem to have a single letter in three copies, sent to Kisrā, Caesar, and the Negus.

through a set of memorable oppositions: Qurʾanic versus Persian history, Muslim (and for a time, Byzantine) believers versus Meccan and Persian unbelievers (even idolators), and the Prophet's rule by Islam versus Kisrā's mere kingship. In the following, final case we even see traditionists narrowing in on a source of blame for late Sasanian Iran's troubles: a woman.

The final decades of Sasanian rule were full of conflict, as I have already outlined. In 622, Heraclius started a counteroffensive, freeing Asia Minor from Sasanian control and initiating a reversal in the ongoing Byzantine-Persian wars that saw him advance all the way to Ctesiphon in the beginning of 628. In February 628, Khusraw Parvīz was assassinated, and his successor, Shīrawayh, was forced to conclude a peace agreement with the Byzantines on terms that saw the Sasanians give up the territories of Armenia and the western part of Mesopotamia in that year and Syria, Palestine, and Egypt the following year.[64] Persia's leadership fell to pieces as Shīrawayh reportedly killed nearly all male contenders for the throne (as already mentioned in Chapter 3). A rapid succession of leaders followed, culminating in Yazdagird III, the last of the Sasanian kings, who reigned from 632 until his death in 651.

Among those who governed for a while during these chaotic years was a daughter of Khusraw Parvīz. Muḥammad reportedly learned of this woman's rule and prophesied devastating results. In the Hadith collection of al-Bukhārī, it is reported that "when it reached the Messenger of God that the Persians had made a daughter of Kisrā their king, he said: 'No people shall prosper if a woman rules over them' (*lan yaflaḥ qawm wa-law amarahum imraʾa*)." Muḥammad's witness is named as the companion Abū Bakra, who provides the statement after saying that it profited him as advice afterward on the Day of the Camel, when he decided not to plot with the group led by ʿĀʾisha, the Prophet's widow, against the then-caliph ʿAlī.[65]

Variations of Muḥammad's statement to Abū Bakra are repeated in numerous legal and historical texts. The Battle of the Camel often provides the context for Abū Bakra's recollection, whereas the text's

[64] Beate Dignas and Engelbert Winter, *Rome and Persia in Late Antiquity: Neighbours and Rivals* (Cambridge: Cambridge University Press, 2007), 44–9, 148–51.

[65] Al-Bukhārī, *Ṣaḥīḥ*, 4:376–7 (within the chapter entitled "Kitāb al-Fitan"). A further citation of the tradition runs along similar lines; it occurs within the "Kitāb al-Maghāzī" chapter of the *Ṣaḥīḥ*, under the heading "The Writing of the Prophet to Kisrā and Caesar." *Ṣaḥīḥ*, 3:183–4 (its placement here supporting my point about the interlocking of traditions).

FIGURE 5.1. Drachma of Queen Būrān, 630 (1 AH). The State Hermitage Museum, St. Petersburg. Photograph © The State Hermitage Museum/photo by Vladimir Terebenin, Leonard Kheifets, Yuri Molodkovets.

information about Kisrā's daughter provides a critical context for Muḥammad's statement. The early Hadith authorities who transmit the report seem to be Basran, which is of interest given the setting of the Battle of the Camel near Basra.[66] The *Muṣannaf* of Ibn Abī Shayba includes one version of it in its chapter on the first civil war. Four of the other major early Sunni collections also cite it: besides al-Bukhārī's *Ṣaḥīḥ*, it appears in the *Musnad* of Aḥmad b. Ḥanbal; the *Sunan* of al-Tirmidhī (d. 279/892), and the *Sunan* of al-Nasāʾī (d. 915/302).[67] Al-Tirmidhī, for

[66] As noted by Mohammad Fadel, "Is Historicism a Viable Strategy for Islamic Law Reform? The Case of 'Never Shall a Folk Prosper Who Have Appointed a Woman to Rule Them,'" *Islamic Law and Society* 18, no. 2 (2011): 131–76, at 141.

[67] See the useful summary of the Hadith sources in Fadel, "Is Historicism a Viable Strategy," 140–3 and 151–8.

example, reports that Abū Bakra said that when Kisrā died, he heard the Prophet say: "Whom have they appointed as a successor?" He was told, "His daughter." The Prophet then said: "No people shall prosper if a woman rules over them." Abū Bakra explains: "When ʿĀʾisha arrived," that is, to Basra, "I remembered the statement of the Messenger of God, and so God safeguarded me by it."[68] That is, he did not side with ʿĀʾisha against ʿAlī. Aḥmad b. Ḥanbal features the report eight times in his *Musnad*. In one of these cases, Abū Bakra reports that the Prophet was lying down with his head in ʿĀʾisha's lap when a man came to inform him that the Persians had lost a battle. Muḥammad fell to the ground in prostration to God, then rose, asking the messenger questions, and the messenger answered them. Among the news that the messenger brought was that a woman now ruled the Persians. The Prophet declared three times: "Men are doomed when they obey women!"[69]

For those promoting patriarchical views, the failure of Persia provided a credible scenario for the Prophet's statement. The text – and the authority it carried because of its wide circulation in the early, authoritative Sunni collections – proved to be useful for advocates of androcentric ideas, and it is treated accordingly by Ibn al-Jawzī (d. 597/1200), admittedly beyond our time period, who gives the "context" (*sabab*) of the Prophet's statement in this way:

> When Shīrawayh killed his father, Kisrā, he reigned for only eight months (or it is said six months). Then he died, and his son Ardashīr reigned after him. He was seven years old. Then he was killed, and Būrān, a daughter of Kisrā, ruled after him. That reached the Messenger of God, and so he said: "No people shall prosper if a woman rules over them."

In what follows, Ibn al-Jawzī explains that prosperity refers to successful pursuit of one's goals. Managing one's affairs to achieve success requires perfection of judgment, which women lack. The Prophet's statement indicates that women must not act as rulers, serve as judges, or contract their own marriages.[70]

Today, the Prophet's statement is commonly cited alongside Qurʾan 4:34, the interpretation of which has been controversial. ʿAbdullah Yūsuf ʿAlī translated the verse as "Men are the protectors and maintainers of

[68] Al-Tirmidhī, *al-Jāmiʿ al-ṣaḥīḥ*, 4:527–8 (within the "Kitāb al-Fitan," no. 2262).

[69] Ibn Ḥanbal, *Musnad*, 5:61 (no. 84); see also 5:53 (no. 30), 58 (no. 67), 63 (nos. 103, 106–7), 67 (no. 137), and 68 (no. 147).

[70] Ibn al-Jawzī, *Kashf al-mushkil min ḥadīth al-ṣaḥīḥayn*, ed. ʿAlī Ḥusayn al-Bawwāb, 4 vols. (Riyadh: Dār al-Waṭan, 1997), 2:16.

women."[71] When, in 2007, the Grand Mufti of Egypt, Ali Gomaa, said that Islam does not prevent a Muslim woman from becoming leader of her country, his opponents cited the Qur᾽anic verse, the tradition, and the case of Persia as evidence of his wrong-headedness. And opponents of female national leaders in Pakistan, Bangladesh, Turkey, and Indonesia have also cited Muḥammad's statement and Persia's failure in support of their positions. In the United States, when Ingrid Mattson was named the first female president of the Islamic Society of North America in 2006, there were some members, though perhaps not many, who also brought up the Hadith against such a possibility and cited Persia's problems. Those sympathetic to women's struggles for empowerment today have also highlighted the failure of Persia under its queen, but in their case, it has served as a specific, and therefore restricted, context in which to situate the Prophet's statement. Considering "the authorial voice of Abū Bakrah in relation to the authorial voice of the Prophet," Khaled Abou El Fadl, for example, argues that Abū Bakra "is consistently cast into the role of the conservative legitimist who defends the traditional role of men, eschews involvement in politics and is stubborn in adhering to whatever he believes is right." It is ironic, however, that "many of the traditions coming through him are highly politicized." The specific tradition, considered here, can be "taken as a condemnation of ῾Ā᾽isha's political role." It is possible, furthermore, that Abū Bakra was "someone who saw little value in women." Then, "if that is the case, is it possible that the Prophet had commented on the developing situation in Persia by saying, 'A people who are led by *this* woman will not succeed?' If that is the case, is it possible that Abū Bakrah misheard the statement because he was receiving it through his own subjectivities?"[72] Meanwhile, the Egyptian scholar Muḥammad al-Ghazālī (not to be confused with the luminary of Seljuk times) has argued for the irrelevance of the tradition, since it applies, in his view, to the internal turmoil then prevailing in Persia; the Prophet meant only that Persia was doomed to fall, not that all women were unfit for public office.[73]

71 For contemporary debates about this verse, see esp. Amina Wadud, *Qur'an and Woman: Rereading the Sacred Text from a Woman's Perspective*, 2nd ed. (New York: Oxford University Press, 1999), esp. 69–74.

72 Khaled Abou El Fadl, *Speaking in God's Name: Islamic Law, Authority and Women* (Oxford: Oneworld, 2001; repr., 2003), 111–14. Other points of consideration include the integrity of Abū Bakra (or lack thereof) and his place in the politics of his own day, amid the conflict between ῾Ā᾽isha and ῾Alī.

73 Muḥammad al-Ghazālī, *al-Sunna al-nabawiyya bayn ahl al-fiqh wa-ahl al-ḥadīth* (Herndon, VA: International Institute of Islamic Thought, 1989). Discussed by Jonathan

Still, while granting the importance of the tradition for the status of women at different points in history, for many of the earliest traditionists, women's place in society was not the point of first concern. They were not defending patriarchy; they saw no need to do so.[74] Instead, they employed a discourse about gender firstly for the purpose of meditating on the conflict-ridden history of the early Muslim community (thus the report's appearance among other Hadith relevant to the *fitna*). For this meditation, the decline of the Sasanians served as a useful point of reference. They also found Abū Bakra's report helpful for writing about the decline of the Sasanians as a subject unto itself. There is often a strong element of triumphalism in the second type of recollections, and an interest in omens forecasting the Sasanians' decline and fall. Neither of these preoccupations have much to do with the question of whether women are fit to rule (or serve as judges or contract their own marriages). Both concerns help explain why, for example, al-Bukhārī places versions of Abū Bakra's report within the "Kitāb al-Fitan" and "Kitāb al-Maghāzī" chapters of his *Ṣaḥīḥ*, rather than elsewhere in his book.[75]

Two examples illustrate the usefulness of Abū Bakra's report for historians' narratives about the Sasanians and their decline, although one could cite many more. In the first, found on the penultimate page of Ibn Qutayba's *al-Maʿārif* amid discussion of Persia's kings, the author reports that during Būrān's one-and-a-half-year reign, the *kharāj* tax was not collected and wealth (*al-amwāl*) was distributed between the army and the nobility – an unfortunate situation from the state's point of view, and one that would have been familiar in Ibn Qutayba's own day, when the treasury's resources were being depleted. Ibn Qutayba then repeats a version of the Prophet's statement: "A people that entrusts its leadership to a woman will not prosper." The greater burden of blame may fall on Shīrawayh and his murderous reign, but the fact of Būrān's gender shows just how desperate the situation had become.[76] In another case, al-Masʿūdī, in a section of his *Tanbīh* treating the Sasanians, gives the

A. C. Brown, *Hadith: Muhammad's Legacy in the Medieval and Modern World* (Oxford: Oneworld, 2009), 163 and 172, n. 32.

74 Nor did they see a reason to oppose patriarchy by applying the exegetical tools of Muslim tradition to Abū Bakra's report, as noted by Fadel, "Is Historicism a Viable Strategy," 150–3. Fadel notes that only one of the early Hadith collections, that of al-Nasāʾī, "made an explicit connection between Abū Bakra's *ḥadīth* and qualifications for political office."

75 Fadel makes a similar argument; see ibid., 154–5.

76 Ibn Qutayba, *al-Maʿārif*, 666. Ibn Qutayba also cites the report at the start of his *ʿUyūn al-akhbār* (1:1) within its "Kitāb al-Sulṭān"; it would appear that a government ruled by two *amīrs* is as disastrous as one run by a woman.

precise length of the reigns of the dynasty's last monarchs – some a matter of months – before he comes to Būrān, who, he writes, ruled for a year and six months. Her reign, we learn, was in the second year of the hijra, and it was during that year that the Prophet learned that she had been made queen and heard of the partisanship and discord that wreaked havoc among the Persians. And so the Prophet said, "If a woman runs a people's affairs, they will not prosper."[77]

For traditionists such as Ibn al-Jawzī, the Sasanian era was nearly five hundred years in the past, and perhaps of limited interest. He could, however, make good use of it as context to explain the Prophet's statement. But what he takes for granted was more than context to other reporters, particularly of earlier times. For them, it was useful to inject the subject of Būrān's gender into their recollections, with a set of expected norms that supported a damning vision of the past.

Conclusion

By the mid-ninth century, we have in Muslim sources – including prophetic biography, Qurʾan commentaries, and works of Hadith – a raft of interlocking, prejudicial reports that depict Persia's past as one of idle tales, polytheists and idolaters, tyrannical and wicked kings, and disaster. Epic was trivialized, while Zoroastrianism was defined in terms unintelligible to any practitioner. Kisrā missed his chance; Būrān had none. The past has little, if anything, to say to the present – it is finished, a point emphatically made by the Prophet when he pronounced that no people shall prosper if a woman rules over them.

This past did not speak for itself, but came into existence as part of a metanarrative that deeply conditioned the expectations that subsequent generations had for knowledge about Iran's history and the sorts of questions that they asked when confronting it. Built on a set of logically consistent, narrated oppositions – a Qurʾanic versus a Persian past, Muslim and (for a time) Byzantine believers versus Meccan and Persian unbelievers, and rule by Islam versus rule by *mulk* (royal power) – traditions about Iran seemed plausible because they resonated with wider

[77] Al-Masʿūdī, *al-Tanbīh*, 102–3. See also the account of al-Maqdisī; he reports that it was during the queen's reign that Persia experienced the defeat at Dhū Qār and the defeat of the Sasanians by the Arabs – a battle ordinarily dated to the reign of her father. The Prophet reportedly said about this battle: "It is the first time that the Arabs got the upper hand of the Persians, and it is through me that God has helped them." Al-Maqdisī, *al-Badʾ wa-l-taʾrīkh*, 3:172–3; L. Veccia Vaglieri, "Dhū Ḳār," in *EI*[2].

bodies of memory relating to Iran as well as to the earliest days of Islam, the Qurʾanic revelation, and the Prophet's life. This memory helped to generate a cultural expectation that any past could be *jāhiliyya*. Accordingly "the justice of Anūshirvān," which I discussed in the introduction to Part 2, appears in al-Thaʿālibī's book under a heading advertising two-word phrases for "the kings of the *jāhiliyya*" and the "caliphs of Islam."[78]

[78] "Fīmā yuḍāfu wa-yunsabu ilā mulūk al-jāhiliyya wa-khulafāʾ al-Islām"; al-Thaʿālibī, *Thimār al-qulūb*, 178–9.

6

Asserting the End of the Past

Scholars have often commented upon how the earliest stories about the conquests glorified the deeds of the Arab victors and were embellished with details, such as tribal genealogies, that served their descendants as well. In Chapter 3, I showed that Iranians also played this game. If there were winners – Arabs and certain Iranians – in the conquests, there were also losers, whose memory fared less well. Beginning with the battle of al-Qādisiyya, this chapter explores the ways in which dramatic and engaging accounts in third/ninth- and fourth/tenth-century histories tend to transform and diminish the identities of the losing side, namely, Sasanian soldiers, religious communities, and elite families. While such persons and institutions were admittedly pushed aside, much conquest reporting also appears to stretch the truth. The possible reasons for this ask for investigation.

Motivated to Do God's Work and Will

Memory of defeat has often played a major role in the imagination of communities, justifying solidarity, cultural resistance, and, frequently, violence against their oppressors. Such narratives trade in nostalgia and call for a return to lost grandeur and pride. The survival of the Jews after repeated defeats, as recorded in the Hebrew Bible, inspired later national movements with the lesson that a people's religious culture could prove stronger than political and military force. So, too, the sites of loss – whether battlefields, resting places, sites of ambush, or breached city walls – often become eternal monuments to brief, yet irreversible moments

FIGURE 6.1. The battle of al-Qādisiyya. From a manuscript of Firdawsī's *Shāh-nāmah*, 1614. © The British Library Board.

of defeat. Even when history validates the victor's conduct in war, the loser rarely accepts his motives as just.[1]

The battle of al-Qādisiyya, which took place in either 636 or 637[2] to the southwest of al-Ḥīra, offers an apparent counterexample to such military reporting, with Iranian and non-Iranian traditionists alike celebrating the Persians' bloody defeat. It was an especially important battle because it opened the way for the Arab Muslims' entry across the Euphrates into the Sasanian heartlands in Iraq and Iran and crushed the Persians, who were led by the illustrious commander Rustam in the service of Yazdagird III. Al-Qādisiyya and the death of Rustam have provided high drama for generations, up to and including our own day, when the story has been manipulated in the service of a poisonous politics. In 1980, it was the subject of an eponymous film produced on the eve of the Iran-Iraq war under the supervision of ʿIzzat Ibrāhīm al-Dūrī, deputy chairman of Iraq's Revolutionary Command Council. During the filming, al-Dūrī stated: "We are most certainly moving toward decisive battles. Our present position forces upon us decisive battles against the enemies so as to open the arduous road leading to the renewal of our glory and our civilisation." A few months later, war broke out. Several Iraqi units carried names from the original al-Qādisiyya, and Iraqis came to refer to the war as "Saddam's Qādisiyya" or "the second Qādisiyya."[3]

A large part of the power of the battle as a focus of memory lay in the evidence it gave of God's assistance to the Muslims. The account of the Arab historian Ibn Aʿtham al-Kūfī shows the Arabs' sense of a religious mission and furnishes an example. He seems to have written his *Kitāb al-Futūḥ* in the first part of the third/ninth century, though the hands of later generations are also at work in it.[4] The following

1 Although bearing a very different historical consciousness, post–World War II Germans are an exception. It is no coincidence that World War II and the Holocaust have generated some of the most stimulating scholarship on memory.

2 Regarding the dates and chronology of, and participants in, the conquests, see esp. Fred McGraw Donner, *The Early Islamic Conquests* (Princeton, NJ: Princeton University Press, 1981); Robinson, "The Rise of Islam"; and Daniel, "The Islamic East."

3 On the film, entitled *al-Qādisiyya* (directed by the Egyptian director Salah Abou Saif), see Ofra Bengio, *Saddam's Word: Political Discourse in Iraq* (New York: Oxford University Press, 1998), 172–5. This film has been available from time to time on YouTube.

4 This frequently studied but little cited text has a complicated history, on which see especially M. A. Shaban, *The ʿAbbāsid Revolution* (Cambridge: Cambridge University Press, 1970), xvii–xix; Shaban, "Ibn Aʿtham al-Kūfī," in *EI*[2]; Lawrence I. Conrad, "Ibn Aʿtham and His History," unpublished paper presented at the Sixth International Colloquium on "From Jahiliyya to Islam" (Institute for Advanced Studies, Hebrew University, Jerusalem, Sept. 5–10, 1993); Conrad, "Conquest of Arwād"; and Borrut, *Entre mémoire et pouvoir*,

is a summary of what he has to say about the battle. We learn that the Muslims suffered significant losses in their first encounter with the Persians in Iraq at a site called Jisr (Arabic for "bridge"), located near al-Ḥīra. They were overwhelmed by the Persians' military strength but also hurt by their own internal squabbles. But things changed when the Caliph ʿUmar appointed Saʿd b. Abī Waqqāṣ in charge of all of the Muslims in Iraq, saying: "I hope that God will conquer by your hand!"[5] The Muslims subsequently approached Yazdagird with an "invitation" to accept Islam by reciting a profession of the faith or to pay the tax on non-Muslims (*jizya*), the third alternative being combat. Their main agent was a man of high standing among the Arabs named al-Mughīra b. Shuʿba, who told Yazdagird that Muḥammad "informed us before his death of all the lands which God, mighty and glorious, would open by our hands, and your country and palace were among them."[6] Yazdagird, not surprisingly, responded unsympathetically: in lieu of the *jizya* (which, he learned, would involve a whip being held over the Persians' heads), he instructed one of his men to place a load of dirt atop the head of one of the Arab nobles, with a note for their leader warning that he, Yazdagird, would be sending someone to bury him and his companions in the ditch of al-Qādisiyya.[7]

The fighting was difficult; the Persians greatly outnumbered the Muslims and possessed not only horses but also elephants. Ibn Aʿtham reports that Muslim mothers urged their sons to martyrdom.[8] Yet, despite the odds Saʿd and his men persisted, though Saʿd himself could not join in the fighting owing to unbearable sores on the interior of his thighs that made riding a war horse impossible. The tide of the battle changed when a brave former drunk, Abū Miḥjan, rode atop Saʿd's horse and armed with his weapons into battle. In the fighting, the Muslims proclaimed

91–3. More skeptically, see Marina Pyrovolaki, "*Futūḥ al-Shām* and Other *Futūḥ* Texts: A Study of the Perception of Marginal Conquest Narratives in Arabic in Medieval and Modern Times" (D.Phil. thesis, University of Oxford, 2009), ch. 3, "Ibn Aʿtham: The Making of a Historian and the *Futūḥ al-Islām*." The sections of Ibn Aʿtham's book that I treat in this chapter seem to contain early third/ninth-century material, as he gives more attention than do later chroniclers to the identity of the Persians, whose descendants may have been more known to him.

5 Ibn Aʿtham, *Kitāb al-Futūḥ*, ed. Muḥammad ʿAbd al-Muʿīd Khān and ʿAbd al-Wahhāb al-Bukhārī, 8 vols. (Hyderabad: Osmania Oriental Publications Bureau, 1968–75), 1:168–73.

6 Ibid., 1:199. After describing the battle of Jisr, Ibn Aʿtham treats exchanges with Byzantium before returning to the situation in Iraq and the battle of al-Qādisiyya.

7 Ibid., 1:200.

8 Ibid., 1:206–7.

their convictions with shouts of "God is most great!" and by declaring, "Power belongs alone to God, the Almighty, the Great!" By the time the Muslims had pushed their opponents to the bank of the Euphrates, they had killed more than ten thousand horsemen and taken a great deal of booty. They then drove on toward al-Madāʾin. At last, in the vicinity of the Sasanian capital, one of the Muslims, Hilāl b. ʿAlqama, recognized Rustam and charged at him:

> Rustam shot at him with an arrow and pierced the Muslim's foot in its stirrup. The Muslim struck him a blow and knocked him down dead. Then he removed the arrow from his foot, dismounted to Rustam, and removed the crown (*al-tāj*) and whatever else was on Rustam. And he left him dead and despoiled and mounted his horse.[9]

Having killed Rustam off in his narrative, Ibn Aʿtham moves on to relate events at al-Madāʾin and to give an account of the Arabs' crossing of the Tigris.

Rustam's death made for a good story, as can be seen even more vividly in al-Ṭabarī's account of the battle, which is far longer than any other (pieced together from previous reports, it occupies nearly 150 pages in the Leiden edition of the *History*).[10] Toward the beginning, the Arabs invite the Persians to Islam or, alternatively, to pay the *jizya* or to engage in battle; the Persians, led by Yazdagird and Rustam, either reject the offer outright, in some reports al-Ṭabarī features, or give serious consideration to the Arabs' invitation, in others. But in the end, they opt for war. Events unfold until Rustam, hiding in the shade of a mule and its litter, is badly injured when an Arab, Hilāl b. ʿUllafa, cuts the ropes fastening the mule's litter, which collapses onto Rustam's spine.[11] Rustam manages to drag himself to a nearby canal and to throw himself into it, but before he can swim to safety, the Arab, in pursuit, wades into the water, grabs Rustam's leg, and drags him to the canal's bank, where he strikes Rustam in the forehead with his sword, killing him. Al-Ṭabarī continues:

> Then [Hilāl] dragged him farther and threw him at the feet of the mules. He seated himself on Rustam's throne and exclaimed, "By the Lord of the Kaʿba,

[9] Ibid., 1:212.

[10] Al-Ṭabarī cites Sayf b. ʿUmar (d. 180/796) throughout this portion of his *Taʾrīkh* (he credits a recension through Shuʿayb b. Ibrāhīm and al-Sarī b. Yaḥyā). On Sayf and his *Kitāb al-Futūḥ al-kabīr wa-l-ridda*, see esp. Ella Landau-Tasseron, "Sayf b. ʿUmar in Medieval and Modern Scholarship," *Der Islam* 67, no. 1 (1990): 1–26. Toward the end of his account, al-Ṭabarī introduces a separate account by Ibn Isḥāq.

[11] The names ʿAlqama and ʿUllafa resemble each other in the Arabic script.

I have killed Rustam! Come to me!" Men gathered around him without noticing or seeing the throne, proclaiming, "God is most great!" and calling out to each other. At this point the polytheists (*mushrikūn*) lost heart and were defeated.[12]

One learns that in the aftermath thirty thousand Persians followed Rustam's example, throwing themselves into the canal, with the Arabs pursuing them up and down its bank, massacring them. On this day, al-Ṭabarī writes, the Muslims killed "ten thousand" men, "over and above those whom they had killed on the previous day."[13] A group of Christians enquired of Saʿd b. Abī Waqqāṣ: "O commander, we have seen the body of Rustam near the gate of your castle, but he had the head of another man; the blows have disfigured him [beyond recognition]." At this, we are told, "Saʿd laughed."[14]

Al-Ṭabarī's account is structured as a series of episodes that move toward Rustam's death.[15] The topos of the call to Islam appears again and again, as the story repeatedly shows violence as the consequence of rejecting this "invitation." Presented as direct speech, it consists of the options of conversion, payment of the *jizya*, or war, and it emphasizes the Arabs' prior state (the *jāhiliyya*) as a time of spiritual and physical deprivation. When Yazdagird comments, "I know of no other nation on earth that was more miserable, smaller in numbers, and more rancorous than you," one of the Arabs even expands his point: certainly, the Arabs used to eat beetles, scorpions, and snakes; to raid and kill one another as a religion; and to practice female infanticide – but all of that was *before* Islam.[16]

Like many moments in world history, the battle of al-Qādisiyya opens itself to interpretation. A century or two after Ibn Aʿtham and al-Ṭabarī, the Muʿtazilite theologian ʿAbd al-Jabbār (d. 415/1025) – who was born in Asadābād, a small town in western Iran to the southwest of Hamadhān, and who spent much of his career in Baghdad and Rayy – offered proofs

12 Al-Ṭabarī, *Taʾrīkh*, I:2336–7; *The History of al-Ṭabarī*, vol. 12, *The Battle of al-Qādisiyyah and the Conquest of Syria and Palestine*, trans. Yohanan Friedmann (Albany: State University of New York Press, 1992), 123–4.

13 Al-Ṭabarī, *Taʾrīkh*, I:2337.

14 Ibid., I:2340; *History of al-Ṭabarī*, 12:127.

15 According to al-Ṭabarī (from Sayf), this took place at al-Qādisiyya, not outside al-Madāʾin as in Ibn Aʿtham's account. For another account of the killing, see al-Ṭabarī, *Taʾrīkh*, I:2356–7 (from Ibn Isḥāq).

16 Al-Ṭabarī, *Taʾrīkh*, I:2240–2; *History of al-Ṭabarī*, 12:36–9. On this topos, see Noth, *Early Arabic Historical Tradition*, 146–67.

for the superiority of Islam over other religions in his *Tathbīt dalāʾil al-nubuwwa* (Confirmation of the Proofs of Prophecy).[17] One such proof rests on how the Prophet and the Qurʾan had "promised" (*waʿada*) the success of Islam and Muslim rule. ʿAbd al-Jabbār begins with a quotation from the Prophet: "Verily God sent me as a messenger and promised me that my religion would prevail over all [other] religions and my ruling power (*ṣulṭānī*) would be victorious over that of Kisrā and Caesar. So overcome the kings, and my sovereignty and that of my helpers and followers will surpass that of every king on earth."[18] Qurʾanic verses follow in support of this prediction: "[It is] He who sent His messenger with the guidance and the religion of truth to make it prevail over all religion; God is sufficient witness" (48:28) and "They wish to extinguish God's light with their mouths, but God refuses [to do] anything other than to perfect His light, even though the Unbelievers (*al-kāfirīn*) dislike that" (9:32). For ʿAbd al-Jabbār, the conquests brought victory over the Sasanian regime, but more significantly, they heralded the victory of Islam over other religions (*diyānāt*); as he states: "It was as [God] said and as he related." He goes on to present a lengthy theological argument, in which, among other matters, he treats objects of Zoroastrian belief. The history of the conquests supports his case: it fits into a broader narrative about the inevitable triumph of Islam, which begins with Muḥammad's life, his death, and the so-called "wars of apostasy" (*ridda*), followed by the defeat of Persia and reporting on al-Qādisiyya. ʿAbd al-Jabbār recalls with irony Yazdagird's statement that he would bury the Arabs in the ditch at al-Qādisiyya.[19]

Fred Donner has characterized the conquests in general as a "remarkable testament to the power of human action mobilized by ideological commitment as a force in human affairs."[20] Indeed, when the centrality of the Islamic mission is highlighted, this is what classical authors seem to show us. The repeated use of the word *mushrik*, signifying "polytheist," to refer to the Persians underscores their rejection of the invitation to

[17] Christianity occupies a significant portion of ʿAbd al-Jabbār's attention in this book, on which see Gabriel Said Reynolds, *A Muslim Theologian in the Sectarian Milieu: ʿAbd al-Jabbār and the Critique of Christian Origins* (Leiden: Brill, 2004), 1–74. See also ʿAbd al-Jabbār, *Critique of Christian Origins: A Parallel English-Arabic Text*, ed. and trans. Gabriel Said Reynolds and Samir Khalil Samir (Provo, UT: Brigham Young University Press, 2010).

[18] ʿAbd al-Jabbār b. Aḥmad, *Tathbīt dalāʾil al-nubuwwa*, ed. ʿAbd al-Karīm ʿUthmān, 2 vols. (Beirut: Dār al-ʿArabiyya, 1966), 2:314.

[19] ʿAbd al-Jabbār, *Tathbīt dalāʾil al-nubuwwa*, 2:320–1.

[20] Donner, *Early Islamic Conquests*. See also R. Stephen Humphreys, *Islamic History: A Framework for Inquiry*, rev. ed. (Princeton, NJ: Princeton University Press, 1991), 88–9.

Islam through the employment of a Qur'anic term that exegetes in their Qur'an commentaries identified as the Arab polytheists and worshippers of idols in Muḥammad's lifetime.[21] Similarly, the term *fatḥ*, used in the conquest literature generally, has a primary sense of "opening" but points to the idea that the "expansion was an act of God's favor, a divine blessing bestowed upon His prophet and those faithful Believers who followed him."[22]

It is noteworthy that ʿAbd al-Jabbār spells out in theological terms what Ibn Aʿtham and al-Ṭabarī merely described historically, namely, the victory of Islam over other religions. By contrast, for Ibn Aʿtham and al-Ṭabarī, the supersession of the Sasanian Empire as a political event is at least as much an interest, and equally belongs to a fundamentally kerygmatic interpretation of the conquests as they describe the defeated throughout as imperial soldiers, and civilian populations and their religious rituals and beliefs play little or no role in the drama. The identity of the residents of al-Qādisiyya before the war is not important; afterward, the term *ahl al-Qādisiyya* refers to the Arab victors. For historians writing at the center of the ʿAbbasid Empire, such a perspective fits, for they would be sensitive to their own place in a sequence of empires. They do not celebrate the defeat of Persians or ordinary Zoroastrians as such, but rather the defeat of a past regime and its imperial religion. A story related by al-Ṭabarī thus depicts Rustam, on the outskirts of Kufa, dreaming that ʿUmar entered the Persian camp accompanied by an angel, who put a seal on the weapons of the Persians, tied them in a bundle, and handed them to ʿUmar.[23]

Images of God-given victory and violence endured amid disagreements on the identity of Rustam's killer, with the phrase "God killed Rustam," *qatala Allāh Rustam*, employed in recognition of uncertainty on the question, and as various poets vaunted their tribesmen's valor in killing Rustam. One of the Muslims who claimed credit, Zuhayr b. ʿAbd Shams al-Bajalī, reportedly boasted:

> I am Zuhayr and I am the son of ʿAbd Shams.
> I felled by [my] sword the great man of Persia,
> Rustam – a man of pride and fine silk.
> I obeyed my Lord and satisfied myself.[24]

21 See my discussion of homology in Chapter 5, as well as Hawting, *Idea of Idolatry and the Emergence of Islam*, Chapter 2.

22 Donner, "Arabic *fatḥ* as 'Conquest.'" Regarding a "Believers" movement as a form of militant monotheism, see Donner, *Muhammad and the Believers*.

23 Al-Ṭabarī, *Taʾrīkh*, I:2266.

24 Al-Balādhurī, *al-Buldān wa-futūḥuhā*, 302–3.

Such reporting may belong to a much wider pattern of history as told by the winners, in which the losing side suffers in memory. Still, more sympathetic visions could emerge and exist alongside those of al-Ṭabarī and his fellow reporters, especially in works composed under the patronage of Iranian dynasties. One senses mild sympathy in Balʿamī's Persian adaptation of al-Ṭabarī's work, completed under the Samanid governorate and representing a new phase in memory. There are significant differences between Balʿamī's version and al-Ṭabarī's original, including the former's omission of chains of transmission and resolution of some of the ambiguities in the latter, not to mention its extreme brevity; as noted in Chapter 1, his text can in no sense be read as a straight translation of al-Ṭabarī's *History*. For this episode, the details that Balʿamī recalls about Rustam's demise portray the death of an opponent who, while not a Muslim, is never called a polytheist (*mushrik*). Yazdagird's soldiers, no longer called "polytheists" but generally the "ʿAjam" or, on occasion, "unbelievers" (sing. *kāfir*, pl. *kāfirān*) are put to flight by the sight of the head of their general raised on a spear.[25] More profoundly, in Firdawsī's *Shāh-nāmah*, the story of Rustam's death has shades of tragedy, especially in a letter Rustam was supposed to have written to his brother on the eve of his death, in which he predicted the downfall of Persia.[26] Rustam is killed by a worthy opponent, the commander Saʿd himself – the latter no victim of illness.[27] Von Grunebaum aptly summarized the contradiction likely experienced by Firdawsī in recounting these last episodes of his epic, the unexplored future of Iran lying beyond his pages. As a Persian, Firdawsī was "irremediably humiliated by the Sassanian defeat; as a Muslim he should have felt elated at a development that had brought the true faith to his people and to himself."[28]

[25] Balʿamī, *Tārīkh-nāmah-yi Ṭabarī*, ed. Muḥammad Rawshan, 3 vols. (Tehran: Nashr-i Naw, 1366*shamsī*/[1987]), 1:451–2. Cf. *Chronique de Abou-Djafar-Mo'hammed-ben-Djarir-ben-Yezid Tabari* (an unfortunate title, knowing what we now do about the nature of Balʿamī's "translation"), trans. M. Hermann Zotenberg, 4 vols. (Paris: Imprimerie Impériale, 1867–74; repr., Paris: Éditions d'art Les Heures Claires, [1977?]), 3:385–400. Regarding the Samanids, Balʿamī, and translation, see also Travis Zadeh, *The Vernacular Qur'an: Translation and the Rise of Persian Exegesis* (London: Oxford University Press, 2012), 302ff.

[26] Firdawsī, *Shāh-nāmah*, 8:413ff.

[27] Firdawsī, *Shāh-nāmah*, 8:429ff. Cf. also Balʿamī, *Tārīkh-nāmah-yi Ṭabarī*, 1: 451–2.

[28] G. E. von Grunebaum, "Firdausī's Concept of History," in *Islam: Essays in the Nature and Growth of a Cultural Tradition* (Menasha, WI: American Anthropological Association, 1955), 173.

Killing "Polytheists"

In their discussions of al-Qādisiyya, Ibn Aʿtham and al-Ṭabarī show the passage of the Sasanian Empire and the victory of Islam but care little for Iranian society beyond military elites. While Qurʾan commentators, as discussed in Chapter 5, became more careful in how they identified pre-Islamic Persians in some contexts, historians of the conquests often refer to all of the Arabs' opponents as "polytheists" (*mushrikūn*) – as if to erase their religious affiliations. This is the case even when the setting – a Christian monastery (*dayr*), for example – would suggest otherwise.

Toward the end of a short seventh-century Nestorian work known as the *Khūzistān Chronicle*, we find an account of the Arab conquest of the region and of Shūsh and Shūstrā, or as Arabs came to know the towns, al-Sūs and Tustar. The *Chronicle* was completed, at the latest, by the 680s and is of interest because its detailed reporting and proximity to the events can serve as a control against which to compare the later Arabic texts.[29] It notes that "at the time of which we have been speaking, when the *Tayyāyē*" – that is, the Arabs – "conquered all the territory of the Persians and Byzantines, they also overran Bēt Hūzāyē, conquering all the strong towns." There remained only Sūs and Tustar, which were extremely well fortified and controlled by the Persian forces commanded by Yazdagird and one of his generals, called "Hormīzdan the Mede" (known in the Arabic sources as al-Hurmuzān or al-Hurmuzdān). We are told that the Arabs were led by their general Abū Mūsā (al-Ashʿarī, the famed military leader of the conquests) who built Basra as a settlement for the Arabs, just as Saʿd, son of (Abū) Waqqāṣ, had built Kufa. When Abū Mūsā went up against al-Hurmuzān, the latter used delaying tactics until he had collected an army. He petitioned Abū Mūsā to desist from taking captives and laying waste to the land, and he promised to send tribute in return. This arrangement worked for two years, and then al-Hurmuzān, trusting the strength of his walls, broke the peace by killing the Arabs' ambassadors, including Giwargis, bishop of Ulay; he also imprisoned Abraham, metropolitan of Porath. Al-Hurmuzān sent many troops against the Arabs, but they were routed, and then the Arabs besieged Sūs, taking it after only a few days. The Arabs killed all of Sūs's distinguished citizens and seized a building called the House of Mār Daniel, taking the treasure that was

[29] See the lucid analysis of the *Chronicle*'s composition and dating by Chase F. Robinson in "The Conquest of Khūzistān: A Historiographical Reassessment," *Bulletin of the School of Oriental and African Studies* 67, no. 1 (2004): 14–16 (taking into account the history of scholarship on the *Chronicle*).

FIGURE 6.2. Susa (Sūs, Iran), tomb of Daniel, 1903–36. Ernst Herzfeld Papers, Freer Gallery of Art and Arthur M. Sackler Gallery Archives, Smithsonian Institution, Washington, DC. Gift of Ernst Herzfeld, 1946. Drawing by Ernst Herzfeld (D-219).

kept there and that, according to the account, had been preserved on the king's orders "since the days of Darius and Cyrus" (see Figure 6.2). The Arabs also broke open and took a silver chest containing a mummy – according to many it was Daniel's, but others held that it belonged to King Darius. They also besieged Tustar, fighting for two years to take it. Finally a man from the province of Bēt Qaṭrāyē, who lived in Tustar, befriended someone who owned a house on the walls of the city and entered into a conspiracy with him. The two of them went to the Arabs, promising them: "If you give us a third of the spoil of the city, we will let you into it." The conspirators dug a tunnel under the walls and let in the Arabs, who proceeded to spill "blood there as if it were water." They "killed the Exegete of the city and bishop of Hormīzd Ardashīr [Ar. Sūq al-Ahwāz], along with the rest of the students, priests, and deacons, shedding their blood in the very [church] sanctuary." As for al-Hurmuzān, the Arabs took him alive.[30]

[30] I would like to thank Sebastian Brock for making available to me his unpublished translation of the *Chronicle* (I draw from paras. 48–50). This section of the *Chronicle* is also translated by Robinson in "Conquest of Khūzistān," 17–18, from which I have also

Studying the *Chronicle*, Chase Robinson has found the Arabic tradition to be surprisingly faithful to several of the facts as reported in the Nestorian text, such as the principal role played by Abū Mūsā al-Ashʿarī, the historicity of a siege, and the role (but not the identity) of a traitor in securing Tustar's defeat. Robinson's comparison also yields broader insights, including that the conquest traditions that we now have are generally "composite reconstructions, assembled out of discrete units, rather than pieces of a now-lost coherent whole."[31] But on one interesting point, only briefly remarked upon by Robinson, there is a significant difference between the Arabic reporters and the *Chronicle*: in our major Arabic sources we do not find recollection of any Christians having been among the dead at Tustar.[32] Of course, the *Chronicle*, as the work of a Christian author, might see events through a Christian lens, but it would seem a reasonable assumption that there were Christian dead at Tustar. Instead of reference to Christianity, however, one of the main and early ways that the Arabic traditionists refer to the Tustarīs is along ethnic lines as "non-Arabs" or "Persians," while their opponents are described as Muslims or Arabs. And so, at the start of Ibn Aʿtham's treatment of the conquest of Khūzistān, he mentions that ʿUmar wrote a letter to Abū Mūsā asking him to rally his companions and "the people of Basra and the rest of the Muslims" to go fight the "non-Arabs" (*al-aʿājim*) at Tustar, Sūs, Manādhir, and their environs. ʿUmar promised: "Know that the Muslims are under the protection of God, and that of His creatures, the Muslim is the most protected by God," as he entrusted the Muslims to Abū Mūsā's supervision and care.[33] After a series of events, seventy or so Muslims sneaked under cover of night into the town, only to find in the morning that its door was bound with three locks, and the keys were with al-Hurmuzān. Muslims both inside and outside the walls yelled "God is most great." This roused the Persians, including al-Hurmuzān,

benefited. Their translations are based on the text edited by Ignazio Guidi as *Chronicon anonymum*. Scholars have made good use of the *Chronicle*; see esp. Robert G. Hoyland, *Seeing Islam as Others Saw It: A Survey and Evaluation of Christian, Jewish and Zoroastrian Writings on Early Islam* (Princeton, NJ: Darwin Press, 1997), 182–9; James Howard-Johnston, *Witness to a World Crisis: Historians and Histories of the Middle East in the Seventh Century* (Oxford: Oxford University Press, 2010), 128–35; and Savant, "The Conquest of Tustar: Site of Memory, Site of Forgetting," in *Violence in Early Islamic Thought*, ed. István Kristó-Nagy and Robert Gleave (Edinburgh: Edinburgh University Press, forthcoming).

31 Robinson, "Conquest of Khūzistān," 37. Robinson notes that his comparison supports the earlier view of Noth; see his *Early Arabic Historical Tradition*, esp. 5–6.

32 Robinson, "Conquest of Khūzistān," 33.

33 Ibn Aʿtham, *Kitāb al-Futūḥ*, 2:3–4.

his *asāwira* (elite cavalry), and *marzubāns*, from their homes and fortifications. Amid exclamations of "God is most great," a fight ensued, with the Muslims inside fighting while struggling to get the gate opened. Many of them were killed, leaving only three alive when the last lock was finally opened and the main force of Muslims rushed in and began "killing and plundering." Al-Hurmuzān fled to the town's citadel with his retinue and whatever they could carry. With the town now open and its people scattered, the Muslims took booty, setting aside the allotted share for the caliph ʿUmar before securing the surrender of al-Hurmuzān.[34]

Other historians similarly stress the intensity of the fight but write out Tustar's Christians. Ibn Khayyāṭ al-ʿUṣfurī draws together a number of reports dealing with the length of the Muslims' siege of Tustar, the manner by which they entered the town, the role of individual Muslims and a traitor, the fate of al-Hurmuzān, the division of the booty, and the prayers missed amid the fighting – but has nothing to say about the identity of the *ahl Tustar*.[35] The terminology is similarly vague in the reports passed on by al-Balādhurī, who narrates in one report that a non-Arab man (*rajul min al-aʿājim*) sought good terms for himself and his family in exchange for leading the Muslims to a gap in the defenses of the *mushrikīn*. He focuses his attention especially on al-Hurmuzān and his supporters, relating that on the battlefield the Muslims killed nine hundred of al-Hurmuzān's troops and captured six hundred others, who were executed.[36] From another report, we learn that afterward, Abū Mūsā also "killed anyone who was in the citadel who did not have a guarantee of safety," though he passed al-Hurmuzān on to ʿUmar, who let him live.[37] Al-Ṭabarī, likewise, focuses his attention on the Muslims' successes and on al-Hurmuzān and the Sasanians – with armies from Fārs, Jibāl, and Ahwāz – but not the residents of Tustar in recounting the Muslim victory: "From the day the siege began until the time God conquered Tustar for the Muslims, al-Barāʾ b. Mālik killed one hundred adversaries, in addition to those he slew on other occasions." Among the Basran fighters, Majzaʾa b. Thawr, Kaʿb b. Sūr, and Abū Tamīma "killed similar numbers of enemy soldiers." Among the Kufans there we also some men who killed a great number of the enemy, including Ḥabīb b. Qurra, Ribʿī b. ʿĀmir, and ʿĀmir b. ʿAbd al-Aswad. Furthermore, during

34 Ibid., 2:20–3. The Muslims are shown the way by a Tustarī.
35 Ibn Khayyāṭ al-ʿUṣfurī, *Taʾrīkh*, 1:138–42.
36 Al-Balādhurī, *al-Buldān wa-futūḥuhā*, 427.
37 Ibid., 426.

the siege, "there were a number of enemies wounded who have to be added to the numbers killed by them."[38]

Christians as such are not the subject of violence in any of these accounts, nor are they part of the story. That we are witnessing repression of memory is suggested by al-Ṭabarī's recollection of the siege and conquest of Sūs, which denies any use of violence against Christians. According to the story, the military leader al-Nuʿmān b. Muqarrin,[39] before departing from Sūs for Nihāwand, engaged the enemy in combat. Some monks and clerics (*al-ruhbān wa-l-qissīsūn*) taunted the Muslims from the city's battlements: "O Arabs, do not bother, for no one will conquer this fortress but the Antichrist, or forces that have the Antichrist in their midst." Their shouting, we are told, enraged the Muslims. An Arab, Ṣāfī b. Ṣayyād, strode to the gate of Sūs and kicked it with his foot, shouting "Open up," whereupon it blew open, and as chains snapped and locks broke, the other gates opened up too. The Muslims then stormed inside, and the "polytheists" (*al-mushrikūn*) surrendered by stretching out their hands and shouting "Peace, peace!" The Arabs magnanimously agreed to peace even though they had had to enter the city by force.[40] In contrast to the accounts of the taking of Tustar, this report about the conquest of Sūs preserves the identity of the city's Christian inhabitants, perhaps because of the tomb of Daniel and its association by Muslims with the "Palace of Shūshān" in the biblical book of Daniel as well as the possibly greater notoriety and survival of Christians there.[41]

Why were Tustar's Christians not identified? Why did historians such as al-Ṭabarī not use the town's conquest to show, for example, the superiority of Islam over Christianity? Immersed in the Arabic sources and accustomed to such terminology across conquest reporting, today's scholars of the conquests generally take little notice of the term *mushrik*, perhaps because they see it as a polemical term reflecting the Muslims' fashioning of themselves as monotheists. This is a reasonable reading of

[38] Al-Ṭabarī, *Taʾrīkh*, I:2553–4; *The History of al-Ṭabarī*, vol. 13, *The Conquest of Iraq, Southwestern Persia, and Egypt*, trans. G. H. A. Juynboll (Albany: State University of New York Press, 1989), 134.

[39] Brother to Suwayd and Nuʿaym, who were also active in the eastern conquests; see Chapter 1, and also al-Sahmī, *Taʾrīkh Jurjān*, 4. On this family at the conquests, see Donner, *Early Islamic Conquests*, esp. 428–9.

[40] Al-Ṭabarī, *Taʾrīkh*, I:2564–5; *History of al-Ṭabarī*, 13:145–6.

[41] Regarding Syriac Christian churches, see "Shuster" and "Suse" in Fiey, *Pour un Oriens Christianus Novus*, 133 and 135–6.

the sources, and perhaps even of the Qur'an's own usage.[42] The term features prominently in the early numismatic evidence as an important indicator of the Muslims' sense of themselves as a community distinct from others. The Umayyad caliph ʿAbd al-Malik (r. 65–86/685–705) issued coins featuring Arabic inscriptions, including Qur'an 9:33, "[It is] He who has sent His messenger with the guidance and the religion of truth, to make it prevail over all [other] religion, even though the polytheists (*mushrikūn*) dislike that." This verse, known as the *risāla* verse, was reused when the ʿAbbasid caliph al-Ma'mūn (r. 198–218/813–33) reformed the currency. Similarly, Qur'an 112, which proclaims that God has no partner, featured on the coinage and on the Dome of the Rock and has reasonably been read as opposing Christian trinitarianism.[43] There was also the Qur'anic term *kufr*, or unbelief, which some jurists interpreted to signify that any non-Muslim religion is like any other.[44] In other words, an established vocabulary existed that was employed in various contexts that often did efface the identity of Christians and other faith groups. Furthermore, an "elephant in the room" at Tustar was al-Hurmuzān's later relationship with ʿUmar, the Caliph's murder by the hand of a Persian slave, and the possible guilt of al-Hurmuzān – this episode bearing on a number of issues, including *fitna*, or conflict, within the Muslim community itself and the loyalties of converts to Islam. Historians also had other post-conquest axes to grind, such as the spoils and who should have received credit for the victory. Taking these aspects of history writing into account, details about the losers hardly mattered.

But in some of the silence, we likely also have another kind of evidence: evidence of the sensitivities of communities in transition, in which legal-minded scholars, such as al-Ṭabarī, may have felt some discomfort with conquest-era violence against People of the Book, which would partially explain the many references to the topos of the "invitation"

42 See Hawting, *Idea of Idolatry*, Chapter 2.

43 See Max van Berchem, *Matériaux pour un Corpus inscriptionum Arabicarum*, part 2, *Syrie du Sud*, 3 vols. (Cairo: Imprimerie de l'Institut français d'archéologie orientale, 1922–3, 1927), 2:223ff.; Oleg Grabar, "The Umayyad Dome of the Rock in Jerusalem," *Ars Orientalis* 3 (1959): 52ff.; Tayeb El-Hibri, "Coinage Reform under the ʿAbbāsid Caliph al-Ma'mūn," *Journal of the Economic and Social History of the Orient* 36, no. 1 (1993): 58–83; Jere L. Bacharach, *Islamic History through Coins: An Analysis and Catalogue of Tenth-Century Ikhshidid Coinage* (Cairo: American University in Cairo Press, 2006), 15–19; Heidemann, "Numismatics," 656–7 and 659; and Donner, *Muhammad and the Believers*, 208–9.

44 See Yohanan Friedmann, *Tolerance and Coercion in Islam*, 54–86 ("Classification of Unbelievers").

to Islam.[45] This silence deserves more consideration. In the words of Thomas Sizgorich, the militant devotionalism expressed in our Muslim sources should likely be read as testimony to a common late antique pattern of ascetic warriors and as memorializing "a *koinē* of signs, symbols, and narrative forms with which the other communities of late antiquity had for centuries contested questions of divine revelation, prophetic legitimacy, communal integrity and eruptions of the numinous into the lived experience of individuals and communities." Muslim authors participated in these patterns and in the process "inextricably (and unknowingly) bound their community to a constellation of kindred communities arrayed from Ireland to Yemen and from the Atlantic coast of Iberia to eastern Mesopotamia."[46] The late antique world in which Islam emerged really was one of "pious violence" and "pious warriors," where militant devotion to faith was expected, inscriptional propaganda appealed to soldiers paid in coinage, and spokespersons for post-conquest communities – historians included – established boundary lines through narratives that distinguished Muslims from their neighbors and in which the original points of conflict became sites of memory.

The problem was that by the third/ninth and fourth/tenth centuries the nature of the communities in which Muslims lived had changed enormously – in size, in composition, and also in interconnections with Christians and Jews, as we know from other types of evidence, including polemics. Muslims now had real neighbors to consider, so some elements of the old stories just would not do. Iranian Muslims – like all Muslims – could not, nor did they wish to, forget the conquests, which had unfolded on such a vast and significant scale as a sign of God's blessing. But they needed to remember them carefully. It was not in their interest to stir up trouble with Christians, Jews, or Zoroastrians, nor, it should also be said, to recognize their own ancestors amid the vanquished. This meant rewriting history to erase the identity of its losers. Such rewriting developed a vocabulary that presented monotheistic Christians as polytheists and that

[45] Noth, *Early Arabic Historical Tradition*, 146–67. Robinson broaches the topic well into his article, when he writes: "That the Islamic tradition says nothing of the killing of local Christians is to be explained not only by its relative indifference to (and absence of solid information about) the fate of the conquered, but also by the political circumstances in which it stabilized. Clearly defined legal rights and peaceful co-existence, the latter commonly articulated in the Prophetic prohibition of killing monks, are developments of the post-conquest period" ("The Conquest of Khūzistān," 33).

[46] Thomas Sizgorich, *Violence and Belief in Late Antiquity: Militant Devotion in Christianity and Islam* (Philadelphia: University of Pennsylvania Press, 2009), 13.

likely existed well before al-Ṭabarī's day, but it was maintained thanks in part to scholars such as al-Ṭabarī, who could have presented history more along the theological lines of ʿAbd al-Jabbār, in the process rendering explicit the losses to Christians, but chose instead to maintain the anonymity of the victims. And so, while Muslims continued to elaborate their own convictions through ever longer and more integrated narratives about their ascetic values, God-given strength, and devoted militancy against all odds, their original opponents faded into a set of meaningless categories – enemies, polytheists, unbelievers, and so forth.

This willful neglect is also suggested by how historians such as al-Ṭabarī write about Zoroastrian sites at the time of the conquests and afterward. As Iranians converted to Islam, Zoroastrianism suffered a dramatic decline. Today, Zoroastrians number in the tens of thousands[47] in a country dotted with former sites of Zoroastrian ritual.[48] The decline is not – to put it mildly – well documented in our Arabic sources. Even when scholars have sought to identify the three major fires named in the Avesta and in Pahlavi literature, the Ādur Farnbāg, Ādur Gushnasp, and Ādur Būrzīn-mitrō, they have often been forced to work by conjecture. Today, when some documenters of Iran's Zoroastrian heritage study the religion's fate after the conquests, they point to the fear and intimidation wrought by the invading armies, the movement of fires from place to place, the pillaging of fire temples, and the building of mosques on their sites. Still, among Muslims, the destruction of fire temples generated nothing like the literary interest accorded to al-Qādisiyya or Tustar, nor does history seem to have passed on extensive documentary evidence from Zoroastrians themselves. For example, scholars of Zoroastrianism have sought to recover the history of the Ādur Farnbāg (also known in our sources as the Ādur Farrōbay, Ādur Farra, or Ādur Khurra) near the ancient city of Dārābgird in the province of Fārs. The fire's origins could be traced to Khwārizm and to the legendary figure of Jamshīd, and under the Sasanian Anūshirvān it was reportedly moved to the village of Kāriyān in Fārs.[49] At some point, according to Jamsheed Choksy, it was "divided

[47] The Iranian government has estimated that Zoroastrians in the country today number thirty to thirty-five thousand; Zoroastrian groups in Iran claim to have sixty thousand adherents. United States Department of State, "July-December, 2010 International Religious Freedom Report: Iran," Sept. 13, 2011; http://www.unhcr.org/refworld/docid/4e734c92c.html.

[48] On these, see Schippmann, *Die iranischen Feuerheiligtümer*.

[49] See Schippmann, *Die iranischen Feuerheiligtümer*, 86–94 ("Kāriyān, Fārs"), documenting a much wider variety of reports on this fire. See also A. V. Williams Jackson, "The

into two portions hidden to safeguard against extinguishment by Arab Muslims." These protective actions were prescient because in 670 CE the Umayyad governor of Iraq ordered the temple in Kāriyān razed, but the flame was restored in Kāriyān and another started at Fasā from the safeguarded portion of the fire. The threat continued, however, and in 1174 CE, the Kāriyān fire was moved to the nearby village of Sharīfābād "to burn inconspicuously within side chambers of [a] mudbrick *ātashgāh* [fire-temple], safe from extinguishment by zealous Muslims."[50] This all may be true, but not a single source narrates the entirety of this account, which Choksy has pieced together from different sources. This would suggest that neither Muslims nor Zoroastrians wished to remember the events as he relates them. This is not to say that one *cannot* write a history of Christians, Zoroastrians, and Jews at the time of the conquests based on our existing sources, including those in Arabic. Still, often one will have to read against the grain of the record or even within it.

Long ago, Ernest Renan noted how problematic historical knowledge is for modern national solidarity, since it can reveal the violence that produced the present unity. His point was that nations are not natural entities that can be defined through objective factors such as shared ethnicity, language, or religion; rather, they come into being through "a series of convergent facts" and processes, and require a high degree of amnesia regarding what divided their members in the past. Renan wrote:

> The essence of a nation is that all individuals have many things in common, and also that they have forgotten many things. No French citizen knows whether he is a Burgundian, an Alan, a Taifale, or a Visigoth, yet every French citizen has to have already forgotten (*doit avoir oublié*) the massacre of Saint Bartholomew, or the massacres that took place in the Midi in the thirteenth century.[51]

As Benedict Anderson has noted, Renan's point might seem straightforward, but a few moments of reflection will suggest how strange it is that

Location of the Farnbāg Fire, the Most Ancient of the Zoroastrian Fires," *Journal of the American Oriental Society* 41 (1921): 81–106; and Mary Boyce, *Zoroastrians: Their Religious Beliefs and Practices*, 2nd ed. (London: Routledge, 2001), 123–4.

50 Among his sources was Ibn al-Faqīh's *Kitāb al-Buldān*. See Choksy, "Altars, Precincts, and Temples: Medieval and Modern Zoroastrian Praxis," *Iran* 44 (2006): 331, and *Conflict and Cooperation*, 97. Cf. Mary Boyce, "Ādur Farnbāg," in *EIr*.

51 Ernest Renan, "What Is a Nation?" (trans. Martin Thom), in *Nation and Narration*, ed. Homi K. Bhabha, 8–22 (London: Routledge, 1990), 11, edited according to Benedict Anderson's better reading of the French in Benedict Anderson, *Imagined Communities*, 199–200.

he expects modern French nationals to have memories of events roughly three hundred and six hundred years in the past. Nor is the idea of having to "have already forgotten" straightforward. Anderson points out that, "In effect, Renan's readers were being told to 'have already forgotten' what Renan's own words assumed they naturally remembered!" Instead, "we can be confident that, left to themselves, the overwhelming majority of Renan's French contemporaries would never have heard of 'la Saint-Barthélemy' or 'les massacres du Midi.'"[52] Rather, what Renan's remarks reveal (consciously or not) is a "systematic historiographical campaign, deployed by the state mainly through the state's school system, to 'remind' every young Frenchwoman and Frenchman of a series of antique slaughters which are now described as 'family history.'"[53] This is not a particularly French phenomenon, but rather a characteristic way of narrating the biography of a nation and its history.

This modern parallel may help us to further understand what our sources on the Iranian conquest are doing. What might be a modern phenomenon in its circumstances has precedents throughout history and, in the case of our period, in the ways in which audiences are repeatedly reminded of the losers that have passed into oblivion. Renan's point regarding the "essence" of a nation – "that all individuals have many things in common" but also that "they have forgotten many things" – holds equally with regard to the shared memory of Muslims, including Iranians. Seen from this perspective, we can, in particular, identify in narratives of the conquests reminders to "have already forgotten" the "polytheistic" losers, whose identities are shaped to fit the family history of Muslims. As traditionists stress the end of eras, the amnesia is selective and the traces significant. Readers were meant to know the existence but not the identity of the losers. Were the goal simply oblivion, omission would have been a better method, as illustrated by the way in which violence against Zoroastrians and the Ādur Farnbāg is (not) recalled. The next case, of a family written out of history, represents another case of a reminder to forget and also illustrates this dual strategy of memory/forgetting.

52 Anderson queries: "Who but 'Frenchmen,' as it were, would have at once understood that 'la Saint-Barthélemy' referred to the ferocious anti-Huguenot pogrom launched on 24 August 1572 by the Valois dynast Charles IX and his Florentine mother; or that 'les massacres du Midi' alluded to the extermination of the Albigensians across the broad zone between the Pyrenees and the Southern Alps, instigated by Innocent III, one of the guiltier in a long line of guilty popes?" (*Imagined Communities*, 200).

53 Ibid., 200–1.

Toppling Noble Families

Memory of the Christian population of Tustar fared poorly among the historians, who turned the vanquished into polytheists in fashioning their narratives. Specific references to Iranian families from pre-Islamic times do, however, survive in the sources, though often with some confusion in which we can detect manipulation of the record. A good illustration is the way in which al-Ṭabarī presents the story of the fall of a prominent family in Rayy at the time of the conquests, and his likely wish to stamp out their memory.

In her recent work on the decline and fall of the Sasanian Empire, Parvaneh Pourshariati has emphasized the alliance structure that supported it, its transformation during the conquests, and the ways in which its heirs continued under Muslim rule. She provides a deep analysis that takes good advantage of the Iranian side of our literary sources and the details about late Sasanian and early Islamic Iran that they provide. By also giving extensive attention to the onomastic, numismatic, and sigillographic record, she draws attention to the dynastic families of the Sasanians (Pārsīg) in roughly western and southern Iran and of the Parthians (Pahlav) in northern and eastern Iran, or what she terms the "Sasanian-Parthian confederacy."[54] She argues that the Sasanian state collapsed largely because this decentralized and complicated arrangement eventually failed. Most significantly, perhaps, she has presented a picture of late Sasanian Iran dramatically at odds with the highly centralized polity envisioned by Arthur Christensen in the 1930s and widely accepted by historians of late antique Iran.[55]

With respect to Rayy, Pourshariati discovers, in large measure through al-Ṭabarī, an intra-Parthian struggle between the "Parthian dynastic family of the Mihrāns" on the one hand and the family of a certain al-Zīnabī on the other. The struggle resulted in the toppling of the Mihrān family,

[54] Pourshariati defines Pārsīg as "from or belonging to the region of *Fārs*, whence Persian. By extension, the faction associating itself with the Sasanians," whereas the Pahlav are an "ethnic group, originally called Parni or Dahae. Their name is derived from the Achaemenid term for the region, Parthava, to which they migrated. By extension, Pahlav or Parthian is also used to refer to the Arsacid dynasty, and related dynastic families from this region." Pourshariati, *Decline and Fall of the Sasanian Empire*, 504.

[55] Pourshariati, *Decline and Fall of the Sasanian Empire*, esp. "Introduction." Cf. Christensen, *L'Iran sous les Sassanides*, but also the review essay of Touraj Daryaee: "The Fall of the Sasanian Empire to the Arab Muslims: From *Two Centuries of Silence* to *Decline and Fall of the Sasanian Empire: The Partho-Sasanian Confederacy and the Arab Conquest of Iran*." *Journal of Persianate Studies* 3, no. 2 (2010): 239–54.

FIGURE 6.3. Vahrām (Bahrām) VI (590–91). Collection of Robert Schaaf. Photo by Thomas K. Mallon-McCorgray.

whose ancestors included Bahrām Chūbīn, who had seized power from the Sasanian house in 590–1 CE (see Figure 6.3).[56] Pourshariati considers the conquest-era downfall of Bahrām Chūbīn's family "one of the most important transformations that took place in the political structure of this important region of the Sasanian domains in the wake of the Arab conquest."[57] The toppling of the Mihrāns, she notes, also resulted in the promotion of a "likely age-old rival," the family of al-Zīnabī.[58]

Al-Ṭabarī does show that Rayy fell as a result of internal conflicts. He reports that al-Zīnabī had originally opposed the Arabs, but then had a change of heart and surrendered, contrary to the wishes of the ruler, a grandson of Bahrām Chūbīn named Siyāwakhsh. Al-Zīnabī and the Arabs contrived a plan to surprise this grandson. First, al-Zīnabī secretly entered the town by a back way with some of the Muslim horsemen, after which Nuʿaym b. Muqarrin launched a surprise attack at night. The grandson and his supporters stood firm until they heard, from behind them in the town, cries of "God is most great!" from the Arab horsemen. Then the Mihrāns, Siyāwakhsh, and their allies were "put to flight," and the Arabs slaughtered their opponents. Al-Ṭabarī recounts that the spoils God gave to the Muslims at Rayy were about the same as those at al-Madāʾin – that is, God was very generous. Al-Zīnabī signed a treaty with Nuʿaym on behalf of the people of Rayy, and Nuʿaym made

[56] See esp. A. Sh. Shahbazi, "Bahrām vii. Bahrām VI Čōbīn," in *EIr*.
[57] Pourshariati, *Decline and Fall of the Sasanian Empire*, 251.
[58] Ibid., 252. Also drawing heavily on al-Ṭabarī, see Zarrīnkūb, "Arab Conquest of Iran and Its Aftermath," 19 (without expressly naming al-Ṭabarī), and Kennedy, *Great Arab Conquests*, 176 –7.

him governor with the Sasanian title of *marzubān* (Persian, *marzbān*).[59] The "family of al-Zīnabī" subsequently enjoyed the greatest honor. By comparison, the "family of Bahrām fell from grace." Nuʿaym even destroyed the area of the town occupied by the family (*akhraba Nuʿaym madīnatahum*), known as the old town, and al-Zīnabī gave orders for the building of the new town of Rayy. The name of Bahrām Chūbīn does not occur again in al-Ṭabarī's reporting.[60]

It is somewhat surprising, however, that other historians prior to and roughly contemporary with al-Ṭabarī present accounts of Rayy's conquest that mention neither the family of Bahrām Chūbīn nor the support given to the Arabs by al-Zīnabī. These sources do not seem interested in the rivalries that Pourshariati describes and may even be ignorant of them. Al-Balādhurī does make mention of an al-Farrukhān b. al-Zīnabadī, whom, he notes, the Arabs know as al-Zīnabī (he subsequently refers to him as Ibn al-Zīnabī). Al-Balādhurī states, however, that this Ibn al-Zīnabī *fought* the Arabs at Rayy.[61] In al-Ṭabarī's account, al-Zīnabī represents the people of the town in their treaty with the Arabs but is not much of an advocate for them because he has usurped the power of the Mihrāns and, in alliance with the conquerors, imposed a treaty on them. Al-Balādhurī's Ibn al-Zīnabī, however, takes up the cause of the local population and sets as a condition of the treaty with the Arabs that the local people be considered *dhimmī*s (i.e., under official protection so long as they acknowledge the domination of Islam) and be permitted to pay the *jizya* and the *kharāj*.[62] Afterward, al-Balādhurī provides a variety of reports on Rayy's conquest and early administration.[63]

59 *Marzaba-hu*. As noted in Chapter 3, the term *marzubān* (the Arabized form of Middle Persian *marzpān* or New Persian *marzbān*) refers to a Sasanian regional governor whose responsibilities were often military in character; here they seem to be administrative as well. See Kramers and Morony, "Marzpān," in *EI*[2], and Gignoux, "L'organisation administrative sasanide."

60 Al-Ṭabarī, *Taʾrīkh*, I:2650–1 (where al-Ṭabarī cites Sayf b. ʿUmar) and I:2653–5 ("They report [also]"); *The History of al-Ṭabarī*, vol. 14, *The Conquest of Iran*, trans. G. Rex Smith (Albany: State University of New York Press, 1994), 21–2 and 24–6; see also vol. 40, *Index*, by Alex V. Popovkin and Everett K. Rowson (Albany: State University of New York Press, 2007), 102, s.v. "Bahrām VI." Following al-Ṭabarī, see Ibn al-Athīr, *al-Kāmil fī al-taʾrīkh*, 2:405 and 407.

61 Al-Balādhurī, *al-Buldān wa-futūḥuhā*, 364.

62 Ibid. In later days, these terms denoted poll and land taxes, respectively, but the meaning of the terms at the time of the conquests is unclear; see Kennedy, *Great Arab Conquests*, 8 and 19–20.

63 Al-Balādhurī cites Abū Mikhnaf (d. 157/774) as an authority (versus Sayf b. ʿUmar for al-Ṭabarī). Qudāma b. Jaʿfar (d. 337/948) uses wording very close to that of al-Balādhurī; Qudāma b. Jaʿfar, *Kitāb al-Kharāj*, 374ff. Qudāma in general relies on al-Balādhurī for this part of his book; see Heck, *Construction of Knowledge in Islamic Civilization*, 156.

In his *History*, al-Ṭabarī often reports contradictions in the record, but here he gives no indication of a contradictory record. It seems that al-Ṭabarī wanted his readers to know about the success of al-Zīnabī and his family and sought to present the conquest of Rayy in the clearest way possible. His account seems more concerned with the losers – that is, the family of Bahrām Chūbīn – than with the winners. In contrast to his lucid treatment of the Mihrāns, al-Ṭabarī's account of al-Zīnabī and his family, and particularly their names, is confused, Pourshariati's careful efforts at reconstruction notwithstanding. As Pourshariati herself states: "We ought to have been given more information about the party to whom the power of the Mihrāns in Rayy was transferred."[64]

The problem with this picture painted by al-Ṭabarī is that the family of Bahrām Chūbīn did not go away, as Pourshariati in fact argues elsewhere.[65] The Arabic sources make mention of the family's descendants, most importantly, the Samanids in Iran and Transoxiana (204–395/819–1005).[66] For the Samanids' autonomous governorate – widely regarded for its patronage of Persian letters – descent from Bahrām Chūbīn was useful for claiming an antique genealogy. Bahrām Chūbīn had opposed the Sasanians, which perhaps added to the value of his pedigree in the Samanids' view, whereas for al-Ṭabarī the family may have appeared as a long-enduring challenge to ruling authority, Sasanian and

Cf. Ibn Aʿtham, *Kitāb al-Futūḥ*, 2:62ff., which supplies an altogether different account and onomastic record (the manuscripts of Ibn Aʿtham's text might turn up still more variety on the Persian side; see 2:66, n. 1).

64 Pourshariati, *Decline and Fall of the Sasanian Empire*, 252.

65 See esp. Pourshariati, *Decline and Fall of the Sasanian Empire*, 463–4, and Parvaneh Pourshariati, "The Mihrāns and the Articulation of Islamic Dogma: A Preliminary Prosopographical Analysis," in *Trésors d'Orient: Mélanges offerts à Rika Gyselen*, ed. Philippe Gignoux, Christelle Jullien, and Florence Jullien, 283–315 (Paris: Association pour l'avancement des études iraniennes, 2009). In a footnote to her Rayy discussion in *Decline and Fall of the Sasanian Empire*, 252, n. 1455, Pourshariati states: "As with all other significant upheavals in the histories of the dynastic families, however, it is reasonable to assume that these transformations could not have totally destroyed the actual land-ownership, wealth, and power of the Mihrān family. Pending further research on precisely how land ownership from those who controlled these lands during the Sasanian period transferred to those who came to control the land under Muslim rule, this assertion remains conjecture."

66 E.g., Abū al-Rayḥān al-Bīrūnī, *al-Āthār al-bāqiya ʿan al-qurūn al-khāliya* (Beirut: Dār al-Kutub al-ʿIlmiyya, 2000). For the Samanid claim regarding Bahrām Chubīn, see esp. Clifford Edmund Bosworth, "Heritage of Rulership in Early Islamic Iran," 58; Meisami, *Persian Historiography*, 33–4; Peacock, *Mediaeval Islamic Historiography*, 118–23.

now ʿAbbasid.[67] As also with al-Qādisiyya and in many other instances, Balʿamī's adaptation of al-Ṭabarī's text suggests a difference of sensibilities. For Balʿamī, who wrote directly under the Samanids (he was patronized by al-Manṣūr b. Nūḥ, r. 350–65/961–76), al-Ṭabarī's account of the conquest of Rayy must have posed a problem. How could he, under the patronage of this family and serving as its vizier, deny its post-conquest success – at a time, furthermore, when a rival dynasty, the Buyids, was asserting its control over Rayy against the claims of the Samanids?[68] Yarshater noted that in writing about Bahrām Chūbīn's lifetime, Balʿamī drew on other sources "to amplify Ṭabarī's account."[69] For Bahrām's descendants, Balʿamī relies here on al-Ṭabarī – he knows Siyāwakhsh as Rayy's governor (*malik*) at the time of the conquest, and his rival as a *dihqān* by the name of "Zīnī, the father of Farrukhān." But while noting the elevation of Zīnī and his sons and the destruction of the old quarter, Balʿamī skips al-Ṭabarī's statement that the family of Bahrām Chūbīn "fell from grace."[70] Al-Ṭabarī's strategy, stressing the displacement of the family of Bahrām Chūbīn, was no longer an option for Balʿamī, active under the Samanids, so he improved the story of Rayy's conquest by a deft subtraction, even if he could not get around the fact of Siyāwakhsh's defeat. He thus weakened a record of events that served the Samanids' rivals. More profoundly, this divergence suggests that al-Ṭabarī

[67] One of Bahrām's brothers is remembered as not having rebelled and as having stuck by Kisrā, and a sister (whom Bahrām had married) is said to have reproached Bahrām for a speech against Kisrā. Do these traditions present a deliberately nuanced view of the family's Sasanian loyalties, a view that may have been useful to its descendants? Al-Ṭabarī, *Taʾrīkh*, I:997–8.

[68] In 352/963 Manṣūr b. Nūḥ commissioned Balʿamī to translate al-Ṭabarī's *Taʾrīkh*. The Buyid ruler of Rayy, Rukn al-Dawla, had assumed the title of *shāhan-shāh*, which appeared on coins of 351/962. Meisami has described this context and argued that "Balʿamī's detailed treatment of the story of Bahrām Chūbīn seems designed to validate the Sāmānid claim to rule of the East (and in particular of Khurasan, of which Rayy was considered a part)." Meisami, *Persian Historiography*, 24, 33–5.

[69] Yarshater, "Iranian National History," 360; cf. the finely nuanced analysis of Peacock, in *Mediaeval Islamic Historiography*, esp. "Balʿamī's Reshaping of Ṭabarī's *History*" and "The Contents and Purpose of Balʿamī's Alterations to Ṭabarī's *History*" (Peacock does not consider Balʿamī's treatment of the conquest of Rayy). Peacock shows that while Balʿamī alters the "highly negative portrayal of Bahrām Chaūbīn in the *History*," he does not present a picture of Bahrām's career that is especially romanticized, nor does he make in this passage any reference to Bahrām's connection to the Samanid dynasty (whereas he does draw such a connection in the introduction to his work).

[70] Balʿamī, *Tārīkh-nāmah-yi Ṭabarī*, ed. Rawshan, 1:523–5; see also Balʿamī, *Chronique de Abou-Djafar*, 3: 489–91. Cf. al-Ṭabarī, *Taʾrīkh*, I:2653–5.

and Balʿamī belonged to two distinct phases of coming to terms with the pre- and early Islamic Iranian past.

A Subversive Memory?

In each of the preceding cases, memory was fashioned by an outsider with an interest in glorifying the conquests by showing what they represented for Islam, for Muslim government and its imperial reach, or for its elite subjects. Identities were likely written out for reasons of peace and communal harmony but also for political expediency, to erase evidence that might fuel a later generation's ambitions. Through such manipulation, reporters could alter collective memory. Traditions circulated in works whose audiences could not have judged their veracity – a reader in either Ibn Aʿtham's or al-Ṭabarī's day, in Cairo or Baghdad, likely had no reason to doubt these works' versions of the facts concerning the conquest of Tustar or Rayy two or three centuries earlier, nor to take umbrage at their underlying vision.

Closer to the ground, the past was likely less plastic, as it was harder to deny the identity of the losing side. Consider the case of Qum, one of the most important centers today for the Shiʿa and home to the shrine of Fāṭima al-Maʿṣūma (d. 201/816–17), the sister of the eighth Shiʿi Imam, ʿAlī al-Riḍā (d. 203/818). Qum does not figure prominently in the earliest Arabic writings about the conquests. The material record shows settlement in the region since ancient times, but it was possible, in the seventh/thirteenth century, for a well-read geographer such as Yāqūt (d. 626/1229) to describe Qum as a city that came into existence only with Islam (*madīna mustaḥdatha islāmiyya*), stating, as if for emphasis, that non-Arabs have no history in it (*lā athar li-l-aʿājim fīhi*).[71] By contrast, we have the Persian-language *Tārīkh-i Qum* and its deep reservoir of memories about the city's origins and history before and after the conquests. Academic studies on the history of Qum must make use of this book, which claims to be a Persian version of a twenty-chapter Arabic text completed by Ḥasan b. Muḥammad b. Ḥasan Qummī in the year 378/988–9 for his patron Ismāʿīl b. ʿAbbād (d. 385/995), who was a literary man in his own right and served as vizier to the Buyid sultans

[71] Regarding the material record, see esp. "Qum (Qom), ʿIrāq-i ʿAǧamī," in Schippmann, *Die iranischen Feuerheiligtümer*, 415–21, and Andreas Drechsler, "Qom i. History to the Safavid Period," in *EIr*. For Yāqūt's description, see Yāqūt, *Buldān*, 4:175–7, s.v. "Qum."

Mu'ayyid al-Dawla (r. 366–73/977–83 or 984) and Fakhr al-Dawla (r. 373–87/983–97).[72] Ḥasan was a local Imāmī Shi'i scholar, an Arab of Yemeni origin, and a descendant of the Ash'arī family that had ruled Qum in the past. He was well connected and had a brother who served as a tax collector.[73] No manuscript of his Arabic text survives; all we have is a Persian version in five chapters, prepared in 805–6/1402–4 by one al-Ḥasan b. 'Alī b. Ḥasan b. 'Abd al-Malik Qummī. Although scholars have treated al-Ḥasan b. 'Alī as the book's "translator," in its present form, the ninth/fifteenth-century book may well be the result of different hands, which should bear on how we read it.[74] The way the text, at the very beginning of the book, presents the role of al-Ḥasan b. 'Alī himself is particularly noteworthy: he is labeled a *mufassir* and *mu'awwil*, two terms suggesting the interpretive dimensions of his work.[75]

The fourth chapter of the *Tārīkh-i Qum* contains a description of the Arabs' takeover of Qum that is remarkable for the degree of violence it attributes to the Ash'arī Arabs and for its depiction of them as chauvinists.[76] In this account, the Arabs come to Qum during fractious times in Iraq under the governorship of al-Hajjāj b. Yūsuf (d. 95/714). They are led there by Aḥwaṣ b. Sa'd, who had been a supporter of the failed revolt of Zayd b. 'Alī b. al-Ḥusayn b. 'Alī b. Abī Ṭālib (d. 122/740) in Kufa and had been imprisoned by al-Hajjāj (this sequence involves some confusion regarding dates since Zayd's rebellion occurred

72 For an important example, see Andreas Drechsler, *Die Geschichte der Stadt Qom im Mittelalter (650–1350): Politische und wirtschaftliche Aspekte* (Berlin: Klaus Schwarz, 1999), e.g., 81ff.

73 *Tārīkh-i Qum*, ed. Jalāl al-Dīn Ṭihrānī (Tehran: Majlis, 1934; repr., Tehran: Intishārāt-i Tūs, 1982), 11–12, 39, 165; cited by Andreas Drechsler, "Tārik̲-e Qom," in *EIr*.

74 Of the many descriptions of the text (besides those of Drechsler), see esp. those of C. A. Storey, *Persian Literature: A Bio-Bibliographical Survey*, vol. 1 (London: Royal Asiatic Society, 1927–39 and 1953), pt. 1, 348–9 (no. 453), and pt. 2, 1291–2; Ann K. S. Lambton, "An Account of the *Tārīkhi Qumm*," *Bulletin of the School of Oriental and African Studies* 12, no. 3/4 (1948): 586–96 and "Qum: The Evolution of a Medieval City," *Journal of the Royal Asiatic Society*, n.s., 122, no. 2 (1990): 322–39 (esp. 325–6); Ḥusayn Mudarrisī Ṭabāṭabā'ī, *Kitāb-shināsī-yi āsār-i marbūṭ bih Qum* (Qum: Ḥikmat, 1353 *shamsī*/1974), 10ff. (the author questions whether there ever existed a complete Persian translation of the book); 'Alī Aṣghar Faqīhī, "Tārīkh-i Qum," in *Dānish-nāmah-yi jahān-i Islām* (online ed.; Tehran: Bunyād-i Dā'irat al-Ma'ārif-i Islāmī, n.d., http://www.encyclopaediaislamica.com); and regarding the episode I discuss here, Takamitsu Shimamoto, "Some Reflections on the Origin of Qom: Myth and History," *Orient* 27 (1991): 98–100, and Parvaneh Pourshariati, "Local Histories of Khurāsān," 61–4.

75 *Tārīkh-i Qum*, 2.

76 *Tārīkh-i Qum*, 244–65; it is the second of two sections in this chapter.

long after the death of al-Ḥajjāj).[77] They settle peacefully in the territory of Qum, exchanging gifts with the local population. As guests, the Arabs win the locals' special trust and additional land when one year, during Nawrūz celebrations, the area suffers raids from the residents of Daylam, to the northwest of Qum in the Alburz mountain range, and the Arabs, under the leadership of Aḥwaṣ, repel the invaders. The Arabs subsequently acquire even more property, administer justice in their lands, defend Qum from warring Daylamites, and build a mosque, the first in the territory.[78] Speaking to a local landowner named Khurrabandād, Aḥwaṣ and his brother ʿAbd Allāh pledge:

> You are as brothers in religion, foster brothers, and supporters of us. We accept advice and guidance and are bound with you in a confirmed treaty and a perpetual covenant. You have come to occupy the place of brothers, fathers, and sons among us. Neither of us needs to withhold advice, and whatever he owns in this world, he shares liberally with friends and brothers, so his fortune is evident, and he is not cheap with it. On our behalf, you are helping, acting as brothers, and advising sincerely, and you share in our possessions, provisions, and blessings. You have a right to a share in that. We do not accept the word of anyone who detracts from or makes accusations about what is your right, and we gird ourselves against enemies. Both of us charge our sons with [fulfilling] these treaties, agreements, stipulations, and covenants, and by God – may He be glorified and exalted – we are hopeful that these [agreements] will result in order and good behavior that fulfills our rights, and in the confirmation of these stipulations and treaties that we proclaim. From speech comes action.[79]

The text goes on to recount how a slave girl belonging to Khurrabandād told him of a dream in which she saw him in a large garden, the walls of which had collapsed. A group of people in the garden rebuilt the walls and placed a building in it. In the middle of the garden, there were two large cypress trees that fell down, and from the roots of these sprang many young, green shoots. Khurrabandād explains that the garden represents the Arabs' dwellings; the two trees, ʿAbd Allāh and Aḥwaṣ; and the shoots, their descendants. According to the text, Khurrabandād knows that the Arabs will soon constitute a great power (*dawla*). He shares the happy news with the Arabs themselves.[80] Apparently wishing to also secure their own future, Khurrabandād, a local ruler named

[77] Compare the start of the first part of Chapter 4 on p. 242. Lambton avoids identifying Zayd, instead referring to "the ʿAlid rebellion in Kufa"; see "An Account of the *Tārīkhi Qumm*," 596.

[78] *Tārīkh-i Qum*, 250–1.

[79] Ibid., 251.

[80] Ibid., 252.

Yazdanfādhār,[81] and the leaders and nobles of the district ask the Arabs for a written treaty (*kitābī va ʿahd-nāmah*). The Arabs agree, and a document is created, which all parties sign to their mutual benefit and which is then stamped with the seal of Saʿd b. Malik.[82]

So far, so good. Filled with optimism, the Arabs and the ʿAjam (that is, the Iranians) abide by the treaty at first, but with the passage of time, the leaders of the ʿAjam die, and their heirs, seeing the Arabs' prosperity, reconsider the benefits of the treaty. This is when things begin to go wrong. The Iranians say to themselves:

> If this line (*qawm*) of Arabs remains mighty and in power (*dawlah*), they will take over this district, seize the glory, and take the reins of control out of our hands. If we do not fix things with them and find an opportunity to despoil them, we will be ruined and die away.[83]

The ʿAjam decide to expel the Arabs, and send a message to them saying so. In the back-and-forth that follows, the Arabs offer to make amends for any oversights, remind the ʿAjam of the treaty, and stall for time. The ʿAjam, unbending and increasingly menacing, continue with their demands, insisting that the Arabs sell them their properties.[84] Aḥwaṣ then conceives a ploy: he sells the Arabs' properties to the ʿAjam as demanded but uses the money from the sale to purchase seventy slaves. He assigns each slave to a village (*dīh*) and its princely residence (*sarāy*), promising the slave that if he kills the present owner, he can take the owner's place. This the slaves do incognito.[85]

The story captures the reader's attention with several twists that lead toward the conclusion. It thus takes some persuading for Aḥwaṣ to convince his brother ʿAbd Allāh to move to Qum in the beginning, and subsequently, ʿAbd Allāh suspects Aḥwaṣ of making a bad decision to come to Qum. Aḥwaṣ proves his sharp acumen when he surprises ʿAbd Allāh with the heads of seventy village landlords, deposited in a vaulted entrance hall (*dihlīz*) leading into ʿAbd Allāh's residence, but when ʿAbd Allāh, while leaving for the dawn prayer, discovers the heads, he is shocked at the macabre sight. Aḥwaṣ justifies his actions by referring

[81] Or perhaps Yazdanfādhār is a title; see Daniel, "The Islamic East," 463. Cf. Lambton, "An Account of the *Tārīkhi Qumm*," 596.

[82] *Tārīkh-i Qum*, 252–3.

[83] Ibid., 253–4; cf. 248.

[84] Ibid., 254–5.

[85] Ibid., 255–6.

to the broken treaty and notes that God provided him with an opportunity. ʿAbd Allāh expresses fear of a reprisal. "They will annihilate and overpower us! What will we do, and what will we say?"[86] Aḥwaṣ then introduces another ploy: he tells ʿAbd Allāh to go immediately to the mosque and to pray publicly for the Arabs, and then orders all the heads to be thrown into a pit. As he hoped, when morning comes and the ʿAjam discover the pit, they are astounded by God's intervention on the Arabs' behalf. The *Tārīkh-i Qum* reports: "Some of them became Muslims at the hands of the Arabs and some of them took shelter with the Arabs. Others dispersed and scattered to the cities. The district was freed of the enemies of ʿAbd Allāh and Aḥwaṣ, and it became Muslim on account of them."[87] The story ends here with the conversion of Qum.[88]

Given the story's placement in a history whose primary audience was the residents of Qum, it may seem puzzling that conversion is so intimately connected to the treachery of the original Iranian population. One might expect a local history composed by Muslims long after the events in question to downplay resistance by the indigenous population, as likely occurred with historians in Jurjān and Sīstān. What we seem to have, instead, is the opposite. The story shows the local people's treachery: the children of Khurrabandād and Yazdanfādhār violate an agreement, one that their fathers had requested. But if one considers the way the *Tārīkh* represents the actions of the Arabs and the ʿAjam, the Ashʿarī Arabs, especially Aḥwaṣ, come off even worse. Following the poor decisions of the ʿAjam, the Arabs gain full control, and since "the district was freed of the enemies of ʿAbd Allāh and Aḥwaṣ," there could be no further local resistance. The story describes in ruthless terms the brothers' strategy of suppression and Aḥwas's ploy, for example, when he instructs the slaves to kill the village leaders:

> Go and mix with them when they are occupied with drinking and extravagance so they will not be able to distinguish you from their own people. When you are with them, you will recognize the chief (*raʾīs*) of each people and find an opportunity to kill him. Take his head and bring it to me. And if you are in doubt and do not know which of them is the leader, elder, or chief, kill anyone who gives off a good scent.[89]

[86] Ibid., 256–7.
[87] Ibid., 257.
[88] Cf. ibid., 262–3.
[89] Ibid., 255–6.

When the text asserts that the slaves carried out their mission without a single error, it emphasizes the method's violence: "None of them, in observing and killing his lord, had made an error, and not one of the villages' chiefs escaped death by them."[90]

Insofar as conversion of the population results from this ploy, it is represented as an unintended consequence. The Arabs seem disinterested in spreading their religion, although they do build a mosque, destroying a fire temple in the process.[91] When Aḥwaṣ sends the slaves off to kill the village leaders, a local Iranian man, seized by the Arabs, becomes a *mamlūk* to Aḥwaṣ, claims to be an Arab, and asks Aḥwaṣ for an Arab name. The request angers Aḥwaṣ, who threatens to kill him. The *mamlūk* flees, but he then earns the respect of Aḥwaṣ by returning with the heads of four village leaders. With the other successful slaves, he presents the heads to Aḥwaṣ. In a symbolic gesture, Aḥwaṣ kisses the man's head and says: "You are one of my sons, heirs, and successors. Which name is most beloved by you, so that I may bestow it on you?" The *mamlūk* replies: "Give me the name Shaybān." The *Tārīkh-i Qum* states: "He made him a member of his own family and lineage (*va az jumlah va aṣlān-i khūd gardānīd*)."[92] But while he is "adopted," he does not take a particularly Muslim name, unlike many converts to Islam.

What purposes did such memory serve? For the descendants of the Ashʿarī Arabs, the story and its annihilation of opposition might stake a claim for singular authority in a past that, while not heroic, was cleverly managed and portrayed as the result of events initiated by the conquered population. That is, the text might represent the winning side's view. But there is another possibility. Like many Persian histories, the *Tārīkh-i Qum* has a complicated provenance and came into existence in Persian centuries after its composition in Arabic in the late fourth/tenth century. Much of the text appears genuinely archaic, including Arabic poetry scattered across its chapters (though absent from this section). A good portion of the text also provides accounts of the Ashʿarīs that, from their perspective (and from that of the reputed Ashʿarī author), could have been seen as more edifying in the fourth/tenth century and could comfortably enough have taken shape then. But there are also features of the text that are less easily explained, including traces of multiple authors' involvement,

[90] Ibid., 256.

[91] Ibid., 251. The text states that they built the mosque on the ancient site of a fire temple. No objections are mentioned. Cf. 262 (representing another report).

[92] Ibid., 256.

such as repetition between its chapters. For example, the first chapter also treats Aḥwaṣ in the context of his construction of the first mosque in Qum, apparently for the purpose of outlining how Qum was made into a district independent of Iṣfahān.[93] There is also the confusion over dates within the account narrated here (Zayd's rebellion occurring after the death of al-Ḥajjāj), and also between the first and second sections of the fourth chapter, suggesting a varied record and an imperfect attempt to establish a chronology linking Qum to Kufa. Such ambiguity may reside in an original Arabic text, owing to the author's use of multiple sources, but it seems more likely that what we have in hand is a more composite text.[94] One possibility is that the "translator," al-Ḥasan b. ʿAlī, took a more active role than so far generally assumed and pulled together different pieces of text, including the fourth/tenth-century text he names but also others, some of later provenance. In the case of the story of Qum's conversion retold here, he refers to his sources ambiguously, for example as "narrators from the Arabs in Qum."[95] Al-Ḥasan b. ʿAlī may have composed the text himself, or he may have found it; it may also represent a write-up of an oral tradition.

Whatever the story's origins, the account appears to reflect the memory of a group that was not altogether happy with the outcome of history; perhaps it comprised members of another, rival Arab lineage, or Arabs with different ʿAlid loyalties, or non-Arabs in Ḥasan b. ʿAlī's time who, while acknowledging the town's Ashʿarī history, wished to plant doubts about the integrity of its early Ashʿarī residents.[96] In their account, Aḥwaṣ presents his actions as justified by the non-Arabs' disloyalty and as enabled by God's support, but he hardly comes off as a victim, nor does the text seem to condone his actions; rather, ʿAbd Allāh's horror, and that of the residents of Qum, suggest he has crossed a moral line. Under such problematic circumstances, the sudden and complete conversion of the original population (a literary representation of history if ever there was one) devalues what may well have been a more substantial contribution made by the Ashʿarīs to Qum's religious heritage.

[93] Ibid., 36–7.

[94] The *Tārīkh*'s author states that he originally intended to write two books, one on the city itself and one on the Ashʿarīs of Qum; ibid., 12–13. On the sources listed in the book, see esp. Lambton, "An Account of the *Tārīkhi Qumm*," 587, and Mudarrisī Ṭabāṭabāʾi, *Kitāb-shināsī-yi ās̱ār-i marbūṭ bih Qum*, 17–31.

[95] *Tārīkh-i Qum*, 245, and similarly throughout the story; compare with the first section of the chapter in ibid., 242 (note also the dating by the ascension and death of Yazdagird).

[96] See, for example, ibid., 37.

Conclusion

While our authors embellished the Arab side of the record, they often passed over the Iranian side with far less care. They were not interested in the residents of al-Qādisiyya, but rather in those who had won the battle. Polemical aims partially explain their approach, since a victory over a "polytheist" enemy made the conquests into a war in the name of religion. For many believers, the conquests represented edifying tales of the heroic deeds of the first Muslims, their courage in the face of larger numbers, and their triumph over a great empire. They accomplished God's work against polytheism. That the Sasanians, the enemy, were hardly "polytheists" mattered little – these accounts were not carefully parsed theological treatises but epic drama, with a tendency to exaggerate the good and the bad, the winners and the losers. Such works had room for many themes and little concern for modern standards of data or evidence. Often they dramatized issues that are hardly obvious to modern readers, such as the origins of *fitna* and division within the Muslim community in the case of al-Hurmuzān and Tustar. But there was more than such religious polemic at work. If we look closely at the stories these works tell, we can discern an underlying wish to assert the end of different pasts: that of the Sasanians, who make an ignominious departure from the world stage, but also that of Zoroastrians and Christians. The past, we are told, is over – even if such writing itself suggests that the legacy of the past continued to trouble authors three or four centuries afterward.

While Iranians such as al-Ṭabarī could see bloodbaths as part of a militant devotionalism, other traditionists viewed the conquests in more ambiguous terms. Al-Ṭabarī's Persian interpreter, Balʿamī, subverts al-Ṭabarī's vision and shows how subsequent generations could wrestle with their famous predecessors' texts so as to make memory of the past support one's vision of the present. Local historians could also, with some authority, claim to preserve what was forgotten and, in doing so, seek to reshape the memory of their audiences. By the ninth/fifteenth century, it was possible not only to give abundant detail about Qum but to present in grotesque terms the sort of violence that Ibn Aʿtham and al-Ṭabarī had glorified, in the process subverting a dominant theme of Arabic traditions – the divine hand behind the conquests. In the end, then, much was forgotten about Sasanian era soldiers, elites, and their families, but because history writing is accretive, there was often a chance to add new details and remold memory of the conquests. There could be no final word or perspective, but only an intermediate view.

Conclusion

Jan Assmann has shown that memory is an ongoing work of "reconstructive imagination" in which the past is processed and remade.[1] A society's stories help to generate its sense of itself and furnish it with truths by which to live. Each generation becomes conscious of itself by the ways in which it adapts these truths. Without such creative intervention, stories lose their relevance and become material for archives, not for memory. Memory can be bolstered by archives, but much of archival material is neither remembered nor memorable. For historians of memory, one important challenge is to identify socially and culturally significant memory from the vast corpus of writing about the past and, connecting it to its likely contexts, to consider the frameworks that generated it.

This study has proposed that Iran and its conversion to Islam represent such a framework. In writing about the past, generations of Iranians engaged with many questions that arose following the conquests, with the adoption of Islam, and at various stages of history running to approximately 1100 CE. They proposed answers to these questions, and so, too, did non-Iranians. How much cultural autonomy would Iranians retain in their new Muslim "family"? They could be distinct among Muslims but not separate, as traditionists assert when they insert a prophet such as Noah into a locality's history or pepper the preface to the *Shāh-nāmah* with references to Muḥammad and ʿAlī. What about changes to the social fabric of Iran, including the relative positions of Arabs and non-Arabs?

[1] Assmann, *Moses the Egyptian*, 14.

Such concerns are expressed in a myriad of ways, for example, in genealogies and reports of ancestry, slave or free; in the elevation of Salmān as a Prophetic companion; in pseudepigraphic texts of a legal nature, preserved and cited as evidence for special privileges; and in overstatements and understatements of the size and power of religious communities. To what extent were "Islamic" values compatible with pre-Islamic ideals? While works in the genre of "mirrors for princes" might pass on the ideals of Ardashīr, Khusraw Anūshirvān, and the latter's famed vizier, Buzurgmihr, their authors made sure to position this advice carefully, as for example in the *Naṣīḥat al-mulūk* attributed to al-Ghazālī. Even the broader questions historians today ask were part of this framework, especially questions regarding the continuity or rupture that the conquests represented.

Such a framework became a long-lasting creation, and its impact is still felt today when modern readers seeking to read "original" and early sources turn to works such as al-Ṭabarī's *History* or the local histories of Fārs, Iṣfahān, Jurjān, Sīstān, or Qum. Focusing upon this framework allows us to see our sources as engaged with a variety of issues and as shaping the possibilities for future remembrance. Within the general sweep of historiography, the situation of Iranians represented just one inflection, but it was an important one: many of the key founding moments of Islam and Muslim rule concerned Iran, and a significant role in shaping tradition common to all Muslims was played by historians, litterateurs, and scholars of Qurʾan and Hadith whose knowledge and experience were acquired in Iranian contexts. The pre-Islamic past, the Prophet's life, and the conquests considered in this study might be the most outstanding instances where inflections of memory occurred, but there are others that deserve attention from a history of memory perspective but that I have touched on only lightly, if at all. These include the founding moments of Iranian Muslim dynasties, the shaping of bureaucratic institutions, the molding of classes of scholars and jurists, and the formation of sectarian loyalties. A focus on memory might allow us to shed light on the layers of writing and rewriting about a dynasty such as the Buyids or about connections between a *madhhab* and a locale, such as Iṣfahān or Qum. As Iranians adopted Islam in the period from the third/ninth to the fifth/eleventh century, we should expect the changing nature of loyalties to locale, profession, lineage, and ethnie to yield assertions in our sources about precisely such issues as cultural autonomy, social hierarchy and privilege, the nature and binding qualities of "Islamic" values, and the extent to which the present represented a revolutionary break with the past or, rather, but a moment in the plodding sequence of history. This is not to suggest that we should always read our sources simply as expressions of such ideas and loyalties, but particularly when symbolic moments are summoned forth and displayed, we ought to be awake to their messages, and to the various layers of writing and rewriting, and interpretation and reinterpretation.

In terms of hermeneutics, I have considered many case studies or, to use Nora's expression, sites of memory. Given the highly complex situation of Iran in the third/ninth–fifth/eleventh centuries, this is the only even remotely secure way to approach the diversity of our traditionists' contexts. One can identify patterns and trends – for example, when traditionists rewrite Persia's past as a purely local past or replace it with a Muslim past – but one could not provide a satisfactory master narrative outlining a single shift in historical consciousness. Our sources themselves, particularly those composed in Iraq under the ʿAbbasids, do often speak in such metanarrative terms. But as I have argued, much as we may wish to believe that we are discovering the significance and meaningfulness of the past solely through our own diligent study, the sources often reach across time to guide us, including through their choices of where to start and stop their stories, how to contextualize the past, and what to reveal and conceal. Details in narratives are often important signifiers of broad, interpretive schemes and perspectives, much as this may disappoint historians today who search for authentic and verifiable residues of the past, or kernels of truth. The last years of the Sasanians were surely chaotic, with Khusraw Parvīz's deposition followed by the bloody reign of his son, Shīrawayh. But when traditionists turned this past into narrative, they created a kerygmatic and teleological record, and a memory by which future generations, as well as historians, have understood the last Sasanians. Other times, the vision was more parochial, as with Qum, but no less guiding.

A comparative approach that looks at cases across time, geography, and genre – such as the story of al-Rabīʿ and the pile of bodies he created at the conquest of Sīstān, or that of al-Qādisiyya and the fate of Rustam – shows us how profoundly, and under what widely varying circumstances, traditionists reconceived the past to take Iranian perspectives into account. When did they begin to do so? I have proposed roughly the second half of the third/ninth century as a starting point, toward the end of what Claude Gilliot termed the "imperial period." The changing political circumstances, including the increase in local, Iranian patronage of traditionists, surely played a role, but their importance should not be overestimated; broader cultural forces were at work, as Islam became deeply woven into the fabric of Iranian societies, as reflected in local histories and their own narratives about the growth and development of Muslim communities in new "centers" (to use Bulliet's term). Texts before the middle of the third/ninth century seem to have little concern for the sensibilities of Iranians – Prophetic biography being the best example (although we have also seen the same for *tafsīr* and early Hadith collections). Persians do appear to some extent in the mapping of peoples proposed by Ibn al-Kalbī, but his central point of focus was Arab tribes. Ibn Hishām and Ibn Saʿd, both drawing upon the influential work of Ibn Isḥāq, present Salmān as abandoning Persia, evoking ideas of hijra, and either joining an Arab companion of the Prophet as a "brother" or becoming, in a figurative manner at least, a member of the Prophet's family. Neither traditionist pays much attention to Salmān's Persian roots. Ibn Saʿd's interest in al-Ḥasan al-Baṣrī, similarly, lies in myriad aspects of al-Ḥasan's person and career – but only minimally in his family's possible Iranian origins. By contrast, one finds only slightly later narratives making much more of Salmān's Persianness, the Persian origins of the institution of the *dīwān*, and the Iranian mother of the fourth Imam. The reconfiguration of memory continued past the period under principal investigation here, as can be seen in the production of local histories in the sixth/twelfth, seventh/thirteenth, and eighth/fourteenth centuries, in the multitude of translations and recasting of works – into Persian as well as from Persian versions back into Arabic, as occurred with the *History* of al-Ṭabarī – and in the production of commentaries on earlier works, such as Ibn Qutayba's manual for court secretaries or the *Nahj al-balāgha*. These were developments of a trend initiated in the third–fifth/ninth–eleventh centuries, when Iranians were written into an Islamic past. Given discrepant views, it is probably in the second half of the third/ninth and the fourth/tenth centuries that we should locate the first significant struggles over memory. What followed was a general revamping of memory that allowed the inclusion of pre-Islamic Iranian characters, themes, and lore, not as a renaissance but rather as a recognized part of the communities to which they had always belonged.

Given trends in current scholarship, it also bears stressing that in the narratives of the third/ninth to fifth/eleventh centuries that I have examined one finds only weak reference to *Īrān* as an ongoing concern and instead, when geography is at issue, more robust references to localities. Nor is there much of a corresponding idea of "Iranians," but rather ideas about local peoples and identities, or Persians as the most frequently mentioned ethnic affiliation for Iranians. This is the case for the Arabic sources (the language of the major body of material we have for the period), but it is also the case for sources in New Persian from the end of my period, although the *Shāh-nāmah*, set in pre-Islamic times, is something of an exception in its employment of "Iran." Furthermore, throughout the period from the third/ninth to the fifth/eleventh centuries, the most symbolically weighted events of early Islamic history could only be remembered with reference to a body of tradition that had its roots in ʿAbbasid Iraq – whether a traditionist worked in Iṣfahān in the fourth/tenth century or in Sīstān in the fifth/eleventh – although traditionists from locales such as Hamadhān and Shīz likely also shaped recollections in Iraq. The weakness of an Iranian identity, as such, and the importance of Iraq as a cauldron for memory do make writing about Iranian identity and memory in the post-conquest period a complicated affair, but the only alternative is to turn a blind eye to this state of fragmentation.

More than forty years ago, Albrecht Noth identified "Iran" as a salient theme of early historical tradition. By "Iran" he meant "traditions on the Iranian Sasanian Empire and the precedents which it set for Islam," especially as connected to the conquests (*futūḥ*). Iran was the only one of Noth's themes that had a regional focus, and it was the last and most perfunctorily treated in a list that otherwise featured more readily obvious and staple topics of historical writing, namely, *ridda*, *fūtūḥ*, *fitna*, administration, *sīrat al-khulafāʾ*, and *ansāb*.[2] The changing perspectives and sensitivities of the sources I have examined suggest that Noth put his finger, if imprecisely, on an early phase of historical writing, when Iran represented a distinct object of interest, especially in relation to an "other" group of people, Arabs. Neither Arabia nor the Arabs represent a theme for him, presumably because they were so present in the material for his other themes. By the late third/ninth and fourth/tenth centuries, however, and particularly in local histories, Iran and Persians become far more present within the other themes. The result of this integration is that, like Arabs, their distinctively Iranian or Persian character can become invisible.

If in writing about the past groups ask themselves what they must remember, they also ask themselves what they must forget. The processes by which Gayūmart became for Iranian Muslims a first king, rather than a human progenitor, or by which the late Sasanians, Kisrā and Būrān

[2] Noth, *Early Arabic Historical Tradition*, 26–39, esp. 39.

included, came to stand in opposition to prophetic rule, were broadly political and oppositional in character, involving negotiations that we occasionally, though too seldom, can discern. It is rare, in fact, that we can identify objects of erasure, as I have sought to do, for example, in the case of the Christians at the conquest of Tustar and the family of Bahrām Chūbīn in al-Ṭabarī's account of the defeat of Rayy.

Far from a passive process, forgetting can be an extremely creative enterprise, in which members of a society in transition confront sources of anxiety, such as a former empire, the religion it patronized, and its elites. Among themselves, they work out what can no longer serve as a basis for social solidarity, as they substitute one founder for another, redraw the sacred boundaries of their homeland, or adopt a new chronology in which past events of significance can no longer be meaningfully narrated and so remembered. Much of what I have described follows the model of a palimpsest, with traditionists writing over the record of past generations, although I have also tried, where possible, to show that there were limitations to creativity and that often what we have is reframings of the past, as with Salmān or the *Shāh-nāmah*, not wholesale revision. When the Takht-i Sulaymān and Persepolis acquired associations to a prophetic history, they became part of a new sacred map. This map, superimposed upon a fading Achaemenid and Sasanian past, oriented Iranians spatially and chronologically to a wider Near Eastern – Syrian, Iraqi, Arabian, and Iranian – landscape and to a progression of prophets that culminated in Muḥammad. The topography of Baghdad excited the interest of generations of its inhabitants, but its shadow as the caliphal capital occluded memory of Ctesiphon and the Ṭāq-i Kisrā a short distance away as ʿAbbasid era chroniclers and poets made the Sasanian metropolis into an expressive relic. As traditionists transformed the past into authoritative narratives, filters such as labels, homologies, icons, and gender narrowed its possibilities or, more precisely, negatively conditioned the expectations of Muslims for knowledge about Khusraw Parvīz and the late Sasanians in particular. In the end, therefore, modern historians forming their own narratives must often read against the grain of their sources, or within it, to try to discern how earlier generations have assembled the past. In doing so, historians may shape the memory of their readers through the ways in which they themselves write and rewrite, and filter and sift, the historical material, but only insofar as they can persuade their contemporaries that they have created a meaningful narrative.

Bibliography

Electronic Resources

Electronic database sources have greatly enriched this study because they are searchable and can aid in tracking the repetition of traditions and in judging how widely disseminated a report was – a key issue for memory. They also can support the study of variations in matters of detail, structure, and emplotment, and turn up traditions in unexpected sources and genres. For a number of reasons, however, electronic sources can provide only a starting point and cannot replace the printed editions upon which they are based. In my notes, I cite only the printed editions that I have consulted. Many of these databases are available on the internet. I have found particularly helpful the following:

Al-Jāmiʿ al-kabīr li-kutub al-turāth al-ʿarabī wa-l-islāmī. Produced by al-Turāth.

Maktabat ahl al-bayt. Produced by Muʾassasah-yi Āyat Allāh al-ʿUẓmā al-Mīlānī.

Al-Maktaba al-shāmila. Produced by Muʾassasat al-Maktaba al-Shāmila. Available at http://shamela.ws.

Primary Sources

ʿAbd al-Jabbār b. Aḥmad (d. 415/1025). *Critique of Christian Origins: A Parallel English-Arabic Text*. Edited and translated by Gabriel Said Reynolds and Samir Khalil Samir. Provo, UT: Brigham Young University Press, 2010.

———. *Tathbīt dalāʾil al-nubuwwa*. Edited by ʿAbd al-Karīm ʿUthmān. 2 vols. Beirut: Dār al-ʿArabiyya, 1966.

Abū Nuʿaym al-Iṣfahānī (d. 430/1038). *Dhikr akhbār Iṣbahān*. Edited by Sven Dedering. 2 vols. Leiden: E. J. Brill, 1931–4.

———. *Maʿrifat al-ṣaḥāba*. Edited by ʿĀdil b. Yūsuf al-ʿAzzāzī. 7 vols. Riyadh: Dār al-Waṭan li-l-Nashr, 1998.

Abū al-Shaykh al-Iṣfahānī (d. 369/979). *Ṭabaqāt al-muḥaddithīn bi-Iṣfahān wa-l-wāridīn ʿalayhā*. Edited by ʿAbd al-Ghafūr ʿAbd al-Ḥaqq Ḥusayn al-Balūshī. 4 vols. Beirut: Muʾassasat al-Risāla, 1987–92.

———. *Ṭabaqāt al-muḥaddithīn bi-Iṣfahān wa-l-wāridīn ʿalayhā*. Edited by ʿAbd al-Ghaffār Sulaymān al-Bindārī and Sayyid Kasrawī Ḥasan. 4 vols. in 2. Beirut: Dār al-Kutub al-ʿIlmiyya, 1989.

Abū Tammām (d. 231–2/845–6). *Dīwān al-Ḥamāsa*. Edited by Muḥammad ʿAbd al-Munʿim Khafājī. 2 vols. Cairo: Maktabat Muḥammad ʿAlī Ṣubayḥ, 1955.

Abū ʿUbayd al-Qāsim b. Sallām (d. 224/838). *Al-Amwāl*. 2nd ed. Edited by Muḥammad Khalīl Harrās. Cairo: Dār al-Fikr, 1975.

———. *The Book of Revenue (Kitāb al-Amwāl)*. Translated by Imran Ahsan Khan Nyazee. Reading: Garnet, 2002.

Abū Yusūf (d. 182/798). *Abū Yūsuf's Kitāb al-Kharāj*. Vol. 3 of *Taxation in Islam*. Translated by A. Ben Shemesh. Leiden: E. J. Brill, 1969.

———. *Kitāb al-Kharāj*. Bulaq: al-Maṭbaʿa al-Mīriyya, 1302/[1884–5].

ʿAlī b. al-Jahm (d. 249/863). *Dīwān ʿAlī b. al-Jahm*. Edited by Khalīl Mardam Bey. 2nd ed. Beirut: Lajnat al-Turāth al-ʿArab, n.d.

Al-ʿAqīqī, Yaḥyā b. al-Ḥasan al-Madanī (d. 277/891). *Kitāb al-Muʿaqqibīn min wuld al-Imām Amīr al-Muʾminīn*. Edited by Muḥammad al-Kāẓim. Qum: Maktabat Āyat Allāh al-ʿUẓmā al-Marʿashī al-Najafī, 2001.

Asadī Ṭūsī, ʿAlī b. Aḥmad (d. ca. 465/1073). *Garshāsp-nāmah*. Edited by Ḥabīb Yaghmāʾī. Tehran: Kitāb-khānah-i Ṭahūrī, 1975.

Al-Aṣmaʿī (d. 213/828) [attr.]. *Nihāyat al-arab fī akhbār al-Furs wa-l-ʿArab*. Edited by Muḥammad Taqī Dānish-Pazhūh. Tehran: Anjuman-i Āsār va Mafākhir-i Farhangī, 1996.

Al-Balādhurī (d. ca. 279/892). *Al-Buldān wa-futūḥuhā wa-aḥkāmuhā*. Edited by Suhayl Zakkār. Beirut: Dār al-Fikr, 1992.

———. *The Origins of the Islamic State*. Vol. 2. Translated by Francis Clark Murgotten. New York: Columbia University, 1924.

Balʿamī (d. ca. 363/974). *Chronique de Abou-Djafar-Mo'hammed-ben-Djarir-ben-Yezid Tabari*. Translated by M. Hermann Zotenberg. 4 vols. Paris: Imprimerie Impériale, 1867–74. Reprint, Paris: Éditions d'art Les Heures Claires, [1977?].

———. *Tārīkh-i Balʿamī: Takmilah va tarjumah-yi Tārīkh-i Ṭabarī*. Edited by Muḥammad Taqī Bahār and Muḥammad Parvīn Gunābādī. 2 vols. Tehran: Zavvāl, 1974.

———. *Tārīkh-nāmah-yi Ṭabarī*. Edited by Muḥammad Rawshan. 3 vols. Tehran: Nashr-i Naw, 1366 *shamsī*/[1987–8].

Al-Bayhaqī, Aḥmad b. al-Ḥusayn (d. 458/1066). *Shuʿab al-īmān*. Edited by Abū Hājar Muḥammad al-Saʿīd b. Basyūnī Zaghlūl. 9 vols. Beirut: Dār al-Kutub al-ʿIlmiyya, 2000.

Al-Bīrūnī, Abū al-Rayḥān (d. 440/1048). *Al-Āthār al-bāqiya ʿan al-qurūn al-khāliya*. Beirut: Dār al-Kutub al-ʿIlmiyya, 2000.

———. *Chronologie orientalischer Völker*. Edited by C. Eduard Sachau. Leipzig: F. A. Brockhaus, 1878.

———. *The Chronology of Ancient Nations*. Translated by C. Eduard Sachau. London: W. H. Allen, 1879. Reprint, Whitefish, MT: Kessinger Legacy Reprints, n.d.

Al-Buḥturī (d. 284/897). *Dīwān al-Buḥturī*. Edited by Ḥasan Kāmil al-Ṣayrafī. 5 vols. Cairo: Dār al-Maʿārif, 1963–8.

Al-Bukhārī (d. 256/870). *Al-Jāmiʿ al-ṣaḥīḥ*. Edited by M. Ludolf Krehl. 4 vols. Vol. 4 partly edited by Th. W. Juynboll. Leiden: E. J. Brill, 1862–1908.

Al-Burrī, Ibrāhīm b. Abī Bakr (d. 690/1291). *Al-Jawhara fī nasab al-nabī wa-aṣḥābuhu al-ʿashara*. Edited by Muḥammad al-Tūnjī. 2 vols. Al-ʿAyn: Markaz Zāyid li-l-Turāth wa-l-Taʾrīkh, 2001.

La Caverne des trésors: Les deux recensions syriaques. Edited and translated by Su-Min Ri. 2 vols. Corpus Scriptorum Christianorum Orientalium. Leuven: E. Peeters, 1987.

Al-Dīnawarī, Abū Ḥanīfa (d. ca. 281 or 282/894–5). *Al-Akhbār al-ṭiwāl*. Edited by ʿIṣām Muḥammad al-Ḥājj ʿAlī. Beirut: Dār al-Kutub al-ʿIlmiyya, 2001.

Firdawsī, Abū al-Qāsim (d. 411/1020). *Shāh-nāmah*. Edited by Djalal Khaleghi-Motlagh. 8 vols. plus 2 note vols. New York: Bibliotheca Persica Press, 1988–2008.

———. *The Sháhnáma of Firdausí*. Translated by Arthur George Warner and Edmond Warner. 9 vols. London: Kegan Paul, Trench, Trübner & Co., 1905–25.

Al-Gharnāṭī, Abū Ḥayyān (d. 745/1344). *Al-Baḥr al-muḥīt fī tafsīr*. Vol. 7. Beirut: Dār al-Fikr, 1983.

Al-Ghazālī, Abū Ḥāmid (d. 505/1111). "*Al-Ghazali: Nasihat al-muluk*." Edited by H. D. Isaacs. M.A. thesis, University of Manchester, 1956.

———. *Ghazālī's Book of Counsel for Kings (Naṣīḥat al-mulūk)*. Translated by F. R. C. Bagley. London: Oxford University Press, 1964.

———. *Naṣīḥat al-mulūk*. Edited by Jalāl al-Dīn Humāʾī. Tehran: Majlis, 1315–17 *shamsī*/[1936–9].

———. *Naṣīḥat al-mulūk*. 2nd ed. Edited by Jalāl al-Dīn Humāʾī. Tehran: Anjuman-i Āṯār-i Millī, 1351 *shamsī*/[1972].

———. *Al-Tibr al-masbūk fī naṣīḥat al-mulūk*. Edited by Muḥammad Aḥmad Damaj. Beirut: al-Muʾassasa al-Jāmiʿiyya li-l-Dirāsāt wa-l-Nashr wa-l-Tawzīʿ, 1987.

Ḥamza al-Iṣfahānī (d. after 350/961). *Kitāb Taʾrīkh sinī mulūk al-arḍ wa-l-anbiyāʾ*. Berlin: Kaviani, 1340/1921 or 1922.

Hishām b. Muḥammad al-Kalbī (d. 204/819 or 206/821). *Ǧamharat an-nasab: Das genealogische Werk des Hišām ibn Muḥammad al-Kalbī*. Edited by Werner Caskel. 2 vols. Leiden: E. J. Brill, 1966.

The Histories of Nishapur [Kitāb Aḥvāl-i Nīshāpūr]. Edited by Richard N. Frye. Cambridge, MA: Harvard University Press, 1965.

The Holy Bible. Revised Standard Version. 1974.

Ibn ʿAbd Rabbih (d. 328/940). *Kitāb al-ʿIqd al-farīd*. Edited by Aḥmad Amīn, Aḥmad al-Zayn, and Ibrāhīm al-Abyārī. 7 vols. Cairo: Lajnat al-Taʾlīf wa-l-Tarjama wa-l-Nashr, 1940–53.

Ibn Abī al-Ḥadīd (d. 656/1258). *Sharḥ Nahj al-balāgha*. Edited by Muḥammad Abū al-Faḍl Ibrāhīm. 20 vols. Cairo: ʿĪsā al-Bābī al-Ḥalabī, 1959–63.

Ibn Abī Ḥātim (d. 327/938–9). *Tafsīr al-Qurʾān al-ʿaẓīm: Musnadan ʿan al-Rasūl Allāh wa-l-ṣaḥāba wa-l-tābiʿīn*. 14 vols. Sidon and Beirut: al-Maktaba al-ʿAṣriyya, 2003.

Ibn Abī Shayba (d. 235/849). *Muṣannaf*. Edited by Mukhtār Aḥmad al-Nadwī. 15 vols. Karachi: Idārat al-Qurʾān wa-l-ʿUlūm al-Islāmiyya, 1987.

Ibn ʿAsākir (d. 571/1176). *Taʾrīkh Madīnat Dimashq*. Edited by ʿUmar al-ʿAmrawī. 80 vols. Beirut: Dār al-Fikr, 1995–8.

Ibn Aʿtham (d. third/ninth century). *Kitāb al-Futūḥ*. Edited by Muḥammad ʿAbd al-Muʿīd Khān and ʿAbd al-Wahhāb al-Bukhārī. 8 vols. Hyderabad: Osmania Oriental Publications Bureau, 1968–75.

Ibn al-Athīr, ʿIzz al-Dīn (d. 630/1233). *Al-Kāmil fī al-taʾrīkh*. Edited by C. J. Tornberg. 15 vols. Leiden: E. J. Brill, 1851–76.

Ibn Bābawayh al-Qummī [al-Shaykh al-Ṣadūq] (d. 381/991). *A Shīʿite Creed: A Translation of Iʿtiqādātu ʾl-Imāmiyyah (The Beliefs of the Imāmiyyah) of Abū Jaʿfar, Muḥammad ibn ʿAlī ibn al-Ḥusayn, Ibn Bābawayh al-Qummī, known as ash-Shaykh aṣ-Ṣadūq (306/919–381/991)*. Rev. ed. Translated by Asaf A. A. Fyzee. Tehran: World Organization for Islamic Services, 1982.

———. *ʿUyūn akhbār al-Riḍā*. Edited by Mahdī al-Ḥusayn al-Lājūrdī. 2 vols. in 1. Najaf: al-Maṭbaʿa al-Ḥaydariyya, 1970.

Ibn al-Balkhī (fl. fifth–sixth/twelfth century). *Description of the Province of Fars in Persia at the Beginning of the Fourteenth Century A.D.* Edited and translated by Guy Le Strange. London: Royal Asiatic Society, 1912.

———. *The Fársnáma of Ibnu'l-Balkhí*. Edited by Guy Le Strange and Reynold A. Nicholson. London: Luzac, 1921.

Ibn al-Faqīh (fl. second half of the third/ninth or beginning of the fourth/tenth century). *Kitāb al-Buldān*. Edited by Yūsuf al-Hādī. Beirut: ʿĀlam al-Kutub, 1996.

———. *Mukhtaṣar Kitāb al-Buldān*. Edited by Michael J. de Goeje. Leiden: E. J. Brill, 1885.

Ibn Funduq, Abū al-Ḥasan ʿAlī b. Zayd al-Bayḥaqī (d. ca. 565/1169). *Lubāb al-ansāb wa-l-alqāb wa-l-aʿqāb*. Edited by Mahdī Rajāʾī and Maḥmūd Marʿashī. Qum: Maktabat Āyat Allāh al-ʿUẓmā al-Marʿashī al-Najafī al-ʿĀmma, 1410/[1989–90].

Ibn Ḥabīb, Muḥammad (d. 245/860). *Al-Muḥabbar*. Edited by Ilse Lichtenstädter. Hyderabad: Maṭbaʿat Jamʿiyyat Dāʾirat al-Maʿārif al-ʿUthmāniyya, 1942.

Ibn Ḥanbal, Aḥmad (d. 241/855). *Musnad*. Edited by Samīr Ṭāhā al-Majdhūb et al. 8 vols. Beirut: al-Maktab al-Islāmī, 1993.

Ibn Ḥawqal (fl. fourth/tenth century). *Kitāb Ṣūrat al-arḍ*. Beirut: Dār Maktabat al-Ḥayā, 1979.

Ibn Ḥazm, ʿAlī b. Aḥmad (d. 456/1064). *Jamharat ansāb al-ʿArab*. Edited by É. Lévi-Provençal. Cairo: Dār al-Maʿārif, 1948.

Ibn Hishām, ʿAbd al-Malik (d. 218/833 or 213/828). *The Life of Muhammad: A Translation of Ibn Isḥāq's Sīrat Rasūl Allāh*. Translated by A. Guillaume. Karachi: Oxford University Press, 1955. Reprint, 1978.

———. *Al-Sīra al-nabawiyya*. Edited by Muṣṭafā al-Saqqā, Ibrāhīm al-Abyārī, and ʿAbd al-Ḥafīẓ Shalabī. 2 vols. Cairo: al-Bābī al-Ḥalabī, 1955.

Ibn Isfandiyār (d. after 613/1216). *An Abridged Translation of the History of Ṭabaristán Compiled about A.H. 613 (A.D. 1216) by Muḥammad b. al-Ḥasan b. Isfandiyár*. Translated by Edward G. Browne. Leiden: E. J. Brill, 1905.

———. *Tārīkh-i Ṭabaristān*. Edited by ʿAbbās Iqbāl. 2 vols. in 1. Tehran: Majlis, [1941].

Ibn al-Jawzī (d. 597/1200). *Kashf al-mushkil min ḥadīth al-ṣaḥīḥayn*. Edited by ʿAlī Ḥusayn al-Bawwāb. 4 vols. Riyadh: Dār al-Waṭan, 1997.

———. *Al-Muntaẓam fī taʾrīkh al-mulūk wa-l-umam*. Edited by Muḥammad ʿAbd al-Qādir ʿAṭā and Muṣṭafā ʿAbd al-Qādir ʿAṭā. 18 vols. Beirut: Dār al-Kutub al-ʿIlmiyya, 1992.

———. *Talbīs Iblīs*. Edited by Muḥammad Munīr al-Dimashqī et al. Beirut: Dār al-Rāʾid al-ʿArabī, n.d. [198?].

Ibn Kathīr (d. 774/1373). *Tafsīr al-Qurʾān al-ʿaẓīm*. 7 vols. Beirut: Dār al-Andalus, 1966.

Ibn Khallikān (d. 681/1282). *Wafayāt al-aʿyān*. Edited by Iḥsān ʿAbbās. 8 vols. Beirut: Dār al-Thaqāfa, 1968–72.

Ibn Khayyāṭ al-ʿUṣfurī, Khalīfa (d. 240/854). *Taʾrīkh*. Edited by Suhayl Zakkār. 2 vols. Damascus: Wizārat al-Thaqāfa wa-l-Siyāḥa wa-l-Irshād al-Qawmī, 1967–8.

Ibn Manẓūr (d. 711/1311–12). *Lisān al-ʿArab*. 15 vols. Beirut: Dār Ṣādir, [1955–6].

Ibn Qutayba (d. 276/889). *Adab al-kātib*. Edited by Max Grünert. Leiden: E. J. Brill, 1900.

———. *Faḍl al-ʿArab wa-l-tanbīh ʿalā ʿulūmihā*. Edited by Walīd Maḥmūd Khāliṣ. Abu Dhabi: al-Mujammaʿ al-Thaqāfī, 1998.

———. *Al-Maʿārif*. Edited by Tharwat ʿUkāsha. Cairo, 1960. Reprint, Cairo: al-Hayʾa al-Miṣriyya li-l-Kitāb, 1992.

———. *The Superiority of the Arabs and an Exposition of Their Learning: A Translation of Ibn Qutaybah's Faḍl al-ʿArab wa l-tanbīh ʿalā ʿulūmihā*. Edited by Riḍā al-ʿArabī. Translated by Sarah Bowen Savant and Peter Webb. Reviewed by James E. Montgomery. New York: New York University Press, forthcoming.

———. *ʿUyūn al-akhbār*. 4 vols. Cairo: Maṭbaʿat Dār al-Kutub al-Miṣriyya, 1925–30.

Ibn Saʿd (d. 230/845). *Al-Ṭabaqāt al-kabīr*. Edited by Eduard Sachau et al. 9 vols. Leiden: E. J. Brill, 1904–40.

Ibn al-Sīd al-Baṭalyawsī (d. 521/1127). *Al-Iqtiḍāb fī sharḥ Adab al-kuttāb*. Edited by Muḥammad Bāsil ʿUyūn al-Sūd. 3 vols. Beirut: Dār al-Kutub al-ʿIlmiyya, 1999.

Al-Iṣṭakhrī, Abū Isḥāq al-Fārisī (d. mid-fourth/tenth century). *Al-Masālik wa-l-mamālik*. Edited by M. J. de Goeje. Leiden: E. J. Brill, 1927.

Al-Jāḥiẓ, ʿAmr b. Baḥr (d. 255/868–9). *Al-Bayān wa-l-tabyīn*. 2nd ed. Edited by ʿAbd al-Salām Muḥammad Hārūn. 4 vols. Cairo: Maktabat al-Khānjī, 1960–1.

Al-Jahshiyārī, Ibn ʿAbdūs (d. 331/942). *Kitāb al-Wuzarāʾ wa-l-kuttāb*. Edited by Muṣṭafā al-Saqqā, Ibrāhīm al-Abyārī, and ʿAbd al-Ḥafīẓ Shalabī. Cairo: Muṣṭafā al-Bābī al-Ḥalabī, 1938.

Jarīr b. ʿAṭiyya (d. ca. 110/728–9). *Dīwān Jarīr bi-sharḥ Muḥammad b. Ḥabīb*. Edited by Nuʿmān Muḥammad Amīn Ṭāhā. 2 vols. Cairo: Dār al-Maʿārif, 1969–86.

———. *Naqāʾiḍ Jarīr wa-l-Farazdaq*. Edited by Anthony Ashley Bevan. 3 vols. Leiden: E. J. Brill, 1905–12.

Al-Jawālīqī, Mawhūb b. Aḥmad (d. 539/1144). *Al-Muʿarrab min al-kalām al-aʿjamī ʿalā ḥurūf al-muʿjam*. Edited by Aḥmad Muḥammad Shākir. [Cairo]: Dār al-Kutub, 1969.

Al-Khaṭīb al-Baghdādī (d. 463/1071). *Taʾrīkh Baghdād*. 14 vols. Cairo: Maktabat al-Khānjī, 1931.

Khūzistān Chronicle. Edited by Ignazio Guidi as *Chronicon anonymum*, in *Chronica Minora*, vol. 1–2. Corpus Scriptorum Christianorum Orientalium. 1–2. Scr. Syri 1–2. Paris: Imprimerie nationale, 1903.

Khūzistān Chronicle. Translated by Sebastian Brock. Unpublished manuscript.

Al-Maqdisī, al-Muṭahhar b. Ṭāhir (fl. 355/966). *Al-Badʾ wa-l-taʾrīkh*. Edited and translated by Clément Huart. 6 vols. Paris: Ernest Leroux, 1899–1919. Reprint, without the translation, Baghdad: Maktabat al-Muthannā, n.d.

Al-Marzūqī, Aḥmad b. Muḥammad (d. 421/1030). *Sharḥ dīwān al-Ḥamāsa*. Edited by Aḥmad Amīn and ʿAbd al-Salām Hārūn. 4 vols. Cairo: Lajnat al-Taʾlīf wa-l-Tarjama wa-l-Nashr, 1951–3.

Al-Masʿūdī, Abū al-Ḥasan (d. 345/956). *Le livre de l'avertissement et de la revision*. Translated by Bernard Carra de Vaux. Paris: Imprimerie nationale, 1896.

———. *Murūj al-dhahab wa-maʿādin al-jawhar*. Vols. 1 and 2. Edited by Charles Pellat. Beirut: Manshūrāt al-Jāmiʿa al-Lubnāniyya, 1965–6.

———. *Al-Tanbīh wa-l-ishrāf*. Edited by Michael J. de Goeje. Leiden: E. J. Brill, 1893.

Al-Māwardī (d. 450/1058). *Al-Ahkam as-Sultaniyyah: The Laws of Islamic Governance*. Translated by Asadullah Yate. London: Ta-Ha, 1996.

———. *Aʿlām al-nubuwwa*. Edited by Muḥammad al-Muʿtaṣim bi-llāh al-Baghdādī. Beirut: Dār al-Kitāb al-ʿArabī, 1987.

———. *Kitāb al-Aḥkām al-sulṭāniyya wa-l-wilāyāt al-dīniyya*. Edited by Samīr Muṣṭafā Rubāb. Sidon and Beirut: al-Maktaba al-ʿAṣriyya, 2000.

———. *Al-Nukat wa-l-ʿuyūn: Tafsīr al-Māwardī*. Edited by Khiḍr Muḥammad Khiḍr. 4 vols. Kuwait: Wizārat al-Awqāf wa-l-Shuʾūn al-Islāmiyya, 1982.

The Meaning of the Holy Qurʾān. Translated by ʿAbdullah Yūsuf ʿAlī. 7th ed. Beltsville, MD: Amana Publications, 1995.

Al-Mubarrad (d. ca. 286/900). *Al-Fāḍil*. Edited by ʿAbd al-ʿAzīz al-Maymanī. Cairo: Dār al-Kutub al-Miṣriyya, 1956.

Mujāhid b. Jabr al-Makkī (d. between 100/718 and 104/722). *Tafsīr Mujāhid*. Edited by ʿAbd al-Raḥmān al-Ṭāhir b. Muḥammad al-Sūratī. Doha: Maṭābiʿ al-Dawḥa al-Ḥadītha, 1976.

Muqātil b. Sulaymān (d. 150/767). *Tafsīr Muqātil b. Sulaymān*. Edited by ʿAbd Allāh Maḥmūd Shiḥāta. 5 vols. [Cairo]: al-Hayʾa al-Miṣriyya al-ʿĀmma li-l-Kitab, 1979–89.

Muslim b. al-Ḥajjāj (d. 261/875). *Ṣaḥīḥ Muslim*. 2nd ed. Edited by Muḥammad Fu'ād 'Abd al-Bāqī. 5 vols. Beirut: Dār al-Fikr, 1978.

Al-Nīsābūrī, Abū 'Abd Allāh Ḥākim. *Tārīkh-i Nīshābūr: Tarjamah-yi Muḥammad b. Ḥusayn Khalīfah-yi Nīshābūrī*. Edited by Muḥammad Riḍā Shafī'ī Kadkanī. Tehran: Āgah, 1375/1996.

Al-Nuwayrī, Aḥmad b. 'Abd al-Wahhāb (d. 733/1333). *Nihāyat al-arab fī funūn al-adab*. 33 vols. Cairo: Maṭba'at Dār al-Kutub al-Miṣriyya, 1923–2002.

Qudāma b. Ja'far (d. 337/948). *Kitāb al-Kharāj wa-ṣinā'at al-kitāba*. Edited by Muḥammad Ḥusayn al-Zubaydī. Baghdad: Dār al-Rashīd, 1981.

Al-Qummī, 'Alī b. Ibrāhīm (d. 328/939). *Tafsīr*. Edited by Ṭayyib al-Mūsawī al-Jazā'irī. 2 vols. Najaf: Maktabat al-Hudā, 1387/1967–8.

Qummī, Ḥasan b. Muḥammad b. Ḥasan (fl. 378/988–9) [attr.]. *Tārīkh-i Qum*. Trans. [attr.] Ḥasan b. 'Alī b. Ḥasan Qummī. Edited by Jalāl al-Dīn Ṭihrānī. Tehran: Majlis, 1313 *shamsī*/1934. Reprint, Tehran: Intishārāt-i Tūs, 1982.

The Qur'ān. Translated by Alan Jones. Cambridge: Gibb Memorial Trust, 2007. See also *The Meaning of the Holy Qur'ān*.

Al-Qurṭubī, Muḥammad b. Aḥmad (d. 671/1272). *Al-Jāmi' li-aḥkām al-Qur'ān*. Vol. 14. Cairo: Dār al-Kutub al-Miṣriyya, 1364/1945.

Al-Rāfi'ī, 'Abd al-Karīm b. Muḥammad (d. 623/1226). *Al-Tadwīn fī akhbār Qazwīn*. Edited by 'Azīz Allāh 'Uṭāridī. 4 vols. Beirut: Dār al-Kutub al-'Ilmiyya, 1987.

Al-Ṣaffār al-Qummī, Abū Ja'far (d. 290/902–3). *Baṣā'ir al-darajāt fī faḍā'il Āl Muḥammad*. Qum: Ṭalī'at al-Nūr, 1384 *shamsī*/[2005].

Al-Sahmī, Abū al-Qāsim Ḥamza b. Yūsuf b. Ibrāhīm (d. 427/1038). *Ta'rīkh Jurjān*. Hyderabad: Osmania Oriental Publications, 1950.

Al-Sam'ānī, Manṣūr b. Muhammad (d. 489/1096). *Tafsīr al-Qur'ān*. Edited by Abū Tamīm Yāsir b. Ibrāhīm and Abū Bilāl Ghanīm b. 'Abbās b. Ghanīm. 6 vols. Riyadh: Dār al-Waṭan, 1997.

Al-Ṣan'ānī, 'Abd al-Razzāq (d. 211/827). *Al-Muṣannaf*. Edited by Ḥabīb al-Raḥmān al-A'ẓamī. 11 vols. Beirut: al-Maktab al-Islāmī, 1970–2.

Sebeos [attr.]. *The Armenian History Attributed to Sebeos*. Translated by R. W. Thomson with commentary by James Howard-Johnston. 2 vols. Liverpool: Liverpool University Press, 1999.

Al-Shahrastānī, Abū al-Fatḥ Muḥammad (d. 548/1153). *Kitāb al-Milal wa-l-niḥal*. Edited by 'Abd al-'Azīz Muḥammad al-Wakīl. 3 vols. in 1. Cairo: Mu'assasat al-Ḥalabī, 1968.

Al-Shaykh al-Mufīd (d. 413/1022). *Al-Irshād fī ma'rifat ḥujaj Allāh 'alā al-'ibād*. Edited by Mu'assasat Āl al-Bayt li-Iḥyā' al-Turāth. 2 vols. Beirut: al-Mu'assasa, 1995.

———. *Kitāb al-Irshād: The Book of Guidance into the Lives of the Twelve Imams*. Translated by I. K. A. Howard. London: Balagha Books, 1981.

Al-Ṣūlī, Abū Bakr Muḥammad b. Yaḥyā (d. 335/947). *Adab al-kuttāb*. Edited by Muḥammad Bahjat al-Atharī. Cairo: al-Maṭba'a al-Salafiyya, 1341/[1922].

Al-Ṭabarānī, Sulaymān b. Aḥmad b. Ayyūb Abū al-Qāsim (d. 360/971). *Al-Mu'jam al-kabīr*. 2nd ed. Edited by Ḥamdī 'Abd al-Majīd al-Salafī. 25 vols. [Beirut: Maktabat al-Taw'iyya al-Islāmiyya], 1404/1983–[1410/1990].

Al-Ṭabarī, Muḥammad b. Jarīr (d. 310/923). *Geschichte der Perser und Araber zur Zeit der Sasaniden aus der arabischen Chronik des Tabari.* Translated by Theodor Nöldeke. Leiden: E. J. Brill, 1879. Reprint, 1973.

———. *The History of al-Ṭabarī.* 40 vols. Albany: State University of New York Press, 1985–2007.

———. *Jāmiʿ al-bayān ʿan taʾwīl āy al-Qurʾān.* Edited by Aḥmad ʿAbd al-Rāziq al-Bakrī et al. 10 vols. Cairo: Dār al-Salām, 2007.

———. *Taʾrīkh al-rusul wa-l-mulūk.* Edited by M. J. de Goeje et al. 15 vols. in 3 series. Leiden: E. J. Brill, 1879–1901.

The Tārikh-e Sistān. Translated by Milton Gold. Rome: Istituto italiano per il Medio ed Estremo Oriente, 1976.

Tārīkh-i Sīstān. Edited by Muḥammad Taqī Bahār. Tehran: Khāvar, 1935.

Al-Thaʿālibī, Abū Manṣūr (d. 429/1038) [attr.]. *Ghurar akhbār mulūk al-Furs wa-siyarihim.* Edited and translated by H. Zotenberg. Paris: Imprimerie nationale, 1900.

———. *The Laṭāʾif al-maʿārif of Thaʿālibī (The Book of Curious and Entertaining Information).* Translated by C. E. Bosworth. Edinburgh: Edinburgh University Press, 1968.

———. *Thimār al-qulūb fī al-muḍāf wa-l-mansūb.* Edited by Muḥammad Abū al-Faḍl Ibrāhīm. Cairo: Dār Nahḍat Miṣr, 1965.

———. *Yatīmat al-dahr fī maḥāsin ahl al-ʿaṣr.* Edited by Muḥammad Muḥyī al-Dīn ʿAbd al-Ḥamīd. 4 vols. in 2. Cairo: Maṭbaʿat Ḥijāzī, 1947.

Al-Thaʿlabī, Aḥmad b. Muḥammad (d. 427/1035). *Al-Kashf wa-l-bayān.* Edited by Abū Muḥammad b. ʿĀshūr. 10 vols. Beirut: Dār Iḥyāʾ al-Turāth al-ʿArabī, 2002.

Theophanes. *The Chronicle of Theophanes Confessor: Byzantine and Near Eastern History, AD 284–813.* Translated by Cyril Mango and Roger Scott. Oxford: Clarendon, 1997.

Al-Tirmidhī, Muḥammad b. ʿĪsā (d. 279/892). *Al-Jāmiʿ al-ṣaḥīḥ.* Edited by Aḥmad Muḥammad Shākir, Muḥammad Fuʾād ʿAbd al-Bāqī, and Ibrāhīm ʿAṭwa ʿAwaḍ. 5 vols. Cairo: Muṣṭafā al-Bābī al-Ḥalabī, 1937–56.

Al-Wāḥidī, ʿAlī b. Aḥmad (d. 468/1076). *Asbāb al-nuzūl wa-yalīhi al-Nāsikh wa-l-mansūkh.* Cairo: Maktabat al-Mutanabbī, n.d.

———. *Al-Wajīz fī tafsīr al-Kitāb al-ʿAzīz.* Edited by Ṣafwān ʿAdnān Dāwūdī. 2 vols. Damascus: Dār al-Qalam, 1995.

Al-Wāqidī, Muḥammad b. ʿUmar (d. 207/822). *Al-Maghāzī.* Edited by Marsden Jones. 3 vols. London: Oxford University Press, 1966.

Al-Yaʿqūbī, Aḥmad b. Abī Yaʿqūb (fl. second half of the third/ninth century). *Taʾrīkh.* Edited by M. Th. Houtsma. 2 vols. Leiden: E. J. Brill, 1883. Reprint, Beirut: Dār Ṣādir, 1960.

Yāqūt al-Ḥamawī (d. 626/1229). *Irshād al-arīb ilā maʿrifat al-adīb [Muʿjam al-udabāʾ].* Edited by D. S. Margoliouth. 7 vols. London: Luzac, 1907–13.

———. *Jacut's geographisches Wörterbuch [Muʿjam al-buldān].* Edited by Ferdinand Wüstenfeld. 6 vols. Leipzig: F. A. Brockhaus, 1866–73.

Al-Zamakhsharī, Abū al-Qāsim Maḥmūd b. ʿUmar (d. 538/1144). *Rabīʿ al-abrār wa-nuṣūṣ al-akhbār.* Edited by ʿAbd al-Amīr Muhannā. 5 vols. Beirut: Muʾassasat al-Aʿlamī, 1992.

Zand-Ākāsīh: Iranian or Greater Bundahišn. Translated by Behramgore Tehmuras Anklesaria. Bombay: Rahnumae Mazdayasnan Sabha, 1956.

Secondary Sources

Abadal i de Vinyals, Ramón d'. "À propos du Legs visigothique en Espagne." *Settimane di studio del Centro italiano di studi sull'alto medioevo* 5 (1958): 541–85.

Abisaab, Rula Jurdi. *Converting Persia: Religion and Power in the Safavid Empire*. London: I. B. Tauris, 2004.

Abou El Fadl, Khaled. *Speaking in God's Name: Islamic Law, Authority and Women*. Oxford: Oneworld, 2001. Reprint, 2003.

Ādharnūsh, Ādhartāsh [A. Azarnouche]. *Chālish miyān-i Farsī va ʿArabī: Sadah-hā-yi nukhust*. Tehran: Nay, 1385 *shamsī*/[2006].

Afsaruddin, Asma. *The First Muslims: History and Memory*. Oxford: Oneworld, 2008.

Album, Stephen. *A Checklist of Islamic Coins*. 3rd ed. Santa Rosa, CA: Stephen Album Rare Coins, 2011.

Ali, Muhammad Mohar. *Sîrat al-Nabî and the Orientalists, with Special Reference to the Writings of William Muir, D. S. Margoliouth and W. Montgomery Watt. Vol. 1B, From the Early Phase of the Prophet's Mission to His Migration to Madinah*. Medina: King Fahd Complex for the Printing of the Holy Qurʾan and Centre for the Service of Sunnah and Sîrah, 1417/1997.

Amanat, Abbas, and Farzin Vejdani. *Iran Facing Others: Identity Boundaries in a Historical Perspective*. New York: Palgrave Macmillan, 2012.

Amīn, Aḥmad. *Ḍuḥā al-Islām*. 3 vols. Beirut: Dār al-Kitāb al-ʿArabī, [1933–6].

Amir-Moezzi, Mohammad Ali. *The Divine Guide in Early Shiʿism: The Sources of Esotericism in Islam*. Translated by David Streight. Albany: State University of New York Press, 1994.

———. "Šahrbānu." In *Encyclopaedia Iranica*.

———. "Shahrbānū, Dame du pays d'Iran et Mère des Imams: Entre l'Iran préislamique et le Shiisme Imamite." *Jerusalem Studies in Arabic and Islam* 27 (2002): 497–549.

———. "Shahrbānū, princesse sassanide et épouse de l'imam Ḥusayn: De l'Iran préislamique à l'Islam shiite." *Comptes rendus de l'Académie des Inscriptions et Belles-Lettres*, Jan.–Mar. 2002, 255–85.

Anderson, Benedict. *Imagined Communities: Reflections on the Origin and Spread of Nationalism*. Rev. ed. London: Verso, 1991.

Anlezark, Daniel. "Sceaf, Japheth and the Origins of the Anglo-Saxons." *Anglo-Saxon England* 31 (2002): 13–46.

Antrim, Zayde. *Routes and Realms: The Power of Place in the Early Islamic World*. Oxford: Oxford University Press, 2012.

Arberry, A. J. *Arabic Poetry: A Primer for Students*. Cambridge: Cambridge University Press, 1965.

Arkoun, Mohammed. *The Unthought in Contemporary Islamic Thought*. London: Saqi Books, 2002.

Armstrong, John A. *Nations before Nationalism*. Chapel Hill: University of North Carolina Press, 1982.

Arnold, T. W. *The Preaching of Islam: A History of the Propagation of the Muslim Faith*. 2nd ed. Delhi: Low Price Publications, 2001.

Assmann, Jan. *Cultural Memory and Early Civilization: Writing, Remembrance, and Political Imagination*. Cambridge: Cambridge University Press, 2011.

———. *Moses the Egyptian: The Memory of Egypt in Western Monotheism*. Cambridge, MA: Harvard University Press, 1997.

Azkāʾī, Parvīz. "Salmān Fārisī." In *Dāyirat al-maʿārif-i Tashayyuʿ*, edited by Aḥmad Ṣadr Ḥājj Sayyid Javādī, Kāmrān Fānī, and Bahāʾ al-Dīn Khorramshāhī, 9:262–5. Tehran: Bunyād-i Islāmī-yi Ṭāhir, 1988–.

Bacharach, Jere L. *Islamic History through Coins: An Analysis and Catalogue of Tenth-Century Ikhshidid Coinage*. Cairo: American University in Cairo Press, 2006.

Bahrami, Mehdi. "A Gold Medal in the Freer Gallery of Art." In *Archaeologica Orientalia in Memoriam Ernst Herzfeld*, edited by George C. Miles, 5–21. Locust Valley, NY: J. J. Augustin, 1952.

Barbier de Meynard, C. *Dictionnaire géographique, historique et littéraire de la Perse et des contrées adjacentes*. Paris: L'Imprimerie Impériale, 1861.

Barthold, W. *An Historical Geography of Iran*. Translated by Svat Soucek. Edited by C. E. Bosworth. Princeton: Princeton University Press, 1984.

———. "Zur Geschichte des persischen Epos." Translated by Hans Heinrich Schaeder. *Zeitschrift der Deutschen Morgenländischen Gesellschaft* 98 (1944): 121–57.

Al-Bashbīshī, Jamāl al-Dīn ʿAbd Allāh b. Aḥmad. *Jāmiʿ al-taʿrīb bi-l-ṭarīq al-qarīb*. Edited by Nuṣūhī Ūnāl Qarah Arslān. Cairo: Markaz al-Dirāsāt al-Sharqiyya, Kulliyyat al-Ādāb, Jāmiʿat al-Qāhira, 1995.

Bashear, Suliman. *Arabs and Others in Early Islam*. Princeton, NJ: Darwin Press, 1997.

———. "The Mission of Diḥya al-Kalbī and the Situation in Syria." *Der Islam* 74, no. 1 (1997): 64–91.

Bell, Richard. *A Commentary on the Qurʾān*. Vol. 2, *Surahs XXV–CXIV*. Manchester: University of Manchester, 1991.

Bengio, Ofra. *Saddam's Word: Political Discourse in Iraq*. New York: Oxford University Press, 1998.

Berchem, Max van. *Matériaux pour un Corpus inscriptionum Arabicarum*. Part 2, *Syrie du Sud*. 3 vols. Cairo: Imprimerie de l'Institut Français d'Archéologie Orientale, 1922–3, 1927.

Berg, Herbert. "Competing Paradigms in the Study of Islamic Origins: Qurʾān 15:89–91 and the Value of *Isnāds*." In *Method and Theory in the Study of Islamic Origins*, edited by Herbert Berg, 259–90. Leiden: Brill, 2003.

———. *The Development of Exegesis in Early Islam: The Authenticity of Muslim Literature from the Formative Period*. Richmond: Curzon, 2000.

Bernheimer, Teresa. "Genealogy, Marriage, and the Drawing of Boundaries among the ʿAlids (Eighth–Twelfth Centuries)." In *Sayyids and Sharifs in Muslim Societies: The Living Links to the Prophet*, edited by Kazuo Morimoto, 75–91. Abingdon: Routledge, 2012.

Blair, Sheila S. "Transcribing God's Word: Qurʾan Codices in Context." *Journal of Qurʾanic Studies* 10, no. 1 (2008): 70–97.

Blois, François de. "Dīvān i. The Term." In *Encyclopaedia Iranica.*
———. "Garšāsp-nāma." In *Encyclopaedia Iranica.*
Borrut, Antoine. *Entre mémoire et pouvoir: L'espace syrien sous les derniers Omeyyades et les premiers Abbassides (v. 72–193/692–809).* Leiden: Brill, 2011.
———. "La *Memoria* Omeyyade: Les Omeyyades entre souvenir et oubli dans les sources narratives Islamiques." In Borrut and Cobb, *Umayyad Legacies*, 25–61.
———. "La Syrie de Salomon: L'appropriation du mythe salomonien dans les sources arabes." *Pallas* 63 (2003): 107–20.
———and Paul M. Cobb, eds. *Umayyad Legacies: Medieval Memories from Syria to Spain.* Leiden: Brill, 2010.
Bosworth, Clifford Edmund. "ʿAjam." In *Encyclopaedia Iranica.*
———. "Azerbaijan iv. Islamic History to 1941." In *Encyclopaedia Iranica.*
———. "Dīvān ii. Government Office." In *Encyclopaedia Iranica.*
———. "Ebn al-Balkī." In *Encyclopaedia Iranica.*
———. *The Ghaznavids: Their Empire in Afghanistan and Eastern Iran, 994–1040.* Edinburgh: Edinburgh University Press, 1963.
———. "The Heritage of Rulership in Early Islamic Iran and the Search for Dynastic Connections with the Past." *Iran* 11 (1973): 51–62.
———. *The History of the Saffarids of Sistan and the Maliks of Nimruz (247/861 to 949/1542–3).* Costa Mesa, CA: Mazda Publishers, 1994.
———. "Ispahbadh." In *Encyclopaedia of Islam.* 2nd ed.
———. "Mīkālīs." In *Encyclopaedia of Islam.* 2nd ed.
———. *The New Islamic Dynasties: A Chronological and Genealogical Manual.* Rev. ed. New York: Columbia University Press, 1996.
———. "Al-Rukhkhadj." In *Encyclopaedia of Islam.* 2nd ed.
———. "Al-Sallamī." In *Encyclopaedia of Islam.* 2nd ed.
———. "Sistan and Its Local Histories." *Iranian Studies* 33, no. 1/2 (2000): 31–43.
———. *Sīstān under the Arabs: From the Islamic Conquest to the Rise of the Ṣaffārids (30–250/651–864).* Rome: Istituto italiano per il Medio ed Estremo Oriente, Centro studi e scavi archeologici in Asia, 1968.
———. "Tārik-e Sistān." In *Encyclopaedia Iranica.*
———. "Al-Thaʿālibī, Abū Manṣūr." In *Encyclopaedia of Islam.* 2nd ed.
Boyarin, Daniel. Review of *Moses the Egyptian: The Memory of Egypt in Western Monotheism*, by Jan Assmann. *Church History* 67, no. 4 (1998): 842–4.
Boyce, Mary. "Ādur Farnbāg." In *Encyclopaedia Iranica.*
———. "Cleansing i. In Zoroastrianism." In *Encyclopaedia Iranica.*
———. "Gōmēz." In *Encyclopaedia Iranica.*
———, trans. *The Letter of Tansar.* Rome: Istituto Italiano per il Medio ed Estremo Oriente, 1968.
———. "Middle Persian Literature." *Handbuch der Orientalistik* 1.4.2.1 (1988): 31–66.
———. "On the Zoroastrian Temple Cult of Fire." *Journal of the American Oriental Society* 95, no. 3 (1975): 454–65.

———. *Zoroastrians: Their Religious Beliefs and Practices*. 2nd ed. London: Routledge, 2001.
Braude, Benjamin. "The Sons of Noah and the Construction of Ethnic and Geographical Identities in the Medieval and Early Modern Periods." *William and Mary Quarterly* 54, no. 1 (1997): 103–42.
Brockelmann, Carl. *Geschichte der arabischen Litteratur*. 2nd ed. 2 vols. Leiden: E. J. Brill, 1943–9.
———. *Geschichte der arabischen Litteratur*. Supplement. 3 vols. Leiden: E. J. Brill, 1937–42.
———. "Al-Māwardī." In *Encyclopaedia of Islam*. 2nd ed.
Brown, Jonathan A. C. *Hadith: Muhammad's Legacy in the Medieval and Modern World*. Oxford: Oneworld, 2009.
Brown, Stuart C. "Ecbatana." In *Encyclopaedia Iranica*.
Browne, Edward G. *A Literary History of Persia*. 4 vols. Cambridge: Cambridge University Press, 1928.
———. "Some Account of the Arabic Work entitled '*Niháyatu'l-irab fí akhbári'l-Furs wa'l-'Arab*,' particularly of that part which treats of the Persian Kings." *Journal of the Royal Asiatic Society*, n.s., 32, no. 2 (1900): 195–259.
Bulliet, Richard W. *Conversion to Islam in the Medieval Period: An Essay in Quantitative History*. Cambridge, MA: Harvard University Press, 1979.
———. *Islam: The View from the Edge*. New York: Columbia University Press, 1994.
———. "Al-Māfarrūkhī." In *Encyclopaedia of Islam*. 2nd ed.
Busse, Heribert. "Cain and Abel." In *Encyclopaedia of the Qurʾān*, 1:270–2.
Caetani, Leone. *Annali dell'Islām*. 10 vols. Milan: U. Hoepli, 1918.
Cameron, Averil. *Procopius and the Sixth Century*. London: Duckworth, 1985.
Canard, M. "ʿAmmūriya." In *Encyclopaedia of Islam*. 2nd ed.
Cauthen, Bruce. "Covenant and Continuity: Ethno-Symbolism and the Myth of Divine Election." *Nations and Nationalism* 10, no. 1/2 (2004): 19–33.
Chabbi, Jacqueline. "Abū Nuʿaym al-Iṣfahānī." In *Encyclopaedia of Islam*. 3rd ed.
Choksy, Jamsheed K. "Altars, Precincts, and Temples: Medieval and Modern Zoroastrian Praxis." *Iran* 44 (2006): 327–46.
———. *Conflict and Cooperation: Zoroastrian Subalterns and Muslim Elites in Medieval Iranian Society*. New York: Columbia University Press, 1997.
Christensen, Arthur. *L'Iran sous les Sassanides*. Copenhagen: Levin & Munksgaard, 1936.
———. *Les Kayanides*. Copenhagen: Andr. Fred. Høst & Søn, 1931.
———. *Les types du premier homme et du premier roi dans l'histoire légendaire des Iraniens*. Vol. 1, *Gajōmard, Masjaγ et Masjānaγ, Hōšang et Taχmōruw*. Stockholm: P. A. Norstedt, 1917.
Clinton, Jerome W. "A Sketch of Translation and the Formation of New Persian Literature." In *Iran and Iranian Studies: Essays in Honor of Iraj Afshar*, edited by Kambiz Eslami, 288–305. Princeton, NJ: Zagros, 1998.
Conrad, Lawrence I. "Abraha and Muḥammad: Some Observations Apropos of Chronology and Literary *Topoi* in the Early Arabic Historical Tradition."

Bulletin of the School of Oriental and African Studies 50, no. 2 (1987): 225–40.

———. "The Conquest of Arwād: A Source-Critical Study in the Historiography of the Early Medieval Near East." In *The Byzantine and Early Islamic Near East*, vol. 1, *Problems in the Literary Source Material*, edited by Averil Cameron and Lawrence I. Conrad, 317–401. Princeton, NJ: Darwin Press, 1992.

———. "Heraclius in Early Islamic Kerygma." In *The Reign of Heraclius (610–641): Crisis and Confrontation*, edited by Gerrit J. Reinink and Bernard H. Stolte, 113–56. Leuven: Peeters, 2002.

———. "Ibn Aʿtham and His History." Unpublished paper presented at the Sixth International Colloquium on "From Jahiliyya to Islam," Institute for Advanced Studies, Hebrew University, Jerusalem, Sept. 5–10, 1993.

———. "Recovering Lost Texts: Some Methodological Issues." *Journal of the American Oriental Society* 113, no. 2 (1993): 258–63.

———. "Theophanes and the Arabic Historical Tradition: Some Indications of Intercultural Transmission." *Byzantinische Forschungen* 15 (1990): 1–44.

Cook, Michael. "The Opponents of the Writing of Tradition in Early Islam." "Voix et Calame en Islam Médiéval," special issue, *Arabica* 44, no. 4 (1997): 437–530.

———. "Pharaonic History in Medieval Egypt." *Studia Islamica*, no. 57 (1983): 67–103.

Cooperson, Michael. "Al-Maʾmūn, the Pyramids, and the Hieroglyphs." In *ʿAbbasid Studies II: Occasional Papers of the School of ʿAbbasid Studies, Leuven, 28 June–1 July 2004*, edited by John Nawas, 165–90. Leuven: Peeters, 2010.

———. "Masʿudi." In *Encyclopaedia Iranica.*

Cornu, Georgette. *Atlas du monde Arabo-islamique à l'époque classique: IXe–Xe siècles*. 2 vols. Leiden: E. J. Brill, 1983–5.

Coser, Lewis A. "Introduction." In *On Collective Memory*, by Maurice Halbwachs, translated by Lewis A. Coser, 1–34. Chicago: University of Chicago Press, 1992.

Crone, Patricia. "The First-Century Concept of *Hiǧra*." *Arabica* 41, no. 3 (1994): 352–87.

———. *From Kavād to al-Ghazālī: Religion, Law and Political Thought in the Near East, c.600–c.1100*. Aldershot: Ashgate Variorum, 2005.

———. *God's Rule: Government and Islam; Six Centuries of Medieval Islamic Political Thought*. New York: Columbia University Press, 2004.

———. "Muhallabids." In *Encyclopaedia of Islam*. 2nd ed.

———. *The Nativist Prophets of Early Islamic Iran: Rural Revolt and Local Zoroastrianism*. Cambridge: Cambridge University Press, 2012.

———. *Roman, Provincial, and Islamic Law: The Origins of the Islamic Patronate*. Cambridge: Cambridge University Press, 1987.

Daftary, Farhad. *The Ismāʿīlīs: Their History and Doctrines*. Cambridge: Cambridge University Press, 1990.

Dakake, Maria Massi. *The Charismatic Community: Shiʿite Identity in Early Islam*. Albany: State University of New York Press, 2007.

Dalley, Stephanie. "Gilgamesh in the Arabian Nights." *Journal of the Royal Asiatic Society*, 3rd ser., 1, no. 1 (1991): 1–17.

———. "The Tale of Bulūqiyā and the *Alexander Romance* in Jewish and Sufi Mystical Circles." In *Tracing the Threads: Studies in the Vitality of Jewish Pseudepigrapha*, edited by John C. Reeves, 239–69. Atlanta: Scholars Press, 1994.

Daniel, Elton L. "The Islamic East." In *The New Cambridge History of Islam*, vol. 1, *The Formation of the Islamic World, Sixth to Eleventh Centuries*, edited by Chase F. Robinson, 448–505. Cambridge: Cambridge University Press, 2010.

———. "Manuscripts and Editions of Balʿamī's *Tarjamah-i Tārīkh-i Ṭabarī*." *Journal of the Royal Asiatic Society*, n.s., 122, no. 2 (1990): 282–321.

Daryaee, Touraj. "The Fall of the Sasanian Empire to the Arab Muslims: From *Two Centuries of Silence* to *Decline and Fall of the Sasanian Empire: The Partho-Sasanian Confederacy and the Arab Conquest of Iran*." *Journal of Persianate Studies* 3, no. 2 (2010): 239–54.

———. "The Mazdean Sect of Gayōmartiya." In *Ātaš-e Dorun: The Fire Within, Jamshid Soroush Soroushian Commemorative Volume*, edited by Carlo G. Cereti and Farrokh Vajifdar, 131–7. [United States]: 1st Books, 2003.

———, ed. and trans. *Šahrestānīhā ī Ērānšahr: A Middle Persian Text on Late Antique Geography, Epic, and History*. Costa Mesa, CA: Mazda Publishers, 2002.

———. *Sasanian Persia: The Rise and Fall of an Empire*. London: I. B. Tauris, 2009.

Davis, Craig R. "Cultural Assimilation in the Anglo-Saxon Royal Genealogies." *Anglo-Saxon England* 21 (1992): 23–36.

Davis, Dick. *Epic and Sedition: The Case of Ferdowsi's Shāhnāmeh*. Fayetteville: University of Arkansas Press, 1992.

———. "The Problem of Ferdowsî's Sources." *Journal of the American Oriental Society* 116, no. 1 (1996): 48–57.

Décobert, Christian. *Le mendiant et le combattant: L'institution de l'islam*. Paris: Seuil, 1991.

Dignas, Beate, and Engelbert Winter. *Rome and Persia in Late Antiquity: Neighbours and Rivals*. Cambridge: Cambridge University Press, 2007.

Donner, Fred McGraw. "Arabic *fatḥ* as 'Conquest.'" Unpublished manuscript.

———. "Centralized Authority and Military Autonomy in the Early Islamic Conquests." In *The Byzantine and Early Islamic Near East*, vol. 3, *States, Resources and Armies*, edited by Averil Cameron, 337–60. Princeton, NJ: Darwin Press, 1995.

———. *The Early Islamic Conquests*. Princeton, NJ: Princeton University Press, 1981.

———. *Muhammad and the Believers: At the Origins of Islam*. Cambridge, MA: Belknap Press of Harvard University Press, 2010.

———. *Narratives of Islamic Origins: The Beginnings of Islamic Historical Writing*. Princeton, NJ: Darwin Press, 1998.

———. Review of *The Prophet and the Age of the Caliphates: The Islamic Near East from the Sixth to the Eleventh Century*, by Hugh Kennedy. *Speculum* 65, no. 1 (1990): 182–4.
Donohue, John J. *The Buwayhid Dynasty in Iraq, 334H./945 to 403H./1012: Shaping Institutions for the Future.* Leiden: Brill, 2003.
———. "Three Buwayhid Inscriptions." *Arabica* 20, no. 1 (1973): 74–80.
Drechsler, Andreas. *Die Geschichte der Stadt Qom im Mittelalter (650–1350): Politische und wirtschaftliche Aspekte.* Berlin: Klaus Schwarz, 1999.
———. "Qom i. History to the Safavid Period." In *Encyclopaedia Iranica.*
———. "Tārik-e Qom." In *Encyclopaedia Iranica.*
Drory, Rina. "The Abbasid Construction of the Jahiliyya: Cultural Authority in the Making." *Studia Islamica*, no. 83 (1996): 33–49.
Durand-Guédy, David. *Iranian Elites and Turkish Rulers: A History of Iṣfahān in the Saljūq Period.* London: Routledge, 2010.
Al-Dūrī, ʿAbd al-ʿAzīz. "Dīwān i. The Caliphate." In *Encyclopaedia of Islam.* 2nd ed.
———. *Al-Judhūr al-taʾrīkhiyya li-l-Shuʿūbiyya.* Beirut: Dār al-Ṭalīʿa, 1962.
Eco, Umberto. "An *Ars Oblivionalis*? Forget It!" Translated by Marilyn Migiel. *PMLA* 103, no. 3 (1988): 254–61.
El Ali, Saleh Ahmad [Ṣāliḥ Aḥmad al-ʿAlī]. "Al-Madāʾin and Its Surrounding Area in Arabic Literary Sources." *Mesopotamia* 3–4 (1968–9): 417–39.
———. "Al-Madāʾin fī al-maṣādir al-ʿarabiyya." *Sumer* 23 (1967): 47–65.
El Cheikh, Nadia Maria. "Byzantines, Exegetical Explanations." In *Encyclopaedia of the Qurʾān*, 1:66–9.
———. *Byzantium Viewed by the Arabs.* Cambridge, MA: Harvard University Press, 2004.
———. "Muḥammad and Heraclius: A Study in Legitimacy." *Studia Islamica*, no. 89 (1999): 5–21.
———. "*Sūrat al-Rūm*: A Study of the Exegetical Literature." *Journal of the American Oriental Society* 118, no. 3 (1998): 356–64.
El-Hibri, Tayeb. "Coinage Reform under the ʿAbbāsid Caliph al-Maʾmūn." *Journal of the Economic and Social History of the Orient* 36, no. 1 (1993): 58–83.
———. *Reinterpreting Islamic Historiography: Hārūn Al-Rashīd and the Narrative of the ʿAbbāsid Caliphate.* Cambridge: Cambridge University Press, 1999.
———. "Ṭabarī's Biography of al-Muʿtaṣim: The Literary Use of a Military Career." *Der Islam* 86, no. 2 (2011): 187–236.
Encyclopaedia Iranica. Edited by Ehsan Yarshater. Online ed. New York, 1996–. http://www.iranicaonline.org.
Encyclopaedia of Islam. 2nd ed. Edited by P. Bearman, Th. Bianquis, C. E. Bosworth, E. van Donzel, and W. P. Heinrichs. 12 vols. Leiden: E. J. Brill, 1960–2004.
Encyclopaedia of Islam. 3rd ed. Edited by Kate Fleet, Gudrun Krämer, Denis Matringe, John Nawas, and Everett Rowson. Leiden: E. J. Brill, 2007–.
Encyclopaedia of the Qurʾān. Edited by Jane Dammen McAuliffe. 6 vols. Leiden: Brill, 2001–6.

Fadel, Mohammad. "Is Historicism a Viable Strategy for Islamic Law Reform? The Case of 'Never Shall a Folk Prosper Who Have Appointed a Woman to Rule Them.'" *Islamic Law and Society* 18, no. 2 (2011): 131–76.

Faqīhī, ʿAlī Aṣghar. "Tārīkh-i Qum." In *Dānish-nāmah-yi jahān-i Islām*. Online ed. Tehran: Bunyād-i Dāʾirat al-Maʿārif-i Islāmī, n.d. http://www.encyclopaediaislamica.com.

Fiey, Jean Maurice. *Pour un Oriens Christianus Novus: Répertoire des diocèses syriaques orientaux et occidentaux*. Beirut and Stuttgart: Franz Steiner, 1993.

———. "Topography of al-Madaʾin (Seleucia-Ctesiphon area)." *Sumer* 23 (1967): 3–38.

Firestone, Reuven. "Pharaoh." In *Encyclopaedia of the Qurʾān*, 4:66–8.

Fowden, Garth. *Quṣayr ʿAmra: Art and the Umayyad Elite in Late Antique Syria*. Berkeley: University of California Press, 2004.

Fragner, Bert G. "The Concept of Regionalism in Historical Research on Central Asia and Iran (A Macro-Historical Interpretation)." In *Studies on Central Asian History in Honor of Yuri Bregel*, edited by Devin DeWeese, 341–54. Bloomington: Indiana University Research Institute for Inner Asian Studies, 2001.

———. *Die "Persophonie": Regionalität, Identität und Sprachkontakt in der Geschichte Asiens*. Berlin: Das Arabische Buch, 1999.

Friedmann, Yohanan. *Tolerance and Coercion in Islam: Interfaith Relations in the Muslim Tradition*. Cambridge: Cambridge University Press, 2003.

Frye, R. N. "Bāwand." In *Encyclopaedia of Islam*. 2nd ed.

———. "Hamadhān." In *Encyclopaedia of Islam*. 2nd ed.

———. "The Political History of Iran under the Sasanians." In *The Cambridge History of Iran*, vol. 3(1), *The Seleucid, Parthian and Sasanian Periods*, edited by Ehsan Yarshater, 116–80. Cambridge: Cambridge University Press, 1983.

Fück, Johann. *Muḥammad b. Isḥāq: Literarhistorische Untersuchungen*. Frankfurt: n.p., 1925.

Gabrieli, F. "Ibn al-Muḳaffaʿ." In *Encyclopaedia of Islam*. 2nd ed.

Garrison, Mark. "Fire Altars." In *Encyclopaedia Iranica*.

Geary, Patrick J. *Phantoms of Remembrance: Memory and Oblivion at the End of the First Millennium*. Princeton, NJ: Princeton University Press, 1994.

Gelder, Geert Jan van. *Close Relationships: Incest and Inbreeding in Classical Arabic Literature*. London: I. B. Tauris, 2005.

Geoffroy, E. "Ummī." In *Encyclopaedia of Islam*. 2nd ed.

Al-Ghazālī, Muḥammad. *Al-Sunna al-nabawiyya bayn ahl al-fiqh wa-ahl al-ḥadīth*. Herndon, VA: International Institute of Islamic Thought, 1989.

Gibb, H. A. R. "ʿAbd Allāh b. ʿĀmir." In *Encyclopaedia of Islam*. 2nd ed.

———. "ʿAlī b. al-Djahm." In *Encyclopaedia of Islam*. 2nd ed.

———. "The Social Significance of the Shuubiya." In *Studies on the Civilization of Islam*, edited by Stanford J. Shaw and William R. Polk, 62–73. Boston: Beacon Press, 1962.

Gignoux, Ph. "L'organisation administrative sasanide: Le cas du *marzbān*." *Jerusalem Studies in Arabic and Islam* 4 (1984): 1–29.

Gil, Moshe. "Additions to *Islamische Masse und Gewichte*." In *Occident and Orient: A Tribute to the Memory of Alexander Scheiber*, edited by Robert Dán, 167–70. Budapest: Akadémiai Kiadó, 1988.

Gilliot, Claude. "Creation of a Fixed Text." In *The Cambridge Companion to the Qur'ān*, edited by Jane Dammen McAuliffe, 41–57. Cambridge: Cambridge University Press, 2006.

———. "La formation intellectuelle de Tabari (224/5–310/839–923)." *Journal Asiatique* 276 (1988): 203–44.

———. "Muḥammad, le Coran et les 'contraintes de l'histoire.'" In *The Qur'an as Text*, edited by Stefan Wild, 3–26. Leiden: E. J. Brill, 1996.

Gnoli, Gherardo. *The Idea of Iran: An Essay on Its Origin*. Rome: Istituto italiano per il Medio ed Estremo Oriente, 1989.

Göbl, Robert. *Sasanian Numismatics*. Translated by Paul Severin. Braunschweig: Klinkhardt & Biermann, 1971.

Goitein, S. D. *Studies in Islamic History and Institutions*. Leiden: E. J. Brill, 1966.

Goldziher, Ignaz. *Muhammedanische Studien*. 2 vols. Halle: Max Niemeyer, 1889–90.

———. *Muslim Studies*. 2 vols. Edited by S. M. Stern. Translated by C. R. Barber and S. M. Stern. Chicago: Aldine, 1966.

Grabar, Oleg. "The Umayyad Dome of the Rock in Jerusalem." *Ars Orientalis* 3 (1959): 33–62.

Graham, William A. *Divine Word and Prophetic Word in Early Islam: A Reconsideration of the Sources, with Special Reference to the Divine Saying or Ḥadîth Qudsî*. The Hague: Mouton, 1977.

Gray, Louis H. "The Kings of Early Irān according to the Sidrā Rabbā." *Zeitschrift für Assyriologie und vorderasiatische Archäologie* 19, no. 2 (1906): 272–87.

Grignaschi, Mario. "La Nihāyatu-l-'Arab fī Aẖbāri-l-Furs wa-l-'Arab." Pt. 1. *Bulletin d'études orientales* 22 (1969): 15–67.

———. "La *Nihāyatu-l-'Arab fī Aẖbāri-l-Furs wa-l-'Arab* et les *Siyaru Mulūki-l-'Ağam* du Ps. Ibn-al-Muqaffa'." *Bulletin d'études orientales* 26 (1973): 83–184.

Grunebaum, G. E. von. *Islam: Essays in the Nature and Growth of a Cultural Tradition*. Menasha, WI: American Anthropological Association, 1955.

Günther, Sebastian. "Illiteracy." In *Encyclopaedia of the Qur'ān*, 2:492–500.

———. "Ummī." In *Encyclopaedia of the Qur'ān*, 5:399–403.

Gutas, Dimitri. *Greek Thought, Arabic Culture: The Graeco-Arabic Translation Movement in Baghdad and Early 'Abbāsid Society (2nd–4th/8th–10th Centuries)*. New York: Routledge, 1998.

Haarmann, Ulrich. "Medieval Muslim Perceptions of Pharaonic Egypt." In *Ancient Egyptian Literature: History and Forms*, edited by Antonio Loprieno, 605–27. Leiden: E. J. Brill, 1996.

———. "Regional Sentiment in Medieval Islamic Egypt." *Bulletin of the School of Oriental and African Studies* 43, no. 1 (1980): 55–66.

Halbwachs, Maurice. *On Collective Memory*. Translated by Lewis A. Coser. Chicago: University of Chicago Press, 1992.

Hämeen-Anttila, Jaakko. "The Corruption of Christianity: Salmān al-Fārisī's Quest as a Paradigmatic Model." *Studia Orientalia* 85 (1999): 115–26.

Hamidullah, Muhammad. "La lettre du Prophète à Héraclius et le sort de l'original." *Arabica* 2, no. 1 (1955): 97–110.

———. *Majmūʿat al-wathāʾiq al-siyāsiyya li-l-ʿahd al-nabawī wa-l-khilāfa al-rāshida*. 3rd ed. Beirut: Dār al-Irshād li-l-Ṭibāʿa wa-l-Nashr wa-l-Tawzīʿ, 1969.

———. "Original de la lettre du Prophète à Kisrà." *Rivista degli Studi orientali* 40 (1965): 57–69.

———. *Le Prophète de l'Islam*. 2 vols. Paris: J. Vrin, 1959.

———. *Six originaux des lettres du Prophète de l'islam: Étude paléographique et historique des lettres du Prophète*. Paris: Tougui, 1985.

Harley Walker, C. T. "Jāḥiẓ of Baṣra to al-Fatḥ ibn Khāqān on the 'Exploits of the Turks and the Army of the Khalifate in General.'" *Journal of the Royal Asiatic Society*, n.s., 47, no. 4 (1915): 631–97.

Hartman, Sven S. *Gayōmart: Étude sur le syncrétisme dans l'ancien Iran*. Uppsala: Almqvist & Wiksells Boktryckeri, 1953.

Hawting, G. R. "The Disappearance and Rediscovery of Zamzam and the 'Well of the Kaʿba.'" *Bulletin of the School of Oriental and African Studies* 43, no. 1 (1980): 44–54.

———. *The Idea of Idolatry and the Emergence of Islam: From Polemic to History*. Cambridge: Cambridge University Press, 1999.

———. "Muḥammad b. Abī Bakr." In *Encyclopaedia of Islam*. 2nd ed.

Heck, Paul L. *The Construction of Knowledge in Islamic Civilization: Qudāma b. Jaʿfar and his Kitāb al-kharāj wa-ṣināʿat al-kitāba*. Leiden: Brill, 2002.

Heidemann, Stefan. "Numismatics." In *The New Cambridge History of Islam*, vol. 1, *The Formation of the Islamic World, Sixth to Eleventh Centuries*, edited by Chase F. Robinson, 648–63, 775–9, and plates. Cambridge: Cambridge University Press, 2010.

Hinz, Walther. *Islamische Masse und Gewichte: Umgerechnet ins metrische System*. Leiden: E. J. Brill, 1955.

Hirschler, Konrad. *The Written Word in the Medieval Arabic Lands: A Social and Cultural History of Reading Practices*. Edinburgh: Edinburgh University Press, 2012.

Hjerrild, Bodil. *Studies in Zoroastrian Family Law: A Comparative Analysis*. Copenhagen: Museum Tusculanum Press, 2003.

Hobsbawm, Eric, and Terence Ranger, eds. *The Invention of Tradition*. Cambridge: Cambridge University Press, 1983.

Horovitz, Josef. "Bulūqjā." *Zeitschrift der Deutschen Morgenländischen Gesellschaft* 55 (1901): 519–25.

———. "Salmān al-Fārisi." *Der Islam* 12, no. 3–4 (1922): 178–83.

Howard-Johnston, James. "The Two Great Powers in Late Antiquity: A Comparison." In *The Byzantine and Early Islamic Near East*, vol. 3, *States, Resources and Armies*, edited by Averil Cameron, 157–226. Princeton, NJ: Darwin Press, 1995.

———. *Witness to a World Crisis: Historians and Histories of the Middle East in the Seventh Century*. Oxford: Oxford University Press, 2010.

Hoyland, Robert G. "Arabic, Syriac and Greek Historiography in the First Abbasid Century: An Inquiry into Inter-Cultural Traffic." *ARAM Periodical* 3, no. 1 (1991): 211–33.

———. *Seeing Islam as Others Saw It: A Survey and Evaluation of Christian, Jewish, and Zoroastrian Writings on Early Islam*. Princeton, NJ: Darwin Press, 1997.

Huart, Cl. "Selmân du Fârs." In *Mélanges Hartwig Derenbourg (1844–1908)*, 297–310. Paris: Ernest Leroux, 1909.

Humphreys, R. Stephen. *Islamic History: A Framework for Inquiry*. Rev. ed. Princeton, NJ: Princeton University Press, 1991.

Inostranzev, M. *Iranian Influence on Moslem Literature*. Pt. 1. Translated by G. K. Nariman. Bombay: D. B. Taraporevala Sons, 1918.

Iqbal, Afzal. *The Prophet's Diplomacy: The Art of Negotiation as Conceived and Developed by the Prophet of Islam*. Cape Cod, MA: Claude Stark, 1975.

Ivanow, W. "Notes sur l''Ummu'l-Kitab': Des Ismaëliens de l'Asie Centrale." *Revue des études islamiques* 6 (1932): 419–81.

Izzi Dien, Mawil Y., and P. E. Walker. "Wilāya." In *Encyclopaedia of Islam*. 2nd ed.

Jackson, A. V. Williams. "The Location of the Farnbāg Fire, the Most Ancient of the Zoroastrian Fires." *Journal of the American Oriental Society* 41 (1921): 81–106.

Al-Jādir, Maḥmūd ʿAbd Allāh. "Al-Thaʿālibī: Nāqidan wa-adīban." M.A. thesis, Baghdad University, 1974.

Al-Jazeera. "Elbaradei urges Mubarak to quit." Jan. 29, 2011. http://www.aljazeera.com/news/middleeast/2011/01/201112919263354 2354.html.

Jeffery, Arthur. "Ghevond's Text of the Correspondence between ʿUmar II and Leo III." *Harvard Theological Review* 37, no. 4 (1944): 269–332.

Judd, Steven C. "Competitive Hagiography in Biographies of al-Awzāʿī and Sufyān al-Thawrī." *Journal of the American Oriental Society* 122, no. 1 (2002): 25–37.

Kamaly, Hossein. "Isfahan vi. Medieval Period." In *Encyclopaedia Iranica*.

Keall, E. J. "Ayvān-e Kesrā (or Ṭāq-e Kesrā)." In *Encyclopaedia Iranica*.

Kemper, Steven. *The Presence of the Past: Chronicles, Politics, and Culture in Sinhala Life*. Ithaca, NY: Cornell University Press, 1991.

Kennedy, Hugh. *The Early Abbasid Caliphate: A Political History*. London: Croom Helm, 1981.

———. "The Financing of the Military in the Early Islamic State." In *The Byzantine and Early Islamic Near East, East*, vol. 3, *States, Resources and Armies*, edited by Averil Cameron, 361–78. Princeton, NJ: Darwin Press, 1995.

———. "From Oral Tradition to Written Record in Arabic Genealogy." *Arabica* 44, no. 4 (1997): 531–44.

———. "From Shahristan to Medina." *Studia Islamica*, no. 102/103 (2006): 5–34.

———. *The Great Arab Conquests: How the Spread of Islam Changed the World We Live In*. London: Weidenfeld & Nicolson, 2007.

———. *An Historical Atlas of Islam/Atlas historique de l'Islam*. 2nd ed. Leiden: Brill, 2002.

———. "Al-Mutawakkil ʿAlā 'llāh, Abū 'l-Faḍl D̲jaʿfar b. Muḥammad." In *Encyclopaedia of Islam*. 2nd ed.

———. *The Prophet and the Age of the Caliphates: The Islamic Near East from the Sixth to the Eleventh Century*. London: Longman, 1986.

———. "Survival of Iranianness." In *The Idea of Iran*, vol. 4, *The Rise of Islam*, edited by Vesta Sarkhosh Curtis and Sarah Stewart, 13–29. London: I. B. Tauris, 2009.

Khaleghi-Motlagh, Djalal. "Ferdowsi, Abu'l-Qāsem, i. Life." In *Encyclopaedia Iranica*.

Khalidi, Tarif. *Arabic Historical Thought in the Classical Period*. Cambridge: Cambridge University Press, 1994.

———. *Islamic Historiography: The Histories of Masʿūdī*. Albany: State University of New York Press, 1975.

Khalidov, Anas B. "Ebn al-Faqīh, Abū Bakr Aḥmad." In *Encyclopaedia Iranica*.

Khatibi, Abolfazl, and John Cooper. "Abū ʿAlī Balkhī." In *Encyclopaedia Islamica*, edited by Wilferd Madelung and Farhad Daftary. Online ed. Leiden: Brill, 2008.

Kiani, Muhammad Yusof. "Excavations on the Defensive Wall of the Gurgān Plain: A Preliminary Report." *Iran* 20 (1982): 73–9.

———. "Gorgān iv. Archaeology." In *Encyclopaedia Iranica*.

Kister, M. J. "Al-Ḥīra: Some Notes on Its Relations with Arabia." *Arabica* 15, no. 2 (1968): 143–69.

Kohlberg, Etan. "Some Imāmī Shīʿī Views on the *Ṣaḥāba*." *Jerusalem Studies in Arabic and Islam* 5 (1984): 143–75.

Kramers, J. H., and M. Morony. "Marzpān." In *Encyclopaedia of Islam*. 2nd ed.

Krawulsky, Dorothea. *Īrān, das Reich der Īlḫāne: Eine topographisch-historische Studie*. Wiesbaden: Dr. Ludwig Reichert, 1978.

———. *Mongolen und Ilkhâne: Ideologie und Geschichte; 5 Studien*. Beirut: Verlag für Islamische Studien, 1989.

Lambton, Ann K. S. "An Account of the *Tārīkhi Qumm*." *Bulletin of the School of Oriental and African Studies* 12, no. 3/4 (1948): 586–96.

———. "Qum: The Evolution of a Medieval City." *Journal of the Royal Asiatic Society*, n.s., 122, no. 2 (1990): 322–39.

———, and J. Sourdel-Thomine. "Isfahan." In *Historic Cities of the Islamic World*, edited by C. Edmund Bosworth, 167–80. Leiden: Brill, 2007.

Landau-Tasseron, Ella. "Sayf b. ʿUmar in Medieval and Modern Scholarship." *Der Islam* 67, no. 1 (1990): 1–26.

Latham, J. Derek. "Ebn al-Moqaffaʿ, Abū Moḥammad ʿAbd-Allāh Rōzbeh." In *Encyclopaedia Iranica*.

———. "Ibn al-Muqaffaʿ and Early ʿAbbasid Prose." In *ʿAbbasid Belles-Lettres*, edited by Julia Ashtiany et al., 48–77. Cambridge: Cambridge University Press, 1990.

Lazard, G. "Abu'l-Moʾayyad Balḵī." In *Encyclopaedia Iranica*.

Lecker, Michael. "The Levying of Taxes for the Sasanians in Pre-Islamic Medina." *Jerusalem Studies in Arabic and Islam* 27 (2002): 109–26.

Leder, Stefan. "Heraklios erkennt den Propheten: Ein Beispiel für Form und Entstehungsweise narrativer Geschichtskonstruktionen." *Zeitschrift der Deutschen Morgenländischen Gesellschaft* 151 (2001): 1–42.

———. "Al-Wāḳidī." In *Encyclopaedia of Islam*. 2nd ed.

Leemhuis, Fred. "Ms. 1075 Tafsīr of the Cairene Dār al-Kutub and Muğāhid's *Tafsīr*." In *Proceedings of the Ninth Congress of the Union Européenne des Arabisants et Islamisants* (Amsterdam, Sept. 1–7, 1978), edited by Rudolph Peters, 169–77. Leiden: E. J. Brill, 1981.

———. "Origins and Early Development of the *Tafsīr* Tradition." In *Approaches to the History of the Interpretation of the Qur'ān*, edited by Andrew Rippin, 13–30. Oxford: Clarendon, 1988.

Leslie, Donald Daniel. "Japhet in China." *Journal of the American Oriental Society* 104, no. 3 (1984): 403–9.

Le Strange, Guy. *The Lands of the Eastern Caliphate: Mesopotamia, Persia, and Central Asia, from the Moslem Conquest to the Time of Timur*. Cambridge: Cambridge University Press, 1905. Reprint, Boston: Adamant Media, 2006.

Levi Della Vida, G. "Salmān al-Fārisī." In *Encyclopaedia of Islam*. 2nd ed.

Levin, Yigal. "Nimrod the Mighty, King of Kish, King of Sumer and Akkad." *Vetus Testamentum* 52, no. 3 (2002): 350–66.

Lewin, B. "Al-Dīnawarī." In *Encyclopaedia of Islam*. 2nd ed.

Lichtenstädter, Ilse. "Muḥammad b. Ḥabīb and His Kitâb al-Muḥabbar." *Journal of the Royal Asiatic Society*, n.s., 71, no. 1 (1939): 1–27.

Lincoln, Bruce. *Death, War, and Sacrifice: Studies in Ideology and Practice*. Chicago: University of Chicago Press, 1991.

Lowenthal, David. *The Past Is a Foreign Country*. Cambridge: Cambridge University Press, 1985.

Lowin, Shari L. "Narratives of Villainy: Titus, Nebuchadnezzar, and Nimrod in the *Ḥadīth* and *Midrash Aggadah*." In *The Lineaments of Islam: Studies in Honor of Fred McGraw Donner*, edited by Paul M. Cobb, 261–96. Leiden: Brill, 2012.

Luria, Aleksandr Romanovich. *The Mind of a Mnemonist: A Little Book about a Vast Memory*. Translated by Lynn Solotaroff. Cambridge, MA: Harvard University Press, 1987.

MacKenzie, D. Neil. "Bundahišn." In *Encyclopaedia Iranica*.

Macuch, M. "Pahlavi Literature." In *The Literature of Pre-Islamic Iran*, companion volume 1 to *A History of Persian Literature*, edited by Ronald E. Emmerick and Maria Macuch, 116–96. London: I. B. Tauris, 2009.

Madelung, Wilferd. "The Assumption of the Title Shāhānshāh by the Būyids and 'the Reign of the Daylam (*Dawlat al-Daylam*).'" *Journal of Near Eastern Studies* 28, no. 2 (1969): 84–108.

Makdisi, George. "*Ṭabaqāt*-Biography: Law and Orthodoxy in Classical Islam," *Islamic Studies* (Islamabad) 32, no. 4 (1993): 371–96.

Malandra, W. W. "Zoroaster ii. General Survey." In *Encyclopaedia Iranica*.

Marashi, Afshin. *Nationalizing Iran: Culture, Power, and the State, 1870–1940*. Seattle: University of Washington Press, 2008.

———. “The Nation’s Poet: Ferdowsi and the Iranian National Imagination.” In *Iran in the 20th Century: Historiography and Political Culture*, edited by Touraj Atabaki, 93–111. London: I. B. Tauris, 2009.

Margoliouth, D. S. *Mohammed and the Rise of Islam*. 3rd ed. New York: G. P. Putnam’s Sons, 1905.

Marzolph, Ulrich. “Islamische Kultur als Gedächtniskultur: Fachspezifische Überlegungen anhand des Fallbeispiels Iran.” *Der Islam* 75, no. 2 (1998): 296–317.

Mashkūr, Muḥammad Javād. *Tārīkh-i siyāsī-yi Sāsāniyān*. Tehran: Dunyā-yi Kitāb, 1987.

Massignon, Louis. *Salmān Pāk and the Spiritual Beginnings of Iranian Islām*. Translated by Jamshedji Maneckji Unvala. Bombay: n.p., 1955.

———. *Salmân Pâk et les prémices spirituelles de l’Islam iranien*. Tours: Arrault, 1934.

Meisami, Julie Scott. “The Past in Service of the Present: Two Views of History in Medieval Persia.” “Cultural Processes in Muslim and Arab Societies: Medieval and Early Modern Periods,” special issue, *Poetics Today* 14, no. 2 (1993): 247–75.

———. *Persian Historiography to the End of the Twelfth Century*. Edinburgh: Edinburgh University Press, 1999.

Melchert, Christopher. *The Formation of the Sunni Schools of Law, 9th–10th Centuries C.E.* Leiden: Brill, 1997.

———. “Ḥasan Baṣri.” In *Encyclopaedia Iranica*.

———. “How Ḥanafism Came to Originate in Kufa and Traditionalism in Medina.” *Islamic Law and Society* 6, no. 3 (1999): 318–47.

———. Review of *The History of an Islamic School of Law: The Early Spread of Hanafism*, by Nurit Tsafrir. *Journal of Near Eastern Studies* 67, no. 3 (2008): 228–30.

Menasce, J. de. “Zoroastrian Literature after the Muslim Conquest.” In *The Cambridge History of Iran*, vol. 4, *The Period from the Arab Invasion to the Saljuqs*, edited by R. N. Frye, 543–65. Cambridge: Cambridge University Press, 1975.

———. “Zoroastrian Pahlavī Writings.” In *The Cambridge History of Iran*, vol. 3(2), *The Seleucid, Parthian and Sasanian Periods*, edited by Ehsan Yarshater, 1166–95. Cambridge: Cambridge University Press, 1983.

Mignan, Robert. *Travels in Chaldæa, including a Journey from Bussorah to Bagdad, Hillah, and Babylon, Performed on Foot in 1827: With Observations on the Sites and Remains of Babel, Seleucia, and Ctesiphon*. London: Henry Colburn and Richard Bentley, 1829.

Minorsky, Vladimir. *Medieval Iran and Its Neighbours*. London: Variorum Reprints, 1982.

———. “Nihāwand.” in *Encyclopaedia of Islam*. 2nd ed.

———. “The Older Preface to the *Shāh-nāma*.” In *Studi orientalistici in onore di Giorgio Levi Della Vida*, 2 vols., 2:159–79. Rome: Istituto per l’Oriente, 1956.

Miquel, André. *La géographie humaine au monde musulman jusqu’au milieu du 11e siècle*. 2nd ed. 3 vols. Paris: Mouton, 1973–80.

Mochiri, Malek Iradj. "A Pahlavi Forerunner of the Umayyad Reformed Coinage." *Journal of the Royal Asiatic Society*, n.s., 113, no. 2 (1981): 168–72.
Modarressi, Hossein [Ḥusayn Mudarrisī Ṭabāṭabāʾī]. *Kitāb-shināsī-yi āsār-i marbūṭ bih Qum*. Qum: Ḥikmat, 1353 *shamsī*/1974.
Mohammadi-Malayeri, Mohammad [Muḥammad Muḥammadī-Malāyirī]. *Iranian Civilization and Culture: Before Islam and Its Impact on Islamic Civilization and Arab Literature*. Translated by Shahrokh Mohammadi-Malayeri. New Delhi: Manohar, 2012.
———. *Tārīkh va farhang-i Irān dar dawrān-i intiqāl az ʿaṣr-i sāsānī bih ʿaṣr-i islāmī*. Vols. 1 and 2. Tehran, 1996–7.
Morgan, David. *Medieval Persia, 1040–1797*. London: Longman, 1988.
Morimoto, Kazuo. "Putting the *Lubāb al-ansāb* in Context: *Sayyid*s and *Naqīb*s in Late Saljuq Khurasan." *Studia Iranica* 36, no. 2 (2007): 163–83.
Morony, Michael G. "The Age of Conversions: A Reassessment." In *Conversion and Continuity: Indigenous Christian Communities in Islamic Lands, Eighth to Eighteenth Centuries*, edited by Michael Gervers and Ramzi Jibran Bikhazi, 135–50. Toronto: Pontifical Institute of Mediaeval Studies, 1990.
———. *Iraq after the Muslim Conquest*. Princeton, NJ: Princeton University Press, 1984.
Mottahedeh, Roy Parviz. "The Eastern Travels of Solomon: Reimagining Persepolis and the Iranian Past." In *Law and Tradition in Classical Islamic Thought: Studies in Honor of Professor Hossein Modarressi*, edited by Michael Cook, Najam Haider, Intisar Rabb, and Asma Sayeed, 247–67. New York: Palgrave Macmillan, 2012.
———. "Finding *Iran* in the Panegyrics of the Ghaznavid Court." Paper presented at the conference "Eastern Iran and Transoxiana 750–1150: Persianate Culture and Islamic Civilization," Institute of Iranian Studies, University of St. Andrews, March 9, 2013.
———. "The Idea of Iran in the Buyid Dominions." In *The Idea of Iran*, vol. 5, *Early Islamic Iran*, edited by Edmund Herzig and Sarah Stewart, 153–60. London: I. B. Tauris, 2012.
———. "Some Islamic Views of the Pre-Islamic Past." *Harvard Middle Eastern and Islamic Review* 1, no. 1 (1994): 17–26.
Motzki, Harald. "ʿAbd al-Razzāq al-Ṣanʿānī." In *Encyclopaedia of Islam*. 3rd ed.
———. "The *Muṣannaf* of ʿAbd al-Razzāq al-Ṣanʿānī as a Source of Authentic *Aḥādīth* of the First Century A.H." *Journal of Near Eastern Studies* 50, no. 1 (1991): 1–21.
———. "The Role of Non-Arab Converts in the Development of Early Islamic Law." *Islamic Law and Society* 6, no. 3 (1999): 293–317.
———, with Nicolet Boekhoff-Van Der Voort and Sean W. Anthony. *Analysing Muslim Traditions: Studies in Legal, Exegetical and Maghāzī Ḥadīth*. Leiden: Brill, 2010.
Mourad, Suleiman Ali. *Early Islam between Myth and History: Al-Ḥasan al-Baṣrī (d. 110H/728CE) and the Formation of His Legacy in Classical Islamic Scholarship*. Leiden: Brill, 2006.

Nastich, Vladimir N. "Persian Legends on Islamic Coins: From Traditional Arabic to the Challenge of Leadership." In *The 2nd Simone Assemani Symposium on Islamic Coins*, edited by Bruno Callagher and Arianna D'Ottone, 165–90. Trieste: Edizioni Università di Trieste, 2010.

Nawas, John A. "A Profile of the *Mawālī ʿUlamāʾ*." In *Patronate and Patronage in Early and Classical Islam*, edited by Monique Bernards and John Nawas, 454–80. Leiden: Brill, 2005.

Newby, Gordon Darnell. *The Making of the Last Prophet: A Reconstruction of the Earliest Biography of Muhammad*. Columbia: University of South Carolina Press, 1989.

Newman, Andrew J. *The Formative Period of Twelver Shīʿism: Ḥadīth as Discourse between Qum and Baghdad*. Richmond: Curzon, 2000.

Newman, Barclay M., Jr. "Matthew 1.1–18: Some Comments and a Suggested Restructuring." *Bible Translator* 27, no. 2 (1976): 209–12.

Neyzi, Leyla. "Remembering to Forget: Sabbateanism, National Identity, and Subjectivity in Turkey." *Comparative Studies in Society and History* 44, no. 1 (2002): 137–58.

Nöldeke, Theodor. *Delectus veterum carminum arabicorum*. Berlin: H. Reuther, 1890.

———. *Geschichte der Perser und Araber zur Zeit der Sasaniden aus der arabischen Chronik des Tabari*. Leiden: E. J. Brill, 1879. Reprint, 1973.

———. *Das Iranische Nationalepos*. Berlin: de Gruyter, 1920.

Nora, Pierre. "Between Memory and History: *Les lieux de mémoire*." Translated by Marc Roudebush. "Memory and Counter-Memory," special issue, *Representations*, no. 26 (1989): 7–24.

———, ed. *Les Lieux de mémoire*. Vol. 1. Paris: Gallimard, 1997.

Noth, Albrecht. "Der Charakter der ersten großen Sammlungen von Nachrichten zur frühen Kalifenzeit." *Der Islam* 47 (1971): 168–99.

———, with Lawrence I. Conrad. *The Early Arabic Historical Tradition: A Source-Critical Study*. 2nd ed. Translated by Michael Bonner. Princeton, NJ: Darwin Press, 1994.

Omidsalar, Mahmoud. "Could al-Thaʿâlibî Have Used the *Shâhnâma* as a Source?" *Der Islam* 75, no. 2 (1998): 338–46.

———. "Dīv." In *Encyclopaedia Iranica*.

Orfali, Bilal Walid. "The Art of Anthology: Al-Thaʿālibī and His *Yatīmat al-dahr*." Ph.D. dissertation, Yale University, 2009.

Özkirimli, Umut. "The Nation as an Artichoke? A Critique of Ethnosymbolist Interpretations of Nationalism." *Nations and Nationalism* 9, no. 3 (2003): 339–55.

Ozouf, Jacques, and Mona Ozouf. "*Le Tour de la France par deux enfants*: Le petit livre rouge de la République." In *Les Lieux de mémoire*, edited by Pierre Nora, 1:277–301. Paris: Gallimard, 1997.

Paul, Jürgen. "The Histories of Herat." *Iranian Studies* 33, no. 1/2 (2000): 93–115.

———. "The Histories of Isfahan: Mafarrukhi's *Kitāb maḥāsin Iṣfahān*." *Iranian Studies* 33, no. 1/2 (2000): 117–32.

———. "Isfahan v. Local Historiography." In *Encyclopaedia Iranica*.

Paul, Ludwig. "The Language of the *Šāhnāme* in Historical and Dialectical Perspective." In *Languages of Iran: Past and Present; Iranian Studies in Memoriam David Neil MacKenzie*, edited by Dieter Weber, 141–51. Wiesbaden: Harrassowitz, 2005.
Peacock, Andrew C. S. *Mediaeval Islamic Historiography and Political Legitimacy: Balʿamī's Tārīkhnāma*. London: Routledge, 2007.
Pellat, Charles. "Dīnavarī, Abū Ḥanīfa Aḥmad." In *Encyclopaedia Iranica*.
———. "Al-Naḍr b. al-Ḥārith." In *Encyclopaedia of Islam*. 2nd ed.
Pettigrew, Mark Fraser. "The Wonders of the Ancients: Arab-Islamic Representations of Ancient Egypt." Ph.D. dissertation, University of California, Berkeley, 2004.
Planhol, Xavier de. "Fārs i. Geography." In *Encyclopaedia Iranica*.
Plessner, M., and A. Rippin. "Muḳātil b. Sulaymān." In *Encyclopaedia of Islam*. 2nd ed.
Pourshariati, Parvaneh. "The *Akhbār al-Ṭiwāl* of Abū Ḥanīfa Dīnawarī: A *Shuʿūbī* Treatise on Late Antique Iran." In *Sources for the History of Sasanian and Post-Sasanian Iran*, edited by Rika Gyselen, 201–89. Bures-sur-Yvette: Groupe pour l'Étude de la Civilisation du Moyen-Orient, 2010.
———. *Decline and Fall of the Sasanian Empire: The Sasanian-Parthian Confederacy and the Arab Conquest of Iran*. London: I. B. Tauris, 2008.
———. "Local Histories of Khurāsān and the Pattern of Arab Settlement." *Studia Iranica* 27, no. 1 (1998): 41–81.
———. "The Mihrāns and the Articulation of Islamic Dogma: A Preliminary Prosopographical Analysis." In *Trésors d'Orient: Mélanges offerts à Rika Gyselen*, edited by Philippe Gignoux, Christelle Jullien, and Florence Jullien, 283–315. Paris: Association pour l'avancement des études iraniennes, 2009.
Prideaux, Humphrey. *The True Nature of Imposture Fully Display'd in the Life of Mahomet, with a Discourse annex'd for the Vindication of Christianity from this Charge, Offered to the Consideration of the Deists of the Present Age*. 8th ed. London: E. Curll, 1723.
Puin, Gerd-Rüdiger. "Der Dīwān von ʿUmar ibn al-Ḫaṭṭāb: Ein Beitrag zur frühislamischen Verwaltungeschichte." Ph.D. dissertation, Rheinische Friedrich-Wilhelms-Universität, 1970.
Pūrjavādī, Naṣr Allāh. *Dū mujaddid: Pazhūhishhā-yi dar bārah-yi Muḥammad Ghazzālī va Fakhr al-Rāzī*. Markaz-i Nashr-i Dānishgāhī, 1381/[2002 or 2003].
Pyrovolaki, Marina. "*Futūḥ al-Shām* and Other *Futūḥ* Texts: A Study of the Perception of Marginal Conquest Narratives in Arabic in Medieval and Modern Times." D.Phil. thesis, University of Oxford, 2009.
Raddatz, H. P. "Sufyān al-Thawrī." In *Encyclopaedia of Islam*. 2nd ed.
Rahman, Afzalur. *Muhammad: Encyclopædia of Seerah*. 7 vols. London: Muslim Schools Trust, 1981.
Reitzenstein, Richard, and Hans Heinrich Schaeder. *Studien zum antiken Synkretismus aus Iran und Griechenland*. Leipzig: B. G. Teubner, 1926.
Renan, Ernest. "What Is a Nation?" Translated by Martin Thom. In *Nation and Narration*, edited by Homi K. Bhabha, 8–22. London: Routledge, 1990.
Retsö, Jan. *The Arabs in Antiquity: Their History from the Assyrians to the Umayyads*. London: RoutledgeCurzon, 2005.

Reuther, Oscar. "The German Excavations at Ctesiphon." *Antiquity* 3, no. 12 (1929): 434–51.

Reynolds, Gabriel Said. *A Muslim Theologian in the Sectarian Milieu: ʿAbd al-Jabbār and the Critique of Christian Origins*. Leiden: Brill, 2004.

Ricœur, Paul. *Memory, History, Forgetting*. Translated by Kathleen Blamey and David Pellauer. Chicago: University of Chicago Press, 2004.

Rippin, Andrew. "Introduction." In *Approaches to the History of the Interpretation of the Qurʾān*, edited by Andrew Rippin, 1–9. Oxford: Clarendon, 1988.

Robinson, Chase F. "The Conquest of Khūzistān: A Historiographical Reassessment." *Bulletin of the School of Oriental and African Studies* 67, no. 1 (2004): 14–39.

———. "The Ideological Uses of Early Islam." *Past & Present*, no. 203 (2009): 205–28.

———. *Islamic Historiography*. Cambridge: Cambridge University Press, 2003.

———. "The Rise of Islam." In *The New Cambridge History of Islam*, vol. 1, *The Formation of the Islamic World, Sixth to Eleventh Centuries*, edited by Chase F. Robinson, 173–225. Cambridge: Cambridge University Press, 2010.

Rodinson, Maxime, A. J. Arberry, and Charles Perry. *Medieval Arab Cookery*. Blackawton, Devon: Prospect Books, 2001.

Roggema, Barbara. *The Legend of Sergius Baḥīrā: Eastern Christian Apologetics and Apocalyptic in Response to Islam*. Leiden: Brill, 2009.

Rosenthal, Franz. "Asāṭīr al-Awwalīn." In *Encyclopaedia of Islam*. 2nd ed.

———. "Ebn Qotayba, Abū Moḥammad ʿAbd-Allāh." In *Encyclopaedia Iranica*.

———. "From Arabic Books and Manuscripts I: Pseudo-Aṣmaʿī on the Pre-Islamic Arab Kings." *Journal of the American Oriental Society* 69, no. 2 (1949): 90–1.

———. "From Arabic Books and Manuscripts III: The Author of the Ġurar as-siyar." *Journal of the American Oriental Society* 70, no. 3 (1950): 181–2.

———. "The Influence of the Biblical Tradition on Muslim Historiography." In *Historians of the Middle East*, edited by Bernard Lewis and P. M. Holt, 35–45. London: Oxford University Press, 1962.

Rubin, Uri. *The Eye of the Beholder: The Life of Muḥammad as Viewed by the Early Muslims*. Princeton, NJ: Darwin Press, 1995.

Rubin, Zeev. "Ḥamza al-Iṣfahānī's Sources for Sasanian History." *Jerusalem Studies in Arabic and Islam* 35 (2008): 27–58.

———. "Ibn al-Muqaffaʿ and the Account of Sasanian History in the Arabic Codex Sprenger 30." *Jerusalem Studies in Arabic and Islam* 30 (2005): 52–93.

Saleh, Walid A. *The Formation of the Classical* Tafsīr *Tradition: The Qurʾān Commentary of al-Thaʿlabī (d. 427/1035)*. Leiden: Brill, 2004.

Sauer, Eberhard W., et al. *Persia's Imperial Power in Late Antiquity: The Great Wall of Gorgān and Frontier Landscapes of Sasanian Iran*. Oxford: Oxbow Books, 2013.

Savant, Sarah Bowen. "The Conquest of Tustar: Site of Memory, Site of Forgetting." In *Violence in Early Islamic Thought*, edited by István Kristó-Nagy and Robert Gleave. Edinburgh: Edinburgh University Press, forthcoming.

———. "Forgetting Ctesiphon: Iran's Pre-Islamic Past, ca. 800–1100." In *History and Identity in the Late Antique Near East*, edited by Philip Wood, 169–86. Oxford: Oxford University Press, 2013.

———, "Genealogy." In *The Princeton Encyclopedia of Islamic Political Thought*, edited by Gerhard Böwering et al., 189–90. Princeton, NJ: Princeton University Press, 2012.

———. "Genealogy and Ethnogenesis in al-Mas'udi's *Muruj al-Dhahab*." In *Genealogy and Knowledge in Muslim Societies: Understanding the Past*, edited by Sarah Bowen Savant and Helena de Felipe. Edinburgh: Edinburgh University Press, 2013.

———. "Isaac as the Persians' Ishmael: Pride and the Pre-Islamic Past in Ninth and Tenth-Century Islam." *Comparative Islamic Studies* 2, no. 1 (2006): 5–25.

———. "'Persians' in Early Islam," *Annales Islamologiques* 42 (2008): 73–91.

Schacht, J. "'Ikrima." In *Encyclopaedia of Islam*. 2nd ed.

Scheler, Max. *Problems of a Sociology of Knowledge*. Translated by Manfred S. Frings. Edited by Kenneth W. Stikkers. London: Routledge & Kegan Paul, 1980.

Schippmann, Klaus. "Azerbaijan iii. Pre-Islamic History." In *Encyclopaedia Iranica*.

———. *Die iranischen Feuerheiligtümer*. Berlin: de Gruyter, 1971.

Schmidt, Eric F. *Persepolis*. 3 vols. Chicago: University of Chicago Press, 1953–70.

Schneider, Rolf M. "Orientalism in Late Antiquity: The Oriental in Imperial and Christian Imagery." In *Ērān ud Anērān: Studien zu den Beziehungen zwischen dem Sasanidenreich und der Mittelmeerwelt*, edited by Josef Wiesehöfer and Philip Huyse, 241–78. Munich: Franz Steiner, 2006.

Schoeler, Gregor. *Écrire et transmettre dans les débuts de l'Islam*. Paris: Presses universitaires de France, 2002.

———. *The Genesis of Literature in Islam: From the Aural to the Read*. Rev. ed. Translated by Shawkat M. Toorawa. Edinburgh: Edinburgh University Press, 2009.

Schwartz, Barry. "Collective Memory." In *The Blackwell Encyclopedia of Sociology*, edited by George Ritzer. 11 vols. New York: Blackwell-Wiley, 2007.

Sears, Stuart D. "The Sasanian Style Drachms of Sistan." *Yarmouk Numismatics* 11 (1999): 18–28.

Serjeant, R. B. "Early Arabic Prose." In *Arabic Literature to the End of the Umayyad Period*, edited by A. F. L. Beeston, T. M. Johnstone, R. B. Serjeant, and G. R. Smith, 114–53. Cambridge: Cambridge University Press, 1983.

Serrano, Richard A. "Al-Buḥturī's Poetics of Persian Abodes." *Journal of Arabic Literature* 28, no. 1 (1997): 68–87.

Sezgin, Fuat. *Geschichte des arabischen Schrifttums*. Vol. 1. Leiden: E. J. Brill, 1967.

Shaban, M.A. *The 'Abbāsid Revolution*. Cambridge: Cambridge University Press, 1970.

———. "Ibn A'tham al-Kūfī." In *Encyclopaedia of Islam*. 2nd ed.

Shahbazi [Shabazi], A. Shapur [Shahpur]. "Bahrām vii. Bahrām VI Čōbīn." In *Encyclopaedia Iranica*.

———. "Goštāsp." In *Encyclopaedia Iranica*.

———. "On the *X*^{w}*adāy-nāmag*." In *Iranica Varia: Papers in Honor of Professor Ehsan Yarshater*, 208–29. Leiden: E. J. Brill, 1990.

———. *Persepolis Illustrated.* Persepolis: Institute of Achaemenid Research, 1976.

Shaked, Shaul. "Cosmic Origins and Human Origins in the Iranian Cultural Milieu." In *Genesis and Regeneration: Essays on Conceptions of Origins*, edited by Shaul Shaked, 210–22. Jerusalem: Israel Academy of Sciences and Humanities, 2005.

———. "First Man, First King: Notes on Semitic-Iranian Syncretism and Iranian Mythical Transformations." In *Gilgul: Essays on Transformation, Revolution and Permanence in the History of Religions; Dedicated to R. J. Zwi Werblowsky*, edited by S. Shaked, D. Shulman, and G. G. Stroumsa, 238–56. Leiden: E. J. Brill, 1987.

———. *From Zoroastrian Iran to Islam: Studies in Religious History and Intercultural Contacts.* Aldershot: Variorum, 1995.

———. "Religion in the Late Sasanian Period: Eran, Aneran, and Other Religious Designations." In *The Idea of Iran*, vol. 3, *The Sasanian Era*, edited by Vesta Sarkhosh Curtis and Sarah Stewart, 103–17. London: I. B. Tauris, 2008.

———. "Some Islamic Reports concerning Zoroastrianism." *Jerusalem Studies in Arabic and Islam* 17 (1994): 43–84.

Shboul, Ahmad M. H. *Al-Masʿūdī and His World: A Muslim Humanist and His Interest in Non-Muslims.* London: Ithaca Press, 1979.

Shils, Edward. *Tradition.* Chicago: University of Chicago Press, 1981.

Shimamoto, Takamitsu. "Some Reflections on the Origin of Qom: Myth and History." *Orient* 27 (1991): 95–113.

Shoshan, Boaz. *Poetics of Islamic Historiography: Deconstructing Ṭabarī's History.* Leiden: Brill, 2004.

Sizgorich, Thomas. "'Do Prophets Come with a Sword?' Conquest, Empire, and Historical Narrative in the Early Islamic World." *American Historical Review* 112, no. 4 (2007): 992–1015.

———. *Violence and Belief in Late Antiquity: Militant Devotion in Christianity and Islam.* Philadelphia: University of Pennsylvania Press, 2009.

Smith, Anthony D. *Chosen Peoples.* Oxford: Oxford University Press, 2003.

———. "Chosen Peoples: Why Ethnic Groups Survive." *Ethnic and Racial Studies* 15, no. 3 (1992): 436–56.

———. "Ethnic Election and Cultural Identity." "Pre-Modern and Modern National Identity in Russia and Eastern Europe," special issue, *Ethnic Studies* 10, no. 1–3 (1993): 9–25.

———. *The Ethnic Origins of Nations.* Oxford: Blackwell, 1986.

———. *Myths and Memories of the Nation.* New York: Oxford University Press, 1999.

———. *The Nation in History: Historiographical Debates about Ethnicity and Nationalism.* Hanover, NH: University Press of New England, 2000.

———. "The 'Sacred' Dimension of Nationalism." *Millennium: Journal of International Studies* 29, no. 3 (2000): 791–814.

Sourdel, Dominique. *Le vizirat ʿabbāside de 749 à 936 (132 à 324 de l'hégire).* 2 vols. Damascus: Institut français de Damas, 1959–60.

Spellberg, D. A. *Politics, Gender, and the Islamic Past: The Legacy of ʿAʾisha bint Abi Bakr.* New York: Columbia University Press, 1994.

Sprengling, M. "From Persian to Arabic." *American Journal of Semitic Languages and Literatures* 56, no. 2 (1939): 175–224.
Stausberg, M. "The Invention of a Canon: The Case of Zoroastrianism." In *Canonization & Decanonization: Papers Presented to the International Conference of the Leiden Institute for the Study of Religions (LISOR) Held at Leiden 9–10 January 1997*, edited by A. van der Kooij and K. van der Toorn, 257–77. Leiden: Brill, 1998.
Stauth, Georg. "Die Überlieferung des Korankommentars Muǧāhid b. Ǧabrs: Zur Frage der Rekonstruktion der in den Sammelwerken des 3. Jh. d. H. benutzten frühislamischen Quellenwerke." Ph.D. dissertation, Universität Giessen, 1969.
Stern, S. M. "Yaʿqūb the Coppersmith and Persian National Sentiment." In *Iran and Islam: In Memory of the Late Vladimir Minorsky*, edited by C. E. Bosworth, 535–55. Edinburgh: Edinburgh University Press, 1971.
Storey, C. A. *Persian Literature: A Bio-Bibliographical Survey*. Vol. 1, pts. 1–2. London: Royal Asiatic Society, 1927–39 and 1953.
Subtelny, Maria. "Between Persian Legend and Samanid Orthodoxy: Accounts about Gayumarth in Balʿami's *Tarikhnama*." In *Ferdowsi, the Mongols and Iranian History: Art, Literature and Culture from Early Islam to Qajar Persia*, edited by Robert Hillenbrand, A. C. S. Peacock, and Firuza Abdullaeva. London: I. B. Tauris, 2013.
Szombathy, Zoltan. "The *Nassâbah*: Anthropological Fieldwork in Mediaeval Islam." *Islamic Culture* 73, no. 3 (1999): 61–108.
Tafazzoli, Ahmad [Aḥmad Tafaẓẓulī]. *Tārīkh-i adabiyāt-i Īrān pīsh az Islām*. Edited by Zhāla Āmūzigār. Tehran: Intishārāt-i Sukhan, 1997.
Tai, Hue-Tam Ho. "Remembered Realms: Pierre Nora and French National Memory." *American Historical Review* 106, no. 3 (2001): 906–22.
Taqīzadeh, Sayyid Ḥasan. "Shāh-nāmah va Firdawsī." In *Hazārah-yi Firdawsī*, 43–107. Tehran: Dunyā-yi Kitāb, 1362 *shamsī*.
Tavakoli-Targhi, Mohamad. "Contested Memories: Narrative Structures and Allegorical Meanings of Iran's Pre-Islamic History." *Iranian Studies* 29, no. 1/2 (1996): 149–75.
———. "Historiography and Crafting Iranian National Identity." In *Iran in the 20th Century: Historiography and Political Culture*, edited by Touraj Atabaki, 5–21. London: I. B. Tauris, 2009.
Toorawa, Shawkat M. *Ibn Abī Ṭāhir Ṭayfūr and Arabic Writerly Culture: A Ninth-Century Bookman in Baghdad*. London: RoutledgeCurzon, 2005.
Toorn, K. van der, and P. W. van der Horst. "Nimrod before and after the Bible." *Harvard Theological Review* 83, no. 1 (1990): 1–29.
Tor, Deborah G. "Historical Representations of Yaʿqūb b. al-Layth: A Reappraisal." *Journal of the Royal Asiatic Society*, 3rd ser., 12, no. 3 (2002): 247–75.
———. "A Numismatic History of the First Saffarid Dynasty (AH 247–300/AD 861–911)." *Numismatic Chronicle*, 7th ser., 162 (2002): 293–314.
Tottoli, Roberto. "Cain and Abel (Qābīl wa Hābīl)." In *Encyclopaedia of Islam*. 3rd ed.

Treadwell, Luke. *Buyid Coinage: A Die Corpus (322–445 A.H.)*. Oxford: Ashmolean Museum Oxford, 2001.
Trevor-Roper, Hugh. "The Invention of Tradition: The Highland Tradition of Scotland." In *The Invention of Tradition*, edited by Eric Hobsbawm and Terence Ranger, 15–41. Cambridge: Cambridge University Press, 1983.
Tsafrir, Nurit. "The Beginnings of the Ḥanafī School in Iṣfahān." *Islamic Law and Society* 5, no. 1 (1998): 1–21.
———. *The History of an Islamic School of Law: The Early Spread of Hanafism*. Cambridge, MA: Islamic Legal Studies Program and Harvard University Press, 2004.
United States Department of State. "July-December, 2010 International Religious Freedom Report: Iran." Sept. 13, 2011. http://www.unhcr.org/refworld/docid/4e734c92c.html.
Utas, Bo. "The Pahlavi Treatise *Avdēh u sahīkēh ī Sakistān* or 'Wonders and Magnificence of Sistan.'" *Acta Antiqua Academiae Scientiarum Hungaricae* 28 (1980): 259–67.
Van Bladel, Kevin. *The Arabic Hermes: From Pagan Sage to Prophet of Science*. Oxford: Oxford University Press, 2009.
Varisco, Daniel Martin. "Metaphors and Sacred History: The Genealogy of Muhammad and the Arab 'Tribe.'" "Anthropological Analysis and Islamic Texts," special issue, *Anthropological Quarterly* 68, no. 3 (1995): 139–56.
Vaziri, Mostafa. *Iran as Imagined Nation: The Construction of National Identity*. New York: Paragon House, 1993.
Veccia Vaglieri, L. "Dhū Ḳār." In *Encyclopaedia of Islam*. 2nd ed.
Wadud, Amina. *Qur'an and Woman: Rereading the Sacred Text from a Woman's Perspective*. 2nd ed. New York: Oxford University Press, 1999.
Wakin, Jeanette, and A. Zysow. "Raʾy." In *Encyclopaedia of Islam*. 2nd ed.
Wansbrough, John. *The Sectarian Milieu: Content and Composition of Islamic Salvation History*. Oxford: Oxford University Press, 1978.
Watt, W. Montgomery. "Al-Ḥudaybiya." In *Encyclopaedia of Islam*. 2nd ed.
———. "Ibn Hishām." In *Encyclopaedia of Islam*. 2nd ed.
Weinrich, Harald. *Lethe: The Art and Critique of Forgetting*. Translated by Steven Rendall. Ithaca, NY: Cornell University Press, 2004.
Wensinck, A. J., and G. Vajda. "Firʿawn." In *Encyclopaedia of Islam*. 2nd ed.
Williams, Alan. *The Zoroastrian Myth of Migration from Iran and Settlement in the Indian Diaspora: Text, Translation and Analysis of the 16th Century Qeṣṣe-ye Sanjān 'The Story of Sanjan.'* Leiden: Brill, 2009.
Wolff, Fritz. *Glossar zu Firdosis Schahname*. Hildesheim: Georg Olms, 1965.
Yamamoto, Kumiko. *The Oral Background of Persian Epics: Storytelling and Poetry*. Leiden: Brill, 2003.
Yarshater, Ehsan. "Iranian Common Beliefs and World-View." In *The Cambridge History of Iran*, vol. 3(1), *The Seleucid, Parthian and Sasanian Periods*, edited by Ehsan Yarshater, 343–58. Cambridge: Cambridge University Press, 1983.
———. "Iranian National History." In *The Cambridge History of Iran*, vol. 3(1), *The Seleucid, Parthian and Sasanian Periods*, edited by Ehsan Yarshater, 359–477. Cambridge: Cambridge University Press, 1983.

Yerushalmi, Yosef Hayim. *Zakhor: Jewish History and Jewish Memory*. Seattle: University of Washington Press, 1996.

Young, James E. Foreword to *Oblivion*, by Marc Augé. Translated by Marjolijn de Jager. Minneapolis: University of Minnesota Press, 2004.

Zadeh, Travis. *Mapping Frontiers across Medieval Islam: Geography, Translation, and the ʿAbbāsid Empire*. London: I. B. Tauris, 2011.

———. "Of Mummies, Poets, and Water Nymphs: Tracing the Codicological Limits of Ibn Khurradādhbih's Geography." In *ʿAbbasid Studies IV: Occasional Papers of the School of ʿAbbasid Studies*, edited by Monique Bernards. Forthcoming: Gibb Memorial Trust.

———. *The Vernacular Qur'an: Translation and the Rise of Persian Exegesis*. London: Oxford University Press, 2012.

Zarrīnkūb, ʿAbd al-Ḥusayn. "The Arab Conquest of Iran and Its Aftermath." In *The Cambridge History of Iran*, vol. 4, *The Period from the Arab Invasion to the Saljuqs*, ed. R. N. Frye, 1–56. Cambridge: Cambridge University Press, 1975.

———. *Dū qarn sukūt*. Tehran: Jāmiʿah-yi Līsānsīyahā-yi Dānishsarā-yi ʿĀlī, 1330 shamsī/[1951]). 2nd ed., Tehran: Amīr Kabīr, 1336 *shamsī*/[1957].

Zetterstéen, K. V. "D̲jalal al-Dawla." In *Encyclopaedia of Islam*. 2nd ed.

Index

Note: References to maps are given in **bold**.

Abadal i de Vinyals, Ramón d', 60
Abarqwayh, 153
ʿAbbasids, 6, 101, 135, 170
ʿAbd Allāh b. Saʿd, 224, 225–26, 228
ʿAbd al-Jabbār, 203–4
ʿAbd al-Malik (caliph), 7, 157, 170, 212
ʿAbd al-Raḥmān b. ʿAwf, 82, 85
Abou El Fadl, Khaled, 194
Abraham, 38n21, 51, 153
  as ancestor to Muḥammad, 32–33
  as ancestor to Persians, 43, 47–49
  as prophet and monotheist, 33–34, 49, 63, 65
Abraham (metropolitan of Porath), 207
Abū al-Bakhtarī, 157
Abū Bakr, 82, 85, 99, 100, 181
Abū Bakra, 191–93, 194
Abū Dardāʾ, 67
Abū Dharr al-Ghifārī, 72, 82, 85
Abū al-Ḥajjāj al-Azdī, 79
Abū Hurayra, 70, 97, 99
Abū Jaʿfar (Muḥammad al-Bāqir), 188
Abū Miḥjan, 201
Abū Mūsā al-Ashʿarī, 124, 207, 209
Abū Nuʿaym al-Iṣfahānī, 75, 79–81
Abū al-Shaykh al-Iṣfahānī, 75, 76–77, 82, 85
Abū Sufyān b. Ḥarb, 99
Abū Tammām, 176
Abū ʿUbayd al-Qāsim b. Sallām, 189
Abū Yūsuf, 97, 112
ʿĀd and Thamūd, 175
Adam, 39, 121, 139, 144
  descent from, 32–33, 121
  as Gayūmart, 42
ʿĀdites, 149–50
Ādur Būrzīn-mitrō, 214
Ādur Farnbāg, 214–15
Ādur Gushnasp, 55, 57, 214
Aḥmad b. Ḥanbal, 170, 181, 192, 193
Ahriman, 120, 122, 141
Ahura Mazdā, 138
Aḥwaṣ b. Saʿd, 223–27, 228
ʿĀʾisha, 97, 100, 112, 170, 191–93
ʿAjam, 107
  as counterpoint to Arabs, 80, 105
  as non-Arabs, 9n18, 70, 80, 148, 176, 209
  as Persians, 9n18, 99, 144, 206, 225–26
Akkad, Moustapha, 184
Alexander the Great, 58, 77
ʿAlī b. Abī Ṭālib, 13, 67, 100, 124, 170
  on Persians, 52
  and Salmān, 61, 67, 71n30
  and Shahrbānū, 104–5, 107–8
  as witness, 82, 83
ʿAlī, ʿAbdullah Yūsuf, 175, 193
Ali, Muhammad Mohar, 173–74
ʿAlī b. al-Jahm, 135
ʿAlī Zayn al-ʿĀbidīn, 102–4, 106

ʿĀmir al-Shaʿbī, 157
Amir-Moezzi, Mohammad Ali, 103, 105
ʿAmmār b. Yāsir, 72, 85
ʿAmr b. al-Layth al-Ṣaffār, 119, 125
Āmul, **xx**, 39, **110**
Anderson, Benedict, 24, 215–16
Anṣār (helpers), 6, 67, 178
  pensions of, 97, 99, 100
anthologizing, 144–45
Aparvīz, 118
Arabian Nights, 6
Arabs
  as ethnic elect, 50–51, 52
  genealogy of, 33, 38
  as identity, 12, 172
  replaced by Persians, 80–81
  tribes of, 33, 38, 51
Ardashīr, 9n20, 59, 193, 231
Armenia, **xix**, 149
Armstrong, John, 60
Arnold, T. W., 92, 185
Arpachshad, descendants of, 33, 149, 150
Asadī Ṭūsī, ʿAlī b. Aḥmad, 121
asāṭīr al-awwalīn, 172–75
Ashʿarīs of Qum, 223, 226, 227, 228
Aṣmaʿī, al-, 97, 156–57
Assmann, Jan, 16–17, 230
astrology, 149, 153
Avesta, 35, 131, 141, 154, 166
Ayyūb b. al-Qirriyya, 157
Azarbaijan, **xx**, 55–56
Āzarmīdukht, 95

Babylon (Bābil), Babylonia, **xx**, 42, 55, 150–51, 153
Bādhān (Sasanian governor), 187–88
Badr, battle of, **xix**, 100, 172
Bahār-i Khusraw, 13
Bahmān, 155
Bahrām Chūbīn, 155
  family of, 218–19, 220–21, 235
Bahrām b. Mihrān Iṣfahānī, 45
Baḥrayn, **xix**, 99
Balādhurī, al-, 210, 219
Balʿamī, 206, 221–22
  sources of, 45
Balkhī, Abū ʿAlī Muḥammad b. Aḥmad al-, 141
Balkhī, Abū al-Muʾayyad, 45, 118
Balūshī, ʿAbd al-Ghafūr, 86
Banū Hāshim, 100
Baradei, Mohamad al-, 162
Basra, **xx**, 192, 207
Battle of the Camel, 191
Battle of the Ditch, 67
Bāwandids, 39n24
belonging, 3, 31, 65, 115
Bernheimer, Teresa, 86
Bible, 37n16
Bilāl, 82, 85, 100, 170
Bīrūnī, al-, 140–41
Bishtāsif (king), 154–55
Blair, Sheila, 73n35
Borrut, Antoine, 15
Brock, Sebastian, 208n30
Brockelmann, Carl, 41n27
Buddhists, 27, 93
Buḥturī, al-, 1, 13–14
Bulliet, Richard, 4–5, 76, 108
Bundahishn, 118, 138, 166
Būrān, 95, 191–93
Burāq, 59
Burrī, al-, 106
Bust (city), **xxi**, **116**, 120, 122, 125
Bust (rural district), 134
Buwayh, Aḥmad b., 7
Buyids, 6, 7–8
Buzurgmihr (vizier), 231
Byzantine Empire, **xix**, 6, 96, 149
Byzantines, 99, 188
  genealogy of, 38
  as monotheists, 178–81, 182

Caesar, 48–49, 176. *See also* Heraclius
Cain and Abel, 165–67
Chaldeans, 154
Children of Israel, 148, 154, 155, 161
  as kin to Persians, 38, 49
  See also Jews
Choksy, Jamsheed, 4n7, 214–15
Christensen, Arthur, 217
Christianity, in story of Salmān, 63–65, 75, 77
Christians, 92, 123, 204n17
  European, genealogies of, 37
  oblivion of, 27, 207, 209–11, 213–14, 235
  as People of the Book, 182
  as source of historical knowledge, 36, 92, 94
clientage (*walāʾ*), 68, 82, 85, 86n88, 87
coinage, 7–8, 117, 212

companions (*ṣaḥāba*), 6
conquest of Mecca by Muslims, 100
conquest of Persia by Arabs, 6, 91, 92–93
  kerygmatic interpretations of, 91–95, 120–21, 129, 203–5
  treaties in, 113, 219
conversion
  to Islam, 5, 17, 66, 68
  to Persianness, 17
  to Zoroastrianism, 154–55
Copts, 161. *See also* Christians
Crone, Patricia, 141
Ctesiphon, **xix**, 2, 13, 21–22, 61, 235
cultural memory, 17n41
Cypress of Bust, 134–35

Ḍaḥḥāk, al-, 42, 56, 149–51
Daniel, Elton, 45
Daryaee, Touraj, 11n25
Davis, Craig, 37n18
Davis, Dick, 146
Daylamites, **xx**, **110**, 224
Debié, Muriel, 140n10
*dhimmī*s (protected people), 219
Dhū al-Qarnayn, 40, 77
*dihqān*s (landed gentry), 63, 108, 221
Dīnawar, **xx**, 151–52, **152**
Dīnawarī, al-, 94, 148, 152, 177
disobedience to God, 153–54, 159
dīwān (pension register), 86, 96–100
  etymology of, 96, 97
Donner, Fred, 47n50, 91n5, 204–5
Drory, Rina, 172
Dūrī, ʿIzzat Ibrāhīm al-, 200
Durkheim, Émile, 18

Eco, Umberto, 24, 136
Egypt, **xix**, 160–61, 164
El Cheikh, Nadia Maria, 178, 179, 181
election, 49–50
  of Arabs, 50–51, 52
  of Arabs and Persians, 104, 106
Ērān, 9–10. *See also* Iran, Iranians

Farīdūn, 40, 150–51
Fāris, 9, 11, 52, 69, 71n29. *See also* Persians
Fārs, **xx**, 11, 49, 57, **58**, 149
  meaning of, 9, 10n23
  See also Persia
Fārs-nāmah, 57, 231
fatḥ, *futūḥ* (opening, conquest), 205, 234
Fayrūzān, al-, 99, 101
Firdawsī, 146n32, 177, 206
  Shāh-nāmah, 35, 46n46, 46n49, 118, 145–47
fires, Zoroastrian, 55, 57, 78, 164–66, 214–15
fitna (civil strife), 107, 170, 212, 234
fiṭra (state of nature), 31, 60
Flood, story of, 37, 38, 41, 149
forgery of documents, 85–86. *See also* pseudepigraphy
forgetting
  as failure of memory, 21
  need for, 215–16
  reasons for, 22–24, 235
  strategies of, 137
  as superimposition, 24, 136, 235
France, collective memory of, 20–21, 215–16
Furs, 9, 10n23, 11, 38, 69. *See also* Persians

Garshāsp, 121–22
Gayūmart, 40, 41, 146, 159
  children of, 42, 138–39, 141, 159
  as first king, 57, 145, 146, 147
  relationship to Adam, 42, 144, 159
  in Zoroastrian myth, 138, 141
genealogies, 31–54
  prophetic, 32–33, 36, 121
  uses of, 32, 38, 53
Ghassān (descendant of Salmān's brother), 83
Ghassanids, 187n52
Ghazāla. *See* Shahrbānū
Ghazālī, Abū Ḥāmid al-, 141
Ghazālī, Muḥammad al-, 194
Ghaznavids, 7, 117, 126, 133
Ghurar akhbār mulūk al-Furs wa-siyarihim, 133n9
Gibb, H. A. R., 28
Gilliot, Claude, 72, 232
Giwargis (bishop of Ulay), 207
Gnoli, Gherardo, 9
Goldziher, Ignaz, 27
Gomaa, Ali, 194
Grignaschi, Mario, 156
groups as loci of collective memory, 19–20, 115

Grunebaum, G. E. von, 206

Haarmann, Ulrich, 164
Hādī, al- (caliph), 102
Hagar, 52, 102
Ḥajjāj, al- (governor), 114, 123
Halbwachs, Maurice, 18–20
Ham (son of Noah), 37, 38, 151
Hamadhān, **xx**, 6, 54–55, 151, **152**, 164
Hämeen-Anttila, Jaakko, 65n11
Ḥamza b. ʿAbd Allāh, 124
Ḥamza al-Iṣfahānī, 44, 46
Ḥanafism
  in Iṣfahān, 76
  in Jurjān, 112
Ḥanbalism in Jurjān, 112
ḥanīf (true monotheist), 65
Ḥārith b. Abī Shamir, al-, 187n52
Hārūn al-Rashīd (caliph), 102, 112, 156–57
Ḥasan, al-, 113, 124
Ḥasan al-Baṣrī, al-, 90–91, 122
Hawdha b. ʿAlī al-Ḥanafī, 187n52
Hephthalites, 55, 149
Heraclius, 178–79, 191
  invited to Islam by Muḥammad, 92, 184–85, 187
hijra, 66
Hilāl b. ʿAlqama (ʿUllafa), 202–3
Ḥīra, al-, **xx**, 175n14
histories, local, 56–57, 108–9, 127
history
  Iranian accounts of, 34–36, 41–43, 138–39
  Islamic vs. Iranian, 40, 45, 138, 147
  limits to rewriting of, 168, 222, 235
  national vs. religious, 36
  prophetic, 41, 43, 148, 158
  Qurʾanic vs. Persian, 177
  universal vs. local, 139–40, 145, 147
homologies, 177–83
Ḥudhayfa, 67, 82
Hurmuzān, al-, 48–49, 101n43, 212
  at the conquest of Tustar, 207–10
Ḥusayn, al-, 113, 123, 124
  and Shahrbānū, 102–5
Hūshang, 40, 42–43, 57, 146

Iblīs, 141, 165
Ibn ʿAbbād, Ismāʿīl, 222
Ibn ʿAbbās, ʿAbd Allāh, 38
Ibn ʿĀmir, ʿAbd Allāh, 119
Ibn ʿAsākir, 87
Ibn Aʿtham, 200, 205
Ibn Bābawayh, 71
Ibn al-Balkhī, 57
Ibn al-Faqīh, 55, 57
Ibn Funduq, 106
Ibn Hishām, 66, 173, 177
Ibn Isfandiyār, 115
Ibn Isḥāq, 66, 77
  Kitāb al-Mubtadaʾ, 44, 157
Ibn al-Kalbī, 31n1, 43, 57
Ibn Kathīr, 163
Ibn Khayyāṭ al-ʿUṣfurī, 189, 210
Ibn al-Muqaffaʿ, 56, 157–58
  Siyar al-mulūk, 35, 44, 46, 118
Ibn Qutayba, 52, 71n29, 105, 134, 195
  attitudes toward Persians, 97–98
Ibn Saʿd, 66, 67, 90
Ibn ʿUmar, ʿAbd Allāh, 68, 113, 180
Ibn al-Zubayr, ʿAbd Allāh, 113, 117, 170
icons, 183–90
identities
  confused, 150
  erased, 207, 209–14, 221, 235
  overlapping, 11–12, 18, 115
  role of past in, 17, 24–25, 172
idolators (*ahl al-awthān*), 181
ijtihād (independent judgment), 41
invitation to Islam, 185–86, 201, 202, 203, 213
Iqbal, Afzal, 186
Iran, idea of, 9–10, 34, 233
Iran, Iranians
  meaning of terms, 9–11, 147n34
  use of terms, 233–34
  See also Persia; Persians
Iran as historical theme, 234
Iran before Islam
  dearth of memories about, 22
  traditionists' attitudes toward, 158, 159, 168, 196
Īrān b. Rustam b. Āzādkhū b. Bakhtiyār, 119–20
Īrān-shahr, 9–11
Iraq as source of memory, 7, 32, 36, 57, 177, 234
Isaac, 34
  as ancestor to Jews, 33
  as ancestor to Persians, 43, 47, 48–49, 51–53

Iṣfahān, **xx**, 151, **152**
as birthplace of Pharaoh, 164
as birthplace of Salmān, 77, 78–79
eponymous founder of, 55
history of, 73–77
Isfandiyār, 173, 175
Ishmael, 33, 34
as ancestor to Arabs, 32
descent from Hagar, 52
Islam
in contemporary Iran, 3
origins of, 5–6, 39
in pre-conquest Iran, 122, 126, 127
Islamic law, 92
Ismāʿīlīs and Salmān, 61
Ispahbadhs, 49
Iṣṭakhr, **xx**, 2, 48–49, **58**, 58–59
as birthplace of Pharaoh, 161, 162, 163
Iṣṭakhrī, Abū Isḥāq al-, 59
īwān (throne hall), 2, 13, 135n16

jāhiliyya (pre-Islamic times), 172, 177, 197, 203
Jāḥiẓ, al-, 46, 51, 167
Jalāl al-Dawla (Buyid ruler), 8
Jamshīd, 40, 149, 153
and al-Ḍaḥḥāk, 149–50
as first king, 149
as originator of fire worship, 166, 214
and Persepolis, 58–59
Japheth (son of Noah), 37, 38, 151
Jarīr b. ʿAṭiyya, 48, 51
Jayy, **xix**, **xx**, 73
Jerusalem, **xix**, 57, 153–54, 155, 178
Jesus, 56n89, 140, 178, 185
genealogy of, 32
and Salmān, 65, 78
Jews, 27, 73, 92, 198, 213
genealogy of, 51, 53
as source of historical knowledge, 36, 40
in story of Salmān, 63, 75, 82
See also Children of Israel
Jibāl, **xx**, 54, **152**, 151–53
Jurjān, **xx**, **110**, 109–16

Kaʿba, 47, 154
kadhdhāb (liar), 173, 174
Kāriyān, **xx**, **58**, 214
Kay Qubādh, 40, 149
Kayanids, 155
Kayūmarthiyya, 139
Kennedy, Hugh, 100
kerygma, 91–95, 120–21, 129, 170, 203–5
kharāj tax, 195, 219
Khārijites, 117, 119, 121n116, 123–25
Khaṭīb al-Baghdādī, al-, 87
Khiḍr, al-, as ancestor to Persians, 40
Khurāsān, **xxi**, 71n29, **110**, 134
eponymous founder of, 149
Khurrabandād, 224–25
Khusraw Anūshirvān, 2, 77, 132, 231
Khusraw Parvīz, 93, 155, 191
daughter of, 95, 191–93
invited to Islam by Muḥammad, 92, 187–90
Khūzistān, **xx**, 207. *See also* Tustar
Khūzistān Chronicle, 207
Khwārizm-Shāhs, 133
kings, as honored by God, 143
kingship in Iranian history, 34, 140, 144, 147
origins of, 145, 159
traditionists' attitudes toward, 43, 131, 159, 164, 183
kinship as principle of social organization, 31
Kirmān, **xxi**, 149
Kisrā, 13, 48–49, 176
daughter of, 95, 108, 191–93
invited to Islam by Muḥammad, 184–85, 186–90
See also Khusraw Anūshirvān; Khusraw Parvīz; Yazdagird III
Kufa, **xx**, 207
Kurds, 148, 150
Kūthā Rabbā, 153

labels as aids to memory and forgetting, 171–77
lahw al-ḥadīth (diverting tales), 175, 176
Leo III the Isaurian, 61n1
lieux de mémoire. *See* sites of memory
light, divine, 104
lineages, 38, 115. *See also* genealogies
loyalties, 3, 17, 60, 158
conflicting, 66, 168
to Islam, 3, 66, 88, 127, 212
Luria, Alexandr Romanovitch, 22

Madāʾin, al-, 2, 13–14, 22, 202
Māfarrūkhī, al-, 76

Magians. *See* Zoroastrianism
malik al-mulūk (king of kings), 8. See also *shāhān-shāh*
mamlūk (slave), 227
Maʾmūn, al- (caliph), 112, 212
Manicheans, 27, 92
Manṣūr, al- (caliph), 135n16
manumission, 85
Manūshihr, 40, 43, 53, 151
Manushkhūrnar b. Manūshkhūrnak b. Wīrak, 53
Mardāvīj b. Ziyār, 110
Margoliouth, D. S., 173
*marzubān*s (Sasanian regional governors), 117–18, 210, 219
Mashī and Mashyāna, 40, 42, 138–39, 141, 159
Masʿūdī, al-, 9n18, 47, 54, 144
Mattson, Ingrid, 194
mawālī (clients), 31, 68, 80, 123
Māwardī, al-, 8, 163
Mecca, **xix**, 154, 178
  pre-Islamic Persian pilgrimage to, 47–48
Meisami, Julie Scott, 45, 46n46, 126n137, 221n68
Melchert, Christopher, 67, 111
memory, 3–4
  lack of reliability of, 21
  reshaping of, 15, 129, 136, 222, 230
  as socially constructed knowledge of past, 19–20
  techniques of, 14–15
merit, 99, 100
  vs. noble birth, 68, 69
Message: The Story of Islam, The (film), 184–85
Mignan, Robert, 1
Mihrāns, 217–19, 220n65
Miqdād b. al-Aswad, al-, 72, 82, 85, 175
miʿrāj (Muḥammad's ascension to Heaven), 174, 183
mnemohistory, 16–17, 95, 128–29, 230
monuments, ascription of Islamic associations to, 32, 57–59
Moses, 149, 178
  as ancestor of Children of Israel, 38
  in European history, 16–17
  vs. Pharaoh, 160
Muʿāwiya, 124, 170
Mubarrad, al-, 105
Mughīra b. Shuʿba, al-, 201
Muhājirūn (emigrants), 6, 67, 178
  pensions of, 97, 99
Muhallabids, 115
Muḥammad, 2, 5–6, 178
  annunciation of prophethood of, 63–64, 65, 78
  displeased with Persians, 184, 189
  family of, 31, 124
  genealogy of, 32–33
  letters to other rulers from, 92, 184–90
  statements about female rulers by, 191–94
  statements about Persians by, 11, 52–53, 69–71, 144
  and tolerance, 172
  wives of, 97, 100
Mujāhid b. Jabr al-Makkī, 161–62
Muqātil b. Sulaymān, 161
Mūsā b. ʿĪsā al-Kisrawī, 46
Musaylima, 174
Mutawakkil, al- (caliph), 101, 134–35

Nabat (*al-Nabaṭ*), 38
Naḍr b. al-Ḥārith, al-, 172–77
narratives, study of, 16, 17
Naṣīḥat al-mulūk, 141–43
Nawas, John, 68n20
Nebuchadnezzar, 153–54
Negus of Abyssinia, 92, 187
Newman, Andrew, 72
Nihāwand, **xx**, 54–55, **152**
Nihāyat al-arab fī akhbār al-Furs wa-l-ʿArab, 156–58
Nimrod, 1, 150–51, 153
  sons of, 151
Nīshāpūr, **xix**, **xxi**, 6, **110**, 152
Noah, 42, 55, 121
  as ancestor to Muḥammad, 33
  as ancestor to Persians, 37–39, 149
  as ancestor to Pharaoh, 163
  as father to world's peoples, 37–38, 149
Nöldeke, Theodor, 156n65
Nora, Pierre, 20, 232
Noth, Albrecht, 234
Nuʿaym b. Muqarrin, 218–19
Nuʿmān b. Muqarrin, al-, 211
Nuwayrī, al-, 165

orality, 15

Pahlav, 11, 217

pahlavāns (warriors), 120
Pārsīg, 217
Parthians, 217
past, shared, 18, 115, 129, 216
Patriarch of Alexandria, 184, 187n52
Paul, Jürgen, 76, 79
Peacock, Andrew, 45
pensions, 68, 97, 98–100
People of the Book (*ahl al-kitāb*), 181, 182, 212
Persepolis, **xx**, **58**, 58–59, 235
Persia, 8–11
Persian Muslim culture, 18
Persian Muslim self-awareness, 18, 81
Persians
genealogy of, 38, 40, 47, 149
as identity, 12, 17–18, 72
meaning of term, 8–11
piety of, 69–71, 79–80
as polytheists, 178, 180–83, 204, 229
replacing Arabs, 80–81
sensitivity to, 73, 98, 178, 213
Pharaoh as Persian, 160–64
Pleiades Hadith, 69–71, 80
polytheists (*mushrikūn*), as label, 180, 204, 206, 207, 211–12, 229
Pourshariati, Parvaneh, 217–18, 220
prophets, 33–34, 143
pseudepigraphy, 82n67, 143. *See also* forgery of documents
Puin, Gerd-Rüdiger, 96

Qādisiyya, al-, battle of, **xx**, 200–3
Qāsim b. Muḥammad b. Abī Bakr, al-, 102
Qaṭarī b. al-Fujāʾa, 124
Qazwīn, **xx**, 90–91, **152**
Qudāma b. Jaʿfar, 118
Qum, **xx**, 6, 72, 151, **152**, 222–26, 228
Qummī, ʿAlī b. Ibrāhīm al-, 188
Qummī, al-Ḥasan b. ʿAlī b. Ḥasan, 223, 228. See also *Tārīkh-i Qum*
Qummī, Ḥasan b. Muḥammad b. Ḥasan, 222–23. See also *Tārīkh-i Qum*
Qurʾan commentaries, 163–64
Qurʾan vs. *asāṭīr al-awwalīn* (fables of the ancients), 173–75
Quraysh, 100, 104
Qutayba b. Muslim, 114
Qutayla, 176
Qutb, Sayyid, 162

Rabīʿ b. Ziyād al-Ḥārithī, al-, 117–18, 119–20
Rāmhurmuz, **xx**, 78
Rayy, **xix**, **xx**, 6, **110**, 151, **152**
conquest of, 217–20
religious tolerance, 93, 123
Renan, Ernest, 215–16
representation, in writing history, 168
Ricœur, Paul, 19, 21
Robinson, Chase, 209, 213n45
Rosenthal, Franz, 41
Rukhad, 122
rulership, types of, 153–54
Rustam (of Persian epic tradition), 117, 155, 173, 175
Rustam (Sasanian commander), 200, 202–3, 205–6

Sabians, 48n54, 92
Saʿd b. Abī Waqqāṣ, 2, 201, 203, 207
and Salmān, 69
as witness, 85
Saʿd b. Malik, 225
Saʿd b. Saʿīd, 111
Sadd-i Iskandar, 109, **110**
Saffarids, 6, 101, 117, 119, 124, 126
Ṣāfī b. Ṣayyād, 211
Sahmī, al-, 110, 112, 115–16
harmony in reporting of, 113–15, 129
Taʾrīkh Jurjān, 110–16, 127, 231
Saʿīd b. Zayd, 85
Sālim b. ʿAbd Allāh b. ʿUmar b. al-Khaṭṭāb, 102
Salmān al-Fārisī
as author of the Qurʾan, 61n1
biography of, 62–64, 77–79, 81
descendants of, 82, 84, 86–87
as member of *ahl al-bayt*, 67, 83, 86
modern views on, 61
as opposite of al-Naḍr, 177
purported manumission contract of, 82–83, 87
purported testament for family of, 83–85, 87
and Shiʿism, 71–72
Samʿānī, al-, 164
Samanids, 6, 101, 220–21
Ṣanʿānī, ʿAbd al-Razzāq al-, 69
Sarah (wife of Abraham), 52
Sāsān, 1, 47, 48, 58

Sasanian Empire, **xix**, 6, 96
as counterpoint to Muḥammad and Islam, 170–71
fall of, 93–95, 187–89, 217
Muslim views on, 133, 155
sayyids/sharīfs (Muḥammad's descendants), 31
Schoeler, Gregor, 77
Seljuks, 6, 126
Serrano, Richard, 13, 14
Seth (son of Adam), 144
Shadīd b. ʿImlīq b. ʿĀd, 150
Shāfiʿism
in Iṣfahān, 76n44
in Jurjān, 111, 112
shāhān-shāh (king of kings), 7, 9, 110
Shahrbānū, 102–8
Shahrestānīhā-ī Ērān-shahr, 11n25
Sharīʿatī, ʿAlī, 162
Shem (son of Noah), 37, 149, 157, 158
as ancestor to Muḥammad, 33
as ancestor to Nimrod, 153
as ancestor to Persians, 41
descendants of, 38
Shiʿism, 67
vs. ʿAlidism, 86
Persian, 12, 105, 107
and Salmān, 71–72
and Shahrbānū, 102–5, 107
Shīrawayh, 94, 187, 191, 193
Shīrāz, **xx**, 56, **58**
Shīz, **xx**, 56n89
Shuʿūbiyya, 28, 52, 98, 102, 105
Sijistān. *See* Sīstān
Sīstān, **xxi**, **116**, 116–28, 129
sites of memory (*lieux de mémoire*), 20–21, 128, 186, 213, 232
Siyāmak, 146
Siyāwakhsh, 218, 221
Sizgorich, Thomas, 213
slaves as mothers, 52, 102–4, 105
Smith, Anthony D., 49–50, 60
Solomon, 57–59, 121, 153–54
as ancestor to Persians, 40, 49
throne of, 154, 155
sources, 3, 7, 14
Arabic as language of, 7, 35, 131
limitations of, 27, 35–36, 128–29
Sūdān, 39
Suhayb al-Rūmī, 85
Ṣūl, Ruzbān, 113, 114, 116n95
Ṣūlī, al-, 99, 100–1, 102, 113
Sūratī, ʿAbd al-Raḥmān al-, 161
Sūs, **xix**, **xx**, **152**, 207–8, 211
Suwayd b. Muqarrin, 113

Ṭabarī, ʿAlī b. Muḥammad, 118
Ṭabarī, Muḥammad b. Jarīr al-, 39, 43–44, 177, 221
on the battle of al-Qādisiyya, 202, 205
on the conquest of Rayy, 220
on the conquest of Sūs, 211
originality of, 40–41
on Persian genealogy, 32, 39, 43, 138
on Pharaoh, 162
sources of, 44, 45
Taʾrīkh al-rusul wa-l-mulūk, 35, 46, 231
Ṭabaristān, **xx**, 57, **110**, 109–10
Ṭāhir b. ʿAbd Allāh (governor), 134–35
Takht-i Sulaymān, 58, 235
Ṭalḥa b. ʿUbayd Allāh, 85, 100, 124, 170
Tāq-i Kisrā (Arch of Khusraw), 1–2, 22, 235
Taqīzadeh, Sayyid Ḥasan, 145
Tārīkh-i Qum, 222–28, 231
Tārīkh-i Sīstān, 127, 231
Tawḥīdī, Abū Ḥayyān al-, 152n50
Taymī, Jawāb al-, 111
Thaʿālibī, al-, 132–34, 197
Thaʿlabī, al-, 165
Thawrī, Sufyān al-, 111
Tour de la France par deux enfants, 20
tradition, 3
"invented", 10n20, 24
traditionists, 4, 13, 128, 129
attention to Persia by, 73, 109, 140
creative use of sources by, 167–69
editorial choices of, 137, 147, 148, 168
traditions (reports about the past), 4, 12–13
Trevor-Roper, Hugh, 24
Tsafrir, Nurit, 76
Turks, 39, 148
Ṭūs, **xxi**, 152
Tustar, **xx**, 48–49, **152**
conquest of, 207–10

Uhud, battle of, 100
ʿUmar b. al-Khaṭṭāb, 69, 105, 201, 209
as creator of *dīwān*, 96–97, 98–100
and al-Hurmuzān, 210, 212
and Shahrbānū, 103, 104
as witness, 82, 85
Umayyads, 6, 100, 170

ummiyyūn (people lacking a scripture), 182
unbelievers (*kuffār*), as label, 206, 212
Uthayl, 176
ʿUthmān, 85, 100, 123

viziers, 6, 101

Wahb b. Munabbih, 38–39
walāʾ (clientage), 68, 82, 85, 86n88, 87
walāya (sacred transmission), 104
Wansbrough, John, 91
White Palace, 22, 95n21, 135n16
women
  as rulers, 95
  as slave mothers, 51–52, 102–4, 105
Wonders and Magnificence of Sīstān, 36
Wushmgīr b. Ziyār, 110

Xwadāy-nāmag, 34–35
  difficulties establishing text of, 22, 35, 46
  as source for al-Dīnawarī, 155
  as source for al-Ṭabarī, 44

Yahūdiyya, 73
Yaʿqūb b. al-Layth al-Ṣaffār, 119, 124–26
Yaʿqūbī, al-, 94, 103
Yāqūt al-Ḥamawī, 222
Yarshater, Ehsan, 221
Yazd, **xx**, 57, **152**
Yazdagird III, 40, 144
  and chaotic end of Sasanian Empire, 93, 95, 191
  daughter of, 102–8
  at al-Qādisiyya, 201, 203
  at Tustar, 207
Yazdanfādhār, 225
Yazīd b. Muʿāwiya, 124
Yazīd b. al-Muhallab, 113, 114–15, 116n95
Yazīd III (caliph), 106n56
Yerushalmi, Yosef Hayim, 21
Young, James, 23

Zamzam, Persian origins of name, 48
Zaranj, **xxi**, **116**, 117–18, 119
Zīnabī, al-, 217–20, 221
Ziyarids, 110
Zoroaster, 55, 134, 154, 167
Zoroastrian historiography, 36, 41–43, 138–39, 141
Zoroastrianism
  in contemporary Iran, 3, 214
  conversion to, 154–55
  decline of, 214–15
  Muslim traditionists' interest in, 27, 131, 147, 159, 214
Zubayr b. al-ʿAwwām, al-, 85, 124, 170
Zuhayr b. ʿAbd Shams al-Bajalī, 205

Titles in the Series

POPULAR CULTURE IN MEDIEVAL CAIRO Boaz Shoshan
EARLY PHILOSOPHICAL SHIISM: THE ISMAILI NEOPLATONISM OF ABŪ YAʿQŪB AL-SIJISTĀNĪ Paul E. Walker
INDIAN MERCHANTS AND EURASIAN TRADE, 1600–1750 Stephen Frederic Dale
PALESTINIAN PEASANTS AND OTTOMAN OFFICIALS: RURAL ADMINISTRATION AROUND SIXTEENTH-CENTURY JERUSALEM Amy Singer
ARABIC HISTORICAL THOUGHT IN THE CLASSICAL PERIOD Tarif Khalidi
MONGOLS AND MAMLUKS: THE MAMLUK–ĪLKHĀNID WAR, 1260–1281 Reuven Amitai-Preiss
HIERARCHY AND EGALITARIANISM IN ISLAMIC THOUGHT Louise Marlow
THE POLITICS OF HOUSEHOLDS IN OTTOMAN EGYPT: THE RISE OF THE QAZDAĞLIS Jane Hathaway
COMMODITY AND EXCHANGE IN THE MONGOL EMPIRE: A CULTURAL HISTORY OF ISLAMIC TEXTILES Thomas T. Allsen
STATE AND PROVINCIAL SOCIETY IN THE OTTOMAN EMPIRE: MOSUL, 1540–1834 Dina Rizk Khoury
THE MAMLUKS IN EGYPTIAN POLITICS AND SOCIETY Thomas Philipp and Ulrich Haarmann (eds.)
THE DELHI SULTANATE: A POLITICAL AND MILITARY HISTORY Peter Jackson
EUROPEAN AND ISLAMIC TRADE IN THE EARLY OTTOMAN STATE: THE MERCHANTS OF GENOA AND TURKEY Kate Fleet
REINTERPRETING ISLAMIC HISTORIOGRAPHY: HĀRŪN AL-RASHĪD AND THE NARRATIVE OF THE ʿABBĀSID CALIPHATE Tayeb El-Hibri
THE OTTOMAN CITY BETWEEN EAST AND WEST: ALEPPO, IZMIR, AND ISTANBUL Edhem Eldem, Daniel Goffman, and Bruce Masters
A MONETARY HISTORY OF THE OTTOMAN EMPIRE Şevket Pamuk
THE POLITICS OF TRADE IN SAFAVID IRAN: SILK FOR SILVER, 1600–1730 Rudolph P. Matthee
THE IDEA OF IDOLATRY AND THE EMERGENCE OF ISLAM: FROM POLEMIC TO HISTORY G. R. Hawting
CLASSICAL ARABIC BIOGRAPHY: THE HEIRS OF THE PROPHETS IN THE AGE OF AL-MA'MŪN Michael Cooperson
EMPIRE AND ELITES AFTER THE MUSLIM CONQUEST: THE TRANSFORMATION OF NORTHERN MESOPOTAMIA Chase F. Robinson
POVERTY AND CHARITY IN MEDIEVAL ISLAM: MAMLUK EGYPT, 1250–1517 Adam Sabra
CHRISTIANS AND JEWS IN THE OTTOMAN ARAB WORLD: THE ROOTS OF SECTARIANISM Bruce Masters
CULTURE AND CONQUEST IN MONGOL EURASIA Thomas T. Allsen

REVIVAL AND REFORM IN ISLAM: THE LEGACY OF MUHAMMAD AL-SHAWKANI Bernard Haykel
TOLERANCE AND COERCION IN ISLAM: INTERFAITH RELATIONS IN THE MUSLIM TRADITION Yohanan Friedmann
GUNS FOR THE SULTAN: MILITARY POWER AND THE WEAPONS INDUSTRY IN THE OTTOMAN EMPIRE Gábor Ágoston
MARRIAGE, MONEY AND DIVORCE IN MEDIEVAL ISLAMIC SOCIETY Yossef Rapoport
THE EMPIRE OF THE QARA KHITAI IN EURASIAN HISTORY: BETWEEN CHINA AND THE ISLAMIC WORLD Michal Biran
DOMESTICITY AND POWER IN THE EARLY MUGHAL WORLD Ruby Lal
POWER, POLITICS AND RELIGION IN TIMURID IRAN Beatrice Forbes Manz
POSTAL SYSTEMS IN THE PRE-MODERN ISLAMIC WORLD Adam J. Silverstein
KINGSHIP AND IDEOLOGY IN THE ISLAMIC AND MONGOL WORLDS Anne F. Broadbridge
JUSTICE, PUNISHMENT AND THE MEDIEVAL MUSLIM IMAGINATION Christian Lange
THE SHIITES OF LEBANON UNDER OTTOMAN RULE, 1516–1788 Stefan Winter
WOMEN AND SLAVERY IN THE LATE OTTOMAN EMPIRE Madeline Zilfi
THE SECOND OTTOMAN EMPIRE: POLITICAL AND SOCIAL TRANSFORMATION IN THE EARLY MODERN WORLD Baki Tezcan
NON-MUSLIMS IN THE EARLY ISLAMIC EMPIRE: FROM SURRENDER TO COEXISTENCE Milka Levy-Rubin
THE LEGENDARY BIOGRAPHIES OF TAMERLANE: ISLAM AND HEROIC APOCRYPHA IN CENTRAL ASIA Ron Sela
LAW AND PIETY IN MEDIEVAL ISLAM Megan H. Reid
THE ORIGINS OF THE SHIʿA: IDENTITY, RITUAL, AND SACRED SPACE IN EIGHTH-CENTURY KUFA Najam Haider
POLITICS, LAW, AND COMMUNITY IN ISLAMIC THOUGHT: THE TAYMIYYAN MOMENT Ovamir Anjum
THE POWER OF ORATORY IN THE MEDIEVAL MUSLIM WORLD Linda G. Jones
ANIMALS IN THE QUR'AN Sarra Tlili
THE LOGIC OF LAW MAKING IN ISLAM: WOMEN AND PRAYER IN THE LEGAL TRADITION Behnam Sadeghi
EMPIRE AND POWER IN THE REIGN OF SÜLEYMAN: NARRATING THE SIXTEENTH-CENTURY OTTOMAN WORLD Kaya Şahin
WOMEN AND THE TRANSMISSION OF RELIGIOUS KNOWLEDGE IN ISLAM Asma Sayeed

Printed in the United States
By Bookmasters